A Complete Guide to Full-time RVing

A Complete Guide to

Full-time RVing:

Life on the Open Road

Third Edition

BILL AND JAN MOELLER

TRAILER LIFE BOOKS

To Bob and Mildred—for their love
of books and their love of RVing

All photographs are by the authors unless otherwise credited.

Editorial Director: Bob Livingston
Production Manager: Ann Forman
Copy Editor: Rena Copperman
Interior Illustrations: Randy Miyake
Cover Design: Bob Schroeder
Interior Design and Typesetting: Robert S. Tinnon

This book was set in Minion and Formata and
Printed and bound by R. R. Donnelley and Sons.

9   8   7   6   5   4   3   2   1

ISBN:0-934798-53-2

Contents

CHAPTER 1

The Full-timing Lifestyle: What Is It? Is It for You?   1

Why We Became Fulltimers • Attractions of Fulltiming • Can You Be a Fulltimer? • Who Are Fulltimers?

CHAPTER 2

How Much Will Fulltiming Cost?   25

The Full-timing Rig • Membership Campgrounds: Worth the Cost? • Living Within Your Budget

CHAPTER 3

Where Will the Money Come From?   51

Work Awhile, Travel Awhile • How Can I Find Work? • A Plan for Early Fulltiming

CHAPTER 4

Special Situations and How to Handle Them   73

Mail Forwarding • Fulltimers and Telephones • Message Services • Operating Capital • Registration and Licenses • Voting • Medical Concerns • Vehicle Concerns

CHAPTER 5

Getting Started   115

Begin by Reading About the Lifestyle • Talk to People Living the
Full-timing Life • Try RVing Before Buying • To Sell or Not to Sell
Your House • Moving into an RV • Delayed Fulltiming

CHAPTER 6

Selecting the Full-timing Rig 131

Practical RVs for Fulltiming • Selecting an RV to Suit Your
Lifestyle • Shopping for an RV • Why We Selected Our Rig •
A Motorhome or a Trailer: Some Comparisons • What Size Should
the RV Be? • The Weight Factor • The Tow-Vehicle Factor •
Slideout Rooms • Windows • Battery Compartments • Propane-
Cylinder Compartments • Holding Tanks • Optional Equipment •
A Used Rig? • Financing the RV • Shopping Tips

CHAPTER 7

Selecting a Full-timing RV: Interiors 177

Basic Floorplans • Storage • Baths • Bedrooms • The Living-
Room and Dining Areas • Galleys • Windows • Color Schemes •
Try Before Buying • An Overview

CHAPTER 8

Making Your RV More Livable 205

Privacy Curtains • Pictures and Decorative Accessories • Baths •
Tables and Chairs • Doors • Other Modifications

CHAPTER 9

Remodeling an Old or New RV 213

The Big Three • Comfort and Convenience Modifications • Major
Remodeling • A Picnic-Table Workshop

CHAPTER 10

Storage 245

Storage in a Movable House • Clothing Storage • Galley Storage • Book Storage • Audiocassette Storage • Other Storage Units • Constructing Storage Units • Personal and Business-Paper Storage • Outside Storage • Storage in Pickup Beds • Containment • Fulltiming and Storage

CHAPTER 11

An RV Office for Working Fulltimers 281

Computer Selection • Computer Storage • The All-Important Telephone Connection • What Does the Future Hold? • Other Communication Equipment

CHAPTER 12

Electronic Entertainment and Information 299

Weather Reports and Travel Information • Television • VCRs and VCPs • Stereos and Audio Players • Ham Radios • Weather and CB Radios • Useful Computer Programs for Travelers

CHAPTER 13

Electricity and Electrical Equipment 319

The 120-Volt AC System • The 12-Volt DC System • Trouble-free Electrical Systems

CHAPTER 14

Water, Sewage, and Propane 367

The Water System • Water Quality • Water Conservation • Water Heaters • Holding Tanks • Sewer Accessories • Plumbing and Cold Weather • Propane

CHAPTER 15

Climate Control 389

Insulation • Heating • Condensation • Storm Windows • Cold-Weather Situations • Cooling • Hot-Weather Site Selection

CHAPTER 16

Rig Maintenance: Inside and Out 405

Housecleaning Tools • Dusting • Carpeting, Drapery, and
Upholstery Care • Bath Maintenance • Caring for Woodwork and
Wall Coverings • Roof-Vent Maintenance • Cleaning Supplies •
Dealing with Odors • Pest Control • Exterior Cleaning •
Leakproofing the RV • Vehicle and Engine Maintenance • Tires •
Maintenance and Repair Equipment

CHAPTER 17

Campgrounds 423

How to Find a Campground • Types of Campgrounds •
Campground Site Selection • Campground Hazards •
Traveling Without Campground Reservations • Camping in
Noncampgrounds • Cold-Weather Camping • Camping Etiquette

CHAPTER 18

Setting Up and Breaking Camp 445

Using Checklists • Hitching and Unhitching • Leveling •
Stabilizing the RV • Chocking • Aids for Outside Work •
Utility Hookups • Keys

CHAPTER 19

Driving and Handling Practices 465

Take It Easy • Take It Slow • No Schedule Is the Best
Schedule • Avoiding Crowded Highways • Dealing with
Inclement Weather • Handling Long, Heavy Rigs • Up and Down
Hills • Backing an RV • Practice Makes Perfect •
Driving Through Campgrounds

CHAPTER 20

Customizing the Cockpit 485

Extra Cockpit Storage • Helpful Cockpit Items

CHAPTER 21

Recreational Transportation 495
Boats • Bicycles • Other Vehicles • How About Renting? •
Protecting Your Equipment

CHAPTER 22

Safety, Security, and Protection 503
Locks • Windows • Campground Safety Procedures • An Encour-
aging Word • Safety Equipment for the RV • Emergency Cards •
A Record of Important Numbers

CHAPTER 23

Fulltiming with Children and Pets 517
RV Accommodations for Children • Traveling with Children •
Children Visiting Fulltimers • Traveling with Pets

CHAPTER 24

The Fun and Rewards of Fulltiming 529
Clubs and Camaraderie • Fulltimers as Conservationists •
Full-timing Activities • A Fulltimer's Year

Index 549

Acknowledgments

We gratefully acknowledge the help of all the fulltimers and RVers who, knowingly and unknowingly, contributed to this book. You gave us much valuable information and many useful ideas. Without your input, this book would have been far less complete.

Our thanks to all the RV manufacturers who provided us with photographs and the manufacturers of RV products who were so helpful when we needed clarification on technical points.

We were fortunate to have Rena Copperman as the editor and Bob Tinnon as the art director, who, along with Randy Miyake and Bob Schroeder, handled the complicated job of both designing and producing the book.

Our special thanks to Bob Livingston, who coordinated the project and worked closely with us from beginning to end.

Preface

Fulltiming—having an RV for a home—is different than living in a fixed dwelling. It, like any lifestyle, has its own idiosyncrasies; however, with fulltiming the problems are few and the pleasures are many. It's a lifestyle that offers the freedom to live where you want, when you want, and how you want.

In our travels, we constantly meet people who want to become fulltimers but don't quite know how to go about changing their lifestyle; they also want information about what living in such a way entails. We are always happy to answer questions, but in a brief or even lengthy conversation, it's impossible to cover everything the potential fulltimer needs to know.

This was the main reason for writing this book. We hope it will dispel doubts, answer questions, give you ideas, and provide the incentive needed to get you started. If you are already a fulltimer, you'll find it contains a wealth of useful information for you as well.

In compiling this book, we have drawn upon many of our own experiences, but because everyone's fulltiming is different, we have also included the experiences of many others engaged in the lifestyle. We don't expect people to do it "our way," if another way works better for them.

Whether your fulltiming includes traveling all the time or just seasonally, whether you do it in a motorhome or trailer, whether you have an income or need to earn money as you go, you'll find information that applies to your own individualistic way of fulltiming.

As we write this, in the 29-foot fifth-wheel trailer that is our only home, we are beginning our eighteenth year of fulltiming. We are just as satisfied with this delightful lifestyle now as we were in the early years of our fulltiming.

CHAPTER 1

The Full-timing Lifestyle: What Is It? Is It for You?

As we are writing this, our RV is parked in Central Ferry State Park on the Snake River in southeastern Washington. The lush greens of the vegetation in this man-made oasis contrast with the grasses in the tawny shades of late summer that cover the high, nearly treeless hills through which the Snake wends its way in this arid country. It's a barren landscape but beautiful, especially in late afternoon when the sun turns the grasses to gold and casts deep shadows, making the folds of the hills stand out in sharp relief.

The Snake River here is in just one of its many incarnations. We know this because fulltiming has afforded us the opportunity to explore this fascinating river from beginning to end. We've camped on its bank where it's a rushing mountain stream flowing south out of Grand Teton National Park before it turns to the northwest to enter Idaho.

Once in Idaho, a few miles after it again begins to flow south, the river is tamed for a while by the dam at American Falls that turns it into a broad reservoir.

Not far from here, though, the river runs wild and free again. It's especially beautiful in Massacre Rocks State Park (Figure 1.1). The river, which now has a tropical blue-green color, runs between dark brown, almost black, basalt cliffs. It's visible from many of the campsites in the park, some of which are high above the river, others lower down and close to the water. Each time we have stayed here we have been treated to the sight of a flock of white pelicans wheeling above the river, stark against the dark cliffs.

Just east of the city of Twin Falls, the Snake tumbles down in two waterfalls: Twin Falls, after which the town is named, and Shoshone Falls, aptly called the "Niagara of the West." In the spring, before most of the river water is diverted for irrigation, the Snake plunges over Shoshone Falls, thundering magnificently as it drops 212 feet, rainbows arcing in the spray (Figure 1.2).

Entering the town of Twin Falls from the north, we and other travelers suddenly come upon one of the most spectacular views of the Snake as we cross the Perrine Bridge that spans it; looking very small, the river runs at the bottom of a 486-foot deep chasm.

Further west in Idaho, we camped at Three Island State Park to take a look at the place where Oregon Trail emigrants crossed from the south side of the Snake to the north side.

The emigrants continued westward along the Snake, following it until just after it crossed what is now the Oregon border. There they camped before saying farewell to the river they had followed for hundreds of miles. We camped there too; it's now Farewell Bend State Park.

Not many miles north of Farewell Bend, the Snake has carved out Hell's Canyon, America's deepest gorge. The dirt road down into the canyon is long, bumpy, rutted, and steep, so for this visit to the Snake we left our trailer parked on the plateau and made the trip down in our pickup truck.

When we visited Pasco, Washington, we saw the end of the Snake—now a wide, placid stream running between low banks—where it empties into the Columbia River.

We didn't follow the Snake River from start to finish all at once and didn't consciously set out to follow it at all. It has taken us fifteen years of being traveling fulltimers to become so familiar with the Snake. We kept encountering it in our travels, seeing new sec-

> **"**Traveling with our home gives us the freedom to come and go as we please, and stay as long as we want in places that we especially like.**"**

Figure 1.1 The Snake River is visible from many of the campsites in Massacre Rocks State Park near American Falls, Idaho.

tions of it sometimes, and other times purposely returning to other sections we had previously visited because we enjoyed them so much.

There are many other aspects of our country that we have also explored in depth, some on purpose, some by happenstance, such as the Snake River. It is the full-timing lifestyle that allows us to travel to these places. Traveling with our home gives us the freedom to come and go as we please and stay as long as we want in places that we especially like.

We are fulltimers with no fixed schedule; we go more or less where our fancy takes us. We wouldn't have so much freedom if we had an itinerary to follow. If bad weather interferes with our plans,

Figure 1.2 In the spring, water from melting snow turns Shoshone Falls into one of our country's most magnificent waterfalls.

which are always loose and flexible, we can wait until it improves, all the while ensconced in the comfort of our snug home on wheels. Rainy days don't ruin our vacation because, as fulltimers, we are on vacation all year long.

If we visit popular tourist areas, we usually go there in the off-season. That way, we need no advance reservations at campgrounds, we often have the pick of the campsite we want, we avoid lines at attractions and restaurants, and the highways in and around the area are relatively uncrowded. As fulltimers, we've seen the wonders of Yellowstone National Park in the spring and fall, but never in the summer, and we usually visit the Grand Canyon in the winter.

Spring and fall are our favorite seasons and, being fulltimers, we can live in our home and follow spring as it moves north and autumn as it moves south, thus prolonging the seasons. One year we lingered in Maine until the leaves were in the full glory of a New England autumn. The brilliant foliage stayed with us as we took over a month to travel south to Virginia. Another year we were in Georgia when the early spring flowers and trees began to bloom, and much later in Indiana we experienced the same blossomings.

The way we live as fulltimers is the way we most enjoy it, but other fulltimers have their own ways of pursuing the lifestyle. Some travel most of the time, as we do. Others spend much of their time staying put in a favorite place, or use a mixture of traveling and staying put that suits them.

This is what fulltiming is all about—being able to go where you want, when you want, see new places, revisit old ones, and make friends wherever your fulltiming takes you.

WHY WE BECAME FULLTIMERS

We have had a mobile lifestyle, one way or another, for more than twenty-six years now.

After years of being employed at hectic, high-pressure jobs, we decided—one cold, snowy, January day—that there must be more to life than working at jobs that allowed us to spend only occasional weekends and vacations doing what we really wanted, which was to travel.

Another source of dissatisfaction: When we did manage to get away, we never had enough time to spend at our destination. There were so many places we wanted to see and explore in depth, but there was no way we ever would be able to visit even a small percentage of them as long as we were tied down by our jobs.

We wanted to change our lifestyle for other reasons as well: Neither of us likes the chores that are involved in maintaining a house and yard. And, even though we enjoyed traveling and living in the various RVs we owned, we did not like the packing, unpacking,

> **"This is what fulltiming is all about—being able to go where you want, when you want, see new places, revisit old ones, and make friends wherever your fulltiming takes you."**

loading, and unloading that went with it. The time spent readying our rig was often out of proportion to the leisure time that would be spent in it. More than once we decided it wasn't worth the effort and stayed home. This was usually a bad trade-off; as long as we were at home we felt compelled to take care of the lawn or tackle the many other projects that needed doing.

One of the most important reasons for our needing a lifestyle change was that the stresses of our work were beginning to have adverse effects on our health. If we continued on as we were, we figured we would eventually have some serious problems.

We believe in these axioms:

Don't put off until tomorrow what you can do today.
Do it now; tomorrow may never come.

Knowing that the best-laid plans may never come to fruition, we didn't want to wait for retirement, which at that time was more than twenty years away. So, on that January day, we decided to arrange for a mobile lifestyle just as quickly as we could.

Our stressful jobs had one positive factor: We received from them a better than average income. Even though most of our extra money was spent on travel and vehicles to travel in (at different times we had a van, a pickup camper, a 17-foot travel trailer, and sailboats ranging in size from 20 to 30 feet) we had managed to save some.

We knew that selling the house, the furniture, and the maintenance equipment we had accumulated would give us a decent nest egg. It would not, however, generate enough income to allow us to live on the interest. We calculated that we had enough money to live for probably four years without skimping too much. Four years of living exactly the way we wanted now, we decided, was much better than waiting for the uncertainty of what our retirement years would bring. There was plenty of time to worry about what we would do when we ran out of money four years hence. We decided to go for it. Being able to travel full time, for however long it lasted, was worth some risk-taking.

"Being able to travel full time, for however long it lasted, was worth some risk-taking."

If our health problems didn't clear up (they did), we reasoned, at least we would have spent some time doing what we wanted to do. No matter what happened, we would never have to join the countless others who preface many of their statements with:

"If only I had . . ."
"I wish I could have . . ."
"If things had been different . . ."
"If I had it to do over again . . ."
"I've always been sorry I didn't . . ."

We have extended our mobile lifestyle for many years more than four, and we intend to keep on fulltiming for many more years. We have never once regretted our decision to become full-timers. In fact, we believe it was one of the best moves that we ever made.

ATTRACTIONS OF FULLTIMING

The opportunity to travel is what attracts most people to the full-timing lifestyle, and this way of life offers it in abundance. As a fulltimer you can visit relaxing places where the lifestyle is leisurely, or take off to out-of-the-way areas in search of rugged adventure. You can do it at your own pace and in your own style. Fulltiming can be as individualistic as you want to make it.

It's More Than Just Traveling

The full-timing lifestyle has many more advantages than just traveling. Living in an RV is a less complicated way of life than living in a fixed dwelling. Not as much maintenance is required because RVs are smaller than houses and apartments, they are constructed of materials that need little care, and there is no yard to take care of. Because the lifestyle is not so complex, fulltimers have more time to do the things they want to do; they aren't faced with so many chores they think they should do.

Fulltiming is not rigidly structured. Most nonfulltimers' lives are dominated by schedules. Work days are generally fairly inflexible. Nonfulltimers arise at a certain hour, go through a prescribed personal routine, arrive at work—going over the same route day after day, month after month, year after year—and carry out virtually the same duties on the job every day. At the end of the day, they go home over the same route that they traveled earlier. Evenings are filled with other scheduled events, activities they must participate in, and tasks that must be done. Weekends are often just as structured as days spent on the job because most of this "free" time is taken up with specified chores and duties.

Even nonfulltimers' sleep is controlled by schedules. If you don't travel full time, you need a good night's sleep to be alert and ready for the next day's scheduled events.

When a vacation is in the offing, it too is precisely defined by when it begins and when it ends. The activities during a vacation are also preplanned with little or no leeway allowed for variations. Fulltimers have the freedom to set their own schedules and generally can do what they please, when they please.

Fulltiming can be a very economical way to live, although many don't find out about this aspect of living in an RV until they have done it for a while. (We have never encountered anyone who became a fulltimer for this reason alone.) When we started fulltiming we were not aware of how inexpensive it could be.

It's a common misconception among some that certain compromises and sacrifices have to be made when living in an RV. This isn't so. Today's RVs are designed so that they have all the necessities and conveniences anyone needs for comfortable living. When fulltiming in a modern RV you're never "camping out" and making do with spartan living accommodations and doing without creature comforts. In fact, your RV may be more luxurious than the home you're now living in. Fulltiming can be, and should be, comfortable, convenient, safe, easy, and fun.

> **"**When fulltiming in a modern RV you're never "camping out" and making do with spartan living accommodations and doing without creature comforts.**"**

The lifestyle can be a relatively carefree existence, but none of us can drive off into the sunset without a care in the world. No one should expect fulltiming to be an escape from reality or a panacea for all problems. If you are realistic about what it can offer, you aren't likely to be disappointed or disillusioned.

CAN YOU BE A FULLTIMER?

Most fulltimers are retirees since these are the people who are no longer tied down to a job, but many engaged in the lifestyle are a long way from retirement. Fulltiming is open to anyone who wants to undertake it, young or old. Still, many don't seize the opportunity at hand and choose instead to plan ahead for fulltiming sometime in the future.

Most of us are acquainted with people who had their future all planned, who were eagerly anticipating the day when this "future" would begin, but a death, illness, or other unfortunate circumstance occurred, and they found themselves having to either alter their plans, or put them on hold, or forget about them altogether.

This may not happen to you, but then again, it could; the longer you put off anything, the greater the risk of something interfering with your plans. Even if nothing so drastic as a death or a serious illness occurs, long-range plans have a way of being continually superseded by other occurrences. Eventually, they may be pushed out of the schedule entirely. What's more, if plans are made for well into the future, when the time comes to act, you may find that you are too set in your ways, or perhaps, by then, you may decide that it's too difficult or inconvenient to change, so your life continues on in the same old way.

Don't Let Excuses Get in the Way

Some people seem to go out of their way to find excuses for not enjoying their lives and doing what they want with them. Are you one of those who would like to be a fulltimer, but who says, "I can't until I retire," or, "I can't until the mortgage is paid off," or, "I can't until the kids are through school"?

None of these "I can'ts" is reason enough, by itself, to keep anyone from fulltiming. To be sure, legitimate "I can'ts" exist that may prevent someone from pursuing the full-timing lifestyle, but many "I can'ts" are invalid. They are set up by those who don't actually want to be fulltimers. They like to talk about it, but when it comes right down to it, they wouldn't change lifestyles even if the opportunity for doing so presented itself without any obstacles. We know from our own experience and that of others that, if the desire for fulltiming is really there, a way can be found to do it.

Fulltiming for the Disabled

A physical disability is often used as an "I can't," but some determined people participate in fulltiming even though they have serious handicaps. Many times we have had campground neighbors with RVs with a removable ramp or a lifting device at the doorway for use by a person confined to a wheelchair.

One such woman started fulltiming in a travel trailer. While she and her husband were towing their trailer, she wasn't comfortable when sitting in the truck seat of their tow vehicle, and it was painful for her to shift from the wheelchair to the seat. They replaced the trailer with a motorhome and now have an arrangement by which her wheelchair can be locked securely in place while they are under way.

Yet another woman's husband is the one who must be in a wheelchair. She does all the driving and parking of their rig. Her husband cooperates by doing chores he can handle from the wheelchair, such as some of the cooking.

Then there are Vera and Cecil: They had been active RVers for years, but when Vera developed kidney problems, they gave up RVing because of the daily treatments she needed at a dialysis center.

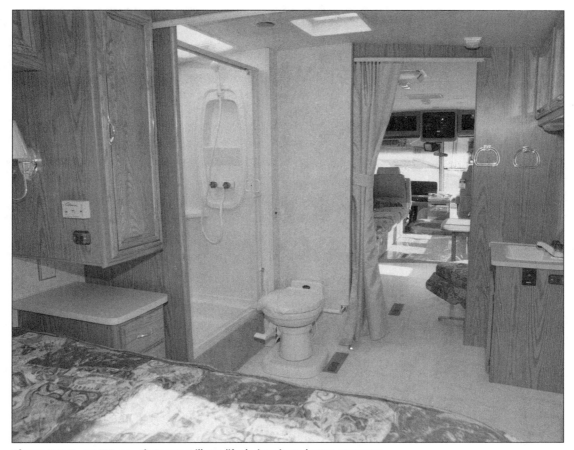

Figure 1.3 Some RV manufacturers will modify their units to better accommo-date those with disabilities, as in this motorhome with extra-wide aisles and an easily accessible bath. (Courtesy Winnebago Industries, Inc.)

After a number of months, Cecil, who is more of an "I can" than an "I can't" person, set out to investigate if there was a way he could give Vera the treatments at home. He did extensive research on his own and consulted with medical professionals, one of whom was Vera's understanding, cooperative doctor. He found that with proper training he could perform the dialysis himself. Cecil took the necessary courses, and soon Vera was able to have the three daily treatments she needed at home. Since the equipment used for Vera's treatment—continuous ambulatory peritoneal dialysis (CAPD)—is portable and relatively simple to operate, and the necessary supplies are readily obtainable throughout the country, Cecil reasoned that the dialysis could be performed in an RV. He proposed to Vera that they buy a motorhome and take it to Yuma, Arizona, to visit their niece. Vera was apprehensive but agreed to try it; she hated being tied down. At the beginning of the trip, they stopped each time the dialysis was needed, but it wasn't long before Cecil figured out a method for doing the dialysis while they were under way.

They spent six weeks in Yuma, and so successful was the venture that they have since taken many other RVing trips.

Because she can travel again, Vera's morale and physical well-being have improved enormously. Oh, we forgot to mention the ages of this intrepid couple: When we first heard about them, Vera was seventy-six and Cecil was eighty-two.

In the strictest sense of the word, Vera and Cecil are not fulltimers. "Not yet anyway," says Cecil, but they could be. They should be an inspiration to those who think they can't be fulltimers because of a restrictive medical condition.

We know of fulltimers who have varying degrees of paralysis, others who need a constant supply of oxygen, and many who have crippling or debilitating diseases, but these afflictions don't stop them from pursuing their chosen lifestyle. They take advantage of the numerous devices, both portable and those incorporated into their RVs, that allow them to be mobile and functional. In addition to releasing them from being housebound, RVing takes their minds off their troubles and gives them a great sense of freedom.

If you have a physical disability and have been living in a house or apartment without any major problems, chances are that a recreational vehicle can be found that is suitable for you to live in (Figure 1.3). In fact, an RV may even be a better dwelling for you than any other. Being smaller than a fixed dwelling, it takes less time and effort to go from one room to another, and there are easily reach-

"If you have a physical disability and have been living in a house or apartment without any major problems, chances are that a recreational vehicle can be found that is suitable for you to live in.**"**

able, sturdy handholds throughout. Another important point: When traveling in your own RV, you always have a bathroom with you. You don't have to be concerned with using public facilities that may present problems. (See Chapter 24, "The Fun and Rewards of Fulltiming" for information on a club for those with disabilities.)

Fulltiming for the Retired

No doubt you have noticed, as we have, that some seniors seem older than others of the same age. It's our opinion that this generally occurs when older people get into a retirement rut. All too often these people not only retire from a job, they retire from life because they vegetate.

Retired fulltimers, by the very nature of their existence, can't easily be in this state. Something new and interesting to see is always around the next bend of the road or over the next horizon. When the means for traveling exists, as it does with all who choose fulltiming for their retirement lifestyle, bogging down or getting into a rut shouldn't happen.

We're not advocating our lifestyle of constant travel for every fulltimer—just a change in perspective every few months for those who tend to settle into one spot and stay there. Use the mobility fulltiming affords to see new things, meet new people, and experience living in different locales. Fulltimers' golden years can truly be golden if they take advantage of all the lifestyle offers.

CAN YOU ADJUST TO FULLTIMING?

Although many people sincerely believe they want to be fulltimers, they may not be able to give up the security that conventional living represents to them. For example, some cannot imagine living solely in a movable dwelling. For such people, security means having a permanent, fixed place anchored securely to its foundation to come home to. Those who have such ideas can never experience the total freedom that fulltiming offers.

Others have qualms about doing without the personal attention of their regular doctors and dentists if a medical or dental problem arises when on the road. Would you be able to adjust to this situation, or that of not having a known and trusted mechanic to call on for your rig repairs?

When living the life of a traveling fulltimer and an emergency arises, you may be far from your regular service and professional people. It's easier than may be expected to find the professionals and service people you need on the road (see Chapter 4, "Special Situations and How to Handle Them"), but will you be at ease with strangers doing the work?

You may also have to give up the security that comes from having friends and relatives nearby. You are bound to make more friends wherever you go, but will you feel as comfortable and secure with the new friends as with the old?

All these points must be considered before making the decision to become a fulltimer.

It may be that simply not knowing what fulltiming is all about or having misconceptions about the lifestyle holds back many from pursuing their dream. We have had people who were contemplating fulltiming anxiously ask us such questions as:

"How do you find a place to stay?"
"How do you store everything you need?"
"How do you arrange to get your mail?"
"How do you keep enough ready cash on hand?"

All these questions, and more, are answered in the ensuing chapters, but we mention them here to illustrate the concerns of some about problems that may be lurking in the full-timing lifestyle.

It's always wise to find out as much as you can about any new venture before embarking on it. But remember, thousands of us are out here fulltiming who once were in the same unenlightened state as you may be. We have found answers to the questions, solved the problems, overcome obstacles, and found that, in general, fulltiming is easy to do.

Fulltiming with a Partner

Ideally, if you are planning to pursue the full-time lifestyle with a spouse or a partner, he or she should be as enthusiastic about it as you are. In our case, each of us wanted to become a fulltimer as much as the other so, undoubtedly, this is one of the reasons we have been so satisfied with our chosen way of life.

Some people, however, make plans blissfully unaware that what they want to do is not necessarily what their partners want. If you talk about what you are planning and receive little or no input from your partner, if he or she is evasive when discussing it, or lukewarm about the idea in general, you may be in for some unpleasantness.

Fred and Sylvia, a couple in their early sixties, met and married after their respective spouses had died. When we met them, they had been married for about five years. They were outgoing, fun to be with, and seemed to have a good relationship. One day when Sylvia was away, Fred told us how he had looked forward to being a fulltimer and, now that he was, he was having the time of his life. His eyes danced as he said, "At last I feel as if I'm really living."

Unfortunately, Sylvia harbored other feelings. She told Jan that she had agreed to try fulltiming "so Fred can get it out of his system." She went on to say that she certainly didn't want to spend the rest of her life living in a trailer, and she was sure Fred would see it her way eventually. They had been traveling for only four months, but Sylvia was already anxious to get back to her house and garden.

Over the years we have lost touch with Fred and Sylvia so we don't know how, or if, they worked out their differences, but we hope they reached some sort of a compromise.

Another couple we met, Rich and Teresa, weren't able to work out their differences. Rich, an avid fisherman, convinced his wife that they should sell their house and become fulltimers so they could see some of the country, which both wanted to do. They hadn't been traveling long when Rich found the fishing spot of his dreams on the Pacific Coast and parked their trailer in a nearby campground to fish for a spell.

They ended up staying there for months and never traveled any farther. Teresa, who wasn't interested in fishing at all, sat around the trailer with little to do once she had it arranged the way she wanted. Eventually she tired of this sort of fulltiming; Rick was having fun but she wasn't. After living in their trailer for about two years, they sold it and bought a house on the coast.

Now Teresa is happy taking care of the house and yard and being involved in community activities while Rick continues with his fishing. Probably Rich intended to travel when he proposed the idea of fulltiming, and Teresa probably would have been content with such a lifestyle. They might have continued as fulltimers if Rich hadn't gotten bogged down in one place. Had they pursued the lifestyle, he might have found lots of other dream fishing places and Teresa would have had the benefit of traveling to new places and not become so bored.

The time to find out about your partner's wishes and feelings is not after you have moved into your RV. Talk it over beforehand and be honest. Find out if you both have the same ideas of what fulltiming for you will encompass. Many people never think to come right out and ask their partner if he or she wants to become a fulltimer. Ask. It can be very illuminating.

Mutual desire alone may not be enough for satisfying fulltiming if you and your partner aren't compatible. Some couples, to put it bluntly, simply don't like each other. Sometimes these couples have stayed together for the sake of the children or some other family or monetary reason, but often they remain together because it's easier to go on in the same old way than to change.

Such couples usually have areas in their home or on its grounds where they can get away from each other. This option may not be available once they become fulltimers. By the very nature of the lifestyle, couples must spend more time together in closer quarters since RVs are a good deal smaller than any fixed dwelling. Disagreements have no room to "spread out" in the confines of the average RV. What's more, in a small environment, little annoyances have a way of festering into major irritations.

Compatibility is the basis for a good relationship anywhere, but it's especially important for fulltimers. The odds are against the lifestyle being a curative for any domestic problems; if they exist there is a good chance they will become worse when fulltiming—a sad but true fact.

Living harmoniously with each other is only one facet of an ideal full-timing partnership. Many partners get along well, but their likes and dislikes vary widely. Your fulltiming will be richer and more rewarding if you and your partner have at least some similar interests.

At the outset of your new lifestyle, it will be much easier to choose the size and type of rig if you both have the same point of view. Consider how you would work it out if you want a large motorhome and your partner prefers a compact fifth-wheeler. If you reach a happy compromise on the type of full-timing rig, how satisfying will your fulltiming be if one of you likes away-from-it-all environments and hunting, and the other prefers campsites in urban parks with full hookups and easy accessibility to shopping instead?

What if you like a change of seasons and your partner wants to follow the sun? Do you want to travel most of the time while your partner prefers to stay put for long periods?

Before committing yourselves wholeheartedly to fulltiming, differences should be discussed and compromises worked out. Do this before you sell your current dwelling or buy an RV. If you and your partner have any doubts at all about each of you enjoying fulltiming, don't cut off the avenues of escape entirely. Leave some options open just in case you can't make it work for you.

"Compatibility is the basis for a good relationship anywhere, but it's especially important for fulltimers."

A Life Without Schedules

You and your partner may have an ideal relationship and similar desires, but can you adjust to being unfettered and free to come and go as you want? Many cannot. They have been tied down by jobs, family responsibilities, and other circumstances for such a long period that they find it difficult to break loose. If they do, they feel as if they are adrift. Not being able to adjust to their new-found freedom, they put themselves back on schedules that are just as restrictive as the ones in the lives they have left behind. As a consequence, some turn fulltiming into a job.

Jim was one of these people. He and his wife, Susan, had taken an early retirement and set off in a brand new rig. When we met them in a campground in North Carolina, they were giving up fulltiming after less than a year, and were on their way "home" because Jim hadn't found the lifestyle to be as he expected. We were rather new at fulltiming then and enjoying every minute of it, so we were interested to find out if Jim had discovered something about the lifestyle that we were not aware of. We asked him what the problem was. "Too much traveling," he said disgustedly. He elaborated: "You get up early every day and do three or four hundred miles, then pull into a campground all tired out late in the day, and you do the same thing seven days a week. At least when I had a job I got the weekends off." Yes, those were his exact words.

Admittedly, Jim is an extreme example of someone who was not able to adjust to the full-timing way of life, but we have met others who had the same problem to a lesser extent.

Art and Verna lived part of the year in a house and the rest of the year in their trailer, which they took to Arizona each winter. We encountered them in New Mexico when they were on their way to a family reunion in Massachusetts. They wanted to do some sightseeing along the way and had allowed themselves a month for this purpose. They proudly showed us their neatly typed itinerary, which listed the number of miles to be covered each day—not small distances, we noted. With few exceptions, nearly every night was to be spent in a different campground. There were no al-

> **"N**ot being able to adjust to their new-found freedom, they put themselves back on schedules that are just as restrictive as the ones in the lives they have left behind.**"**

lowances for bad-weather days and staying over if repairs of some kind were needed. It was a tight schedule that involved lots of driving. Such a schedule was necessary, it was explained, so they would arrive in time for the reunion. We didn't ask, but we wondered why they simply hadn't left earlier and allowed more time. They were retired, so they could have taken all year to make the trip if they wanted to.

In Montana we became acquainted with another couple, Shirley and Harry, who were having similar problems. Shirley needed someone to talk to, and Jan happened to be available. She learned that Harry's doctor had suggested he take an early retirement because he was pushing himself too hard in his work. From Michigan, where they lived, they took their 29-foot trailer and set off to tour all the western states.

*"**S**ome people can't slow down or break away from set routines."*

While they had no schedule and could take all the time they wanted, Shirley complained that she couldn't get Harry to slow down. He worked just as hard at traveling as he had at his job. They, or rather Harry, drove all day, every day. He rarely let Shirley drive even though she was willing to do her share. Harry didn't enjoy driving especially; it was just that he always had to be doing something; he couldn't relax.

On vacations it's necessary to plan carefully for the optimum use of your time, but none of these couples was on a time-limited vacation. They were all free as birds but did not realize it and certainly did not take advantage of their situations.

We recently met an English couple who did have a time limit on exploring the United States. For reasons they didn't disclose, they allowed themselves two years for their "vacation." They were traveling in a motorhome they had purchased when they arrived in the States. Their "schedule" was this: Drive no more than 100 miles a day, and stay at least two nights at each stop. They admitted they probably wouldn't be able to see everything they wanted to with this schedule, but they knew they would better appreciate what they did see and avoid the exhaustion that often accompanies trying to do too much in too short a time.

Free Yourself from Structure

"The Grand Canyon and the Blue Ridge Mountains will be there tomorrow, next week, next year, or ten years from now. Take your time. Relax and enjoy.**"**

Some people can't slow down or break away from set routines. When there is nothing they must do, they invent things to do. If they can't come up with concrete projects, they often create schedules. Then, adhering to the schedule becomes a suitable project. Once it's formulated, the schedule is followed religiously and the schedule's creator usually becomes upset when anything interferes with what he or she has laid out. People like this set up their own restrictions against the free and easy life they might have if only they could cut loose.

You won't get the most out of fulltiming unless you can free yourself from a rigidly structured life. Learn to allow plenty of time to travel to events that are held on specific dates. Also realize that you don't have to be in a hurry to get to any place. The Grand Canyon and the Blue Ridge Mountains will be there tomorrow, next week, next year, or ten years from now. Take your time. Relax and enjoy.

Our full-timing life is so flexible that some days when we set out we don't know for sure where we will be spending the night. We select a spot once we are on the road. After camp is set up in such a place we come to the realization that no one, absolutely no one in the whole world, knows where we are. It's an interesting feeling to experience. We don't consciously plan such disappearances, which are always short-lived—we don't want to drop out of society altogether, but because we have such an unstructured, unscheduled way of traveling, we often find ourselves in this situation.

One year, in February, we were heading to Panama City, Florida, after a month's stay in Mobile, Alabama. The traffic on the interstate was heavy, and we had to wait in line to eat and at filling stations to refuel. We figured that the crowds and traffic would only increase the farther we went into Florida. This is not the type of traveling we enjoy and, not having a schedule, we don't have to put up with it. We quickly reached a mutual decision. We exited the interstate, got back on to head in the opposite direction, and ended up spending the remainder of the winter along the Gulf Coast in Mississippi, Louisiana, and Texas.

We aren't advocating that others undertake fulltiming the way we do—it's probably too unstructured for many. We use the above examples from our own experiences to illustrate how the lifestyle can be adapted to what suits you as long as you don't allow yourself to be restrained by inflexible schedules.

Fulltiming Versus Vacations

No one should judge fulltiming by unpleasant experiences they may have had when vacationing in an RV, especially on shorter trips. The RV you use for vacations may not be suitable for fulltiming; it may be the wrong type, or too small for living in long-term. Occasional trips in such a rig aren't like "real" fulltiming and shouldn't color your attitude toward the lifestyle.

First of all, on a vacation, you'll never experience the free feeling that comes from knowing you won't have to return home by a certain time. Then there is the thrown-together, messy, helter-skelter atmosphere sometimes found in rigs that are used solely for vacations. When packing an RV for a trip there is a tendency to cram things into any places that can be found for them. As a result, it's often difficult to locate what you want when you want it.

A vacation RV isn't in use constantly, and you may find that some of its equipment that hasn't been used for some time may not work as it should, or at all, just when you are counting on it. You might be able to fix the problem if you can remember where you stashed the needed tools—if you remembered to bring them in the first place. Food and other supplies may run out at inconvenient times, and extras may not be on hand as they might be at home.

When vacationing, your routine is not a normal one. Normal is when you are at home, where things are kept in specific places, and where items that are used on a regular basis can be located easily.

You know when you are running low on such things as flour and toothpaste, and you replenish them before the supply runs out. Your toothbrush is always where it belongs as well; it has never been left behind somewhere.

When you are fulltiming, your RV is your home. It can be, and should be, managed just as any other home. If it is, your fulltiming will be totally unlike vacationing; there will be no continuing, petty annoyances and inconvenient situations to put up with, and you should never have to make do or rough it.

It may, however, take some time before you get your full-timing lifestyle in order so that you don't feel like a harried vacationer. The first day you set off you may think that Murphy's Law—if something can go wrong it will—was invented just for you. As on a vacation, there will probably be some glitches at first.

Hang in there. You'll have to give yourself time to settle into the routines of this different lifestyle, time to get the feel of it. It may be rocky at first, but eventually things will sort themselves out and you'll be able to enjoy yourself to the fullest.

WHO ARE FULLTIMERS?

Fulltimers are young, middle-aged, and old, those who are retired and those who are employed, parents with school-age children, those with no children, and those whose children are grown and on their own. Fulltimers are families, couples, and singles.

Some fulltimers live in their RVs year-round and travel much of the time, rarely spending more than a month in any one place. They have no home other than their RV. (This is the type of full-timing we do.)

Others live exclusively in their RVs but spend the winter months in one location and the summer in another. The only major traveling they do is following the seasons twice a year. They often seasonally rent the same site in the same park year after year.

Others may travel during part of the year, living in their RVs while doing so, and return periodically to a fixed, permanent dwelling that is their primary home and where they live most of the time.

Some mild controversy has arisen over who can correctly and rightfully call themselves fulltimers. Whether someone qualifies in another's perception as a fulltimer is not important. Labels, names, and designations don't mean a thing as long as you are doing what you want and having fun.

A site on the World Wide Web of interest to both fulltimers and potential fulltimers is http://www.fulltiming-america.com.

CHAPTER 2

How Much Will Fulltiming Cost?

Fulltiming can be an economical way to live, although some expenses will be the same as those of a nonmobile lifestyle, some will increase, and some will decrease. How much it costs can be controlled in large measure by the decisions you make before venturing into the lifestyle and when you are actually on the road.

THE FULL-TIMING RIG

Preliminary cost control begins with the selection of the full-timing rig. The would-be fulltimer has lots of options available when choosing an RV: It may be new or used, large or small, a luxury or utilitarian model, a motorhome, a travel trailer, or a fifth-wheel trailer.

What you can afford to pay for the type of unit you want is the next consideration. If you purchase a used trailer and already own a proper tow vehicle, you can be on the road in a suitable, fairly recent model RV for around $15,000, or you can spend well into the six-figure range for a new, luxurious motorhome.

Most new trailers cost much less than new motorhomes because they don't have an engine and drivetrain. But if a tow vehicle must be purchased along with the trailer, the total cost of the rig can be comparable to that of a mid-priced motorhome.

Preowned Units

For those who can't afford a new unit, there is always a selection of good, used RVs to choose from. Preowned motorhomes and trailers are available for prices ranging from one-third to one-half the cost of new units. Sometimes a tow vehicle is offered with a trailer when sold by a private party.

Once we were parked in a site next to a new-looking, big, pricey motorhome in Skidaway Island State Park near Savannah, Georgia. During a conversation with Jack, the owner of the motorhome, he told us how he had acquired his impressive RV. "I certainly couldn't afford to buy this new," he said.

He went on to tell us that the previous owner had spared no expense in having the motorhome customized just the way he wanted it. He had used it for a short time before his business failed at about the same time he was getting a divorce. He had to raise some cash quickly so he sold his motorhome for much less than it cost him. Jack was the happy buyer of what was a fantastic bargain.

Many preowned units, like Jack's, have been used only for vacations and occasional weekends, so they have low mileage and little actual wear, even though they may be many years old.

Some RVers who have been planning to become fulltimers may already have an adequate rig. One way or another, it's not too difficult to find some sort of affordable rig in which to get started.

Equipping a Tow Vehicle

When you take delivery of a new motorhome it's ready for the road, but a new or preowned tow vehicle may not be outfitted with all, or any, of the equipment needed for pulling a trailer.

If you're ordering a tow vehicle from the manufacturer be sure to order it with the towing package.

Before a trailer can be towed, a hitch of the proper type is needed. For a travel trailer, you'll need a load-distributing hitch, a receiver, and a sway control. A fifth-wheel trailer requires a hitch that is mounted in the bed of a pickup truck—the only suitable tow vehicle for this type of trailer.

The tow vehicle also needs a trailer brake controller, and unless factory equipped with a towing package, a wiring harness, probably a heavy-duty transmission oil cooler, and possibly heavy-duty shock absorbers.

The cost of the towing assembly and its installation is often offered as a package by the trailer dealer when a trailer is purchased.

If you don't buy a trailer from a dealer, a place that does RV repairs or one that specializes in hitch installations can install the equipment.

What About Extra Equipment?

Motorhomes and trailers come equipped with just about everything needed to live comfortably. All modern units are completely furnished, tastefully decorated, and have the basic major appliances built in. You can add lots of other options and upgrade some standard equipment on new units as your budget allows, but today's RVs are all ready for living in except for adding such items as pots and pans, dinnerware, flatware, linens, clothing, and personal items.

Some optional equipment adds to the enjoyment of fulltiming. The major and most expensive items of optional equipment wanted by most fulltimers are an air conditioner—two of them may be needed if the unit is large—and an awning.

The fulltimer should have a few other miscellaneous items (these are discussed in the appropriate chapters), but most aren't especially costly, and purchasing them shouldn't dent anyone's budget. Used units already may have many accessories and extra equipment.

Auxiliary Transportation for Motorhomers

Those who opt for a motorhome probably will want an auxiliary vehicle (also called a dinghy, tag-a-long, or toad) so the motorhome won't have to be their only means of transportation. Once the motorhome is parked, whether for the night, week, month, or season, it's neither convenient nor practical to break camp for shopping and sightseeing trips.

Some people may already own a suitable vehicle for this purpose. If not, the initial cost has to be figured into the budget. And for both present and new owners, the continuing costs of operating the auxiliary vehicle must be considered. With the auxiliary vehicle and the motorhome, there are two engines to be maintained and repaired.

Unless someone will be driving the auxiliary vehicle as you travel, a towing apparatus will be needed. This can be a simple tow bar or a more elaborate, and more expensive, tow dolly.

Some motorhomers use a motorcycle as an auxiliary vehicle, and store it in a rack installed on the back of the motorhome, although this is not a recommended practice.

Operating Costs

Towing a car, just like towing a trailer, increases the fuel consumption of the towing vehicle. Since fuel is one of the major expenditures for most traveling fulltimers, the miles per gallon you are likely to get is an important consideration when purchasing the rig.

If you have any doubts about the importance of this expenditure, take a careful look at Table 2.1. Obviously, having a motorhome or tow vehicle that is fuel efficient results in significant savings.

It is, however, very difficult to determine what the fuel consumption will be for a particular rig. Mileage figures are affected

TABLE 2.1
A Comparison of RV Fuel Costs*

MPG	Gallons to Travel 5,000 Miles	Average Cost per Gallon	Total Fuel Cost
16	312.5	$1.30	$406.25
12	416.7		541.71
9	555.5		722.15
6	833.4		1,083.42

*Figures rounded to the nearest tenth.

by so many variables—driving habits, the condition of the vehicle's engine, whether it's maintained properly, the weather and areas in which the vehicle is driven, the loaded weight of the rig—that EPA ratings or the word of someone who is trying to sell you a unit give only an indication of how much fuel may be consumed.

A fact that cannot be disputed is: The amount of fuel consumed increases in direct proportion to the size and weight of the unit. Therefore, fuel expenses won't be so high if you purchase a small or lightweight RV.

Although motorhomes have a reputation for being fuel guzzlers—many average less than ten miles per gallon—a tow vehicle pulling a large, heavy trailer also consumes lots of fuel. If a truck is used as a tow vehicle, a half-ton truck is the most economical as far as fuel is concerned, but a three-quarter-ton or one-ton or even larger truck may be needed to pull a heavy trailer.

Vehicles with high axle ratios (numerically) are necessary for towing any type of heavy load. As the axle ratio increases (numerically), fuel consumption also increases.

In relation to operating costs, another point to consider is the number of wheels a unit may have. Some big trailers have three axles and six wheels instead of the two axles and four wheels found on smaller trailers. Motorhomes have dual rear wheels, and larger rigs may have tandem axles, adding two more wheels. Eventually, all the tires on all the wheels have to be replaced. In addition is the continuing expense of servicing all the wheel bearings and brakes.

Should You Keep a Home Base?

While the most economical traveling can be done in a unit that is easy on fuel, much of the cost of fulltiming depends on the type of home base you maintain or whether you maintain a home base at all. Of course, if you have no home base, you have nothing to maintain, therefore no expenses connected with it.

A home base should not be confused with a legal residence; for many they are one and the same, but a legal residence does not necessarily have to be your home base and vice versa. (Legal residences are discussed fully in Chapter 4, "Special Situations and How to Handle Them.")

Not having a home base is one of the reasons we've been able to live so economically as fulltimers. The only home we have anywhere, the only dwelling we own, is our trailer. In fact, we couldn't afford to travel as we do if we had the additional expense of maintaining a house or any other fixed home base. On our budget, it has to be one or the other; however, we are perfectly content with our mobile dwelling and have never felt the need to have any place to go back to periodically.

The closest thing we have to a home base (the term is a misnomer because it's neither our home nor our base) is our mailing address, which is that of a relative. We visit this "home base" infrequently, and when we do, we continue to live in our trailer while we are there. (In all the years we have been fulltiming, we have spent every night in our RV except for three. Each of these times our trailer was in a repair shop overnight.)

One of the alluring aspects of fulltiming is the freedom it offers, but much of the freedom gained is eroded when you have a fixed-dwelling home base. In many ways, fulltimers with a home base have only a little more freedom than do full-time house dwellers going off on an annual vacation.

More Costs, More Work

Many fulltimers and those contemplating the lifestyle feel they must have a place other than their RV they can call home. This is unfortunate for those on tight budgets, because keeping up such a place is a burdensome, extra expense. Fulltimers who maintain any sort of a permanent residence other than their RV will spend more than those who do not. It doesn't matter whether the residence is a house, a condominium, an apartment, a mobile home, a park-model trailer, a campsite rented on an annual basis, or a campsite purchased outright. Certain expenses are incurred with all of them. A fixed dwelling situated on a piece of land that you own or are paying for is the type of home base that costs the most.

The Costs of a House

If you have a house you intend to keep as your home base, total up the amount you must pay for it annually: maintenance, repairs, insurance, taxes, perhaps mortgage payments. Can you afford to keep it if you are a fulltimer? If you can, will it be worth it? Or could the money spent on the house, which may be used for only a few weeks a year, be put to better use?

As long as you have the house, you'll have to spend money to keep it up in order to protect your investment and have a decent place to come back to. Major repairs, such as replacing the roofing, have to be done as needed. When the washer or other major appliance gives up the ghost, it has to be replaced. You'll also have to allocate some funds for insurance and the annual taxes. No real estate taxes are so low that they are an insignificant amount to fulltimers who have to watch what they spend.

Renting the house to defray expenses doesn't often work out because the rent that can be charged usually does not take care of all the costs. In addition, if you aren't there to oversee the property, you may have to pay someone to do the job.

It's one thing when you own property for the purpose of renting it; it's quite another matter when you are renting out your own home. Generally, tenants don't maintain the place as an owner would. Bad tenants may neglect it to the point of ruin. Something else to consider: If the property is rented, it may not be available for you to live in whenever you want to.

Each time you return to the house, you have to secure it before you leave again. All utilities have to be shut off or disconnected; newspaper delivery may have to be canceled; windows and doors have to be double-checked to be sure they are all closed and locked; chores, such as cleaning out the refrigerator, must be done; timers and alarms on security systems have to be set and activated; and arrangements have to be made for the disposition of mail. If you'll be away for some time during the warm months of the year, someone should come around periodically to take care of the yard work. And someone should be available to check on the house when you are away.

In addition to all these going-away preparations, dwellings in climates subject to freezing temperatures need to be winterized before you head for the Sunbelt. You'll have to decide if you want the expense, and perhaps the danger, of leaving the furnace on, or if you'd rather take the time to drain all the water lines and protect from freezing anything that needs it. If you have ever winterized an RV you know what a time-consuming job it is. The process is magnified tremendously when dealing with all the systems in a house. Arrangements should be made for someone to shovel the walkways in case of snow. Uncleared walks, like untended yards, and any other indication that the house is vacant, may make it a prime target for thieves and vandals.

When you return, whatever the season, you'll have to make the place livable for the time you'll spend there before it has to be made secure again. It's an endless cycle.

You can only hope you never return to find the basement full of water, termites at work, the roof caved in, or the place stripped bare by thieves. If nothing so drastic happens, it will be amazing if reactivating the systems is all you have to do when you arrive. Something always needs to be done around a house even if one is living in it all the time; houses left unattended seem to need a lot more work, so you can count on doing the odd jobs and repairs that have piled up in your absence.

If you have a house you will, in effect, be living in two places, so you'll do a certain amount of packing and unpacking. Like the vacationer, you may find that you have forgotten something you'll need and left it where you are not.

What Price Security?

We saw a survey that revealed that most fulltimers who were holding onto a dwelling for a home base were doing so to have a place to return to when they can no longer fulltime or when they voluntarily give up the lifestyle.

If this is the reason you want to keep a fixed dwelling, ask yourself: What could cause my fulltiming to come to an end?

Old age? What is old age in relation to fulltiming? Is it when you are so infirm that you can't perform the functions needed for setting up a campsite? Is it when your driving abilities are no longer as good as they used to be? Speculate as to what age you'll be when you consider yourself to be old.

We have met many fulltimers in their seventies and some in their eighties. If you can't manage to hook up your RV and take care of the little maintenance it requires, how will you ever take care of a house?

Bad health can be a valid reason for giving up fulltiming, but consider whether it makes sense to move back into a house because of what ails you. If heart trouble or emphysema is your problem and you can't overtax yourself, who will take care of your house? On top of your medical expenses, you may have to pay for help to take care of all the maintenance you used to do.

If you need regular medical treatments that can be performed only at a hospital or clinic, you can find these facilities in places other than where the house is.

To bring up a subject discussed earlier, if you need a walker, crutches, or a cane to get around, why put yourself in the position of having to traverse the large rooms and perhaps stairways in a house when you can maneuver more quickly and easily in an RV? There are so many convenient handholds and supports in an RV that a walker may not be needed when moving around in it. Such is not the case in any average room in a house.

Conceivably, you could become tired or bored being a traveling fulltimer, but it's not necessary to have a house if you decide to settle down.

What we are getting at is something that evidently did not occur to any of the survey's respondents: If you stop fulltiming, for whatever reason, you don't necessarily have to give up living in an RV and go back to a fixed dwelling. Why not continue to live in the RV? If you have chosen well, it will be comfortable, efficiently designed, require little maintenance, and have storage space for everything you need and want.

If your traveling home has been a compromise between space and a larger unit's fuel consumption, you can purchase a large unit to live in when you stop traveling. Mileage figures won't be a concern if it's permanently parked or used infrequently for travel.

As a permanent, full-time residence, an RV has a lot to offer over and above being an inexpensive dwelling with low-cost, easy maintenance. No matter how long it's parked, it still retains much of its mobility and probably can be moved without too much trouble. This can be an advantage if, for instance, you find the RV park you have chosen has been built over a toxic waste dump, the neighborhood deteriorates or becomes the target of criminals, air pollution increases in the area, a superhighway is built adjacent to where you are parked, you need or want to move to another climate, or you just don't like the neighbors. If you are a working fulltimer who is out of a job, your home can be moved from a place of high unemployment to a better economic area. Moving an RV is a lot less trouble than moving roomfuls of furniture and having to sell one house in order to be able to buy another.

Many of the people who participated in the survey said that keeping a house gave them a feeling of security. Whether the mortgage is paid off or not, any house continues to cost you money until it's sold. It doesn't matter whether the property is appreciating or depreciating, funds for it come out of your pocket on a regular basis. What sort of security is that?

Some believe that owning a house provides security for the future, but real estate values never stay constant; they can go down as well as up. Owners shouldn't count on a house being worth more in later years. And real estate can only be converted into cash when a buyer is found who is willing to pay the amount you'll accept.

All the foregoing won't make a bit of difference if you want to hang onto your house for sentimental reasons. Many cherished memories are associated with houses. They may be places where children have grown up; they may be filled with things you have built with your own hands or surrounded with plantings you have nurtured and watched grow to maturity from seedlings. For some, the house may not be as important as the possessions in it—family heirlooms, hobbyists' collections, or valuable furniture. Only you can decide if the emotional attachment is really worth the cost and time needed for keeping up a house.

It's true that when most people begin fulltiming they maintain some sort of home base; many do it for the reason we mentioned earlier: to try out fulltiming while having a place to come back to

*"**O**nly you can decide if the emotional attachment is really worth the cost and time needed for keeping up a house."*

in case it doesn't work out—a valid and sensible reason. But some of those who become committed to the full-timing life don't want the expense and nuisance of having a home base and get rid of it when they realize how much it directly affects and hinders their new way of living.

Expenses: A Comparison

One important thing to remember, once you start fulltiming, is that it will be your everyday way of life. You won't be on vacation—even though it may seem like it—so, chances are, your budget won't stand the strain of spending money for extras and luxuries as you might when on a two- or three-week trip.

Many people begin fulltiming with a being-on-holiday attitude—why not celebrate such an event?—but most of us have to be careful not to spend too many of our hard-earned dollars on vacation-type frivolities.

Day-to-Day Expenses

Excluding an initial cutting-loose celebration, many of your expenses will be generally the same as when you lived in a fixed dwelling, unless the beginning of your fulltiming happens to coincide with a drop or increase in income and you need to revamp your budget. Being a fulltimer does not necessarily mean you'll change your habits and priorities.

You aren't likely to alter your eating habits just because of your new lifestyle, so food expenditures will probably remain the same. Most likely, so will the number of times you eat out compared with the number of meals you eat at home.

You'll probably continue with any long-standing personal habits you may have, such as having a libation before dinner, to the same extent as prefulltiming, so the expenses connected with them will remain virtually the same.

Fulltiming will do nothing to affect what you normally spend for periodic medical and dental checkups.

Life and medical insurance costs won't change just because you are living in an RV; however, vehicle insurance rates may increase if you have an expensive rig or if you drive more miles in a year than is considered average.

If you leave a white-collar job, you may be able to save substantially on clothes since you won't have to maintain a business wardrobe. Casual wear is appropriate for fulltiming, and the lifestyle requires no special clothing. Selectivity about the climates in which you spend your time may enable you to do away with heavy winter clothing, but no matter how sunny the clime, some cool- and cold-weather garments will be needed every now and then.

More money may be spent on vehicle fuel and maintenance, depending on the amount of traveling you do.

In addition to sightseeing, many of us want to visit certain attractions we come across in our travels. Admission fees for these and other entertainment expenses can be more or less than you previously spent, depending on what you can afford.

If these expenses were all that had to be considered, fulltiming could cost more than, or just as much as, other nonmobile lifestyles. But you may have noticed that two significant items are missing from the budget categories: taxes and shelter. Both of these can be "adjusted" to make fulltiming a relatively inexpensive way to live.

Shelter Expenses and Tax Concerns

Because fulltimers can choose where they want to register their vehicles, they can decide on a place where wheel taxes or personal-property taxes are low or nonexistent. They can also select a place with no sales tax or a low one for purchasing big-ticket items. If a state income tax must be paid, fulltimers can arrange to "live" in a state that takes less of a bite than others. A good possibility exists as well that some of the taxes a person paid before becoming a fulltimer may no longer be applicable.

The budget category for a fulltimer's shelter is the rent paid for a place to park an RV—in other words, campground fees. It's possible to spend much less on these fees than what may be spent for renting an apartment or maintaining a house, with or without attendant mortgage payments.

Let's say campground fees are $20 for an overnight stay. At this rate the costs for an entire year would be $7,300, or $608 a month. This is what may be paid for rent on a small apartment or payments on a modest mortgage. So where do the full-timing savings come in? We used a $20 overnight fee for our example and, although some campgrounds have fees of $20 or higher, just as many and more have fees that are much lower. Sometimes even free campgrounds can be found.

For the last year our rent has averaged just under $12.00 a night. This included a few (very few) stays in campgrounds that charged $20.00 or more, and one week where no fee was paid because we were parked in a relative's driveway. We were not making any special effort to economize, but we followed our usual practice: if there are several campgrounds in an area where we want to stay, we tend to patronize those with a price below that of the most expensive ones. Our total yearly expenditure for shelter was $4334.27, which averages out to $361.00 a month. In what other lifestyle would the amount spent for shelter be so low?

The shelter figure is lower still when you take into account that our campground fees included all utilities and sometimes cable TV. If we had concentrated on spending as little as possible for each night's stay—which would have meant going out of our way in some instances or doing without hookups for the sake of saving money—our annual expenditure for shelter would have been even lower.

Cost-Cutting Tactics

Once into the full-timing way of life, there are additional ways to economize. Being a do-it-yourselfer for maintenance and repairs, for instance, helps in holding down expenses.

One of the best tactics for saving a good deal of money is simply to cut down on traveling. Go somewhere and stay awhile instead of overnighting so much.

The immediate and considerable saving is on fuel. Instead of fueling up once or twice a day, you may find as much as a week may go by before you need fuel. You'll realize long-range savings because the regular maintenance of the vehicle won't have to be performed so often and, since there is less wear and tear, the need for repairs and replacements is lessened.

Saving on Campground Fees

While the highest campground rate is for overnighting, most private campgrounds have weekly and monthly rates, and some offer seasonal and yearly rates. So if you stay in one campground for a week or longer instead of traveling to a different campground every day or so, another significant saving will be on campground fees.

The common weekly rates amount to receiving one night's stay free: Six nights are paid at the regular overnight rate and the seventh night is free.

Sometimes you can find a place where the weekly rate is discounted even more. We have stayed in numerous places where the weekly rate was less than three or four days at the daily rate.

When we pull into a place intending to stay for overnight and find it has especially attractive weekly rate and it's located in a place we like, we often decide to stay over for a week, or sometimes longer.

Monthly rates average less per day than weekly rates. How they are determined varies widely. In some campgrounds we have found the monthly charge to be less than half the cost it would have been if we paid by the day, yet in other campgrounds the monthly rate was only slightly less than renting the site by the week. Yearly rates are the lowest of all, if they are available. Generally, campgrounds in and around cities and large metropolitan areas are the most expensive as well as being the most crowded.

RV parks in popular vacation areas and resort localities may offer seasonal rates. Although staying for the season, in season, is cheaper than staying at these places on a shorter-term basis, such places may be much more expensive than a campground in a less popular area.

Another way to economize is to avoid places that are advertised as resort campgrounds, such as those that have a swimming pool, tennis courts, a golf course, stables, a marina or boat rentals, a water slide, or saunas. All this fancy equipment has to be paid for and maintained and these costs are reflected in the rates.

For long-term stops, most of us want all the hookups—electricity, water, sewer—but for overnight or a few days, not all these conveniences may be needed. Some RV parks have a base rate for a site and an individual charge for the electricity, water, and sewer. Each hookup may have a different charge; the range is generally from $1 to $3. The higher figure is usually for the electric hookup; sometimes water is included with the electric charge. On top of this may be an additional charge of $1 to $3 if you want to run an electric heater or an air conditioner. To save money in places with individual charges, don't pay for more than you intend to use, and don't hook up to anything you don't need.

In campgrounds where each hookup carries an individual charge, we habitually pay for only an electrical hookup. If we have filled our water tank and dumped the holding tanks at the campground where we stayed the day before, we have no need for anything but electricity and sometimes not even that. Even if we are running low on water and the holding tanks need to be emptied, sometimes we can take care of the filling and dumping at no charge at a highway rest area. We also frequent state, city, and county parks where we can dump on the way in, if we need to, and on the way out, at no charge.

You can see how a little calculated planning can save you some money. Not spending even so little as a dollar can add up to quite a bit if you do it often enough.

Staying in a campground just because it's inexpensive may not be economical if the campground is miles from a place you want to visit or far from a town where you'll be shopping for supplies. Calculate the amount of fuel it will take to make the round trip to your destination, and multiply that figure by the number of times you'll make such a trip. You may find it's cheaper, in the long run, to pay a higher rate at a closer-in campground. For a long-term stay, the costs of going out for a daily newspaper, making regular trips to the post office, and perhaps, having to drive a distance to a public telephone should be figured in. They can mount up.

The attractive rate we found at an out-of-the-way campground wasn't nearly so appealing when we realized we would have to make an eight-mile round trip to purchase a daily paper and a two-mile round trip to use the telephone at the entrance gate—the only public telephone in this large park.

Stay Longer, Save More

Staying a while in one place can lower your campground costs but it can also aid in cost-cutting in another way. You'll be in an area long enough to take advantage of sales and specials on groceries, clothing, vehicle maintenance, replacement items, hair care, meals, even entertainment.

All you need to do is buy the local newspaper and pick up free "shoppers" and visitor guides, then read the ads looking for special offers and clip any coupons you may use. You may find movies at reduced prices, "early-bird" or two-for-one restaurant specials, and senior citizen discounts. Aside from advertising special grocery prices, supermarket ads sometimes contain a number of coupons enabling you to double your manufacturer's coupons, or their ads may contain the valuable information that they double all coupons. Newspapers and shoppers also carry ads for garage sales and flea markets where bargains often can be found.

We vividly remember one day when we saved a whopping $101.19 over what we would have spent if we had done our shopping without previously checking out the local newspaper.

First, we saved money in the supermarket. We had coupon savings of $7.30 because we learned from the newspaper that a particular supermarket was doubling manufacturers' coupons that day and we never do any supermarket shopping without our coupon collection in hand. The amount we saved with coupons was over and above any in-store specials we bought; we didn't keep a record of those.

At that time we were working on a project that required extensive photography. We had noticed a discount catalog store in town and thought it might be a good place to obtain some film-processing mailers we needed. It was. We bought a quantity of them and saved a total of $17.52 over the regular, or undiscounted, price. This turned out to be an especially fortunate purchase because with the amount of mailers we bought, we received a manufacturer's rebate form for five free mailers worth $29.25.

We had a newspaper coupon for vehicle air-conditioner servicing that allowed us to have this needed job done on our truck for less than half the usual price—$17.00 saved. We needed some reference books for our project and knew, again from a newspaper ad, that one of the bookstores in town was giving an across-the-board discount of 20 percent. This amounted to $5.17 on our purchases. We came across an apparel item for which we had been searching for some time. It was on a sale rack for less than half the regular price, resulting in another sizable saving of $15.00. For lunch we used a buy-one-get-one-free coupon we had clipped, so the check for both of us was $7.95. On the way back to the RV park, we noticed a car wash that was having a special that day. We ran our filthy truck through and saved another $2.00.

We had not planned this bargain-finding onslaught; we were just going about our business as we normally do, which is using coupons and taking advantage of specials wherever we can.

We have met some fulltimers who never buy or read any newspapers. One woman said she never reads them because they are full of bad news and they depress her. Another said, "I don't know any of the local people here, and I don't care about what goes on in this town." And some just think that reading the newspaper is a chore and one they don't wish to take on now that they are experiencing their new-found full-timing freedom. But whether or not the news is read, the sum spent for a newspaper can often result in quite a return on the investment for those of us who have to watch what we spend. We don't use all the coupons in the Sunday paper, but we consider this paper to be free most times because the value of the coupons we do use nearly always exceeds the cost of the paper.

The longer we stay in a place, the better we know it, and this too can help save money. We learn which places charge the highest prices, be they restaurants, supermarkets, service stations, or pharmacies, and we patronize other establishments. We have the time and opportunity to become acquainted with local people who often have information about where bargains can be found. Recently we were telling a local resident about a great lunch bargain we had found. She proceeded to tell us about an even better one in a restaurant we had avoided because we thought it was too expensive.

When we stay in one place for a while, we like to be in or near small towns with populations of about 20,000 to 30,000. Towns of this size have a variety of competing businesses and provides us with better opportunities for finding the lowest prices and the best deal. If you stay in a town that has, for instance, one grocery store and one service station, you have no choice but to pay whatever is asked, no matter what the price.

*"**W**e don't use all the coupons in the Sunday paper, but we consider this paper to be free most times because the value of the coupons we do use nearly always exceeds the cost of the paper."*

While you're likely to find many more bargains in big cities than in small towns, often the fuel used to cover the miles to reach them offsets much of what you may save. It may be possible to walk to many places in small towns.

Other Economies

Saving money also results when you practice conservation of consumables. Here are some methods for cutting propane and other expenses:

- If you're purchasing an RV, be sure it's well-insulated.
- Select window coverings that provide insulating qualities.
- Be sure the water heater is set for efficient operation; the flame on ours was too high until we adjusted it.
- Set the water-heater thermostat on low.
- If you have a water heater that is not electronically controlled, try using just the pilot light to keep the water hot in warm weather.
- Set the furnace thermostat low at night and during the times the RV is unoccupied, or turn it off when you leave the RV.
- Use a catalytic heater instead of the furnace.
- In campgrounds with electricity included in the fee, operate the refrigerator in the electric mode, and do as much cooking as you can with a microwave oven and other electric appliances.
- Outfit your RV for boondocking. This allows you to comfortably stay in campgrounds that have no hookups—such campgrounds usually have very low rates—or park free in certain places.
- Arrange to have the water and holding tanks empty if you'll be driving many miles. The less weight hauled around, the less fuel consumed.

- We can estimate fairly accurately how long it takes us to use a cylinder of propane, so we often put off filling the cylinder that's empty until necessary to avoid pulling the weight of two full cylinders.

It won't take more than a month or two of full-time living in your RV to learn how long you can expect a cylinder of propane to last. You'll also be able to determine how long the water in the freshwater tank will last with normal use, and how many days can go by before the holding tanks need to be emptied. You'll have to spend money for the propane eventually; however, at certain times you may not need to spend anything for water and sewer hookups or for a dumping fee if you have a basis on which to estimate how full the tanks are.

MEMBERSHIP CAMPGROUNDS: WORTH THE COST?

Since you'll probably be doing a fair amount of traveling when you're a fulltimer, you may wonder if it's worthwhile to join a membership campground. The answer is: Maybe, maybe not. It depends on your own travel habits and finances.

All the large membership campground associations operate in basically the same way: The initiation, or joining, fee costs thousands of dollars. The cost may be $5,000 or a little lower, but it can be much higher. This amount can be paid all at once or in periodic installments—with a finance charge added on, of course. In addition to the initiation fee are annual dues; a typical amount is $300.

Being a member does not give you the opportunity to buy a lot or campsite; it means you can stay free at the campground where you joined—your home campground—for a given amount of time each year. At some home campgrounds, thirty days is the maximum number of days you can stay in one year; other home campgrounds may have maximums of fewer days.

TABLE 2.2
Membership Campground Typical Annual Costs

Initial membership cost	$7,000	
(Cost per year, amortized over 10 years)		$700
Yearly dues		200
		———
Yearly base cost		$900

You can also stay at other affiliated campgrounds in the association (the majority of which are closed to nonmembers) but perhaps not for as long a period as at your home campground. At these other campgrounds you must pay an extra charge for each night you stay; typically this charge is $4.00, and you must make reservations in advance.

The affiliated campgrounds are promoted as "destination resorts"—the sort of place at which one might spend an entire vacation. While it's true that many of the campgrounds in each association have the amenities of a resort and are in desirable vacation areas, not all the campgrounds in an association meet these criteria.

The largest associations, such as Coast to Coast, Thousand Trails, and NACO have affiliated campgrounds throughout the country, which makes it seem as if joining may be worthwhile for a traveling fulltimer. A common problem, though, is that popular tourist areas are heavily saturated with these campgrounds—campgrounds in the same association may be just a few miles from one another—yet in some states there may be only a few campgrounds, perhaps even none. If you can't count on staying at the campgrounds in your association a large percentage of the time as you travel without having to drive miles out of your way to do so, it will take you quite a while to break even on the expenditure required.

Table 2.2 shows what the yearly base cost might be for a typical membership amortized over ten years. It does not include finance charges, miscellaneous costs, and any assessments that may be made, which will increase the base cost by an unknown amount, and expecting the annual dues to remain the same for ten years is unrealistic. The table also doesn't include the $4 charge that must be paid each time you overnight at an affiliated campground. You'll have to estimate what that amount may be and include it as part of your annual expenditure. Considering all the amounts, nebulous as they are, and projecting if you can stay in enough affiliated campgrounds during the year, may give you a rough idea as to whether a membership may be practical for you.

We figured it out long ago and came to the conclusion that a campground membership wouldn't be cost effective for us, and we were right. We must go where our work takes us, and, for the most part, that has been, and continues to be, in areas where there is a dearth of membership campgrounds. Another reason it wouldn't work for us is because our loose schedule isn't compatible with making advance reservations. On the other hand, we recently talked with a new fulltimer who was our campground neighbor and found that he belonged to four membership campground associations!

Purchasing and Selling an Existing Membership

As a buyer you may be able to purchase a campground membership at a bargain if it's offered for sale by an individual or through a broker. Such a membership can usually be purchased for about 30 to 50 percent of its original cost or less. A transfer fee is almost always involved in a transaction of this sort and can be as much as 20 percent of the original owner's cost. Of course, this means that as a seller of an existing campground membership you'll take quite a loss.

If you are buying or selling through a broker be sure you are dealing with a reputable one. Sellers should be suspicious of a broker who tells you your membership can be sold at close to what you paid for it.

Some people with a campground membership find that they can't sell it because the contract they signed contained a lifetime membership clause (which may be illegal in some states). Such a clause means you agree to keep the membership for life—whether you use it or not. If an illness or partner's death causes you to give up RVing, you would still be liable for all the yearly costs and remaining installments, if any, on the initiation fee. Although reluctant to do so, sometimes the association will buy back a lifetime membership. You'll have to pay a hefty fee for the privilege of selling and, as with any resale, accept a resale price of 30 to 50 percent less than your original cost.

Buyers should look carefully for any clause that states, however obscurely, that you are buying a lifetime membership.

Buyer Beware

From a monetary aspect, if you think it's worth it to purchase a campground membership, there are other aspects to consider in addition to the lifetime provision before you sign on the dotted line.

Carefully scrutinize clauses relating to transferring your membership. If it's non-transferable, it can obligate you in just about the same way as a lifetime membership.

Once you have a membership, you may be offered an upgrade, that is, you pay more money for which you are supposed to receive more benefits. Another name for an upgrade is reloading and in too many instances all that happens is reloading an additional finical burden on the owner. If you are offered an upgrade, investigate it thoroughly to find out if you will indeed benefit from it. Sometimes when a cash problem exists at a campground, upgrades are offered simply to obtain funds to keep the campground operating. Be suspicious if scare tactics are used to get you to buy.

If you feel you have been pressured into signing a contract to join a membership be aware that such contracts are subject to the "three-day-cooling-off rule." This is a federal regulation allowing you to rescind the contract within three days of signing it. Some states have similar rules and may have longer "cooling-off" periods.

We haven't begun to cover all the ramifications of buying, selling, and using a campground membership. Various rules, regulations, and covenants have to be abided by to use or sell your membership. Understand what they are in your particular contract.

Some key points to consider (in addition to those mentioned above) include:

- Know how much is at risk if you default in any way; in some cases, you could lose your entire investment.
- How and when may your membership be sold and what fees are involved?
- What is the ratio of sites to members in the home campground? If it's too many, you may find it difficult to get a reservation.
- What happens if your home park goes bankrupt?
- Can you use other affiliated campgrounds in your area, or must they be a certain distance (100 or 125 miles is typical) from your home park?

Although many states strictly regulate the manner in which membership campground associations can operate, some states have no regulations at all. No matter in which state the membership is sold, buyers, for their own protection, must read and thoroughly understand what they sign.

Other Types of Membership Campgrounds

If you think the type of campground membership described above won't suit you, you might consider a different type. There are some that have no initiation fee and annual dues ranging from about $50 to $200. When you join you'll be able to stay at certain private campgrounds—which are open to the general public—for rates that may be half the usual rate, or as little as $5. Ads for these associations may be found in RVing publications, and membership in certain RV clubs may give you the opportunity to join these associations at reduced annual dues.

LIVING WITHIN YOUR BUDGET

As we have shown, when fulltiming some of your expenses will be the same, some will lessen, and some will increase. Figuring out the expenditures for those budget items that will remain the same is no problem, but the expenses that will be less or more can be determined only by actually living for a few months as a fulltimer. Only then can you know if you are going over budget on such items as fuel and campground fees.

It's wise to be cautious when beginning fulltiming if your funds are limited. For example, don't start off on a quick cross-country trip the first day you begin fulltiming unless you know you can afford it. Nothing is wrong with planning such a major trip across the United States, but do it in small sections at first to get the feel of where your money will be spent and how fast its outgo will be. If it's disappearing too quickly, slow down your traveling.

CHAPTER 3

Where Will the Money Come From?

I t requires money to be a fulltimer, just as it does to live in any other way. You must either have an income of some sort, work as you go, or stop traveling for a while and work until you earn enough money to go again.

Many retirees can count on a monthly social security or pension check or income from investments. This is one of the reasons that most fulltimers are retired persons, and may lead those who are not retired to believe they can't become fulltimers until they too retire. This does not have to be the case. As we have shown, fulltiming can be less expensive than a nonmobile lifestyle, so an early retirement with perhaps a little less money coming in might be considered.

WORK AWHILE, TRAVEL AWHILE

If retirement is far in the future, as it was for us when we started fulltiming, it's conceivable that you could work for a few months and earn enough to tide you over to travel for several months. No matter what your age, it may be possible to earn a living by working as you travel.

Some occupations are ideal for those fulltimers who need to work for a time to earn traveling money: server in restaurants, bartender, cook, construction worker, and many construction-related trades such as electrician, plumber, painter, mason, or carpenter. Many of these jobs are seasonal or for a designated period of time, so they are inherently short term. Nurses are in demand just about everywhere. It rarely matters whether they want to work for a few months or a year; most medical facilities are happy to have them for any length of time.

Fast-food restaurants offer job opportunities for those interested in short-term employment. No one expects employees of such establishments to stay on the job for very long unless they are interested in advancing to a management position.

Other work where a lengthy commitment is not required or expected may be in general maintenance jobs of any kind, such as lawn care, landscaping, janitorial jobs, and cleaning and readying new cars or RVs at a dealership.

Working in orchards and on farms is another way to earn money seasonally. Once we were in Montana when the cherry growers had an exceptionally fruitful season. They needed more cherry pickers than they could find. Many had large signs next to the highway offering free RV space for anyone who would help them out. We were tempted to stop and earn a few extra dollars, but right then the kitty was pretty full so we just bought and ate the delicious fruit others had picked.

Another year, in Virginia, we noticed strawberry pickers were in great demand. In some areas in certain seasons, huckleberries and some kinds of mushrooms can be gathered and sold to buyers who station themselves along the roadsides.

If you have word processing or other computer or office skills, they can be marketed through employment agencies that specialize in temporaries, or you can contract for work independently. Although the focus of agencies for temps used to be office workers, nowadays, no matter what your field, such an agency may be able to find work for you.

> "If you have word processing or other computer or office skills, they can be marketed through employment agencies that specialize in temporaries, or you can contract for work independently."

If much of what you do in your regular job is computer work, it can usually be done on any computer no matter where it is located. Many engineers, designers, and word processors do their work on a computer in their home. In the case of a fulltimer, the home would be an RV. (See Chapter 11, "An RV Office for Working Fulltimers" for more about computers and fulltiming.)

Seasonal work is always available from concessionaires who operate restaurants, gift shops, lodging facilities, service stations, convenience stores, stables, marinas, and the like in national parks. Privately owned resorts have need for the same type of personnel, as well as instructors for activities such as scuba diving, horseback riding, swimming, tennis, and golf. There may be need for qualified people to teach cooking, photography, crafts, and exercise classes.

If you have a skill that allows you to use portable tools and equipment that can be conveniently carried with you, maybe you can think of a way to put them to use for earning money while fulltiming.

Another type of work that lends itself to the full-timing lifestyle is being a property caretaker or house-sitter. In some cases, the caretaker's function is simply to occupy the property when the owner is away so it won't be vacant, but other caretaking positions may involve more work than just "sitting." The caretaker may be called upon to tend a yard or garden, water house plants, or look after pets.

Some property owners may provide a site with hookups for the caretaker's RV, and some may provide just a parking space for the RV and the caretaker lives in the house of the property owner until the owner returns.

Campground hosts are needed in the summer, or year round, in some national parks as well as in parks under the jurisdiction of the United States Forest Service, the Corps of Engineers, and the Bureau of Land Management. State parks also have host positions available.

When hosts have more duties than greeting campers and selling firewood, they may be paid something for their work, but some-

"If you have a skill that allows you to use portable tools and equipment that can be conveniently carried with you, maybe you can think of a way to put them to use for earning money while fulltiming."

times a free campsite is the only compensation for their services. Depending on the campground, the host's site may have no hookups or just electricity, while others can be quite luxurious, having all hookups and a paved pad.

A demand exists for hosts in all areas of the country. You can work in the mountains, the desert, and the forests, and you can count on all Corps of Engineers' campgrounds to be on a body of water.

We have met many full-timing couples who manage private campgrounds on a seasonal basis. A variety of other job opportunities exist in RV parks. The office must be looked after, the buildings and grounds need maintenance, and equipment requires servicing and repair. If you have talents in copywriting, graphic design, illustration, or photography, you may be able to produce ads, brochures, letterheads, and design logos for campgrounds and carry the project through to completion if you have a computer setup for desktop publishing.

HOW CAN I FIND WORK?

If you're looking for a job in a campground, read the notices on the bulletin board in the campground where you are staying for jobs that may be listed there.

Don is a young fulltimer who has a regular job in Wisconsin during the summer. He travels to the Sunbelt in the winter and, since he has no retirement income, is always looking for ways to supplement what he earns in the summer. We met him and his wife, Peg, in a campground in Arizona. They were about to move on when they saw a notice on the bulletin board about two jobs that were available at the campground for the balance of the season. They got the jobs and spent the remainder of the winter there, enjoying the climate and earning money to boot. Before arriving in Arizona, Don and Peg sold Christmas trees in Texas during the holidays.

Hosting opportunities and positions in campgrounds are often advertised in the classified section of RV publications, both national and regional.

A valuable resource for fulltimers seeking campground employment is:

Workamper News
201 Hiram Road
Heber Springs, Arkansas 72543
(501) 362-2637 or (800) 446-5627
E-mail: workamp@arkansas.net
World Wide Web site: http://www.workamper.com

This bimonthly newsletter carries extensive listings of positions in campgrounds all over the country as well as other information useful to working fulltimers. It also sells *Road Work: The Ultimate RVing Adventure* by Arline Chandler, a comprehensive sourcebook for those seeking work while traveling.

Workers On Wheels is a bimonthly newsletter. It doesn't list jobs but carries articles about RVers, how they make money on the road, and also contains useful articles relating to working while traveling. The address is:

Workers On Wheels
4012 South Rainbow Boulevard
Suite K94
Las Vegas, Nevada 89103
(800) 371-1440

The *Camperforce Directory* is a book listing more than 3,000 campgrounds offering employment to RVers. For ordering information write to:

Camperforce Directory
P.O. Box 1212
Cocoa, Florida 32923

Information about caretaking opportunities may be obtained by subscribing to:

The Caretaker Gazette
1845 NW Deane Street
Pullman, Washington 99163-3503
(509) 332-0806
E-mail: garydunn@pullman.com
World Wide Web site: http://www.angelfire.com/wa/caretaker

Income from Writing and Photography

Once people find out that we are fulltimers, one of the first things they usually ask is if we are retired. When we tell them we are not, they are either discreetly or openly curious about how we earn the money on which to live. We are often tempted to tell the truth and say we live by our wits, but we know this wouldn't be satisfying, so we try to give them a little insight about our vocation, which is freelance writing and photography.

Many people might assume this is ideal work for fulltimers—being able to travel while earning a living. It is, in respect to the working conditions. You can set your own hours and choose the place in which you want to work. But very few fulltimers, or non-fulltimers for that matter, can make a living as freelance photographers or writers.

Let's examine the writing first: If you intend to write articles about RV-related subjects, there are just two national newsstand magazines that may buy them: *Trailer Life* and *MotorHome*. The only other markets for such articles might be the several regional RV publications that are sold or given away free in RV-oriented areas of the country, and perhaps some RV club publications.

The magazines pay the most for articles. The other publications pay considerably less, often so little that it's not worth a serious writer's time to do a piece for them. Some of the RV club publications don't pay anything for articles.

Regardless of what is paid for an RV article, consider how many you would need to publish to sustain your lifestyle. One each month? Even if this would provide you with enough money to live on (it wouldn't), the chances of selling an article for each issue of a magazine are practically nil. You have to be an excellent writer turning out articles the magazine can use, to sell even a few articles a year to one magazine. Other writers are also submitting articles, so you may have yours rejected, no matter how good it is, because the magazine already has something scheduled on the same subject.

Okay, you may say, what if I write articles on subjects other than RVing for other magazines? If we were asked the question we would answer, "Try it, certainly, but don't be disappointed if your writing earnings don't begin to pay your way."

It's certainly possible to earn some money by writing even if writing is not your occupation. If you write well and know your subject thoroughly enough to write about it with authority, you may be able to sell occasional articles.

Anyone who wants to sell articles should become acquainted with *Writer's Digest*. It contains listings of publications; particulars about the type of articles needed; how, and to whom, to submit material; payment rates; and other pertinent information. It's available in most libraries.

If you want to pursue photography as a means of making money, the prospect is even more gloomy. Whether you intend to specialize in art photography, the sort of pictures that are usually framed and hung on a wall, or purely commercial work, you'll be hard put to realize any decent return on the considerable investment of equipment, materials, and time it takes to produce a professional product.

It isn't possible to do professional-quality work with one 35-millimeter camera and a lens or two. You'll need a variety of cameras, lenses, and many other expensive accessories, and you need to buy and shoot film in quantity.

"It's certainly possible to earn some money by writing even if writing is not your occupation."

Installing a darkroom in an RV isn't easy, and even if it could be accomplished it wouldn't be practical for doing extensive professional work; therefore, you'll need to have all your developing, processing, and printing done commercially. These costs have to be figured into what you charge for your work.

If you have the equipment and the expertise for turning out top-quality photographs, where can you sell them? If you submit an article accompanied by photographs and it's accepted, you'll usually be paid a higher rate than that for an article without pictures.

As we mentioned before, you might arrange to take advertising photos of a campground and its facilities. You might try soliciting work from businesses in the area where you are staying, but you'll have stiff competition from local professional photographers; they usually need every job they can get so they can make a decent living.

If your work is professional and the subject matter salable, you may be able to concentrate on doing work for a stock photo agency. To make any significant amount of money though, you'll need to have thousands of photographs on file.

No matter what you choose to do photographically, jobs are not plentiful and the field is overcrowded.

We have worked for years (we were professional writers and photographers before we became fulltimers) to be in the position we are today—being traveling fulltimers and making a living as we go. We sell some articles, but the bulk of our income is from royalties on books that often take us years to compile. Note that we said "books"—plural; one book isn't likely to bring in enough to live on. We derive additional earnings from photo sales we make directly and through stock photo agencies with which we are affiliated. It took many years to build up the thousands of photographs we, and the agencies, have on file.

We enjoy our work but to keep producing material for future royalties and sales, we often work long hours and sometimes weeks go by before we have any days off. In order to bring in enough to support our traveling lifestyle we must have a commitment to our projects and be willing to work as long as it takes to meet our deadlines.

Other fulltimers who are successfully self-employed and work at their businesses as they travel necessarily must be as committed as we are, although most of us think it's a fair trade-off for having the freedom to work when and where we please.

Other Work/Travel Options

Representatives for certain manufacturers' products often can work as they travel. If fulltimers want to do this, they usually think of being a rep for an RV product, but the field does not have to be so limited; there are thousands of manufacturers that have nothing to do with the recreational vehicle business that need reps for their products.

As a rep you may not be able to travel when or where you want, and your traveling may be limited to a specific area of the country or a small territory. On the other hand, you may have to travel more than you would like. If you are repping an RV-related product, you'll likely have to attend rallies and RV club get-togethers as well as visit RV-supply stores. This may require you to travel many miles and keep to a tight schedule.

A friend of ours is a representative for a company that manufactures fishing rods and other equipment for anglers. This ties in nicely with his full-timing lifestyle and one of his favorite hobbies, which just happens to be fishing.

Another man works as he goes in an unusual way. We met Lowell several years ago in Florida. Then in his mid-thirties, he was fulltiming with his wife and two children and supporting his family by working as a blacksmith as they traveled.

Lowell specializes in horseshoeing. You may think that this is a little-called-for skill nowadays, but there is work at racetracks, horse farms, riding stables, and rodeos all over the country, so Lowell can count on being paid often and well for his valuable service in just about any place he chooses to go.

Since he works out of the back of his pickup truck, he can set up his portable forge and anvil in minutes and be ready for work. The tools, equipment, and supplies for his trade take up only about a third of the space in the truck's bed.

In a Virginia campground, we met Judd, who is also a fulltimer and whose entire income comes from his work with horses. Judd is a horse dentist, an occupation we didn't know existed until we met him. Judd has a big, luxurious Class A motorhome—horse dentists, like people dentists, can make a good deal of money from their work—and tows a minivan which carries his dental equipment. Sometimes Judd parks his motorhome in a conveniently-located campground and travels to his "patients" in the van. Other times he may park the motorhome at the horse farms and racetracks where he works. The owners of some of the farms on his regular circuit have installed a paved pad and hookups just for his use.

Judd works only the East Coast from New York to Florida, but he, like Lowell, can find work anywhere he wants.

Sometime ago in Montana we met John, a retiree who was fulltiming and still working at his trade—welding. He carried a portable welder in his pickup-truck tow vehicle. He occasionally made some money from other RVers who needed welding done, but he specialized in repairing heavy equipment. John would travel to farms and ranches in the area where he was camping to see if any welding was needed. There was always work for him, he explained, because it was usually inconvenient to take large machinery to a shop where the welding could be done.

If John was going to be in one area for a while, he would post notices about his service with implement dealers, in feed stores, and other places where they would be seen by likely customers. John had arranged with the owner of the campground at which he was staying to use the park's telephone number on his notices, and the owner had agreed to take the calls he received. He was lucky; most campground owners would not be so accommodating.

John did not earn enough to live on from his itinerant work. Perhaps he could have if he had pursued it more aggressively, but it was not necessary because he had a retirement income.

For many years, Fred, a professional bicycle mechanic, has been a fulltimer. He, like John, takes his services to those who need them, spending much of his time in small towns that don't have a bicycle repair shop. The converted bus in which he and his wife live has ample room for the tools of his trade.

We heard about an ingenious full-timing couple who run an upholstery business from their RV. Their large trailer was originally built for hauling dune buggies. They have transformed the front of the trailer into living quarters and converted the rear into their shop. They also make RV products such as tire covers, screens, and shades.

Herb, a fulltimer we know, is a sign maker who carries his equipment in his motorhome. When he stays for a while in one area, he contacts local businesses to let them know he can take care of their sign needs.

Making badges is the business of two full-timing women. Behind their motorhome they tow a utility trailer that holds the badge-making equipment and converts to a stand from which they display and sell their wares. Much of their business is done at RV club rallies, but they also set up shop during extended stays in campgrounds.

Another means of earning money is as acting as wagonmasters. Not only does being wagonmasters for RV tours allow you to take the tour but you can earn money while doing so.

Those who need a workshop in their traveling home should investigate the type of trailer that has a large open rear area. This type is designed for carrying bulky items such as motorcycles and boats, but the space can be easily converted into a workshop. The size of

Figure 3.1 In this fifth-wheel trailer, the open rear area is suitable for a workshop. Living quarters with all the amenities are in the front. (Courtesy Play-Mor Trailers, Inc.)

the cargo area ranges from about 12 feet to 20 feet. The balance of the trailer is the living area.

This type of trailer is made by several manufacturers and available in either travel or fifth-wheel models in lengths ranging from 24 to 40 feet (Figure 3.1).

What About Earning Money from Crafts?

Some fulltimers think about financing all their traveling by selling items they have handcrafted. A few manage to do this but they are in the minority.

It doesn't matter how unique or well done the product is or what it sells for, earning enough to live on may be impossible because of two factors: (1) the logistics of selling the product and (2) the competition you'll encounter.

You'll have to travel to established flea markets and craft fairs to obtain maximum exposure for your wares. Even if you travel long hours and many miles, you won't have the time to cover all of the big events. If your traveling is mainly for the purpose of selling your crafts, travel expenses should be considered when calculating the profit you wish to make.

The fabrication of the item also enters into the logistics. If you are rushing off to market after market, you won't have much time left over to make more of the product.

Competition in all craft areas is keen. If the items you offer for sale aren't top-quality, not many of them will be sold. Many highly skilled people are turning out fine work and some of them may be participating in the same events as you.

If you have visited any flea markets and craft fairs you are probably aware that not much being offered today is unique. Unless you can come up with something that is truly different, you'll probably have to settle for a minuscule share of the market.

When you are making an item just for fun or relaxation, how long it takes to complete it isn't usually important. If, however, you are crafting articles to sell, such as elaborate wood carvings or quilts, which can be quite time consuming to fabricate, you'll have to sell them for a comparatively high price if you expect to be compensated for the time spent making them. The more costly the item, the narrower the market.

Higher-priced items need to be offered for sale in a marketplace where likely buyers are available. To avoid wasting time, you'll have to become familiar with the best outlets for your product. Some flea markets seem to attract a lot of junk sellers, whereas others have a reputation for offering higher-quality merchandise.

If you can turn out a quantity of items in a short time with an attractive price, the market is wider, and you won't have to exercise so much selectivity about where the item is sold.

Selling your work by renting space in a crafter's mall may be a possibility. Although your work is displayed in your space, you don't have to be there to sell it; the permanent staff takes care of sales. You are responsible for keeping your space stocked, which could be a problem if you aren't in the area.

If you are one of those who can make a substantial amount of money from your handiwork, it may affect your full-timing lifestyle. You may need a larger place to store the needed materials

"Higher-priced items need to be offered for sale in a marketplace where likely buyers are available."

and equipment, so you may be faced with buying a larger RV or renting space and remaining in one location to do the work.

We know of one talented person whose income is derived entirely from what he crafts. Some years ago Steve was living in a large town on the Chesapeake Bay working as an advertising artist and making scrimshaw items as a hobby. His work was so good that he began to get orders from friends for custom-made items. He eventually exhibited his work at a craft fair and sold nearly every item.

Like many hobbyists, Steve enjoyed the time spent with his hobby as much as any work he did. As an artist creating for his own pleasure he was free to do the sort of things he wanted; it was much more satisfying than doing the work his advertising clients demanded.

At one time or another many hobbyists wonder if they can make a living from their hobbies. Steve was no different, but he knew he needed a broader market than an occasional craft fair to make enough money to live on.

He made some samples and took them around to places on or near the water he thought might be possible outlets: marine supply stores, nautical gift shops, even the several maritime museums in the bay area. Steve received so many orders he knew he would have a problem filling them if he worked only in his spare time. He took the considerable gamble, quit his job, and began working on the scrimshaw full time. Now Steve is able to live on what he earns from his former hobby.

Scrimshaw, a one-of-a-kind work of art painstakingly carved on ivory, or, nowadays, on a synthetic look-alike, can command a high price. Steve was able to find proper outlets for his work because at the time he went into business for himself he lived in an area where there was always a market for this old sailors' art.

Now that Steve has enough established customers, he supplies them by mail. He can practice his craft wherever he wants and he is free to travel whenever he desires.

The items Steve makes are relatively small—earrings, belt buckles, and other jewelry items, so he does not need storage space for a large amount of raw material. The equipment used for fabricating the items is also compact. A craft such as this fits nicely into the full-timing life since everything can be stored conveniently in an RV and not much work space is needed.

Steve does his own marketing and keeps all the money he makes, but some artists become affiliated with a gallery that displays and sells their work, for which the gallery receives a commission. Most galleries accept only the work of superb artists who have either a reputation in their field or whose work is obviously marketable.

At the outset, it would be realistic for fulltimers with a craft skill to consider selling what they fabricate as a means of earning a little extra money rather than counting on it to be their main or sole source of income.

Making Products for RVers

It's not necessary to sell all or any of your products at flea markets or craft fairs. Often a market exists—albeit a limited one—right in the campground where you are staying. Selling in this market could put a few extra dollars in your pocket.

Dotty is a talented artist who combines her artistic skills with her lifestyle. She does portraits of people and drawings and paintings of RVs, which she sells. Depending on what is wanted by her customers, she creates the work in pencil, pen and ink, or acrylics. Once she received a commission from a proud RV owner to execute his rig in needlepoint. Fortunately, this too is one of her skills.

Dotty knows she can't earn even a modest living from this sort of work but she enjoys doing it. It supplements her income and she welcomes the extra money.

Sewing skills may be put to good use to earn extra money. A small sewing machine that can be tucked away in a cabinet can be used to turn out a great many money-making items. Garments can be made, altered, and repaired for other RVers.

Perhaps you can invent something specifically for RV use, such as pocketed shoe bags to fit on the inside of RV cabinet or wardrobe doors (regular shoe bags are usually too wide). How about making decorative, multicolored wind socks in a size suitable for flying from an RV? Or you can apply the better mousetrap theory and come up with some sort of practical, easy-to-use laundry bag. Laundry storage is the bane of many RVers; a suitable container in which to keep it would be welcomed.

Once you are an RVer and a fulltimer, you'll know from your own experience what products need to be invented or improved. If you're creative, you may be able to come up with something that would cause other RVers to beat a path to your door.

If you can't think of anything to make, any RV accessory catalog should provide a wealth of ideas. We looked through one of our catalogs and found many things that can be made using an ordinary sewing machine: covers for air conditioners, propane cylinders, and spare tires; folding chair storage bags; picnic-table covers; protective wheel covers; curtains and draperies; electric jack covers; and roof-vent covers. All of these items lend themselves to customization.

A skilled carpenter can do everything from major custom work on RV interiors to simple projects such as installing shelves. A carpenter also can build other items that often can't be purchased ready-made, such as a bookcase just for paperbacks.

Our first full-timing trailer had no specific place suitable for storing such books, so Bill made a bookcase for our paperbacks that fit neatly against one end of the galley counter. He later built another that was attached to the vanity in the bedroom. We collaborated on building and installing storage bins in the bed of our pickup truck, and Jan designed, and Bill built, a gun case that fit into a small space in a corner that couldn't have been put to practical use for much else.

Carpenters also have the tools needed to make boards used for leveling RVs. The board needs only to be cut to the desired length and have the ends beveled. Tapered wooden wheel chocks and blocks to go under jacks can also be fabricated easily.

Sharing Your Skills for Money

Any of your own special skills can be used to teach others. You may be able to hold classes in a campground recreation hall or perhaps in or outside your own RV for a limited number of people. You might instruct others in sewing, knitting, crocheting, needlework, cooking, carpentry, photography, writing, painting, drawing, and jewelry making, for example. Classes might be given in fly casting, golf, and tennis techniques, or in any other activity or sport at which you excel.

If you have traveled to interesting places, you could give talks and slide shows about your travels. Include a question-and-answer period afterward so RVers who wish to make the same trip can learn how to prepare for it and how to handle any special problems they may encounter. Talks such as this might also be given to civic clubs and fraternal organizations.

If your background is in finance, you might hold seminars on money management or investing.

In some cases, you may be able to work out an arrangement with the campground management to pay you to give classes. Specific fees should be set up for instruction given in your own RV. Admission could be charged, or donations accepted for talks and seminars.

Don't hide your skills or your desire to work. It's important to let others know what you can and are willing, to do. If you want a job, let people know because, if you expect to earn any money, it will be up to you to make the first move toward that end.

No matter what you do, be sure you aren't violating any campground rules. It's common to find rules posted in campgrounds prohibiting the selling or displaying of merchandise as well as banning solicitation of any type by outsiders or tenants of the park. Many campgrounds have restrictions against the washing or repairing of vehicles.

We were told of a couple who earns money by washing RVs. We don't know how they conduct their business but it must be with the cooperation of the campground owner. Perhaps they have an arrangement whereby they are the only ones permitted to do this work in the park, in which case they may have to pay the owner a certain percentage of their earnings for the water they use. Be certain you know the rules and regulations before you conduct any kind of business in a campground.

If you are selling a product, don't be surprised if other fulltimers are not your best customers. Many fulltimers are living on an income where pennies have to be watched; they can't afford to buy many of the things they would like to have. If the money is available, fulltimers can't collect too many purely decorative items; there simply is not enough space in an RV to keep them. Even utilitarian items must be purchased with an eye toward their storage.

We have a saying about earning extra money. It certainly applies to us and may hold true for you: "The easier it is to see the bottom of the barrel, the more inventive and imaginative we become in putting our skills to work to earn money."

A PLAN FOR EARLY FULLTIMING

It may be possible become a fulltimer and not have to worry about earning money, even if you are too young to receive social security, or if you want to opt for an early retirement but don't have enough equity in a pension fund to provide you with an adequate income.

When you're employed and earning a salary or wages, each paycheck you receive has a considerable amount deducted from it for income tax and social security payments. In addition, there are many expenses connected with working at any job: parking fees, lunches and other meals eaten out because you don't have the time to shop for food and cook, a business wardrobe, dry cleaning, special tools or equipment used in your work, and any transportation costs incurred as a direct result of having to travel to the place where you earn your money. An example of this: A typical, new, six-cylinder, four-door sedan, driven 15,000 miles a year, and being financed costs $.447 cents a mile, or $5,090 a year to operate. Often-overlooked expenses related to working are payments to those who perform maintenance work on your house, yard, and vehicles that you might otherwise do yourself if you had time.

Bob and Kathy were a working couple who kept an accurate record of what they spent. They found that what they paid others to keep up their house and large yard was close to what Kathy earned. (Kathy, with her job, hadn't the time to do the work, and Bob couldn't because he was on the road with his sales job most of the time). When Kathy eventually quit her job, all her job-related expenses disappeared, and since she was now able to take care of the house and yard, that substantial expense was also eliminated. They found, to their surprise, that they were able to live just as well on Bob's income alone.

If you have a house, the insurance, utilities, maintenance, and property taxes take another large chunk from your income—lots more if you are making mortgage payments.

It's a fact: The taxes and social security deductions from your paycheck, job-related expenses, and house payments and expenses can amount to as much as an astounding 80 percent of your gross income. The remaining 20 percent represents the amount of money available for all other living expenses: food, clothing, insurance other than house insurance, transportation, entertainment, and miscellaneous items in your budget.

Think about it. This 20 percent is just about all you'll need to live on if you don't have a job or a house.

Determining Potential Full-timing Income

By following the steps below and using Exhibit 3.1 as a general guide, you can get an idea about whether this plan would work for you:

1. Enter your yearly gross income.
2. Total what is withheld for income taxes, social security, mortgage or rent payments, all house-related expenses, and all job-related expenses.

"The taxes and social security deductions from your paycheck, job-related expenses, and house payments and expenses can amount to as much as an astounding 80 percent of your gross income."

EXHIBIT 3.1
Calculations for Early Fulltiming

Yearly gross income
       ① _____

     Income taxes   _____

     Social security   _____

     Mortgage payments/rent   _____

     House expenses   _____

     Job-related expenses   _____

Total deductions   **②** _____   **③** − _____

Funds after expenses   **④** _____

Net worth from all convertible assets   **⑤** _____

Estimated income from net worth   **⑥** _____

Income taxes on above income   **⑦** − _____

Total estimated fulltiming income   **⑧** _____

3. Subtract the total deductions from your yearly gross income.

4. This is the amount of money available annually for all living expenses once the taxes and house- and job-related expenses are eliminated.

5. Calculate your net worth by computing what you can reasonably expect to receive if you convert your assets into cash by selling your house, cars, furniture, and other items not needed for living in an RV. (If you have been contributing to an employee pension plan and can take a lump-sum payout when you leave your job, include this amount in your net worth.)

6. Calculate how much annual income the converted cash from liquidation of assets would produce if it were invested in United States bank certificates of deposit (CDs).*

7. Calculate the income taxes that must be paid on the interest income, and subtract the tax amount from the amount in step 6.

8. This figure is roughly the amount you'll have available annually for your full-timing lifestyle.

If the amount in step 8 is close to the amount in step 4, you could seriously consider quitting your job, becoming a fulltimer, and living on your investment income. (If you don't have an RV suitable for fulltiming, the purchase of one might alter the figures enough so the plan would not be feasible.)

Should you not come up with enough to sustain you, perhaps you could still become a fulltimer if your income were supplemented with part-time work.

It may seem as if this plan is too simple; there must be a catch in it somewhere. Certainly the plan won't work for everyone; some don't earn enough, haven't saved or invested enough, and may not have assets they can convert into the amount of cash needed. Others may have a large debt load or family financial obligations. But

---

*U.S. bank CDs are used for this example because, being federally insured, there is no risk of losing your money and they pay a guaranteed rate of interest. Other investment opportunities exist that may provide more income, but more risk is involved and no return is guaranteed.

the only catch for some people stems from their attitudes—believing that something so simple and straightforward couldn't possibly work, and being unable to break away from ingrained attitudes.

If you think the plan has possibilities for you, don't do anything hastily. Carefully consider all the ramifications. Then, if you have calculated carefully and thought it through realistically—get the input of an accountant or financial planner if you feel you need it—you'll have an accurate picture of your situation, and you may be able to become a fulltimer sooner than you ever dreamed.

CHAPTER 4

Special Situations and How to Handle Them

Traveling fulltimers are ignored when local, state, and federal rules, regulations, and laws are enacted, the rules being made for the majority who live in one place and whose dwelling is permanently affixed to one spot. In some instances, it's a test of our ingenuity as fulltimers to figure out how to live within these governmental frameworks while adapting them to our way of life without violating rules and breaking laws.

Many fulltimers who travel extensively sometimes experience inconveniences in what are routine situations for those living a nonmobile life. They are easily overcome, though, and the fun and benefits of fulltiming far outweigh any paltry annoyances that may crop up.

MAIL FORWARDING

Prospective fulltimers often think that receiving mail regularly will be their biggest problem. Actually, it's one of the least troublesome areas.

Most of us need to receive certain types of business mail—insurance premium notices, vehicle license renewals, bank statements, and the like—and want to receive personal mail. If you are to receive this mail regularly, you can't have an address that constantly changes. Even in these days of lightning-fast computers, it still takes a while for any business to process a change of address. Your social correspondents won't even try to keep up with myriad address changes. So, if you are to receive mail, you must have one place where it can be sent, and have someone who is dependable to forward it on a schedule that is mutually convenient. The better your mail service, the freer you can be.

Friends and Relatives as Mail Forwarders

Friends and relatives are suitable as mail forwarders only if they are likely to remain at one address for some time and if they are responsible, organized, and understanding.

Depending on the amount of mail you engender, the forwarder should be paid something for the service, if only a token amount. This puts what might be a casual arrangement on a somewhat more businesslike basis and may encourage the forwarder to do his or her job with dispatch. Of course, you also need to make some arrangement to pay for postage for forwarding.

Some fulltimers may be able to work out an arrangement whereby the forwarder also pays their bills. If so, be sure the forwarder, in addition to being responsible, is trustworthy.

In our case, the forwarder is a relative who pays our bills from a joint checking account we have just for this purpose. We keep her informed about what bills to expect. If we have any credit card purchases, we send her a list of the charges each month so she can check it against the bill. Instead of compiling this list all at once, which can take hours if we have a lot of charges, we enter each charge on the day we make it. So we'll have a record of the charges, we use a simple, two-part order book for the entries, which provides us with two copies.

Our mail-forwarder and bill-payer is also our telephone-message-taker. We telephone her on a regular, prearranged schedule so she can give us any messages we may have received. We also use these calls to give her a forwarding address, and to discuss anything that we may need to act on quickly without waiting for the mail to arrive.

Where to Have Mail Sent

We prefer to have all our mail sent to a post office and pick it up there rather than having it sent to a campground where we are staying. One reason for this is that in too many campgrounds the mail is routinely placed where tenants or anyone who enters the office has access to it. But there is another and more important reason: If the mail is delayed, or if we should leave before our mail arrives, we would neither expect nor want campground managers to be responsible for forwarding it; many wouldn't perform this service anyway. If we miss a mail drop at a post office, we can file a change-of-address form so it can be sent to our next convenient stop or returned to our mail-forwarder to be sent to us again later. If your travel plans change so you won't be going to the post office to which your mail has been sent, a change-of-address form can be mailed in.

Our forwarder puts all our accumulated mail into a Priority Mail box or envelope (the post office supplies these at no charge) and addresses it: Bill and Jan Moeller, c/o General Delivery, City, State, Zip Code. If there is more than one package, it's noted on the label, such as: 1 of 2. "Hold for Arrival" is written on the package mainly to let postal workers know that we are travelers, not necessarily to expect them to hold it longer than the usual ten days that they hold General Delivery mail. If you know mail is waiting for you but you think you may not arrive before the ten days are up, you might telephone the post office and explain your situation. Depending on the post office, it may be held longer.

We want to have a means of tracing our mail in case it goes astray so each package is sent certified or insured, so we'll have a numbered receipt. The mail is certified and packages containing merchandise worth more than $50 are insured (a numbered receipt isn't given for insurance under $50). The dollar that certification costs and the relatively small charge for insurance are worth it for the peace of mind they provide.

When we pick up mail, we take along a prepared card with our names printed on it in large, legible letters. We show it to the clerk to prevent any misunderstanding of the spelling of our name. We started this practice after a clerk understood our name to be Moore and told us there was no mail for us; it turned out that there was mail for Moeller, however.

Almost always we have our mail sent to post offices in small towns and prefer places small enough to have only one post office. Most such post offices don't receive much General Delivery mail, so ours stands out and everyone on the small staff is usually aware of it. We're often warmly greeted when we come to get our mail.

We avoid having mail sent to big cities because, in most of them, General Delivery goes to only one branch office, even if the mail has been addressed with the zip code of another branch. In large cities this post office is usually in the downtown area, which is rarely conveniently located for us. Furthermore, at post offices where a large volume of mail is handled, we suspect there is a greater chance of our mail becoming misplaced or lost.

We generally use Priority Mail, which is delivered in two or three days (the three-day delivery is to small towns), but on the rare occasions when we need overnight service we still stick with the post office and use Express Mail.

Post office employees are very fussy about this type of mail and do everything they can to make sure it arrives on schedule (the postage is refunded if it doesn't). If you telephone the post office, you can find out if your Express Mail is there. If not, most postal clerks will inform you of the next Express Mail delivery time—there may be several deliveries a day—and suggest you call back then. Express Mail can be picked up after hours and on weekends, as long as there is someone at the post office. Call the post office and they'll tell you how. Another benefit of Express Mail is that the cost of insurance, up to $500 for merchandise, is included in the postage.

Although postal employees are very helpful where Express Mail is involved, if they go strictly by the book, regulations forbid them to tell you, if you telephone, whether you have any General Delivery mail. Not all postal employees adhere to this, however, and some will tell you, especially if you are dealing with a small post office.

The most inconvenience we experienced from the witholding-of-information regulation was when we were in a campground twenty miles from the nearest post office, which happened to be in a small town. We called from the campground to find out if our mail had arrived. The clerk wouldn't tell us, even though we explained where we were staying. Fortunately, when we got to the post office our mail was there, so we hadn't made a useless forty-mile round trip.

United Parcel Service

Occasionally we order merchandise from a company that ships only by United Parcel Service. UPS will not deliver to a post office box or General Delivery, and the post office will not accept anything from UPS because it is not mail.

If we are staying in a campground long enough to receive a UPS package—from five to seven days on average—we have the package sent to us at the campground. If we aren't sure of where we'll be when the package arrives, we have it sent to our mail-forwarder, who then sends it on to us in a mail shipment.

When we order something and know in advance where we will be staying, we call and ask the campground manager if he or she will accept a UPS package for us. We've never been refused, but we wouldn't have a package sent without letting someone know it was coming.

If you arrange for any advance deliveries, we suggest doing so with only private campgrounds; there's too much red tape to contend with at public campgrounds.

Mail-Forwarding Services

If you don't have a friend or relative you can depend on, using a professional mail-forwarding service is probably the safest, most reliable method for handling your mail. Ads for mail forwarders appear in each issue of *Trailer Life* and *MotorHome* magazines in the classified section under the "Services" heading and may also appear in other RV publications.

All mail-forwarding services operate in basically the same way: They receive your mail and hold it until you notify them of the address to which you want it sent. Many services provide a toll-free telephone number for their customers' use and some offer twenty-four-hour service.

Mail forwarders repackage the mail in their own or post-office-provided envelopes and boxes before forwarding. A monthly flat fee plus postage is charged. Some require that a postage deposit be maintained. With most of them you can request that your mail be sent by Express or Priority Mail.

If you provide the forwarding service with a copy of your itinerary, most will forward mail accordingly.

Privately owned mail and shipping services that have mail boxes for rent may do limited mail forwarding for box renters. Such a service may fit the needs of certain fulltimers.

Some of the RV clubs offering a mail-forwarding service to members are the Good Sam Club, the Escapees RV Club, Family Campers and RVers, Family Motor Coach Association, and the Family Travel Trailer Association. (More about these clubs and others in Chapter 24.)

Subscriptions

When traveling full time, your mail forwarding will be simpler and less expensive if you cancel subscriptions to any periodicals that are readily available on newsstands in the areas where you'll be traveling. You won't have to worry about receiving issues, and you won't have to pay for forwarding postage, which sometimes can be almost as much as the newsstand price. We have never missed an issue of any of the periodicals we read regularly, although occasionally we have had to go to some lengths to find them when we have been in places off the beaten path.

Those Good Sam members who subscribe to *Trailer Life* and *MotorHome* magazines may want to take advantage of the club's Snowbird Service. They can have their copies sent to one address during the summer months and another address during the winter.

FULLTIMERS AND TELEPHONES

Telephoning for RV travelers has always been a problem. Travelers who stay in motels and hotels are likely to have a phone in their room, but RV travelers, having no "room," don't have this convenience.

In places where RVers often go to spend an entire season, it's not uncommon to find campgrounds set up for telephone service for long-term guests. You arrange for service with the local telephone company just as you would for any residence and pay a monthly bill.

In recent years we have discovered an ever-increasing number of campgrounds that provide telephone service at the site for overnight guests. A typical arrangement is this: A daily fee is charged for the telephone hookup—what we usually pay is a dollar a day. You'll be charged for long-distance calls made through the campground's switchboard and pay the bill when you leave, or you can use your calling card and the charges will appear on your own bill. In either case you may have to pay a deposit against calls to be made; a $30 deposit was required in one campground.

In another type of arrangement, no daily fee is charged for the telephone hookup; instead each long-distance call, whether it goes through the campground's switchboard or is made with a calling card, carries a surcharge of one dollar, even if the call is made to a toll-free number—an expensive proposition if you have lots of calls to make. With both of these arrangements, local calls are free.

If you don't have your own telephone, you can rent one from some campgrounds; a deposit may be required for that too, but some campgrounds provide the telephone and an extension cable at no charge.

Pay Telephones

Without a telephone at your site, you'll have to resort to using pay telephones, which can be frustrating. It's less so if you have a calling card, and we recommend that all traveling fulltimers have one. Such a card may be obtained from many telephone companies such as AT&T, LDDS World Com, MCI, Sprint, and others. Shop around for the best rate and always inquire about surcharges. The lowest rate is not the best deal if surcharges are too high; some companies have no surcharges and low rates.

Prepaid calling cards, the type for sale at checkout counters in grocery and convenience stores, have a certain usefulness, but using a regular calling card and being billed for the calls is the least expensive way to go.

You may have occasion to use coins for local calls. If you do, pay attention to the instructions posted on the telephone. You may find some telephones that do not return any coins, so if you can't complete your call you'll have insert an additional amount to call again.

You may have noticed that many pay telephones are operated by companies you have never heard of. These companies, called alternate operator services (AOS), sell their service to private businesses—campgrounds and convenience stores, for example—which then receive a percentage of the charge for each call made.

If you use such a phone you may be asked to pay (usually a quarter) to access your calling-card carrier. As a matter of principle, we won't pay this, so we find another telephone to make our calls. If you do pay the fee, you may be asked to pay again after a certain amount of time has elapsed.

When using your calling card with an AOS telephone, don't proceed with dialing until you hear an operator acknowledge that you are connected to your service, such as: "Thank you for using AT&T." Without this acknowledgment, the call may be billed at the AOS rate. We have heard of callers being charged almost $2 a minute. You may also be charged for all calls made, whether answered or not. One fulltimer, using an AOS campground phone, had to make four calls to the same number before reaching his party on the fifth try. When he received his bill he found he had been charged almost $5 for the four uncompleted calls and much more than he expected for the fifth.

Before becoming fulltimers, many of us are accustomed to having two or more people participate in a call by using extension telephones. But when using a pay telephone, only one person can be in on the conversation.

There is a solution to half the problem at least: a device called a telephone listener. It's nothing more than a suction cup on a wire, connected to a slightly larger than palm-sized, battery-powered amplifier.

To use it, the suction cup is placed on the back of the handset on the ear-piece end, and the wire is connected by inserting the plug in the amplifier, which is then switched on. Another person besides the one on the telephone can then hear the conversation. The listener has an adjustable volume control and requires a nine-volt battery. This device can be obtained at Radio Shack stores for about $10.

> "When using your calling card with an AOS telephone, don't proceed with dialing until you hear an operator acknowledge that you are connected to your service . . ."

The listening device works well. We discovered it by chance as we waited one day to use a pay telephone in a campground. Although we were some distance away, we were surprised to hear every word of the conversation from where we were—the couple at the telephone were making arrangements to meet a friend for dinner. As soon as the caller hung up, we inquired about the device and the next day we bought one.

We keep the listener and a spare battery in a small drawstring bag and store it in our tow vehicle instead of our trailer. If we use a campground telephone, we take it from our truck, which is always parked by our trailer. When we must drive to a telephone without the trailer in tow, it's always with us; we don't have to remember to take it from the trailer.

Using a Telephone Hookup

Many new RVs have a factory-installed exterior telephone connection, so hooking up a telephone is as easy as connecting any other hookup. Simply plug one end of your telephone cable into the campground receptacle and the other end into the receptacle on the RV, then plug your telephone into the interior jack.

If your RV doesn't have such a provision, you can easily route the thin, flat telephone cable through an entry door, window, or outside compartment to the telephone inside. The problem with this arrangement is that it's often unsightly and the cable may be a trip hazard.

A more permanent arrangement can be made. You'll need two, surface-mounted, dual-jack junction boxes (the type that accepts an RJ-11 plug on each end) and two extension cables with modular plugs on each end. These components are inexpensive (most are under $5) and can be found at mass merchandisers and home-supply stores.

Install one junction box inside an outside compartment and another inside the RV, convenient to the telephone's location. For the shortest cable run, put the compartment junction box in a street-side compartment so it will be on the side where the hookups of most sites are located.

A 25-foot extension is usually more than long enough for the run from the campground's receptacle to the junction box in the compartment, but if you have a long RV and use a front compartment you may need a longer extension. (For extensions used outdoors, don't join two extensions together with an in-line coupler unless the connection is well taped; otherwise, moisture can enter at the coupler and affect reception.) The inside extension needs to be just long enough to reach from the junction box in the compartment to the other junction box inside, where the telephone will be plugged in.

Install the junction boxes where convenient by using the screws or mounting tape provided (mounting tape doesn't adhere well to unfinished wood, which is found in some RV compartments).

The inside extension is then plugged into one of the jacks on each of the junction boxes and left permanently in place. To conceal the cable, small holes just slightly larger than the plug may have to be drilled in the side of some compartments so the cable can be routed through. To make a neat installation of visible or concealed cable, special clips for this type of cable can be used to hold it in place.

If the extension interferes with closing the compartment's door, a small channel to accommodate it can be cut in the door frame.

Single-jack junction boxes can be used, but the cable has to be hard-wired to these. This is simple to do if you have the special tool needed for stripping the tiny wires. Otherwise you'll need a sharp knife and a steady hand to avoid nicking any of the wires.

If you can't find dual-jack junction boxes and don't want to bother with wiring the single-jack type, an installation can be made using two in-line couplers in place of the two boxes. Since the coupler's purpose is to join an extension to a telephone, it accommodates two plugs. In-line couplers aren't designed for permanent mounting, but they have flat sides and can be attached with mounting tape.

"A 25-foot extension is usually more than long enough for the run from the campground's receptacle to the junction box in the compartment . . ."

Cellular Phones

After all this discussion about the difficulties with telephoning, you may think having a cellular phone is the way to solve the problem: Your handy phone in your RV can be used to call from wherever you happen to be. That's the catch; wherever you happen to be may not be in an area—a cell—served by a cellular phone system.

Cellular service is generally available across the country in urban and suburban areas and along major highways, but there are pockets, mainly in the western states, where a cellular phone is unusable. After all, a cellular phone is nothing but a two-way radio, and to communicate, the signals must go from your antenna to the cell's antenna. If there are no antennas or the antennas are too far apart, there's no service.

Another problem for some fulltimers is the cost of cellular service. In addition to the monthly charge for the service, you pay for air time (the charge to talk from the phone to the cellular tower) and, if you make calls when you're out of your home area, as you may be a great deal of the time if you're a traveling fulltimer, you'll have to pay roaming charges. Table 4-1 gives you a general idea of the various charges. As you can see, it's the roaming charges that can drive your cellular bill through the roof. In some areas, you may also have to pay a daily fee for each day the phone is used outside your home area; no fee is imposed if the phone isn't used. With this arrangement, costs can be kept down by grouping your calls and making them on one day. On top of all this, when you make long-distance calls you must pay the rates charged by your long-distance provider. When someone calls you, you pay for air time and usually the caller pays for the long distance, but some plans require the cellular-phone owner to pay this charge.

The contract with your cellular service may or may not include an amount of free minutes of local air time. Air time is also charged on calls to toll-free numbers. When roaming, air-time charges are set by the local provider of your current locality. Calls made to 911 are usually free.

TABLE 4.1

Cellular Phone Charges

Service	Cost	Variances
Activation	$40–$50	Varies from free to $50 if you have your own phone
Monthly	$19–$45	Varies depending on service required; free minutes may be offered
Air time	$0.10–$1.00	Varies depending on time of day and day of week
Roaming	$0.38–$1.00	Depends on carrier and whether calls made are outside carrier's area
Daily roaming surcharge	$3–$10	Depends on carrier
Long distance	Variable	Depends on carrier

If you want to keep costs down, give your cellular number to only a few people, such as selected members of your family. Give others who may need to get in touch with you the number of the family member. He or she can then call you, relay the messages, and you can call them back using land-line or cellular service, whichever you choose. Remember, calls you receive are also chargeable.

To initiate service, you must select a plan and sign a contract for a certain period of time. Traveling fulltimers may not need a plan with a good deal of free local air time and low local rates once the free time is used up, because they may make local calls infrequently or not at all. Shop for the plan that best suits your usage; different carriers have different plans. If you are a new cellular user, it makes sense to sign up for the shortest time possible. You may be able to get a contract for six months, although yearly contracts are more common. Attractive deals for longer periods may be offered, but don't commit yourself until you know what your cellular usage will be. If, for some reason, you weren't using the phone—perhaps you stop traveling for a while and have regular phone service during that period—you must still pay the monthly charges for as long as your contract runs. You can always upgrade (and often downgrade) a package but you can't shorten a contract. You may be able to get out of a contract by paying a penalty fee; depending on the carrier, this can be as much as $300.

Competition is keen when it comes to garnering cellular subscribers, and you may find a phone offered for a very low price or even free if you sign up. Often these instruments aren't the best quality—they may even be reconditioned units—and may not have the features you would choose if you were purchasing the phone on your own. Having your own phone may give you more bargaining latitude for better rates when negotiating a contract. If you do purchase the phone outright, you can pay as little as $60 for a used unit to over $700 for the fanciest new models.

When purchasing a cellular phone, you have a choice between an analog or digital model. The analog system currently provides the greatest cellular coverage in the United States. The digital systems are mainly in large metropolitan areas and along interstate highways. Incidentally, just because a phone has a screen with a digital display, it doesn't mean the phone is a digital model; this type of screen display is common to both analog and digital phones.

Analog cellular phones use a form of transmission technology called Advanced Mobile Phone Service (AMPS). This is the technology you'll have with any analog cellular phone from any analog cellular provider. At present, however, there are several different kinds of technologies used in digital cellular phone transmissions, and they are not compatible with each other. Therefore, it's important for digital-phone buyers to purchase the phone from the provider offering the technology that's best for their needs. Right now there's no way of knowing which technology will prevail and become the standard, so there's a chance that the phone you choose today could be useless sometime in the future.

> **"W**hen purchasing a cellular phone, you have a choice between an analog or digital model.**"**

The different digital technologies are: Code Division Multiple Access (CDMA), Time Division Multiple Access (TDMA), Global System for Mobiles (GSM, also called PCS 1900). Both CDMA and TDMA operate on the same 800-megahertz frequencies as analog phones. TDMA is more widely available than CDMA, but the CDMA technology may be the universal system of the future because it's the favored system of many providers. GSM, operating on 1900-megahertz frequencies, is the transmission standard in Europe and is used in some places in the United States.

Fulltimers who want a digital cellular phone and who stay in one area can safely sign up with a digital cellular provider whose technology is prevalent in that area. But before traveling fulltimers sign up, they should look at the cellular company's coverage map to see if they'll have service in the places in which they intend to travel. If the company offers multi-state coverage, check whether the coverage is in only the large cities in the various states; there may be no service outside the metropolitan areas.

A very expensive cellular phone is the dual-mode type, which operates on both analog and digital transmissions. No matter where you are in the country, when the phone is out of range of digital coverage, it automatically switches to the analog mode.

Unquestionably, digital transmission will be the mode of the future, but don't let this dissuade you from purchasing an analog cellular phone; they'll be around for many years to come.

For a detailed explanation of analog and digital technologies see Exhibit 11.1 in Chapter 11.

The most practical cellular phones for most travelers are those with 3-watt transmitting power because they provide the best communication in remote areas; most tiny cellular phones are only 0.6-watt models. Three-watt phones are larger and include permanently mounted phones; transportables, sometimes called bag phones; and some hand-held models. All 3-watt phones and some 0.6-watt models can be fitted with an external antenna, which provides extended range, especially when the phone is used inside a vehicle. With an external antenna, you have the flexibility of using the phone in both

"The most practical cellular phones for most travelers are those with 3-watt transmitting power because they provide the best communication in remote areas . . ."

vehicles in your rig—motorhome/towed vehicle or trailer/tow vehicle—because an antenna can be mounted on each.

The antenna can be the magnetic-mount type or the type that is mounted on a window, or it may be the roof-mounted type that requires drilling a hole for installation. Clip-on antenna extensions are available but it's awkward to use the phone with the antenna in place.

On some phones, the 0.6 wattage can be increased with a 3-watt booster kit. The kit is designed to be permanently mounted and is not portable. Purchasing the kit along with a phone is considerably more expensive than purchasing a 3-watt phone in the first place.

If you don't have an external antenna, when in fringe areas you may find you can't get a strong enough signal to use the phone inside your RV. If so, take the phone outside. The metal in the chassis and frame of motorhomes and the metal exterior of some trailers acts as a shield and may partially block the signal.

The jury is still out on the highly controversial matter of whether health problems—mainly cancer—are caused by electromagnetic fields. Until we know for sure, when using a phone with a built-in antenna in the handset, the safest practice is to hold the antenna as far away from your head as possible and make short calls.

Cellular service is expanding rapidly and covering many formerly cell-less areas, but cellular service may never be available in all areas of the country because of the expense of setting up a cellular system. In sparsely populated areas, there aren't enough users to justify it.

The Cellular Travel Guide is a directory that traveling cellular users may find useful. This fairly thick book has maps showing cellular coverage in all states, what local cellular providers charge, and local customer-service phone numbers. To order contact: Communications Publishing, P.O. Box 500, Mercer Island, Washington 98040; (206) 232-8800.

In the future, telephoning by satellite will be common. This much better system, which has none of the dead spots of land-based cellular systems and offers true global communication is, at present, too expensive for the average user; it's better suited to business applications. (See Chapter 11, "An RV Office For Working Fulltimers," for more information on cellular and satellite systems.)

MESSAGE SERVICES

We have explained about making calls, but what if someone wants to call you? This is impossible unless you are hooked up to standard telephone service, or have a cellular phone and give out your cellular number. If you have neither, those who want to reach you can do so if you subscribe to a telephone-message service; anyone trying to contact you calls the number of the service and leaves a message, and you call your service whenever convenient to get your messages.

Some mail forwarders offer a telephone-message service for a separate fee, and a message service is available to members of some RV clubs. Most services have a toll-free number for those calling to leave messages and also for those calling in to receive messages.

If you have a friend or relative with telephone service, you can set up your own message service. In one arrangement, you have your own telephone number but no telephone. Incoming calls are received and stored by the telephone company. To get your messages, you dial a special message number and enter a personal code. Check with the local telephone company for rates.

Another arrangement is to have your own separate line and install a telephone with an answering machine, or just an answering machine that has remote access. You can call your own number and listen to your messages. The cost for this is the basic rate for a residential telephone; you need no frills or long-distance carrier. If you have the telephone installed in the home of a friend or relative, so it won't be a nuisance, set it so it doesn't ring, and turn down the volume on the speaker of the answering machine to the lowest level.

For only a few dollars more a month your telephone number

can be toll-free. Not only is this a convenience for those who call you, it may be a money-saver for you because you'll incur no long-distance charges when you call in for your messages.

OPERATING CAPITAL

Credit Cards

Before we became fulltimers, we had the usual plethora of credit cards, but we soon found that our full-timing life was made simpler by eliminating many of them. Our advice is: Keep only the credit cards you are sure you'll use, and, of these, keep only those that can be used nationwide. A charge card from a local store won't be useful and, until you close the account, you'll receive monthly or more frequent mailings about sales and specials whether you have charged anything or not.

Many nationwide chain stores and oil companies issue their own credit cards, but most also accept Visa, MasterCard, and Discover. (If you want to save money, avoid refueling at service stations that charge more per gallon when the purchase is paid for by credit card.) You'll have fewer bills to pay and receive less mail if you use only one of these three cards.

The idea is to consolidate and condense in order to reduce the amount of mail you receive and, in the process, to simplify the paying of bills. To make less work for our mail-forwarder/bill-payer we try to use just one card for all charges. Only one bill is received, which cuts down on paperwork and also saves on check charges and postage.

American Express and Carte Blanche memberships have rather high annual dues. Only you can decide if it's worth the cost to have the use of these cards.

If you shop around you may be able to find a Visa or Mastercard with no annual fee. Some companies issue their own credit cards through Visa or Mastercard. As an incentive to use the card, you may be awarded points for each purchase. This amounts to a rebate when you buy a product (usually a big-ticket item) of the issuing company. Some companies give a cash rebate at the end of the year. The amount depends on how much has been charged. You can obtain either a Mastercard or Visa from AT&T, which is also a calling card. Charge purchases may be paid in monthly installments, but all telephone charges must be paid in full each month.

The Discover card has no annual fee and each time you make a purchase with the card, you get a credit for a small percentage of the amount charged. A check for your accumulated credits is sent at the end of the year.

Visa and MasterCard are accepted almost universally wherever credit cards can be used; the Discover card is slightly more limited in acceptance.

If you don't have someone to take care of paying your bills, and you're concerned about receiving your mail in order to pay the bills before incurring any finance charges, you can call the toll-free number on your credit credit card, find out what your balance is, and pay it before you have the bill in hand.

Because credit cards are accepted so universally, we charge as many purchases and services as we can—even groceries. This has several advantages: We don't have to carry so much cash, we receive a cash rebate on all purchases, and until we pay the bill, which may arrive anywhere from a week to a month after we make the purchase, the money in our checking account is earning interest. We know our billing date, and sometimes when we purchase an expensive item, we charge it near that date so it appears on the next month's bill four weeks away.

We always pay our bill in full each month. If we weren't able to do so, we would limit our charges to what we could afford in order to avoid high interest charges.

"Visa and MasterCard are accepted almost universally wherever credit cards can be used; the Discover card is slightly more limited in acceptance.**"**

Debit Cards

A debit card is different from a credit card; when you pay for anything with it, the amount is immediately deducted from your bank account. For this reason, whether we were fulltimers or not, we would not use a debit card for transactions. We prefer using a credit card so we can make a little money every time we spend money by leaving what we would have spent if we paid in cash in our interest-paying checking account until the bill is due.

A debit card can be used for cash advances. The card we used for ATM cash withdrawals was recently replaced with a debit card.

For those who use checks for many of their purchases a debit card may be useful; it's easier to use the card than write a check.

Personal Checks

For travelers, using personal checks can be a problem. Many businesses won't accept checks unless they are drawn on a local bank, and many restaurants accept no checks. But check acceptance depends somewhat on where you are. In some of the laid-back states in the West, such as Wyoming and Montana, you are more likely to find it possible to pay with a check from an out-of-town bank. In Nevada, however, it's rare to find any business that accepts out-of-town checks.

You can pay by check for overnight stays in many campgrounds—except in Nevada. At campgrounds set up to accept credit cards we often use our card for payment. If not, we usually pay by check. If it's a Good Sam campground we always pay by check, because the 10-percent discount Good Sam members receive is applied only if you pay by check or with cash.

Grocery stores have varying policies about out-of-town checks. If you want to pay by check, inquire about the policy before you're in the checkout line.

You shouldn't count on writing a personal check to obtain cash because a check written solely for that purpose can rarely be cashed in any place other than at the bank where you have an account and its branches; however, you may be able to do this if you have a check-guarantee card. Some banks issue Mastercards and Visas with a photo ID that are a combined charge card and check-guarantee card.

Bank Selection

Fulltimers who travel will find it convenient to do their banking if they select a bank with branches in several states. Bank of America, for example, is in ten western states, and other banks in the Midwest and East have multi-state offices. You can take care of your financial affairs at any office, just as though you were in your own bank.

Some fulltimers may want to take advantage of the direct-deposit feature offered by banks. You may instruct the issuers of any checks you regularly receive to send the checks directly to your bank where they are deposited in your account.

Automatic Teller Machines (ATMs)

The best way for most fulltimers to obtain cash is to maintain a bank account and make withdrawals from an ATM.

ATMs are common everywhere, they aren't just in banks. You'll find them in grocery and convenience stores, truck stops, casinos (of course), and ATM kiosks are in some parking lots.

You can obtain cash any time because ATMs are "open" round the clock. When you have an account, your bank issues you an ATM card and provides you with a personal identification number (PIN) that must be used with the card for each transaction.

Unless Congress enacts laws prohibiting ATM charges, you may have to pay a fee for using any of your bank's ATMs, and usually have to pay a fee if you use "foreign" ATMs—those not in your bank's system. You may also have to pay another fee for the usage of the particular ATM where you are making the transaction.

These fees are deducted from your account. The most we have paid for using an ATM is $2.00. We began a transaction at one ATM but canceled it when we found we would be charged $5.00. We're usually charged $1.50. This, coupled with the $1.50 charged by our bank when we use a foreign ATM increases the cost for each withdrawal to at least $3.00.

If you must pay a fee to withdraw your money, it makes sense to take out as much cash as you can. Why pay the same fee to withdraw any less? Our bank has a withdrawal limitation of $250 in a twenty-four-hour day, so $250 is what we always withdraw.

ATMs can also be used for making deposits, and the same fees may be charged.

Cash advances and other banking transactions can be taken care of in the old-fashioned way if you go to a teller, but using an ATM is usually the quickest and most convenient method and may be the cheapest; some banks now have charges for transacting business with a teller.

For safety's sake, don't write your pin number on your ATM card, and don't let anyone look over your shoulder so they can see the numbers you punch in. And try to avoid using an ATM after dark. No matter when you use it, pay attention to those around you and what they are doing. Common prey for thieves are those who have just made a withdrawal from an ATM.

Keep all receipts for checking later against your monthly statement. If you dispose of them, tear them in small pieces or obliterate the information on them, lest thieves find them and use them to access your account.

Before some people begin fulltiming and traveling, they have never had occasion to use an ATM. The procedure is simple, and step-by-step instructions are displayed on the ATM's screen. You are allowed plenty of time to complete each step. The ATM even tells you what to do if you make a mistake or change your mind about something.

Most Visa, MasterCard, and Discover cards can be used to obtain cash from ATMs. In this case, you aren't debiting your account, you are receiving a cash advance; in effect, borrowing from the card issuer. You'll be billed for the amount received from the ATM, plus interest, and maybe a service charge.

American Express cards can be used for obtaining cash through some ATMs, but you'll have to request this service and sign a form that permits immediate withdrawal from your bank account the amount received from the ATM, plus a service charge. If you can't locate an ATM displaying the American Express logo, you can get the location of the nearest ATM in which your card can be used by calling the toll-free number on your card.

Money Market Funds

If you want your money to earn interest and still be readily available, you might consider stashing some of it in a money-market fund (not to be confused with a mutual fund) instead of, or in addition to, a regular or interest-paying bank checking account. One type of fund requires a considerable initial investment; $20,000 is a typical amount. Once the initial investment is made, however, it doesn't matter how low the subsequent balance falls. The companies offering this type of money market fund hope you will use some of your money to purchase stocks and bonds through their firm, paying them the usual commissions, but you aren't required to do so.

Free checks and a Mastercard or Visa card are provided. The checks can be used like any other personal checks to pay for goods and services. The card can be used just like any other credit card for cash advances and to charge purchases, but it is a debit card. You won't receive a bill for your charges; on your monthly fund statement they will be shown as debits, as will cash advances and checks. There is no credit limit other than what you have in your account. An annual fee is charged, which is deducted from your account.

Another type of money-market fund requires a relatively small amount for initially opening the account; $2,500 is a common figure. Free checks (but no debit card) are provided, but when writing checks they must each be for a specified minimum amount. This may be $250 or $500, depending on the fund. (The funds requiring the larger initial investment have no check limitations; they can be written for any amount.) The checks won't do you much good if you need ready cash since you probably won't be able to find places to cash them, but a way to get around this situation would be to write the check before the cash is needed, deposit it in your checking account, and then use your ATM card for cash withdrawals. There is no annual fee for this type of money-market fund.

Although money-market funds typically pay a higher rate of interest than bank checking and savings accounts, there is some risk when investing in a money-market fund. Bank funds are usually insured against loss, up to a certain amount, by the Federal Deposit Insurance Corporation (FDIC) or the Federal Deposit Savings and Loan Insurance Corporation (FDSLIC). Funds with brokerage houses are not usually insured.

REGISTRATION AND LICENSES

Licensing Vehicles

Vehicle licensing is a thorny situation. Each state has its own regulations for the procedure, many of which seem designed to foil the traveling fulltimer. Many states require an annual inspection of vehicles, and some states require a vehicle to be equipped with a state-approved smog device. Some municipalities also require smog inspection.

Before a vehicle can be registered, some states demand a special proof-of-insurance form, filled out by the insurance company—not you—before issuing plates, and some require proof that certain local taxes have been paid. Various states probably have many other legal idiosyncrasies that we have not yet had the displeasure of finding out about.

Each state's laws are precise about when you must register your vehicle. It may be required when you are employed in the state or after you have resided in the state for a certain period of time.

Since we have been fulltiming, we have had vehicles licensed in several states. If the initial registration turns out to be easy, the renewals rarely are. At one time, when we were still in the West after spending the better part of the year there, the registrations on our truck and trailer from an East Coast state were close to expiring. We had long since abandoned any East Coast mailing address so there was no way we could have renewed the registrations by mail. We were concerned about being pulled over for driving with plates that had expired. Even if we were not stopped for out-of-date license plates, we would have had some awkward explaining to do if we had been involved in an accident.

We did what we had done before. We found an RV park in the community where we wanted to license our truck and trailer and checked in for a month. We then went to the motor vehicle office and applied for registration, using the park's address as our address, which it was at the time. The plates were issued on the spot, but we were given temporary registrations. The permanent documents were to be sent to us from the main office in the state capital. Explaining that we were leaving on an extended trip and probably would not be at "our address" when the documents arrived, we asked if they could be sent to another address out of state. This was possible, so we had the registrations sent to the address from which all our mail is forwarded. They arrived in due time and we were officially, but perhaps not quite legally, licensed.

One of the problems with this procedure is that someone along the line may not follow your instructions about where to send the

> **"E**ach state's laws are precise about when you must register your vehicle.**"**

documents; a lot of follow-up writing and telephoning may have to be done while the time runs out on the temporary registration, which is good for only a limited number of days.

To cover your bases, you could leave a self-addressed, stamped envelope with the manager of the campground you used for your address, trusting that he or she would forward it in the event it was mistakenly sent there. Or you could stay put until the license arrives, hoping the delay won't be long enough to interfere with your traveling plans.

We recommend using a self-addressed, stamped envelope whenever you expect to have someone send along anything in an envelope that comes from a motor vehicle division. Most such envelopes are imprinted with the words DO NOT FORWARD.

Many states won't send anything dealing with a registration or driver's license to a post office box; a street address is required. In some states, documents will be sent to a post office box only if it can be verified that you also have a street address. A street address is required when you rent a box from the post office; it may not be a requirement when renting a box from a private mail service, and its street address can be your address.

If you have a mail-forwarding service in certain states, you can use the address of the service for your registration address. Of course, the service must be in the same state as the vehicle registration. Probably no service will handle just your vehicle registrations for you.

Even if we could have successfully renewed our East Coast registration by mail, we might have had another problem: If we had crossed that state's borders with our valid, renewed license plates and current registration, we might have been cited for having an outdated inspection sticker; an annual inspection was necessary in that state.

Every state allows registration renewal by mail. This presents no problem for the nonmobile person who receives mail at a home address. Traveling people will need to have the forms forwarded to them because the forms have to be signed by the owner of the vehicle. Then, later, the new stickers and registration will also have to be forwarded. Depending on your state's policy about how soon the forms are mailed out, you may have to remain in one place until you have the proper documents in hand. Fortunately, the majority of states allow at least a month for the renewals, but our former state allowed only ten days for all this mailing back and forth.

Another complication presented itself when we found that the truck registration expired in a different month than that of the trailer, even though both had initially been registered at the same time.

While it would be convenient to have all registrations with the same expiration date, it may not be possible unless all vehicles are purchased and registered at the same time, or all are reregistered in a new state at the same time—a state that doesn't stagger registrations.

In the last few years, our truck and trailer registration dates fell in the same month until we got them out of whack by buying a new trailer four months before the truck registration was due to be renewed. Now we must contend with two separate registrations each year.

Vehicles can be preregistered before "entry" in many states, but some states require the vehicle to be in the state before it can be registered.

Drivers' Licenses

For fulltimers, the matter of their drivers' licenses must be considered. There is nothing illegal about driving a vehicle with plates from one state while holding a driver's license from another; those who rent cars do it all the time. As far as we can determine, there is also nothing illegal about driving your own vehicle, with the registration in your name but with an address different from that of your driver's license. It could, however, raise some questionable issues if you were ever stopped by the police. You may be able to explain the situation satisfactorily—or you may not.

When we registered our vehicles in a western state, we also got new driver's licenses even though our East Coast licenses were good for two more years. (Other complications could have arisen because we each happened to have a license from a different East Coast state.) We figured the fees involved were a small price to pay to keep the situation as close to the norm as possible.

The norm, however, can be elusive for the fulltimer. Consider how the following might apply to you, as it once did to us: We had driver's licenses that carried the same address as our vehicle registration—the address of the RV park where we were staying at the time we acquired them. We only stayed at the park for a month, and never returned during that year, so we could not be reached at that address. Even though we were still in the state, we couldn't change our address to our current one because it was always changing; we moved from campground to campground and rarely stayed in any one place for longer than a week. We certainly couldn't change our address to that of our mail-forwarding address in another state, where we could be reached at any time. What did we do? We drove very carefully, obeying all laws, hoping we wouldn't be stopped for any reason that would require us to explain why we could not be reached at the address that appeared on our license and registration.

You may be asked to present identification when applying for a driver's license. Sometimes a birth certificate is all that is needed, but some states require three separate pieces of identification. Unless a birth certificate is used, the addresses on the IDs had better match.

If examinations or tests are needed for driver's license renewal, you'll have to be in the state for them. If your state's licenses expire on the driver's birthday and your spouse or partner has a different birthday, you may encounter a logistical problem.

The following illustrates another situation that fulltimers may experience when renewals can't be made by mail: Jan's license expires on her birth date in November. One year, in June, we were about to leave the state from which her driver's license was issued, and there was no chance that we would be back in the state in time to renew it. We waited until the day before we were going to leave the state to inquire if she could renew it that far in advance. We found she could, but the motor-vehicle employee told us that had she tried to renew it just the week before, the computer would have rejected the request.

If Jan's license couldn't have been renewed so early, she would have had to apply for a driver's license in the state where we happened to be when the other expired. Either that or drive without a license (for the better part of a year as it turned out) and risk the consequences.

Fulltimers who live in, or regularly visit, a specific place don't have to face such complicated registration and licensing situations as we do.

If you use a mail-forwarder who handles your vehicle registration, you may be able to use the service for renewing your driver's license.

When you begin fulltiming, you'll have to work out the procedure for getting your registration, plates, and driver's license in a way that is convenient for you while complying with the issuing state's laws. To a great degree, the problems are individual and so are the solutions.

Legal Residency

Many people think that being a fulltimer is a good way to escape paying taxes, but this is not true. As a fulltimer you can only avoid paying stiff local and state taxes by deciding to "live" where the tax rates are lower or, in some cases, nonexistent.

You have the choice of living in the state that is the most beneficial and least expensive for you. You can select one without a state income tax or one in which the personal property tax is low. Vehicle insurance rates vary greatly from state to state and this too may be a factor in your decision.

The state you choose may or may not be your legal residence. Most of us feel more comfortable if we have some place that we can call our legal residence, but nowhere is it written that we must establish one.

Depending on who is defining it, legal residency can be one or more of the following: the state in which you are licensed to drive, in which your vehicles are registered, where you have your permanent mailing address, where you are employed, where you have your bank accounts, where you own property, or where you are registered to vote. Other definitions are even more vague. A legal residence may be where your closest relatives reside or be in the state where you would choose to reside on a permanent basis if you were to stop traveling. (This would never work for us because we haven't yet explored all the places we want to see). You'll find as many opinions about what constitutes legal residency as there are state agencies. Even the definition of domicile in *Black's Law Dictionary* is vague when applied to fulltimers: "That place where a man has his true, fixed and permanent home and principal establishment, and to which whenever he is absent he has the intention of returning."

There probably won't ever be a uniform, standard definition of legal residency (we hope there won't be because fulltimers won't be taken into consideration), but as far as we are concerned, our properly licensed and registered trailer is our legal residence, wherever it happens to be. So far we have had no problem operating this way. If and when we do, we'll handle it as best we can at the time.

Generally, it's necessary to prove that you are, or are not, a legal resident of a particular place only when payment or nonpayment of some kind of tax is in question.

Some people mistakenly believe that the Internal Revenue Service requires you to have a permanent, legal address for filing your income taxes. This is not so. The IRS doesn't care a whit where you file from as long as they get their money. It will benefit you, however, to have an address, permanent or not, legal or not, to which a refund can be sent if one is due.

> **"The** IRS doesn't care a whit where you file from as long as they get their money.**"**

Here is some information about state taxes that may be useful: If you work less than an entire calendar year in a state and you must pay state taxes on your earnings for that period, you may have to use a special state tax form. Once, just before we left a state in which we had been employed for a short time, we dutifully picked up the state income tax form before we left. It wasn't until weeks later, when we were filling out the form, that we found we didn't have the proper one for part-year residents.

VOTING

Some may think that voting when on the road presents a problem, but it can be done either with an absentee ballot, or by residing in a place long enough before the election to be eligible to vote.

Voting anywhere involves registration. Most states require residency for thirty days prior to registering, but some have no durational requirement. In most states, a street address is also required—this is so you can be assigned to a voting precinct—but in a few states a post office box suffices for an address.

Once registered, you can request an absentee ballot be sent to another address. You may register by mail in most states.

A handy publication for those who want to pick a good state in which to "live" is *State Residency Requirements: Selecting an RV Home Base*. It contains particulars on state taxes, vehicle licensing and registration, voting, and fishing-license information. To order a copy contact: Trailer Life Books, 64 Inverness Drive East, Englewood, Colorado 80112; (800) 766-1674.

MEDICAL CONCERNS

Fulltiming, while not a cure-all for ailments, can benefit those with certain conditions. With an RV for a home, those with respiratory problems never need to live in areas where smog is a factor. They can park their homes in places with clean air or in dry or humid atmospheres as their conditions warrant. If pool therapy is needed for a condition, they can select campgrounds with swimming pools.

As we mentioned before, those who have trouble getting around have an easier time of it in a recreational vehicle; RV rooms are small compared to any room in a fixed dwelling, so there isn't as much area to negotiate and handholds are plentiful throughout.

The itinerant lifestyle must be good for people because most of the fulltimers we know are basically a pretty healthy group. Even so, most of us have to see a doctor or dentist occasionally. Periodic checkups can be done by your regular doctor or dentist if you can arrange the appointments to fit your traveling plans. Sometimes, though, we need the services of these professionals when we are in an unfamiliar area.

Locating Treatment

When you need treatment for a medical problem there are a variety of ways to locate help. In some towns there are services that can refer you to the type of doctor you need. Often such a service is provided by a local hospital or nurses' association; the telephone number can be found in the Yellow Pages. If you have a regular doctor, you can telephone him or her and perhaps get a referral to a local fellow practitioner.

Walk-in clinics are another possibility for medical treatment. We've used these several times for minor problems. If you can't find a doctor or clinic, you can always go to the emergency room of a local hospital, whether or not your condition is an emergency.

When we have a dental problem, we often ask the campground manager to recommend a dentist. If the manager can't help us for one reason or another (one woman couldn't because she had never had a cavity in her life), he or she often directs us to another campground resident who can. Local people are usually very helpful in this regard.

Once, when we were parked for lunch in Wyoming, Bill broke a cap on one of his teeth. We decided to stop in the next town to see if we could find a dentist to glue the broken piece back on. The next town was the tiny hamlet of Lyman. Using the telephone book, we located the two dentists in town; they were in the same building. Since we weren't planning to stay over, we drove there with our trailer and parked in a big lot across the street from the dentists' offices.

Both offices were closed. We assumed the dentists were out to lunch, so we waited around for a few minutes. A woman returning to an adjacent insurance office told us that one dentist was out of town and the other was gone for the day. We explained our problem—not much explanation was needed because when Bill smiled, it was plain to see the great empty space where a front tooth should have been. We mentioned that we were headed for another small town about forty miles away. The woman invited us into her office and voluntarily telephoned the dentists at our next stop until she found one who could see Bill. After thanking her for her generous help, we left for our prearranged appointment.

The dentist glued the piece on, but it fell off the next morning soon after we were under way. Not far from where we were going to stay the night, we stopped at a tourist information center hoping someone there could recommend a dentist. The woman on duty unhesitatingly gave us a name in the next town on our route. As soon as we got there we called for an appointment and were told to come right over. This dentist did the job successfully.

Another time a helpful campground owner in Idaho recommended his dentist. Bill liked him so much that we will make an effort to go back and see him should we need any major dental work done.

We know you don't care about the condition of our teeth (though you may have deduced that Bill has more problems than Jan), but the anecdotes make some useful points: You usually can count on local people to recommend qualified medical personnel (you may even be told whom to avoid, as we once were), people

"As a fulltimer, you can usually establish an instant rapport with health-care professionals because most of them are fascinated by the lifestyle."

are generally friendly and helpful when you are from out of town and have a problem, and, more often than not, doctors and dentists find room to squeeze you in if you are just passing through.

Throughout the years, we have visited doctors and dentists in various states from coast to coast. These scattered individuals are the ones we see "regularly" when we need a checkup or if a medical problem arises when we are in their localities. If we aren't near one of the "regulars," we are confident we'll find another we can add to our list.

As a fulltimer, you can usually establish an instant rapport with health-care professionals because most of them are fascinated by the lifestyle. They want to know where you've been and where you're going. They invariably remember you if you make a return visit. Because of the way you live, you are one of their most interesting patients.

Medical Records

If you are a fulltimer who has a condition that may require attention while traveling, you should get a copy of your records from your physician and carry them with you. A doctor who hasn't seen you before will find them helpful and they can be especially valuable in an emergency situation.

Also keep current dental X rays in your RV, so you won't have to keep paying for new ones should you need to see a dentist during your travels. A dentist cannot justifiably refuse to give them to you. You paid for them, they are yours, although some dentists may rightfully insist on keeping the X rays of the teeth they have worked on.

Those taking prescription medications need to have a list containing each medication and the daily dosage. This should be carried on your person. In the event of an accident, it could determine the treatment you receive. If you take a number of medications, the list may be useful to refer to when filling out forms prior to receiving medical attention.

If you have a medical condition that could be life-threatening, such as diabetes or certain heart problems, it would be worthwhile to have your medical identification on a bracelet or necklace. Emergency medical personnel look for these types of ID first rather than searching through a wallet or purse.

Prescriptions

If you take prescription medication regularly, you can get refills by mail by utilizing a mail-order pharmacy. The American Association of Retired Persons (AARP) offers this service to members.

We used to have our prescriptions with a pharmacy located close to our mail-forwarder. She took care of refills and mailed them on to us. This was satisfactory, but we had to remind her about refills far enough ahead so we wouldn't run out of medication before we received our mail. So we can obtain our medications ourselves, we recently changed our procedure and have our prescriptions filled at Wal-Mart stores. Through the pharmacy computer network, any store can provide refills, no matter which store has the prescription on file. In addition to low prices, we chose Wal-Mart because the stores are common where we travel. We always have our doctors give us duplicate prescriptions (none of our medications are controlled substances, so there is no problem with this), and we send one to our mail-forwarder. In case we need a refill when a Wal-Mart isn't convenient, we can count on her to send the medication to us.

Certain chain pharmacies are located in many states—Eckerd, Payless, Osco, and Walgreen's are four that come to mind. Many of the chains have computer-connected stores. If you travel regularly where such pharmacies are located, you can obtain your own prescriptions, as we do at Wal-Mart. The pharmacies in some grocery chains also offer this service.

Surgery

Another advantage to being a fulltimer is that you can travel to the places where you can receive the best medical care. If you need elective or minor surgery, it may be worthwhile to do a little investigating and have it done in an area where hospital costs are reasonable yet standards are high. Rates vary widely across the country.

Another consideration that may affect your decision about traveling to a special place for medical care is if there are any campgrounds in the area, or, better, if the hospital has a place where RVs can be parked. Some do, and each RV site may have hookups.

Medical Insurance

Some fulltimers may have a problem with health insurance coverage once they take to the road.

If you are on Medicare, you'll be covered no matter where you travel in the United States. But if you are insured by a health maintenance organization (HMO) or preferred provider organization (PPO), you should check with your insurer to find out how, or if, your coverage is affected if you leave the area. Some coverage for travelers is rather restrictive.

Most regular health insurance is like Medicare; coverage extends throughout the United States.

Veterans are eligible for treatment at any Veteran's administration (VA) hospital. The hospitals are computer-connected so records are available at any VA hospital.

VEHICLE CONCERNS

In addition to taking care of personal health problems, RVers also need to take care of their rigs if they breakdown and need repairs on the road.

Emergency Road Service

We all hope breakdowns won't occur, but if they do, you'll be better off if you are enrolled in an emergency road service designed to service RV rigs.

All the services have similar basic benefits: emergency towing, lockout and flat tire service, fuel delivery, a toll-free number to call twenty-four hours a day, 365 days of the year. Where an RV-designed service differs from regular road services is mainly in the towing. If necessary, your entire rig, be it a motorhome and a dinghy, or a tow vehicle and a trailer, will be towed or transported to the nearest qualified facility, no matter how far away it is. When it comes to towing, most regular road services are set up to handle only one vehicle and no RVs.

Several such services are available. You'll find their ads in RV publications. If you belong to an RV club, enrolling in such a service may be available at a special rate.

Repairs

When it comes to having your vehicles taken care of when they are "sick," fulltimers can't count too much on local referrals. The mechanic who has solved a problem on one type of vehicle may know nothing about the make and model you have. Mechanics in their own way are more specialized than doctors. A human is a human, but each make of vehicle is a completely different breed.

There is no certain method for locating a qualified mechanic who will be able to solve your particular problem. Those who should know the most about your make of tow vehicle or the automotive components of a motorhome, are the mechanics at a dealership selling that brand. The service department at some small dealerships may not have the equipment necessary for working on vehicles as large as motorhomes.

Precautions

If it's obvious that you are just traveling through, disreputable mechanics at some repair shops and service stations may tell you that repair work is needed when it is not, or they may do something to your vehicle, after which it will, indeed, need to be repaired.

Take steps to prevent this by doing the following:

- Never leave your vehicle unattended in an unfamiliar service station while you are fueling or having the fluid levels checked.
- Watch carefully to see that only what you ask to be done is done.
- Without directions from you, be suspicious if someone looks under the hood, under the vehicle, or pays undue attention to the tires.
- Check all dipsticks yourself before authorizing anything to be added.

We make it a practice to never leave the repair shop when our truck or trailer is being worked on (except in the three instances when we had to leave the trailer overnight; we removed some of the most valuable items from it before we took it to the shop). We stay there and wait for it no matter how long it takes. Most times we really don't have much choice because, if we don't have our truck available, we have no other way of getting around. We always take lots of reading material, and once we did our wash in an adjacent self-service laundry we spied the day before when we made the appointment for the repair.

We believe our presence speeds things up to some degree, and we want to be on hand in case any problems are encountered. If we can get away with it, we periodically stroll into the repair area to see how things are coming along. In places with not-too-strict rules we can often talk to the mechanic, which helps us learn more about our vehicles.

Unfortunately, some dishonest mechanics, if left alone, will find other things that need to be "fixed." They might dutifully call your attention to a fan belt or hose with a split in it or perhaps point out a damaged tire, none of which needed fixing when the vehicle was brought in. Strange how such problems develop in some repair shops after the vehicle is in the shop.

Dishonest mechanics are well aware that their mistakes will not come back to haunt them if you are just passing through. When we are having repair work done, we never reveal this information if we can avoid it. If someone comments on our out-of-state plates, we say we are on an extended stay in town visiting relatives. This lets the mechanic know that if the work is not done satisfactorily, we can come back. This does not turn a bad mechanic into a good one, however. If we have any major repair work done, we do try to stay in the area long enough to be sure everything that was fixed is working properly.

If repairs are done at vehicle dealerships they are often warranted for a given period. It may be possible that another of your vehicle's dealerships in a different place would honor the warranty even though the work was not performed there. If a shop that is a franchise of a nationwide chain—Aamco, Firestone, Goodyear, Midas, and others—does the repair, you'll probably be given a warranty that is good in any of their affiliated shops.

When buying expensive items such as tires, batteries, and other products that have a warranty, if you purchase the item from a nationwide chain, warranty problems can be taken care of in many locations across the country.

Vehicle Insurance

It's important to have your RV rig insurance with a company that understands fulltiming. Many do not, or if they claim they do, have some faulty, preconceived ideas about the lifestyle. Even if such a company issued you a policy, you may have trouble collecting if you have a claim.

> *"When buying expensive items such as tires, batteries, and other products that have a warranty, if you purchase the item from a nationwide chain, warranty problems can be taken care of in many locations across the country."*

The carrier that provides group insurance for members of the Good Sam Club, National General Insurance Company, is a very understanding insurance company. They know that fulltimers may have their vehicles licensed in one state and have a mailing address in another. They also know that insuring a fulltimer's "house" is a good risk because when danger threatens a fulltimer's dwelling, be it hurricane, brush fire, or flood, the fulltimer's home can be moved out of harm's way. Many other insurance companies haven't tumbled to this yet.

We know from our own experience and that of others that the National General Insurance Company claim service is excellent.

When you join the Good Sam Club you'll be provided with information on the Good Sam Vehicle Insurance Plan (VIP). Other clubs also may offer similar insurance to their members.

Other companies that have been insuring RVs and fulltimers for years are: RV Alliance America (11100 NE 8th Street, Suite 900, Bellevue, Washington 98004-4441; (800) 521-2942) and Foremost Insurance Service Center (P. O. Box 2450, Grand Rapids, Michigan 59501; (800) 262-0170, Ext. 407).

RV Alliance America offers a total replacement policy for both motorhomes and trailers. Only new units are eligible for this coverage.

If your travels will take you to Mexico, your regular insurance won't cover your rig. You'll have to purchase insurance from a company that specializes in this type. These companies can be found in cities near the Mexican border.

For travel in Canada, check with your regular insurance company for coverage. Many insurers issue a rider for such travel at no extra cost.

In addition to rig insurance, fulltimers should have personal liability insurance. The liability insurance included in most vehicle coverage is intended to cover situations that arise as a result of the vehicle's being driven, or in the case of a trailer, while it is being towed. Another type of liability insurance is needed to cover the RV when it is parked. A fulltimer's personal liability policy, like a

> **"For travel in Canada, check with your regular insurance company for coverage. Many insurers issue a rider for such travel at no extra cost."**

homeowner's policy, protects you if someone should be injured in or on your property—which for a fulltimer is your rig or your campsite. Even though they don't own the campsite, they may have a hose, electrical cords, or a doormat someone could trip over.

We know of an instance that involved the explosion of a motorhome's propane cylinder. The motorhome was virtually destroyed, and flying debris damaged two other RVs in adjacent sites. The motorhome's owner, not a fulltimer, didn't have this sort of liability coverage, and his insurance company balked at paying for damages since the accident occurred when the vehicle was parked.

If a personal liability provision isn't included in your RV insurance, request that it be added. It's worth the small amount it costs.

The personal property coverage is rarely high enough to take care of the loss of fulltimer's personal property; after all, many of us carry all our worldly goods with us. Coverage can usually be increased with the payment of an additional fee.

Be sure to let your insurance company know if your rig is parked for several months and not on the road. Your rate may be lowered for such a period.

CHAPTER 5

Getting Started

Preparations for fulltiming can begin many years before the event (keeping in mind what can happen to long-range plans), or the switch from one lifestyle to another can be made within weeks, depending on individual situations. Although fulltiming should not be jumped into with reckless abandon, neither should it be postponed if it's something you want to do now and your circumstances allow it.

It's risky to venture into fulltiming if you have had no RV experience at all. Having to learn about RVs at the same time you are learning about fulltiming could be exasperating and discouraging. Some people manage to handle both with equanimity, but some neophyte fulltimers become soured on the lifestyle without giving it a fair chance.

BEGIN BY READING ABOUT THE LIFESTYLE

One of the best ways to get a handle on what fulltiming is all about is by reading *Trailer Life* and *MotorHome* magazines. These magazines are the only regular monthly RV publications available throughout the United States and Canada, and are the only ones that regularly have information about fulltiming. This encompasses articles about the lifestyle, news columns that report on legislation and regulations that affect all RVers, as well as letters to the editor, and ombudsman and troubleshooting columns.

Information in the magazines not specifically about fulltiming may still be of use. For instance, both publications contain many articles on general maintenance of trailers, tow vehicles, and motorhomes. Reports about tests and evaluations of new units may help in selecting a rig for fulltiming. Travel articles are valuable if your fulltiming will include traveling. Many RVers collect articles about places in which they are interested and keep them in a file or scrapbook for future reference.

Members of the Good Sam Club receive the magazine *Highways* each month, and members of other RV clubs may also receive magazines or newsletters. These publications also may contain much that is of interest to fulltimers.

Other publications may be found in campgrounds and RV-supply stores. These are generally regional bimonthly or quarterly periodicals, often distributed free of charge. In them you'll rarely find articles directed exclusively to the fulltimer; nevertheless, they are worth reading.

TALK TO PEOPLE LIVING THE FULL-TIMING LIFE

Talking to fulltimers can be helpful. When we began, we sought out fulltimers in order to get an insight into the lifestyle. Those we encountered were all enthusiastic about fulltiming. But later, when we were fulltimers, we met a couple that had an exceptionally downbeat attitude about the lifestyle. They were suspicious and distrustful of just about everything. They didn't like driving on highways because of potential dangers. They found something to complain about in almost every campground they visited. They lived in constant fear of having things stolen by intruders and even worried about being ripped off by the management of campgrounds. They rarely left a campsite after they were parked because they felt it necessary to be on guard constantly against people who were up to no good; in their opinion, this included just about everyone. Throughout our conversation, all these two did was voice their fears and complain. We marveled that they revealed so much to us—a couple of strangers, whom they probably looked upon with suspicion.

These people didn't enjoy fulltiming, but with their attitude they couldn't enjoy life in any style. Had a novice or prospective fulltimer encountered this couple, he or she might understandably have had qualms about the lifestyle.

Beware of those who paint an excessively gloomy picture of full-timing. Also take with a grain of salt those who say that the lifestyle has no problems at all. No way of living is totally trouble free.

You can easily find people to talk to who are engaged in fulltiming. When you are camping, ask others in the park if they are full-timers. If you don't have an RV, you can still visit campgrounds and talk to campers. Whether or not you are camping, stroll around the sites. Conversations can be started by noting license plates and asking where in that state the people are from. Other good conversational gambits are those about a particular rig: How do you like your diesel? Do you find a fifth-wheel easy to tow? Do those automatic levelers work well?

Most RVers are friendly folk and fulltimers are happy to talk about their lifestyle, so much so that you should allow a few hours for this. Time seems to fly as effusive RVers willingly tell you about interesting places they have visited, campgrounds they like, or don't like, how they live the full-timing life, how their rigs are working out, if they have gone from a smaller unit to a larger one or vice versa, and more. Sometimes lifelong friendships are formed from these encounters.

When fulltimers are enjoying themselves and paint a glowing picture of the lifestyle, you'll have to sift through the information you receive and apply it to your own situation. Your fulltiming won't be exactly like anyone else's, so what suits others may not be right for you.

> **"M**ost RVers are friendly folk and fulltimers are happy to talk about their lifestyle . . ."

TRY RVING BEFORE BUYING

Fulltiming should not be undertaken if you have never driven a rig or never overnighted in an RV. Without these experiences, you have no basis on which to select a rig, and you'll be unable to adequately judge how you like spending time in an RV.

Renting an RV

If you have no RVing experience, it will be much better for you, and perhaps less expensive in the long run, if you rent an RV for a vacation to try out the lifestyle. Even a weekend vacation is better than nothing. As we explained before, a vacation in an RV is not at all the same as living in one full time, but it will give you some idea of what it's like.

When it comes to renting an RV, however, only motorhomes are generally available. Sometimes very small trailers, under 20 feet, are offered as rental units. The reason that rental trailers are small is because they can be towed with a simple, easy-to-install bumper hitch. Other trailers require a large hitch assembly in which the hitch receiver is bolted or welded to the tow vehicle's frame. It's not practical to install a hitch of this type each time a trailer is rented.

Renting a motorhome is a good idea even if you think you'll want a trailer for fulltiming. Living in a motorhome and hooking it up in campgrounds is virtually the same as with a trailer.

Renting too small a unit for a short period of time won't provide you with a realistic full-timing experience, but any time spent in any size RV is better than having no RVing experience at all.

To locate rental RVs look in the Yellow Pages under the heading Recreational Vehicles—Rent and Lease.

We have been to some campgrounds in popular vacation areas where stationary trailers are for rent. These are usually travel trailers, permanently parked, and hooked up to all utilities. By renting one of these units you would not gain any driving or parking experience, but you would have the experience of living in a trailer.

If you have done some RVing, you know at least something about what you'll encounter when you begin fulltiming. You'll probably have driven your rig somewhere, parked it in a campsite, and hooked up the utilities. The broader your RV experience, and the more you have traveled, the better and quicker you'll adapt to fulltiming.

First-Day Experiences

Those who start fulltiming without some earlier experience may have a number of worries along with the excitement and anticipation of starting out. A typical first day might include the following concerns—at least:

- Everything you are taking with you must be loaded, stowed, and secured.
- If the rig is a trailer, it will have to be hitched properly. Don't pull away without raising the hitch jack. If a car is to be towed behind a motorhome, it will have to be hitched. Be sure nothing is left behind on the ground.
- After navigating through city traffic before reaching the highway, comes the concern about how the rig will handle when being passed by large trucks. Aside from the suction the trucks create, will the drivers try to give you a hard time? (Probably not.)
- If fuel is needed, you'll have to maneuver the rig next to the pump; there must be sufficient overhead clearance. Will you find an empty parking space large enough for your rig in a rest area if you want to stop there? How will your rig handle going up or down steep grades? If you run into rain, snow, sleet, fog, or wind will it create problems? You'll have to determine the best speed for your rig in any conditions encountered without having any previous experience on which to base your determinations.
- During the day's run you may wonder if you have stowed everything properly so no damage is occurring.

- You may have to drive through an unfamiliar town or city to find a campground. Will you get there before the rush hour traffic starts? Will the campground you have selected have space for you? Have you allowed enough time so that you won't be driving after dark? A common tendency is to drive too many miles the first day.
- If no pull-through spaces are available in the campground, the RV must be backed into a site. A towed car must be unhitched before the motorhome can be backed.
- Perhaps the site isn't level. If not, leveling has to be taken care of. You'll probably want to hook up the electricity and water, and maybe the sewer. When you finish with these duties it's time to get the appliances going.
- In many new RVs the refrigerator, water heater, and furnace are turned on simply by flipping a switch. In older RVs a little more effort may be required. The owner's manual may have to be located and consulted.
- Once all the foregoing is taken care of, you can then raise the TV antenna and finally relax— that is, if everything has gone smoothly.

Simple hookups may not seem as if they would present any problems, and usually they don't, but when you arrive in a campground tired after a long day of driving, you may find your thinking becomes cloudy and your actions less efficient.

We encountered this phenomenon late one night when a motorhome pulled into the site next to us. A man got out, gave his site a cursory glance, then headed for our trailer. We were the only others in the campground and the manager had locked the office and gone home. The man wanted to know where he could get some electricity; he said there was none at his site. We showed him his outlet—identical to ours and in the same location—which was in a common, gray enamel electrical box with a hinged lid that lifted up to expose the receptacles. The man had seen the box but hadn't thought to lift the lid. He sheepishly explained away his oversight by telling us that he was tired because he had been on the road since early morning.

Another time, a couple parked next to us in a Wyoming campground. We noticed they were spending an inordinate amount of time doing something to their water heater. We went over to see if we could help. We found that between the two of them they simply couldn't figure out how to light the water heater.

After we showed them what to do, they told us they had taken delivery of their RV—a used one, but a recent model—the previous day. They left their home in Missouri and had driven 700 miles on their first day out. They had no RV experience whatsoever. The dealer from whom they purchased their rig evidently had not gone over the systems to show the new owners how to operate them—not an oversight of the dealer, we suspected.

As long as we were being so accommodating, the couple asked us to help them with some other problems. We showed them how to light the burners on their range; this had been a complete mystery to them. They wanted some heat but couldn't figure out how to turn on the furnace. We showed them the thermostat; they hadn't a clue about the furnace being thermostatically controlled.

Those who have no RVing experience before taking off in their rigs could find themselves in situations like this, or worse. Just a little practice goes a long way toward solving these problems when, or if, they arise.

Experiment First

Even if you have been RVing for years but will be fulltiming in a new-to-you rig, a little experimentation to familiarize yourself with your rig and its equipment before you take off will smooth your way, and bring to light any problems so they can be corrected before you leave.

When we went from a travel trailer to a fifth-wheel trailer we had to learn an entirely new way of hitching. This was not made easy for us because we had a defective hitch, but we weren't aware of it at the time. We struggled with it, trying to make it work properly, all the while wondering how fifth-wheels had gotten the reputation for being easy to hitch. If we had had previous experience with hitching fifth-wheels we would have known immediately that we weren't doing anything wrong, but that the equipment was causing the problem.

Practice hitching and unhitching either the trailer to the tow vehicle or the auxiliary vehicle to the motorhome. Going through the maneuvers about a half-dozen times should make you a virtual pro at it, unless you, too, have some equipment that won't work properly. Once you develop a routine for hitching and unhitching, you'll find the procedure to be quite simple.

Once hitched, drive the rig on streets that have little traffic and few or no hills, if possible. Turn corners to find out how wide the rig must swing and in how narrow a space it can be turned safely. Notice the tracking. Be aware of the distance needed to stop when braking. Take the rig to a large parking lot when it's nearly empty and practice backing and parking.

Try all the basic systems—water heater, refrigerator, water pump, range, furnace, electrical—and any others you may have on your rig to find out how they work. Read the instructions for use and apply them until you are completely familiar with each system's operation. Experiment with these simple procedures one at a time. Don't put yourself in the position of having to learn the operation of everything all at once.

Make a short trip to a nearby campground to get some actual field experience. Even if it's an RV park in your town and you stay only overnight, you'll benefit from the experience. If you can't do this, live and sleep in your RV in your own driveway for a day or two.

If it's impossible to arrange for some practice before actually starting your fulltiming, don't plan to drive for more than a few hours the first day. Making this initial day a short one in miles traveled should help you avoid feeling too pressured or harried.

> "Try all the basic systems—water heater, refrigerator, water pump, range, furnace, electrical—and any others you may have on your rig to find out how they work."

You'll give yourself a better chance to enjoy the beginning of your fulltiming, and you may escape having doubts about whether you have done the right thing.

TO SELL OR NOT TO SELL YOUR HOUSE

The most definitive step toward a total commitment to fulltiming is selling your house. This is the biggest decision that has to be made—except, perhaps, the one to become a fulltimer—because once the house is sold, it will be an expensive proposition to go back to living in a fixed dwelling if you change your mind.

Should you sell your house? *Maybe not* if you are planning to try fulltiming for a few years and then return to living in a fixed dwelling. *Probably not* if you or your partner have doubts about whether you'll like the lifestyle. *Definitely not* if you plan on using it as your home base.

If retirement coincides with fulltiming, it may be an opportune time to sell a large family house, experiment with fulltiming, and then perhaps purchase a smaller, fixed dwelling later to use as a home base. Only you are in a position to know what you want to do; what you actually can do often depends on your financial situation.

For many, the decision to become fulltimers means they will have to sell their house in order to have the money to purchase the rig. This was our situation. Making up our minds to sell our house was not difficult for us. We were disenchanted with the responsibilities of home ownership and anxious to be free of the expenses and never-ending chores of keeping it up. In fact, we were so eager to be rid of the house, we placed an ad offering it for sale the Sunday after we made our full-timing decision.

January in Connecticut is not the ideal time to sell houses; they are hardly at their best when buried in snow with ice-covered driveways. But we thought running an ad might give us an idea of what we might expect in the spring, when serious buyers would be out looking. It would be interesting to see if we got any nibbles. As it turned out, we could have sold the house five times over that day and did indeed sell it to one couple. There was no turning back for us at that point.

If you need to sell your house to buy your rig, it's difficult to make definite plans. There's always the possibility that the house won't be sold soon enough to begin your fulltiming as planned. Then again, it may sell so quickly that you aren't ready to start fulltiming when you find a buyer. This is what happened to us. We didn't end up being temporarily homeless however, because we managed to have the closing date set several months ahead. The period from January to the end of April gave us the time we needed to make all the arrangements for our change in lifestyle.

Apartment dwellers don't have this problem. They can schedule their fulltiming to begin when their lease runs out. They have a definite date to work with. You can't count on selling a house precisely when you want to.

Dealing with Your Possessions

Once the house is sold, or before the apartment lease runs out, you'll have to make some crucial decisions about many of your possessions. When you go from living in any kind of a fixed dwelling to an RV, you won't have the room to store everything you own, no matter what size the RV.

Those who will be living in an RV exclusively have two choices regarding the items they won't be taking with them: They can be disposed of or stored. Some possessions can be disposed of by either selling them or giving them away. They can be stored either by renting storage space or by lending them temporarily to family or friends, perhaps with the understanding that if, in the future, the items are wanted, they will be given back.

Giving up possessions is often difficult—so difficult for some that they never become full-time fulltimers. Even though the desire is there, they can't bear to part with many of the things they have accumulated over the years.

Deciding what to keep hinges on two words: want and need. We truly need only a few things to live, but we always want more than just the basics. Life wouldn't be much fun if we had to limit ourselves to just necessities, so a happy balance has to be found between the needed items and the wanted ones.

Since all RVs suitable for fulltiming are completely furnished, you won't need any of the furniture you now own—not one stick of it. Even though we had some good furniture and a few antique pieces, we sold it all. We didn't want the bother of receiving a regular bill for storage, and we figured we could put to better use any money that would have to be spent for storage.

You'll probably need fewer dishes, flatware, and linens in your new life. Cooking utensils, appliances, and tools have to be judiciously sorted according to what you'll need and what you'll have room for. As you are sorting and considering what to take with you, think about how certain items can do double duty; special-purpose and one-purpose kitchen equipment won't be needed if other equipment can do the same job.

Hot dogs can be cooked in other than a hot dog cooker; vegetables can be sliced by hand instead of using a special slicing gadget; an electric skillet is really not needed if you have a same-size skillet than can be used on the range top. Food cooked on a square griddle can be cooked just as successfully in a large skillet.

Before we became fulltimers, we had always done a lot of baking and saw no reason to discontinue the practice just because we would be living in a trailer. We kept our cookie press, which is relatively small and weighs little, but got rid of our heavy rolling pin. The cylinder of the cookie press is what we use now for a rolling pin.

Most RVs suitable for fulltiming have plenty of galley storage space, so regularly used equipment should be retained. Regularly is the key word; when deciding what to keep and what to get rid of, ask yourself: How many times did I use this last year? If the answer is once, or twice, or not at all, the item can probably be disposed of without your missing it.

The clothing storage space in most RVs isn't as extensive as that in houses or apartments so most likely you'll have to get rid of some items in your wardrobe.

A heavy coat may be eliminated if you have a lightweight coat and sweater that can be worn together or separately according to the weather. The lightweight coat could be a parka that can double as a raincoat.

Don't make the common mistake of chucking out too many clothes. Some about-to-be-fulltimers who plan to follow the sun eliminate all items of winter clothing from their wardrobes. In the United States, no matter how far south you go in the winter, jackets and sweaters, even coats, are needed occasionally. Jan bought a winter coat with a zip-in lining—a feature she didn't think she would ever use. But it came in handy last year in southern Arizona when, for several days, the temperature fell to below freezing. She appreciated the hood too, because it also snowed.

Collections—books, glassware, clocks, guns, antique items—and other accumulations of prized possessions, may have to be sold, stored, or reduced to a size or number that will fit into your RV. Often the hardest choices to make are in this area.

We had a difficult time deciding which books from our sizable library to take with us. We were faced with a problem not common to most fulltimers: Because of our writing we needed to keep our large, hardcover dictionary and equally large encyclopedia. We replaced certain other hardbound reference books with lighter, smaller paperback editions. These included a thesaurus; an atlas; identification books for wildflowers, birds, trees, and rocks; and even a few favorite novels that we wanted to reread.

We had a large record collection (this was before CDs were invented) that we couldn't bear to give up but that wouldn't fit into

"In the United States, no matter how far south you go in the winter, jackets and sweaters, even coats, are needed occasionally."

our RV. We transferred all the records to tape cassettes and bought a good quality car stereo for the trailer to replace our large home stereo system.

We also had some favorite paintings. To take them with us, we photographed them, then had prints made in a size that would fit on the wall spaces in our RV.

Even when you have no sentimental attachment to possessions, you may find it difficult to decide what to keep and what to eliminate. When in doubt, keep the item if there is room to store it in your unit. Eliminating such an item later is less costly than having to repurchase it should you find you need it.

MOVING INTO AN RV

Moving from one fixed dwelling to another is not easy. Moving from a fixed dwelling to an RV, which is bound to be smaller, can be difficult and complicated.

Our move would have been simpler if we could have purchased our RV before moving out of our house. If you need to realize the money from the sale of your house to buy your rig as we did, perhaps our experiences will point up difficulties that may arise.

We began the process of disposing of our possessions the day after the buyers put a deposit on our house. We didn't have the deposit money to spend because it was being held in escrow by our attorney, but we knew, unless something out of the ordinary happened, the house sale would be finalized. With the closing at the end of April we had about fourteen weeks to find a suitable RV and get rid of everything we wouldn't be taking with us. This, we found, was not an excessive amount of time for accomplishing what we had to do.

Although we had only a five-room house, and Bill's pack-rat tendencies had always been more than offset by Jan's penchant for *not* collecting things, it still seemed as if we had an uncommonly large number of items to eliminate.

We couldn't afford to give away much since we needed any

money we could raise from selling our possessions. The weather wasn't suitable for holding a yard sale, so we began the disposal process by running classified ads for some of our big furniture items, a car, a van, our small RV, a sailboat, power tools, and yard equipment. It was a rare evening that someone didn't come to look at what we had advertised. Little by little we saw the rooms empty, although lots of items remained. Between telephone calls and visitors, we tackled the sizable jobs of cleaning out closets and cabinets, setting aside items to keep and other items to be included in yard sales later.

We wondered how we would ever find the time to shop for a rig, sell everything we wanted to sell, empty out the house, and move into our RV in the time we had before the closing. We were already weary from juggling schedules and appointments, and our lives were becoming ever more chaotic. Our usually neatly kept house had become an unorganized mess, which didn't help matters.

A spring thaw finally melted the snow in the yard and the ice in the driveway. As soon as the resultant mud dried up somewhat, we held our first yard sale. We had a sale every weekend for the following three weeks.

During this time we did manage to locate a travel trailer we liked and a truck with which to tow it. We had enough money to put a deposit on the units we wanted, but, since we weren't financing them, we couldn't take possession until they were paid for. We wouldn't have the money for this until we had the check for the house, and then we couldn't use the house proceeds until the check cleared. In those days it took from ten days to two weeks for checks to clear. As it happened, the new owner of our house had his canceled check in his possession fully two days before it was "cleared" by our bank. Because we were victims of this then-existing banking regulation, we had to move into a motel for a week and rent a storage unit (monthly rates were all that were available) to temporarily store everything we were going to take with us in our RV. When the check cleared, we paid the balances due and moved into our trailer the same day.

That day we also rented a space in an RV park for a month so we could get settled. As long as we had to pay a month's rent on a storage unit, we could move our things in gradually. Having a whole month to do this was quite a luxury after the hustle and bustle of the previous months. During this time we were able to thoroughly check out all the trailer's systems to see that they were functioning properly before leaving our dealer's area.

DELAYED FULLTIMING

If your plans for taking to the open road are slated for some time well into the future, that's no reason to delay disposing of items you won't need for fulltiming. Any work you can do in advance makes the actual transition that much easier.

Clearing the Closets

One of the best places to start is in clothes closets. We doubt that anyone living in a fixed dwelling doesn't have some clothing that is rarely or never worn. People tend to hang on to such items as long as a place exists for storing them. It should be easy to eliminate all the clothes that you don't wear, that are relegated to the far reaches of the closet because they don't fit properly, are no longer fashionable, or because you simply tired of them. Any accessories that fall into these categories should also be dispensed with.

The closer you get to your full-timing date, the more wardrobe items you can dispense with. Formal clothing won't be needed in your new lifestyle. It's unlikely you'll need any sort of business wardrobe unless you plan to continue working as you fulltime and your job requires business clothes. Neckties have no place in full-timing activities. A few years ago we were attending a get-together of campground residents in the campground's recreation hall. One man showed up in a suit and tie. He was jokingly told that he wouldn't be allowed to participate unless he wore clothes more suitable to the occasion. He promised he would never make such a fashion gaffe again.

Women rarely need dresses; separates suffice for nearly every occasion. A woman of our acquaintance has kept one dress, "Old Blue" she calls it, in case she has to attend any weddings or funerals.

Cleaning Out Packed-away Items

Next easiest to get rid of, after clothing, are items stored away in the attic, basement, garage, storage shed, and unused rooms. Many people have boxes and cartons of things squirreled away in places such as these. Just about anything that is packed away can be eliminated. If the things are stored, they aren't being used, so why keep them? If these repositories of unused items are cleaned out, a monumental job will be over with by the time you are ready to begin fulltiming.

It's a common tendency to fill all empty rooms in a fixed dwelling with furniture; in fact, in some houses many of these rooms seem to serve no purpose other than to hold furniture. They may have been used at some time as bedrooms when children lived at home, or they may be rarely used sewing rooms, dens, or game rooms. Many dining rooms aren't often used for dining when a family room or kitchen contains a suitable dining area.

If you have rooms in your house that aren't used regularly, you can dispose of the furniture in them now and have that much less to do later. Even certain tables, chairs, lamps, pictures, and rugs in rooms that are used all the time can be eliminated without causing any real inconvenience.

Since disposing of possessions is one of the biggest hassles faced by those who are about to be fulltimers, anything that can be done in advance to get rid of what is unneeded and unwanted makes the final elimination much easier.

CHAPTER 6

Selecting the Full-timing Rig

Fulltiming can be done in any type of recreational vehicle. Some people are participating in the lifestyle in vans, mini-motorhomes, tent trailers, and pickup campers. With the possible exception of single fulltimers who need room only for themselves, most people who live in RVs of these types are doing it because they can't afford to buy a larger or more practical unit. Having a home on wheels is more important to them than practicality—even comfort. They make do with their RVs because it's the only way they can fulltime.

Finances permitting, we suspect most of these determined fulltimers would probably prefer to live in an RV that had all the comforts and conveniences of a real home.

PRACTICAL RVS FOR FULLTIMING

The types of RVs that are the most suitable for living in fulltime are Class A and Class C motorhomes, which are self-propelled, and travel and fifth-wheel trailers, which have to be towed (Figures 6.1, 6.2, 6.3, and 6.4). One of these RVs is the choice of the majority of fulltimers.

Figure 6.1 Class A motorhomes are available in lengths ranging from 23 to 45 feet. (Courtesy Fleetwood Enterprises, Inc.)

Figure 6.2 A distinguishing feature of Class C motorhomes is the cabover section, which usually contains a bed; however, in some models this space is devoted to cabinets. (Courtesy Fleetwood Enterprises, Inc.)

Figure 6.3 Travel trailers may be towed by a truck or, if the unit isn't too heavy, a passenger car. (Courtesy Sunline Coach Company)

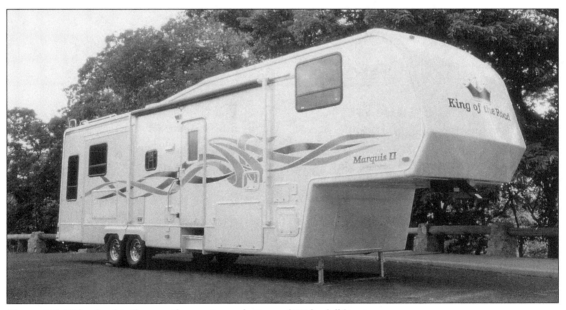

Figure 6.4 Fifth-wheel trailers are the most popular type of RV for fulltimers. (Courtesy King of the Road, RV Division, Chief Industries Inc.)

The difference between a travel and a fifth-wheel trailer is that the front section of the fifth-wheel trailer, the gooseneck, extends over the bed of the pickup-truck tow vehicle and the hitch is located in the center of the truck's bed. Obviously, a truck is the only type of vehicle that can be used for towing a fifth-wheel trailer. Most travel trailers are towed with a truck, but some passenger cars can be used as a tow vehicle if the trailer is not too heavy.

Class A motorhomes resemble buses in shape although many models are sleeker and more streamlined.

Class C motorhomes are built on a van cutaway chassis and have a van cab with the engine located under an extended hood. The distinguishing feature of all Class Cs is the cabover section, which usually contains a bed, but some models may have cabinets there instead.

Within these four basic types, a rig should be selected according to how it will be used and in a size that is right for you and your full-timing companions.

SELECTING AN RV TO SUIT YOUR LIFESTYLE

The size and type of RV you need depends on how and where your fulltiming is done. For instance, those who intend to do a lot of backcountry camping may want a smaller, different type of rig than those who will be staying in established campgrounds with designated sites. Those who travel more than just taking their rig south for the winter and north for the summer will want a maneuverable rig that is easy to drive and to park in a variety of different campground situations.

The climates in which the unit is to be used may also have some bearing on the rig's selection. Many, but not all, of today's RVs are well insulated, and on some units the plumbing can withstand below-zero temperatures without freezing.

Many fulltimers engage in more than just one kind of camping. We have stayed in many places far off the beaten track with no utility hookups whatsoever, and we have spent a good share of our time in campgrounds with paved sites and all hookups. We like a change of seasons and winter may find us in places where the temperature falls below freezing. We enjoy all types of camping, so we wanted a rig that would be as versatile as possible. Your own camping habits should figure in your RV selection.

When it comes to choosing the rig itself, either a motorhome with a towed auxiliary vehicle or a trailer with a towing vehicle, those RVers who have experimented with different types and sizes of rigs should have a good idea of the combination that will be best for them as fulltimers. As for the motorhome or trailer itself, you'll find soon after you begin serious shopping for a full-timing RV that no one unit is absolutely right for all your needs. You'll have to make compromises—perhaps many.

A number of factors, in addition to those mentioned above, must be considered when buying a rig for fulltiming. We hope the information that follows helps in your decision. The selection of an RV that is not right for your needs can be costly. It can also negatively affect your feelings about fulltiming.

SHOPPING FOR AN RV

You'll probably have to do a lot of looking before you can make a reasonably intelligent choice about a full-timing rig. Where to start? If you talk to other RVers about fulltiming, as we suggested earlier, get their opinions on rigs too.

RV shows, which are held regularly in all parts of the country, afford excellent opportunities to see and compare many different brands and types of RVs. Announcements of many of these shows appear in local newspapers, *Trailer Life* and *MotorHome* magazines, and are often posted at RV dealers and RV-supply stores.

Visit as many dealers as you can and look at everything they have to offer that you think may fit your needs. Salespeople are helpful later, but you should do the initial looking on your own; at this point you don't want to be high-pressured. You need to poke around in the units and spend quite a bit of time going over them. Let the salespeople know you are doing some preliminary looking. You may still receive the high-pressure treatment, but at least you will have been honest about not being ready to buy.

We doubt that salespeople can help you decide whether a motorhome or trailer is best for you. Unless they have both types for sale, they will try to convince you that what they are selling is the best choice. Don't expect salespeople to say anything negative about the products they are selling, either. About the only time they downplay one unit is when they are trying to sell you a larger, more expensive model.

We don't mean to imply that salespeople are doing anything wrong or dishonest. On the contrary, these are just good sales tactics, but you do have to be fairly well decided about the type and size of RV you want before the salesperson can be of much help. Then, a good salesperson can be invaluable.

When you are ready to buy and are down to the final comparisons among several units, never feel guilty about taking up too much of a salesperson's time. Ask everything you want to know about the unit you are considering. Making the right selection takes time, and should not be rushed under any circumstance.

No matter what size or type of unit you choose, you'll be spending thousands of dollars. Because so much money is involved, it may be worth your while to travel some miles from home to look at units. We had to travel more than 200 and 300 miles on different trips to see brands of RVs that were not sold in our immediate area.

Your local library should have phone books for your part of the country and in them you can find listings of dealers and the brands they carry.

Advertisements in *Trailer Life* and *MotorHome* magazines may be helpful in finding units and dealers. Information on many units can be obtained by circling the appropriate number on the reader service card (this number usually appears at the bottom or side of the

Figure 6.5 If you can't find a stock trailer to suit you, perhaps a custom unit such as these may fit your needs. (*Top,* courtesy Auto-Mate Recreational Products, Inc.; *bottom,* courtesy Horizons, Inc.)

advertisement). When you receive the literature from the manufacturer it will probably include the name of your closest dealer. Some ads contain a telephone number that can be used for locating dealers as well as for asking questions you may have about the RV.

If you want a trailer, don't overlook a custom-built unit (Figure 6.5). You may be surprised at how inexpensive it is to have a unit built just for you; in some cases it may cost less than a production-line model of the same size.

What About Customizing Production-Line RVs?

Don't expect to find many manufacturers that do customizing on their stock models. Beyond the standard options offered, only a very few manufacturers do any customizing, as we found when we were looking for our second full-timing trailer. If manufacturers customize, most likely it's on their largest, most expensive units. Fewer of these are built, so there is time for some out-of-the-ordinary work on the production-line.

On high-end motorhomes customizing is fairly common, within limitations. You probably can't find a manufacturer that will alter the entire interior to your specifications.

If you want any customizing done, be wary of the salesperson who assures you that "we can take care of it here." Salespeople don't want to let potential buyers get away, so they may promise more than they are capable of delivering. It's difficult to make alterations to a finished unit and have the job look as if it was done at the factory. Very few dealers have the tools needed for doing much custom work on their premises or employ craftspeople that can do such work.

Should your customizing desires be nothing more than having something omitted, you may be unsuccessful in getting the factory to do even this. When we ordered our trailer we did not want the manufacturer to install a dinky, dust-catching, useless spice shelf in the galley and an unreachable-from-the-shower towel ring in the bath. We didn't want to patch the holes that would be left when we removed the items, as we certainly would do if they were put on. When we were told that the worker on the assembly line who would install these items would be idle for a time, we suggested that he or she be given an extra coffee break. Whether the extra break was given we don't know, but the spice shelf and the towel ring were not installed.

We know of a couple who wanted the built-in dinette omitted on their unit, but the factory ignored their wishes and the dinette was installed in the usual way.

We managed to have some customization done because much of what we wanted amounted to taking pieces of furniture from other models and putting them in ours. Nothing was specially built just for us. We persuaded the sales manager at the plant to have the workers install a TV console and a cabinet used in their 32-foot model and a bank of cabinets used in another model. We also wanted to have installed a folding table from their 27-foot model. We got the table but it was not installed; we had to put it in ourselves.

Where to Purchase an RV

Whatever type of RV you decide on, it's wise to purchase a well-known brand from an established manufacturer. One reason for this is that an extensive dealer network usually exists, so if you intend to do much traveling, you can count on having warranty work taken care of and other servicing done when you are away from the dealer from whom you purchased the RV.

Another more important reason for buying this type of RV is to avoid spending your money for a unit that is so shoddily built it may last for only a short time and may be missing some vital components. For example, we heard of a trailer that had no piping connected to the city-water inlet. The unsuspecting owner hooked up and water spurted directly into the interior.

Because trailers can be manufactured less expensively than motorhomes, usually trailers are the type of RV offered for sale by scam artists.

Here are some tips that may help you avoid units like this:

- Be suspicious when a dealer offers you a new unit at a price considerably lower than what brand-name units of the same size are selling for (some dealers sell nothing but this type of unit).
- Ask for a brochure so you can take it home and study it. If you receive a full-color or other decently printed brochure,

it's a good indication the unit is from a reputable manufacturer. If no brochure exists, pass up the "deal."

- Be wary of purchasing a nearly-new unit from a private party, unless it's a brand you recognize and the seller has an established telephone number—not the number of a motel room, for instance. The unit should be parked at the seller's residence or, perhaps, in a storage facility, but not in a motel parking lot. Don't be swayed by a sob story about personal problems that are forcing the seller to let you have the unit at a very low price because he or she needs the money right now. Con artists like this purchase their units, trailers almost exclusively, from certain manufacturers just for the purpose of selling them.

WHY WE SELECTED OUR RIG

When we were faced with selecting an RV for fulltiming, we weren't absolutely sure whether a trailer or motorhome would be best for us. We weighed all the pros and cons many times over and decided on a travel trailer.

We ended up choosing a trailer because it seemed to be the most versatile RV for what we planned to do, and its initial cost and projected future upkeep was affordable for us, as was a pickup truck for a tow vehicle.

The amount we had to spend was not enough for a motorhome in the size we would need. We didn't have a suitable auxiliary vehicle, which we anticipated we would need when the motorhome was parked, so this would have been another expense. And we didn't want to be faced with spending money for the insurance and continuing maintenance for two motorized vehicles, nor did we want the bother.

When we started, we were lucky and made the right rig choice. We fulltimed happily in our trailer for many years, and when we needed a new RV, we again purchased a trailer.

Your fulltiming won't be just like ours, or anyone else's, so your choice of rig may be entirely different than ours.

A MOTORHOME OR A TRAILER: SOME COMPARISONS

There can be no accurate comparison of motorhomes to trailers because it's much like comparing apples to oranges. The two are both fruits, just as motorhomes and trailers are both RVs, but beyond this, the differences between the two are great.

Although the majority of fulltimers live in trailers, many initially think that a motorhome is the best choice for an RV. Perhaps they have used a motorhome for vacations, and it's what they are used to. Some may feel that they won't be able to handle a trailer, and there is often concern about the hitching procedure as well. Undoubtedly, what puts off many people about trailers is the impression that hitching, unhitching, backing, and parking a trailer are mysterious, hard-to-learn procedures. They are not, of course. Otherwise there would not be so many trailerists. These people are no smarter or more skilled than you are.

Towing a trailer is also often thought to be difficult. This too is a misconception. When a tow vehicle is properly matched to a trailer and fitted with the right hitch equipment, you'll hardly know the trailer is behind you.

Auxiliary Transportation

Almost all fulltimers who live in a motorhome have auxiliary transportation of some sort, usually a small car that is towed behind. It may seem like we are putting the cart before the horse to discuss this auxiliary transportation before the motorhome itself, but towing a dinghy is not as straightforward as merely attaching it to the motorhome and taking off. Knowing what is involved may have some bearing on your decision as to whether you want to fulltime in a trailer or motorhome.

Do Your Research

There are so many aspects to be considered about auxiliary towing that a considerable amount of research must be done to be sure of the suitability and compatibility of both the vehicle that will be towed and the motorhome. Two valuable resources are the "Dinghy Towing Guide" that appears annually in the March issue of *MotorHome* magazine, and the booklet, *Trailer Life's Towing Guide*. The booklet may be ordered from Trailer Life Books, 64 Inverness Drive East, Englewood, Colorado 80112; (800) 766-1674.

We cover only the main points of dinghy towing, but you should do your own thorough research before attempting to tow an auxiliary vehicle.

Much of the information you'll need is in the owner's manual. If you own a vehicle you want to use as auxiliary transportation or plan to buy one, consult the owner's manual for the manufacturer's recommendations about whether or not the vehicle can be towed, and, if it can, the restrictions, if any, regarding towing.

Many manufacturers do not authorize towing. Those that do may have limitations on the distance and the speed at which the vehicle can be towed. Don't take the word of salespersons about the suitability of a vehicle for being towed; they often don't know. Use the owner's manual as your authority so there will be no question about the warranty being honored in case of problems.

Towing Equipment

Depending on the manufacturer's recommendations and the towed vehicle's transmission type (automatic or manual), the dinghy can be towed on all four wheels with a tow-bar arrangement, on a dolly that removes the drive wheels from the ground, or the vehicle can be carried on its own trailer.

A tow bar is the simplest and least expensive towing apparatus; a trailer, the most expensive. If a tow bar is used you may need to purchase additional equipment: a device to disconnect the drive shaft, or, if the vehicle has an automatic transmission, a pump to lubricate the transmission.

Towing Weights

The weight of the vehicle you select, the weight of the towing equipment, and the total weight of the motorhome affect the motorhome's gross combined weight rating (GCWR), which should not be exceeded (more about this later in this chapter). Most motorhomes in a size suitable for fulltiming can safely tow a load that weighs from 3,500 to 4,500 pounds.

All states have different regulations regarding the licensing, titling, and brake requirements of tow dollies. The regulations are often so ambiguous and bewildering that even clerks in motor vehicle departments can't give correct answers to questions you may have about it, so you may have to persevere in your research in this area too.

Towing Situations

When deciding whether you want a trailer or motorhome for fulltiming, the situations that will be encountered with the towed vehicle must be considered. Taking along this extra vehicle means that those with motorhomes also have to do a fair amount of towing, hitching, and unhitching.

A motorhome with a small vehicle hitched behind, whether by means of a simple tow-bar arrangement or with a tow dolly, is more difficult to back than a trailer. The vehicle or dolly has a tendency to turn so quickly that there is little the driver can do to control it. The vehicle can jackknife rapidly to the point where damage may be done to it or the towing apparatus.

Compared with hitching a trailer, hitching a vehicle to a motorhome has fewer steps, which is fortunate because the vehicle, or its dolly, has to be unhitched and moved out of the way before the motorhome can be backed successfully. Some campsites are so small that room for a dolly is not available in the site itself and it has to be parked in a special area set aside for this purpose.

A towed vehicle cannot be seen when it's behind a motorhome so you have no way of knowing what's going on back there. This lack of visibility must be taken into account when passing other vehicles; you must always allow room for this unseen vehicle.

Travel and fifth-wheel trailers have their own brakes, which are activated when the tow vehicle is braked. When a vehicle is towed with a tow bar, the motorhome's brakes alone provide the stopping power for the motorhome and the ton or more the vehicle weighs. Tow dollies may or may not have their own brakes.

A hitch receiver mounted on the motorhome's frame is the only safe towing arrangement. Never use a bumper-mounted hitch.

If you don't want the bother of towing a small vehicle, the motorhome will have to be used for all transportation, sightseeing, shopping, and errand running. Aside from this being impractical, if the motorhome is the sole means of transportation it may have to be parked in places where it could be an easy mark for thieves. Motorhome owners are presumed, falsely in many cases, to have more money than other RVers and therefore have more valuables stored in the motorhome. With a small dinghy or a trailer's tow vehicle, you can leave your home with all its valuables in a campground where there is usually more security than in unattended parking lots or on the streets.

Without a vehicle for auxiliary transportation, you'll be hauling around the heavy weight of everything you own each time you go anywhere, which can increase your fuel expenditure.

If you are the type of fulltimer who stays in one place for months at a time, you could eliminate any auxiliary towing problems by leasing a vehicle for the time you are in one area. This could prove to be as cost-effective as owning a vehicle.

Repairs and Servicing

As we see it, one of the biggest drawbacks to having a motorhome is that when the vehicle is in the shop for repair or even routine servicing, so are your possessions and living quarters. Other lodging has to be arranged for if the motorhome is in a shop overnight. No matter how long it remains in the shop there is the likely possibility that mechanics in dirty clothes and shoes will be tracking through your home, and some may take advantage of the situation and relieve you of some of your possessions that are there for the taking. That such incidents occur is evident because it's the rare repair shop that doesn't have a sign posted stating that the management is not responsible for theft, among other things.

Some shops don't have enough overhead clearance for repairs that would require a motorhome to be raised on a hydraulic lift, and some lifts are not capable of lifting the weight of a motorhome.

We have noticed that of the hourly repair rates, those for motorhomes are usually higher than for other vehicles.

Having warranty work taken care of on motorhomes is sometimes a problem. Motorhomes have an engine and chassis from one manufacturer and a body and interior from another. We have heard many stories about how neither manufacturer would take responsibility when it came to honoring the warranty. In these cases, the motorhome owner is usually bounced from one manufacturer to the other, so it may take some time for even simple problems to be resolved. This would be an annoyance if you are staying put somewhere, but if you are traveling, the possibly complicated logistics and the time and effort spent to get satisfaction could cause considerable frustration.

Although a dealership for the brand of engine in the motorhome may be found in most towns, dealers for the make of the motorhome won't be nearly so plentiful.

Driving and Handling

When it comes to driving, motorhomes are most like driving a car or pickup truck because they are one unit. They can be backed easily, and if designed well and equipped with suitable shock absorbers or an air-bag suspension system, they generally have little sway and body roll.

Fifth-wheel trailers are the next best for ease of handling. They track well, sway is almost nonexistent, and backing and maneuvering is not difficult.

The handling of a travel trailer is largely dependent on the hitching apparatus and whether it's installed and used properly. The hitch and receiver must be sturdy enough for the weight of the trailer being pulled. Trailers large enough for comfortable fulltiming are heavy enough to require a weight-distributing hitch, which has two equalizer, or leveling, bars. One sway control, perhaps two if the trailer is long, is also needed. If the equalizer bars, which are adjustable, are attached so that both the trailer and the tow vehicle are on a level plane with the ground, there should be no problem with towing or tracking.

When driving in high winds, even when a sway control is used, there is more of a chance of sway with a travel trailer than with a fifth-wheel or a motorhome. When we had a travel trailer, we usually did not travel when it was extremely windy, although we did tow it several times in fifty-mile-per-hour winds with no problems. The effects of strong winds on the 29-foot fifth-wheel trailer we now have are minimal or nonexistent.

Head winds don't affect the stability of any RV, but when driving into a strong wind, fuel consumption goes up considerably, and we have found that sometimes we can't get up to the speed at which we want to travel. Going west on Interstate 80 across southern Wyoming is where this has repeatedly happened to us. The highway runs along at an altitude of about 6,000 feet for much of its distance in Wyoming and the head winds are fierce.

The tendency of an RV to pull or swerve when being passed by large trucks is greatest with travel trailers, and longer trailers are more affected than shorter ones. The pull is negligible with motorhomes and fifth-wheels. When we were towing a travel trailer we felt the pull in varying degrees nearly every time a big truck passed us, but we never once thought we were in danger of losing control of the rig.

Backing a trailer, although not as straightforward a process as backing a motorhome (without a towed vehicle behind), can be learned quickly. Once learned, the maneuver can be handled easily.

Storage Space

On average, foot for foot, trailers have more living area and storage space, inside and out, than most motorhomes. As near as we can determine, a motorhome would have to be a minimum of four feet longer than a trailer to have an equal amount of storage space.

In recent years storage in some motorhomes has been considerably expanded. Basement-model motorhomes have huge storage areas that run the width of the motorhome under much of the floor area (Figure 6.6). Certain large trailers also have this basement feature.

With fifth-wheels, any storage space lost from the pickup bed because of the hitch being located there is usually made up on the trailer because of the capacious storage area under the gooseneck that most fifth-wheels have.

Figure 6.6 Storage space abounds in this basement-model motorhome. (Courtesy Country Coach, Inc.)

Should you need more storage space in the truck, covers for the entire bed that turn most of the bed into a storage area are available. A typical design has a lid over the hitch location, which is removed for towing. Access to the front of the bed is through two lift-up lids.

Another choice for storage can be a box that fits in the front of the bed. This type of storage unit can be purchased (Figure 6.7) or homemade. If this doesn't take care of your storage needs, you might consider an additional storage unit that fits across the rear of the bed. The tailgate must be removed to install this type of unit.

Climate Control

In any size Class A or Class C motorhome, the dashboard air conditioner is not enough for adequate cooling while driving. If the unit is to be cooled while under way, it must have a roof-mounted air conditioner. Some large motorhomes need two to achieve comfortable cooling. The only way to run such an air conditioner while traveling is with a 120-volt AC generator. A generator may be standard equipment on some motorhomes; if not, it's an option.

Figure 6.7 Extra storage space in a truck's bed is provided by these two storage boxes. The rear box is large enough to accommodate an outboard motor. (Courtesy Creative Industries)

Natural ventilation is generally better in trailers than in motorhomes. Many trailers have opening windows on all four sides, an arrangement that admits a breeze no matter which direction it comes from. The front window on motorhomes, which is the windshield, does not open, of course, and few motorhomes have a window in the back, but if they do, it's rarely the opening type.

Some trailer manufacturers are doing away with rear windows if the unit is a rear-bath model, and finding a front window on any recent model fifth-wheel trailer is a rarity unless the living room is in the gooseneck. But even some of these front-living-room models don't have a front window.

For ventilation, louvered windows are the most efficient because they can be left open in all but a driving rain and angled to catch the slightest breeze. Nevertheless, opening windows on many new motorhomes and some trailers are the sliding type.

Leveling

It's best to have the RV level when parked, and it's necessary with older RVs if the refrigerator is to work properly. Newer refrigerators don't require such critical leveling (check your owner's manual for leveling requirements). Refrigerators aside, a level trailer or motorhome is more comfortable for sleeping and eating, and if the unit is level, you'll have no problem with doors on cabinets, wardrobes, refrigerators, and the bathroom swinging open or shut, or with items rolling off counters.

In campsites that are not level—and many are not—leveling a trailer is usually a simple matter. Side-to-side leveling is accomplished by running the wheels on the lower side up onto a leveling board of the needed height before unhitching. Front-to-back leveling is done simply by raising or lowering the hitch jack, or the front jacks on a fifth-wheel, after unhitching.

A motorhome may need to have boards placed under three wheels to level it fore, aft, and sideways. We have seen many motorhomes that have been leveled, laboriously no doubt, by stuffing all sorts of various-sized pieces of lumber under the front and/or rear wheels. Leveling a motorhome sometimes takes considerably more time than unhitching and leveling a trailer.

Because leveling a motorhome can be such a problem, those who want a motorhome should seriously consider a unit equipped with automatic levelers. Top-of-the-line luxury motorhomes usually come equipped with automatic levelers, but they can be purchased and installed, not cheaply, for use on nearly any motorhome. Some trailers can also be equipped with automatic levelers.

Living Areas

Motorhomes and trailers each have particular advantages and disadvantages when it comes to the living area. We like a trailer because our driving and living areas are separate. Sitting in the same seat for driving and then for relaxing when parked is not appealing to us, no matter how comfortable the seat may be. We prefer more spatial variety than can be achieved merely by swiveling around the front seats of a motorhome to make a temporary living room.

Not having to get out of the RV after you have parked it is a plus for motorhomes. If motorhomers arrive at campground in a pouring rain, once parked in the site they can delay going outside to attach the hookups or take care of other outside duties until the rain stops. Trailerists in this situation have to stay in the tow vehicle, or get wet dashing to the comfort of the trailer.

One fulltimer we know who sometimes overnights in highway rest areas likes a motorhome instead of a trailer because he can leave the area without going outside, as he may want to do if suspicious characters are lurking about his rig.

Other Points About Motorhomes and Trailers

Unlike trucks, cars, and Class C motorhomes, Class A motorhomes may not have a door on either the passenger side or the driver side of the cockpit. Some motorhomes have only one central door on the curb side of the unit. After numerous complaints about this, some manufacturers are now installing a door on the driver's side. But most of these doors are so high off the ground, usually located right above the front wheel, that they may be difficult to use. They would provide a daily dose of exercise, though, for anyone who used them regularly.

This situation does not exist on Class C motorhomes because the living accommodations are installed behind a conventional van cab and the door on each side has been retained, and another full-size door is on the curb side.

On most motorhomes the propane tank is not removable. When it needs to be filled, the motorhome must be driven to the propane supplier unless it's parked in a campground that has propane delivery to the sites (the majority of campgrounds in which we have stayed don't have this service). How the tank is re-filled should be a consideration when planning on a long-term stay in a campground.

Those who have a trailer/tow vehicle rig are in a somewhat better position than those with motorhomes when time comes to upgrade or replace the existing trailer or tow vehicle. They have the option of replacing just one unit. Those with a motorhome have no choice; the whole unit must be replaced.

When it comes to depreciation, motorhomes are much like any other automotive vehicles; the minute you drive it off the lot, it depreciates considerably, whereas a trailer retains more of its value for a longer period.

The foregoing contains facts (not opinions) about motorhomes and trailers. We have pointed them out because some may be overlooked in the excitement of purchasing a rig. Whether these facts amount to advantages or disadvantages about either type of rig depends on the point of view of the purchaser.

WHAT SIZE SHOULD THE RV BE?

Selecting the best size RV for your purposes can be as difficult as deciding what type of rig you need. Aside from the important consideration of its having enough storage space for your needs and those who will be traveling with you, how and where you will use your rig also figures in the size selection, as it does in the type of RV chosen.

If you'll be moving from a fixed dwelling to an RV, don't even think about buying an RV large enough to hold everything you now own, even minus furniture. If such a rig existed, and you could afford it, it wouldn't be much fun to haul all your possessions around with you all the time. Or would it? In Texas we once saw a huge motorhome with several roof storage pods towing a double-deck flatbed trailer. The lower trailer level held a full-size pickup truck; on the upper level was a sizable boat with a large outboard motor on its own trailer.

Start by Thinking Small

The smaller the rig, the more places you'll find to park it, not only in campgrounds, many of which have limitations as to what size RV can be accommodated in their sites, but in shopping center parking lots and on the street.

One of our favorite places to camp is in national forest campgrounds. Many of these campgrounds were built before RVing became so popular and many RVs became so large, so the sites can accommodate only small units. The site size in these campgrounds had a direct effect on the size of the trailer we initially purchased for fulltiming.

National forest campgrounds aren't the only ones that have size limitations. Restrictions on size may be encountered in state parks and even in a some private campgrounds. It isn't that they consider big RVs undesirable, it's just that their sites aren't large enough to accommodate them.

If you plan to do a lot of boondocking (primitive camping where hookups and perhaps even a potable water supply are not available), the capacity of the freshwater and holding tanks is important. We mention this here because the size of these tanks does not necessarily increase in proportion to the size of the trailer or motorhome.

After looking at many trailers we settled on a 23-foot trailer for our first full-timing RV. The particular model we chose had more space than most of the 25-footers we had seen.

We lived in this trailer for over six years. Although we were quite comfortable and had storage space for everything we needed for most of the years, we have come to the conclusion that a 23-foot trailer or slightly larger motorhome is the absolute minimum size for practical fulltiming, and then only if the unit is a special one with plenty of storage space.

A travel trailer's size designation includes the tongue which is about 3½ feet long, so a 23-foot travel trailer has only about 20 feet of actual living space. A 23-foot fifth-wheeler, however, having no hitch protruding from the front, has a full 23 feet of living space.

In the process of doing our work, we accumulated ever more files and reference materials and finally ran out of storage space. After we abandoned our typewriter while we were living in the 23-footer, we needed space where we could comfortably work with our computers (we each had a laptop that we did not always use on our laps). It was time for a larger trailer.

We traded in our travel trailer for a 29-foot fifth-wheel—the same unit we have today.

Fifth-wheels had always attracted us, but when we were considering the type of trailer to buy for our first RV, we knew we would have to utilize the bed of our pickup truck for considerable storage. Pickup-bed covers for use with a fifth-wheel hitch were unknown to us; perhaps they didn't even exist then. That's why we opted for a travel trailer with a canopy for the pickup.

We had found the total combined length of our first rig to be a convenient size, and we didn't want to increase it so much that it would cramp our full-timing style. So when shopping for our present trailer, we looked at fifth-wheels in the 26- to 30-foot range. We were delighted to discover that our 29-footer, when hitched to our truck, measures exactly one inch less in length than the total length of our first rig (this is because 6 of the 29 feet are over the truck's bed when hitched).

We like as small a trailer as possible for a number of reasons: it doesn't require as much fuel to haul it around as does a larger, hence heavier, trailer. It costs less to heat when using the propane furnace, and a small RV doesn't need two furnaces to heat it properly and two air conditioners to cool it. Housekeeping and cleaning don't take much time. And a smaller trailer can be taken to more places because it's easier to drive, park, and maneuver.

We once watched a couple try to park their 40-foot fifth-wheel behemoth in an ordinary, well-laid-out campsite. They managed it only after many attempts that included much turning, pulling forward, and backing. They almost went into a ditch at the campground's entrance because they could not turn sharply enough.

Last week we watched as another large trailer couldn't negotiate a turn in the campground and ended up off the road in the mud. We recently parked our rig in two head-to-head spaces in a parking lot with minimal overhang of either the truck or the trailer. In the next row was a large trailer rig that was parked across five sites.

Drivers of large RV rigs must be especially conscious of routes where they may encounter sharp curves, steep grades, low clearances, and other obstacles. To be safe, they have to keep to interstates, freeways, and main highways using routes suitable for trucks. We know of one couple who took their 35-foot fifth-wheel trailer on a secondary highway and lost their air conditioner and a roof storage pod when they went under an overpass that was too low.

We have standing head room in the bedroom, which is located in the gooseneck. This makes our fifth-wheel 14 inches taller than our travel trailer. More than once we have had to reject staying in certain campsites, even campgrounds, because of trees with too-low branches.

The opportunity for travel is the main reason we are fulltimers, as it is for many others. We've noticed that those with large rigs don't travel as much as those with small rigs, probably because there is more to do to set up and break camp with a large rig. This is something to keep in mind if you intend to do a lot of traveling.

A large rig can be intimidating, especially if you haven't had experience with one before. Recently we checked into a campground on the Oregon coast and were assigned a site. When we reached the spot, we found it was occupied by an obviously brand-new motorhome we judged to be about 40 feet long, with a painted-to-match sport-utility vehicle hitched behind. We drove back to the office, told the manager the site was occupied, and were assigned another site almost next to the original one. The manager remarked, "He was supposed to have been out of there at twelve." It was now two o'clock on a Friday afternoon.

We spent the weekend at the campground. During that time the motorhome remained parked and the SUV remained hitched. Although we saw no people go into or come out of the rig, we as-

> **"M**ore than once we have had to reject staying in certain campsites, even campgrounds, because of trees with too-low branches.**"**

sumed someone was there because lights were on inside at night.

The rig was still parked when we left near noon on Monday. We think we witnessed large-vehicle intimidation. The location of the motorhome manufacturer was only fifty miles inland over a nice, straight highway. We may be wrong, but we figured the owner had taken delivery of the unit and managed to get it to the camp-ground, but driving the big rig further on the curvy, hilly coast highway was something the owner had to stop and think about.

Large RVs, motorhomes in particular, have many systems, and it may take a while to learn what they are and how to use them.

Because our RV is our only home, we need to have a rig capable of carrying everything we own; we have no home base where any-thing can be stored. If you have a place where you can seasonally store items you aren't using, your rig won't have to be large enough to hold all your worldly goods.

It's sensible to purchase a trailer or motorhome that has sleep-ing accommodations for only the number of people who will be regularly living in the unit. Every extra bed or bunk takes up space that may be better used for storage.

THE WEIGHT FACTOR

Some RV buyers are little concerned with the weight of the unit and its weight-carrying capacity, but this should be a primary con-cern for fulltimers since they need to carry so much in their units.

How an RV is constructed affects its weight. Some have light-weight aluminum frameworks; others are constructed with wood, which is heavier. Because of this, many units of the same size may have widely differing weights. Units of the same size but from dif-ferent manufacturers may also have dissimilar weights, so size is not always an indication of what a unit weighs.

Keeping weight down aids in fuel conservation; every 100 pounds of added weight increases fuel consumption by about 2 percent. Overloading an RV can void its warranty and can contribute to unsafe conditions, so fuel economy is not the only good reason for keeping weight down. Lower weight also means less wear on the engine and other moving parts of a vehicle. The less weight tires carry, the longer they last.

Basement models are a blessing and a curse. They hold all manner of things, but stowing too much or too many heavy items in some RVs of this type can cause the unit to be overloaded.

You should do some calculating of weights on any unit you are considering before you purchase it to find out if it has enough capacity for carrying your cargo (we use cargo as a catchall word to define items you may put aboard your RV, excluding what is carried in the water tank and propane cylinders).

Weight Labels

Calculating the weights on an RV built after September, 1996, is fairly simple because that's the date when manufacturers whose units carry the Recreational Vehicle Industry Association seal were required to begin using new weight labeling. On units built before that date, it may be not be possible to calculate the weights. Perhaps the manufacturer may be able to supply you with this information if the RV is a fairly new unit, but if you can't get the information this way, you'll probably have to rely on guesswork. You may find an old weight label on the unit that may give you a little information. Our trailer was built several years ago, and the only information on its weight label is the axle-carrying capacity along with tire and wheel information.

The new weight labels must include the unloaded vehicle weight (UVW) and the net carrying capacity of the vehicle (NCC).

The UVW (the former dry weight) is the weight of the unit without any cargo, fresh water, propane, or dealer-installed accessories. The UVW on a motorhome includes the weight of the unit with a full fuel tank, engine oil, and coolants.

The NCC is the maximum amount of weight the vehicle can

safely carry above the UVW, and includes all the cargo; a full tank of fresh water; full propane cylinders; any dealer-installed accessories; and, for motorhomes, occupants, including the driver, and the hitch weight of a towed vehicle.

The weight of accessories and options installed by the manufacturer should be included in the UVW on each unit. For example, if you ordered a motorhome with certain options, the UVW on your unit will be different from the same motorhome without the options.

Other weights that figure into your calculations are the gross vehicle weight rating (GVWR) and the gross combined weight rating (GCWR). The GVWR is the maximum permissible weight of the RV. It should be equal to or greater than the sum of the UVW plus the NCC.

On motorhomes, the GVWR is determined by the chassis manufacturer. It is up to the manufacturer of the body to build a functional unit within the established GVWR. Some manufacturers do this better than others, as you will see.

The GCVW for motorhomes is the value specified by the motorhome manufacturer as the maximum allowable loaded weight of the motorhome with a towed vehicle.

The GCVR for tow vehicles is the maximum allowable weight of the loaded truck and loaded trailer.

Certain other weight figures that may be helpful may be found in the manufacturer's brochure, but we have looked at some brochures and found vital information missing—one manufacturer did not list weights or tank capacities—and ambiguous footnotes that confused rather than informed us.

The figure you'll be looking for is how much cargo you can carry without being overloaded. You'll have to calculate this, but what you come up with will be an approximate figure because the weight labels carry only approximate weights, and you have no way of knowing how the manufacturers estimate weights.

To aid you in your calculations we have listed the weight of all "wet" consumables in Table 6.1, and weights of popular options and accessories in Table 6.2.

TABLE 6.1
Weight of Wet Consumables

Wet Consumables	Pounds per Gallon
Gasoline	6.15
Diesel	7.10
Water	8.30
Propane	4.25

The process for determining cargo-carrying capacity for motorhomes is to subtract from the NCC the weights of the full water tank and full propane cylinder, occupants, dealer-installed accessories, and tongue weight of a towed vehicle (if you tow a dinghy). What's left is how many pounds of cargo you can carry.

For trailers the process is the same except the occupants and the tongue weight of a towed car are not included.

Motorhome Cargo-carrying Capacities

You may think that motorhomes with the same GVWR, whatever the size, would have approximately the same unloaded vehicle weights. This is not the case. We surveyed nine motorhomes ranging in size from 25 feet 7 inches to 33 feet 10 inches, all with a GVWR of 14,800 pounds. The size differential was not surprising since some units were lightweight models. What was unexpected was the variance in cargo-carrying capacity. The highest UVW was 12,120 pounds and the lowest, 10,711 pounds. Factoring in the weight of a full water tank and a full propane cylinder resulted in cargo-carrying capacities ranging from 1,871 pounds to 3,464 pounds.

Table 6.3 is a comparison between two motorhomes, each with a GVWR of 14,800 pounds, with only a four-inch difference in length between the two. Fuel-tank capacity, which is not included in the table, is almost equal: Motorhome A, 80 gallons; Motorhome B, 78 gallons. To arrive at a cargo-carrying capacity, the weight of

TABLE 6.2
Weight of Selected Aftermarket Accessories

Accessory	Weight in Pounds
Side awning	71–170
Metal weathershield for awning	26–58
Window awning	15–41
Slideout topper	15–40
Storage pod	45–50
Folding chair	6–22
Inverter	8–63
Solar panel (1)	10–26
Automatic levelers	110–200
Tow bar	29–60
Washer/dryer	160–170
Generator	113–272
Satellite dish	13–150
Battery	40–170

occupants must be included, so we have arbitrarily added two occupants, one with a weight of 200 pounds, and another weighing 125 pounds, for a total of 325 pounds.

Adding together the tanks' and occupants' weights along with the UVW, then subtracting the total, results in a cargo-carrying capacity for Motorhome A of 1,546 pounds, and Motorhome B of 3,139 pounds, a difference of 1,593 pounds between the two. You may think that Motorhome A still has a respectable cargo-carrying capacity, but one figure we have omitted from the calculation is the weight of dealer installed-accessories. Adding a few of them can reduce the margin left for cargo to an impractical amount.

Table 6.4 compares cargo capacity and tank capacities in fifteen motorhomes with lengths from 32 feet 4 inches to 34 feet 2 inches. The difference in length between the longest and shortest of these units is only 1 foot 10 inches, but look at the columns headed "GVWR" and "Remaining NCC" and notice the extreme variations between units.

TABLE 6.3
Weights and Cargo Capacities of Two Motorhomes with Equal GVWR*

	Motorhome A (32'4")		Motorhome B (32'8")	
Gross vehicle weight rating (GVWR)		14,800 lbs		14,800 lbs
Unloaded vehicle weight (UVW)		−12,045 lbs		−10,711 lbs
Net carrying capacity (NCC)		2,755 lbs		4,089 lbs
Fresh water	(63 gals) 523 lbs		(66 gals) 548 lbs	
Propane	(85 gals) 361 lbs		(18 gals) 77 lbs	
Total consumables		−884 lbs		−625 lbs
Adjusted NCC allowance		1,871 lbs		3,464 lbs
Weight of two occupants		−325 lbs		−325 lbs
Remaining NCC allowance**		1,546 lbs		3,139 lbs

 *Figures rounded off to nearest whole number
**Does not include dealer installed options and accessories and personal cargo

We have included tank capacities to give you an indication of how motorhomes of this size are equipped. Notice the differences here too.

Even if the unit you buy is not a motorhome in the 32- to 34-foot range, Table 6.3 should make you aware of how cargo and tank capacities can vary in units of nearly the same length.

Trailer Cargo-carrying Capacities

As we noted, from a cargo-carrying standpoint, some motorhome manufacturers are not successful in building practical units within the limitations of the GVWR set by the chassis manufacturer. Trailer manufacturers either construct their chassis or have them made to their specifications. Since they establish the GVWR, it is designed into each individual model. This enables them to build a

TABLE 6.4
Selected Class A Motorhome Weights and Tank Capacities*

Length	GVWR	UVW	NCC	Water tank	Propane cylinder	Remaining NCC
32'4"	14,800 lbs	12,045 lbs	2,755 lbs	63 gals	85 gals	1,871 lbs
32'7"	17,000	14,230	2,770	48	20	2,287
32'7"	14,800	11,619	3,181	56	23	2,618
32'8"	14,800	10,711	4,089	66	18	3,464
32'10"	14,800	11,619	3,181	56	18	2,639
33'2"	17,000	14,075	2,925	60	18	2,350
33'3"	17,000	14,290	2,710	43	18	2,276
33'6"	17,000	14,450	2,550	70	21	1,880
33'7"	16,500	13,823	2,677	76	23	1,948
33'9"	20,000	15,800	4,200	63	21	3,588
33'9"	17,000	13,738	3,262	95	20	2,388
33'10"	14,800	11,567	3,233	63	85	2,349
33'10"	20,000	16,830	3,170	85	20	2,379
34'1"	17,000	14,420	2,580	84	25	1,777
34'2"	16,500	13,247	3,253	70	23	2,574

*Motorhome equipped with a gasoline engine

unit that has an adequate cargo-carrying capacity. Whether they do build them properly is something else again. As with motorhomes, we found some disturbing facts.

Since fifth-wheel trailers are among the most popular full-timing RVs, we used fifth-wheels for our comparison of trailers. Table 6.5 compares two trailers, both with a GVWR of 11,500 pounds. With the UVW, water, and propane added together then subtracted from the GVWR, shows that Trailer B can carry 1,366 pounds more than Trailer A. Again, no dealer-installed accessories are included.

Table 6.6 contains the weights and tank capacities of eighteen fifth-wheels ranging in length from 31 feet to 33 feet 10 inches. The greatest length difference is 2 feet 10 inches. As with mo-

TABLE 6.5
Weights and Cargo Capacities of Two Fifth-wheel Trailers with Equal GVWR*

		Trailer A 32'8"		Trailer B 33'5"
Gross vehicle weight rating (GVWR)		11,500 lbs		11,500 lbs
Unloaded vehicle weight (UVW)		−9,580 lbs		−8,430 lbs
Net carrying capacity (NCC)		1,920 lbs		3,070 lbs
Fresh water	(66 gals) 548 lbs		(40 gals) 332 lbs	
Propane	(14 gals) 60 lbs		(14 gals) 60 lbs	
Total consumables		−608 lbs		−392 lbs
Adjusted NCC allowance		1,312 lbs		2,678 lbs
Weight of two occupants		−325 lbs		−325 lbs
Remaining NCC allowance**		987 lbs		2,353 lbs

*Figures rounded off to the nearest whole number.
**Does not include dealer installed options and accessories and personal cargo.

torhomes, note the variations in cargo-carrying capacities, and differences in water and propane capacities. (A survey of travel trailers of the same sizes showed them to be almost equal in cargo-carrying capacity.)

RVers don't usually travel with full holding tanks, but sometimes it's necessary to haul waste around for a few miles. The weight of full holding tanks can be considerable; a full 30-gallon gray-water tank weighs 249 pounds, for example. If you are borderline on your GVWR, it's not a good idea to travel too often or too far with much in the holding tanks.

Keeping the Weight Down

To keep the weight of our trailer down and to keep our storage areas from becoming overcrowded, we continually clean out cabinets and storage areas. When purchasing nonconsumables, we

TABLE 6.6
Selected Fifth-wheel Trailer Weights and Tank Capacities

Length	GVWR	UVW	NCC	Water tank	Propane cylinder	Remaining NCC
31'0"	9,500 lbs	6,800 lbs	2,700 lbs	42 gals	14 gals	2,292 lbs
31'2"	11,450	9,233	2,217	70	14	1,576
31'3"	11,400	7,985	3,415	50	14	2,940
31'5"	12,000	9,250	2,750	55	14	2,233
31'6"	14,000	10,670	3,330	100	14	2,440
31'9"	10,400	8,610	1,790	50	14	1,315
31'10"	11,470	9,690	1,780	51	14	1,297
31'11"	12,600	8,630	3,970	50	14	3,495
32'5"	12,000	9,740	2,260	74	14	1,586
32'6"	10,400	6,350	4,050	30	14	3,741
32'8"	11,500	9,580	1,920	66	14	1,312
32'9"	13,000	10,100	2,900	83	14	2,151
32'10"	11,800	7,710	4,090	36	14	3,731
33'4"	13,984	9,495	4,489	80	14	3,765
33'5"	11,500	8,430	3,070	40	14	2,678
33'7"	11,890	9,090	2,800	30	14	2,491
33'9"	12,000	9,700	2,300	39	14	1,916
33'10"	11,640	7,900	3,740	24	14	3,481

consider the weight of the item, and on occasion we include consumables in this practice.

One time, knowing our next day's run would be fairly long by our standards—close to 200 miles—and that there were several grades along the way, we took pains to keep the trailer weight down.

A couple of days before we planned to leave, we ran out of potatoes and sugar, both of which we regularly buy in five-pound bags. We also happened to run out of one cylinder of propane. We didn't purchase the potatoes and sugar before we left and didn't refill the propane cylinder. We also arranged to have just enough in the fresh-water tank to take care of our needs during the trip. Because of our weight-saving measures, we lightened our load that day by about 450 pounds.

We don't go to such lengths for a normal day's run (normal for us is under a hundred miles) because it takes a fair amount of planning and the amount saved on fuel is negligible, but if we have enough water in the tank to last for the day's run and enough fuel to get us where we're going, we don't top off either tank before we start out.

THE TOW-VEHICLE FACTOR

If a trailer is selected for fulltiming, it's important to have a suitable tow vehicle, one that is heavy-duty enough to pull the loaded trailer. In years past, a standard light-duty pickup truck could do the job, but nowadays many manufacturers build trailers that are longer, therefore heavier, and require a tow vehicle with more pulling power than any light truck provides.

The maximum weight the largest of the light-duty trucks is rated to tow is 14,000 pounds. Some large fifth-wheel trailers have unloaded vehicle weights approaching, or in some cases exceeding, 14,000 pounds. (We cite fifth-wheel trailers because they weigh

Figure 6.8 Medium-duty trucks are becoming increasingly popular, and necessary, for towing heavyweight trailers. (Courtesy Cabriolet)

considerably more than travel trailers of the same size.) For pulling a loaded trailer that weighs more than 14,000 pounds, a Ford Super Duty F450, F550, or a medium-duty truck is the better choice (Figure 6.8). Super Duty trucks are rated to tow trailers up to 19,500 pounds. Fifth-wheels 37 feet in length are about the size at which the weight can be a critical factor when chosing between a light-duty and medium-duty tow vehicle.

If the tow vehicle isn't suitable, you'll have problems climbing hills, and there may be some you can't negotiate. A rig that does manage to go up must come down, and the downhill aspect is dangerous. The brakes of some light-duty trucks, even when applied in tandem with the trailer brakes, aren't enough to adequately slow the rig, let alone stop it if the trailer is too heavy. It doesn't take too many downhill runs before you'll need to have the brakes repaired on both the tow vehicle and the trailer. If the truck is too light, you probably won't be able to make emergency stops quickly enough on any type of terrain.

Exhaust brakes are standard equipment on some diesel-powered medium-duty trucks and are always available as an option. (Having a brake retarder—a separate braking system—installed on any truck used as a tow vehicle is a good idea.)

When towing a heavy trailer with some light trucks, you may get away with it for a while but eventually vital parts—the transmission especially—wear out and need repairs or replacement.

A medium-duty truck costs much more than a light-duty truck, but as far as money goes you may come out ahead in the long run: You won't have so many wear-and-tear repairs, and you won't have to replace the tow vehicle every few years; a medium-duty truck can last a lifetime. Despite their imposing appearance, such trucks are easy to drive and very comfortable to ride in.

There are two other important reasons for having a proper tow vehicle: If your rig exceeds the GCWR of the tow vehicle, insurance claims may not be paid, and some vehicle warranty-coverage may be denied. This also applies to motorhomes exceeding the GCWR.

For any given tow vehicle, the GCWR rating varies depending on the size of the engine and type (diesel or gasoline), the ratio of the rear axle, whether it has a manual or automatic transmission, and whether it's a standard cab or extended-cab model (the model has nothing to do with the actual pulling power; it's just that the weight of what the truck can tow is lessened by the weight added by the extended cab—one of the reasons we have a standard-cab model). Thus it's possible to have different GCWRs within the same vehicle model. Selecting a diesel-powered vehicle can reduce the GCWR. Here's a comparison of a popular diesel-powered truck with a gasoline-powered truck, identical except for the type of engine: The GCWR of the gasoline model is 19,000 pounds, but largely because the diesel engine itself weighs more, the diesel's GCWR is only 18,000 pounds.

When it comes to light trucks, the engine size and rear-axle ratio are the prime factors to consider. The light trucks capable of pulling the heaviest loads have higher (numerical) axle ratios and high-liter displacement engines. Such equipment is usually standard on three-quarter-ton and one-ton trucks. A half-ton truck can sometimes have a numerically higher rear axle and a more powerful engine installed if the truck is ordered from the factory.

For towing a fifth-wheel trailer, the payload rating, or cargo-carrying capacity, of the truck must be higher than the hitch weight of the trailer plus the weight of the passengers and any equipment carried in the truck. One piece of heavy equipment you'll have to carry is the hitch itself; it may weigh anywhere from 100 to over 200 pounds.

Information on trailer towing is found in the manufacturer's literature; some truck manufacturers publish a separate trailering guide. Read the towing information carefully before making any decisions about a tow vehicle; only by doing so can you make an informed decision and select the best tow vehicle for your purposes.

Once again, don't depend on salespeople to give you accurate information in this regard. They may know a lot about the vehicles

"When it comes to light trucks, the engine size and rear-axle ratio are the prime factors to consider."

they are selling, but often not about using them as tow vehicles. You may find, as we did, that after studying the manufacturers' trailering guides, you'll be able to talk more intelligently about the matter than many of the salespersons you deal with. If we had applied information we had obtained from various salespeople, we would have purchased a tow vehicle entirely unsuited for pulling our trailer.

The vehicle you select for towing should have a factory-installed tow package. This includes a wiring harness, and may include a heavy-duty radiator, auxiliary automatic transmission cooler, beefed-up engine cooling, a higher-amperage alternator and higher amperage-hour battery than standard equipment, heavy-duty flashers, heavy-duty shock absorbers, and a front stabilizer bar. Some towing packages include a hitch receiver and extended mirrors.

Although pickups are the most popular tow vehicles for travel trailers, such trailers, in the medium-size range, can also be pulled by some passenger cars, wagons, and vans.

Each year *Trailer Life* magazine publishes a tow-vehicle guide with ratings for light trucks and other vehicles that can be used for towing. Another good source for information on tow vehicles and towing is *The RV Handbook* by Bill Estes from Trailer Life Books, 64 Inverness Drive East, Englewood, Colorado 80112; (800) 766-1674.

Travel-Trailer Hitch Weights

The A-frames of travel trailers are designed to bear a specific weight. This weight must be considered when fitting the tow vehicle with a hitch; the hitch assembly must be strong enough to take the tongue weight.

Hitch weight affects the towing properties of a trailer. The heavier the weight, the better the trailer tracks. It's more stable, and less fishtailing occurs. If you have a trailer that has any of these problems, perhaps shifting some cargo to the front will alleviate them.

The hitch weight, which is listed among the specifications on the trailer manufacturer's brochure, should be no less than 10 percent of the loaded weight of the trailer.

The proper combination of trailer hitch and tow vehicle can make pulling a trailer an enjoyable task instead of a chore.

SLIDEOUT ROOMS

Slideout rooms are a standard feature on many trailers and some motorhomes; in fact, these days it's difficult to find any but the smallest units without a slideout.

Motorhomes usually have only one slideout located directly behind the cockpit, but some fifth-wheel trailers have three slideouts: one long slideout on the street side opposite the living room and galley areas, another short one on the curb side in the living room, and one in the bedroom. Curb-side and bedroom slideouts are often options. Travel trailers generally have only one long slideout. The long slideout in any unit typically contains a sofa, a dining table, and four chairs.

The great advantage of a slideout is the roominess it provides; there's plenty of walk-through space, and a slideout makes any RV seem airier and not so closed in. An extra benefit may be a window on each end of the slideout.

If you're purchasing an RV with a slideout, here are some points to keep in mind:

Depending on the size of the slideout, it can weigh from about 300 to about 1,500 pounds. If you're thinking about an optional slideout on a unit with skimpy cargo-carrying capacity, find out what the slideout weighs and consider how the weight will diminish the cargo-carrying capacity. Will there be enough allowance left so you can take along the cargo you want and need?

Be sure the slideout can be operated manually. We met a year-round resident of Arizona who lived in his trailer in the winter and in his house in the summer. During the hot season, he parked his trailer, slideout extended, at a location several miles from his house. One year a brush fire was expected to approach the place where he kept his trailer. He rushed to the site so he could move the trailer out of harm's way. When he was ready to retract the slideout, he found that the battery was dead. There was no manual control. By this time the flames were so close that if he was to save the trailer he had to move it immediately, so off he went down the road with the slideout extended.

Find out what is blocked when the slideout is retracted. Almost all slideouts block certain cabinets when retracted, but, in some trailers we've seen, access to the toilet was also blocked. Having a unit like this would preclude using your own facilities when making pit stops during traveling.

As soon as possible after taking delivery of a unit with a slideout, squirt the gasket with a hose so if any leaks appear you can have them taken care of while still under warranty.

If you have a slideout, you should also have a hair dryer. Should you be so unfortunate as to encounter an ice storm, you can use the hair dryer to de-ice the slideout, which will be necessary for either extending or retracting it.

Have an awning installed over each slideout to keep foreign objects off the roof. Tree branches and leaves that fall on the slideout's roof can prevent it from retracting, as can a buildup of snow.

Your slideout should have a secure mechanism to keep it in place when retracted during travel.

If you like to stay in national forest campgrounds, you'll find that many of the sites in these campgrounds are too narrow to accommodate units with slideouts.

WINDOWS

Another problem we would have if we were faced with buying a new trailer today is finding one with enough opening windows.

We don't think any RVer would choose to live in a gloomy, closed-in metal or fiberglass box, yet those are the type of units being offered by some RV manufacturers. Many RVs built today don't have as many windows of any type as their counterparts of previous years.

Front windows on fifth-wheel trailers are almost nonexistent (they were once common), windows are being omitted from baths, and rear windows don't exist on some RVs if the bedroom is in the rear. For years, rear windows haven't been installed on certain motorhomes, and now some trailer manufacturers are omitting them too.

Not long ago we visited a couple in a neighboring campsite who had a travel trailer only a few months old—a rear-bedroom model without a back window. It was quite dark inside; we found the gloominess depressing.

We are further distressed because, of the windows being installed, not enough of them are opening or the opening portion is too small to be effective for ventilation.

We, like many RVers, enjoy the feeling of being close to the outdoors when we are in our RV, a feeling that can't exist in units with few windows.

We have ten opening windows on our 29-footer, and while we doubt we could ever find that many on a new unit, if we had to buy one we wouldn't settle for one with too few opening windows.

BATTERY COMPARTMENTS

Those who boondock and rely on batteries to provide power for their electricity supply instead of a generator should have an RV with room for enough house, or coach, batteries for your needs. We've seen some 40-foot trailers with space for only one battery.

Ideally, the battery compartment of trailers should be located at the front, and motorhomes should have the battery compartment as close to the engine as possible (See Chapter 13, "Electricity and Electrical Equipment," for the reasons this is important.)

PROPANE-CYLINDER COMPARTMENTS

The propane supply on motorhomes, being built-in, can usually be conveniently accessed for refilling. With trailers the cylinders must be removed for refilling.

On travel trailers this usually presents no problem because they are mounted on the A-frame. On fifth-wheels, however, sometimes the cylinders are located in compartments very difficult to access, specifically, the compartments that are under the gooseneck instead of being on the side of the trailer.

If you are considering a trailer with this arrangement, think about how you will handle the cylinders. Removing an empty cylinder—a 30-pound (7-gallon) cylinder weighs 25 pounds—may be fairly easy, but replacing a refilled cylinder, which may weigh 55 pounds, is another matter. Can you handle it in a stooped-over position, as you would be when under the gooseneck?

HOLDING TANKS

In an ideal installation of holding tanks, the gray water (from the shower and sinks) drains into one tank, and the black water (toilet waste) drains into another. We know of several RVers who have unknowingly purchased units in which the shower water is routed to the black-water tank. This is not a good arrangement. Neither is having a black-water tank with a larger capacity than the gray-water tank. Unless the two are of equal size as they are on many units, the gray-water tank should be the larger.

OPTIONAL EQUIPMENT

One RV dealer we know made this statement: "Nobody ever came back to me and complained about having too many options installed." The point he was making was that you probably won't regret having options installed, but you may regret not having them installed.

We share the dealer's view; as much as your budget allows, purchase the options you want when you are buying the RV, especially those that are installed at the factory.

An option being offered frequently for large units is a washer/dryer combination. After hearing what a full-timing friend said about this appliance, we think this is an option we would skip if faced with the decision. She told us that only small loads can be washed and drying takes much longer than in household dryers. So much water is used (water is even used in some dryers to flush away the lint) that it's not feasible to operate the washer/dryer unless you are in a campground with hookups. The electric demands are so great that other high-wattage appliances can't be used when the washer/dryer is operating. Because she was doing her laundry in her RV, our friend also missed the camaraderie of other RVers in the campground laundries.

A USED RIG?

Many RVers may already own a rig they can use for fulltiming. Indeed, many people purchase their vacation RVs with an eye toward future fulltiming.

If you do not own an RV, a new one is not essential for fulltiming. In many ways a used one might be better: It will cost less than a new RV so you may be able to get a better unit than you could afford by purchasing a new one, and the previous owner should have gotten all the bugs out of it.

Preowned RVs are usually good buys. Rarely are they traded in or sold because they are worn out. The most common reasons they are on the market are that the previous owner wanted a different size or type of RV, a death or illness occurred in the family, or the RV owner just wanted a new model of the same unit.

Nevertheless, check over a used unit carefully. With a motorhome, a primary concern will have to be that the engine, transmission, and other automotive components are in good condition.

When inspecting the RV itself, on both trailers and motorhomes, look for cracks in the wheel wells and around pipes. Especially examine the unit for evidence of leaks. Look for water-stain marks and rippled wall surfaces around windows and doors and where the roof joins the sides. Note if caulking has been used on roof and side seams and around the outside of window frames. A leak that has not been taken care of may be an indication of dry rot in the structural members if the RV has a wood frame.

Sponginess in floors may also mean dry rot is present. A distinctive, musty smell often accompanies dry rot. (The floors in some trailers give a little in spots; our first full-timing trailer was purchased new but we noticed some give from the first day we lived in it.)

Used RVs with worn or faded carpeting, upholstery, and draperies are often attractively priced. If such a motorhome or trailer is from a manufacturer that has a reputation for building good, long-lasting units, it may be worth considering. Any money saved may allow you to refurbish the unit yourself or have it done by one of the many companies specializing in this work.

Although some of the scaled-down or special purpose furniture that is used in RVs can't often be found at regular furniture stores, some RV-supply stores sell RV furniture, so replacements can be found, if needed.

FINANCING THE RV

If you need to finance your RV, you should encounter no problems if you have a good credit record. Most dealers will handle the financing or you can work though a bank.

Loans for RVs can be long-term, some running for as long as twenty years. Depending on the lending institution, down payments range from 10 to 20 percent.

Good Sam Club members shopping for a loan can avail themselves of the Sam Cash financing plan handled by the Ganis Corporation. A loan of $15,000 is the minimum Ganis will handle; the maximum isn't fixed but it can be over a half-million dollars.

A minimum downpayment of 15 percent of the cash selling price is required. The term of the loan can be from ten to twenty years. Application can be made by telephone, and approval may be granted in as little as four hours. For information contact: Ganis Corporation, 660 Newport Center Drive, Newport Beach, California 92660; (800) 234-2647.

SHOPPING TIPS

It won't take much shopping before you are hopelessly confused about the various units you have looked at. If you go about your looking in an organized fashion the task will be made easier.

Make a list of what you want and need in an RV. Some of the items on our list of wants were a battery box that would hold two Group 27 batteries, and, since we had decided on a fifth-wheel, ducted air conditioning to the bedroom in the gooseneck, and an area we could use for a computer work station. Another's list might include such items as storage space for fishing rods or golf clubs or a hobby workspace. (Many of the following chapters in this book contain information that may aid you in making up your list.) Take a small notebook or steno pad with you when shopping so you can write down comments and make notes.

After some preliminary looking at a selection of units in all sizes from small to large, you should have some idea of what size RV you need. Since all RVs in a size suitable for fulltiming have a galley, a bath, a dining area, and sleeping accommodations, it comes down to finding a size that sleeps the number of people who will be your full-timing companions and that has enough storage space for what you'll be carrying with you.

Limit your looking to RVs in this size. You'll save time by ignoring those RVs that are too big or too small for your needs. Once we got down to serious shopping, many of the salespeople we dealt with couldn't understand why we wouldn't even look at any units over 30 feet. We knew we would not purchase a large trailer even if we liked it, so why should we waste time looking at such units? Besides, we had already seen lots of large units when we did our preliminary looking to determine the size we would need.

Pick up a brochure on the RV before looking at the unit, not afterwards. As you are going through it make notes on the brochure, or in your notebook, about its good and bad points, and write down questions you want answered. You might even rate the RVs you look at with a simple number or letter system.

A sheet listing options, the price of each, and the total cost of the unit can be found in many RVs. If this is not displayed, get the base price of the unit from the salesperson and the cost of the options you want. Jot down all this information, even though the dealer may offer you a deal at a lower price if you decide to buy.

When you go home to consider which units you like, with the brochures and the notes you have made, you'll have a clearer picture of each individual unit and be able to remember more about it.

Each succeeding visit to dealers should narrow the choices until you are down to just two or three to decide from. We made six visits to one dealer before we finally decided to purchase our trailer from him.

CHAPTER 7

Selecting a Full-timing RV: Interiors

A unit for fulltiming must be considered in a different light than a vacation RV. Fulltimers' needs and requirements are much different from those who live in their RVs only occasionally and for short periods of time.

The actual living that is done in a fulltimer's RV should not differ appreciably from the living done in a fixed dwelling. The closer the two lifestyles are, the more satisfaction you'll receive from fulltiming and from the RV you have selected.

When looking for an RV, don't be overwhelmed by the decor and seeming spaciousness of a unit. Ignore the plants, flowers, decorative accessories, and other trappings placed in display models to make them look as attractive as possible; they may divert your attention from noticing a unit's shortcomings. An eye-catching appearance, although making the unit more appealing, does not contribute one iota to its livability. In interiors, livability is the only thing that should be considered when purchasing a trailer or motorhome for full-time use. At a recent RV show a woman in a trailer we were looking at exclaimed, "This is the most beautiful trailer I've ever seen!" Beautiful it was, but we inspected it thoroughly and found many shortcomings.

BASIC FLOORPLANS

In a size suitable for comfortable fulltiming, only a few basic floorplans are found in the four types of RVs discussed in the previous chapter: Class A and Class C motorhomes and travel and fifth-wheel trailers.

Although a wide-body RV has the width increased by only about six inches, this has allowed manufacturers of motorhomes, especially, a little more versatility in their floorplans.

Class A Floorplans

Class A motorhomes have one basic floorplan because the cockpit must necessarily be in the front. The living room is behind the cockpit because the two swiveling chairs for the driver and the passenger are designed to become a part of this area when the motorhome is parked. Aft of the living room is the galley, which may have the appliances and sink on one side and the dining area on the other. The bath is next to the galley and may be on one side of the unit, or it may be a split bath with a shower on one side and the toilet and sink on the other. The bedroom is in the rear on all recent Class A motorhome models (Figure 7.1).

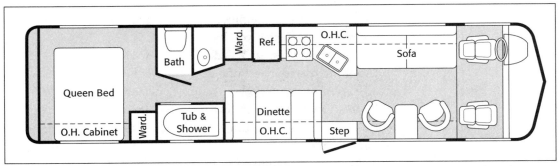

Figure 7.1 The basic floorplan of nearly all Class A motorhomes is from front to rear: cockpit, living room, galley/dining area, bath, bedroom.

Figure 7.2 In addition to increased storage space, a wide-body motorhome has extra seating in the spacious living room and more counter space in the galley. (Courtesy Winnebago Industries, Inc.)

Figure 7.2 shows one of the versatile furniture arrrangements that can be found in the extra interior room of wide-body models. Figure 7.3 is a typical floorplan in a Class A motorhome with a slideout.

Class C Floorplans

A feature of many small Class C motorhomes is a rear bath, and forward of the bath is the galley. Depending on the size of the unit, a dining area may be in the galley or opposite the sofa in the living room area, which is between the galley and the cab. In a rear-bath model, a bed is over the cab and this is the only actual bed in these

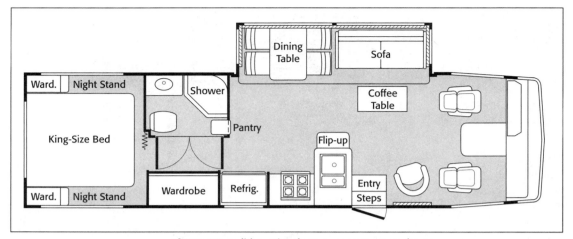

Figure 7.3 A slideout is a feature on some motorhomes.

models. Other sleeping accommodations may be a convertible sofa and dinette, if this is the dining arrangement (Figure 7.4).

A mid-size or large Class C with a rear bedroom has either a side bath or split bath (Figure 7.5).

Small Class As and Class Cs with a rear bedroom may have a bedside bath: All the usual bath equipment is in the rear on the curb side (usually) of the unit and tucked in next to the bed, which is located in the rear street-side corner. Such beds, although usually designated as double beds, are often somewhat narrower than a

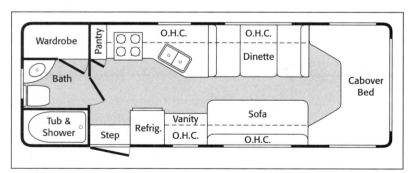

Figure 7.4 A common floorplan is found in Class C motorhome models with a rear bath.

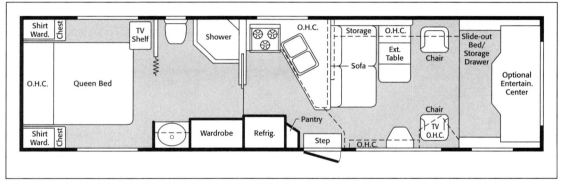

Figure 7.5 The main bed in this Class C motorhome is in the rear, behind the split bath. A bunk, cabinets, or an entertainment center (as shown) may be in the cabover section.

standard, 54-inch double bed. Such a bath is quite tiny, and because of space limitations, may have only a curtain that can be pulled for privacy. See Figure 7.15 on page 189 for an example of this type of bath arrangement, which is also found in some trailers.

Fifth-wheel Floorplans

A popular fifth-wheel floorplan includes a split bath located behind the bedroom, the bedroom being in the gooseneck (the front section of the trailer that extends over the fifth wheel, or hitch). Behind the bath is the living room, and, in the back, a rear galley, which almost always includes a dining area unless the unit is very small (Figure 7.6).

Another common fifth-wheel floorplan has a rear living room and center galley (Figure 7.7).

A floorplan popular a few years ago was with the living room in the gooseneck, the galley adjacent to the living room, and the bath between the rear bedroom and the galley (Figure 7.8). A few manufacturers still offer this floorplan, but it is not common. Some models with a front living room have the bath immediately behind the living room.

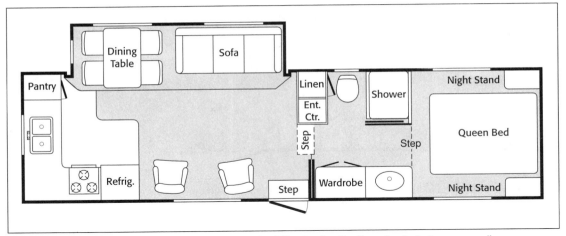

Figure 7.6 A popular fifth-wheel trailer floorplan includes a rear galley.

Figure 7.9 is a floorplan that may be found in a fifth-wheel with triple slideouts.

Some large fifth-wheels may be two-bedroom models. One bedroom is in the gooseneck and the other, containing bunk beds, in the rear.

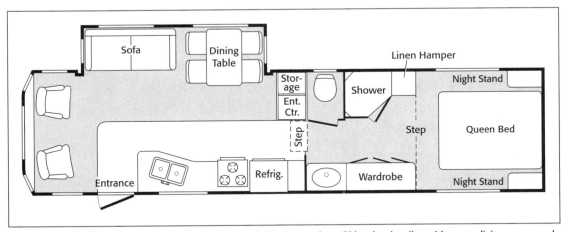

Figure 7.7 Some fulltimers prefer a fifth-wheel trailer with a rear living room and a center galley.

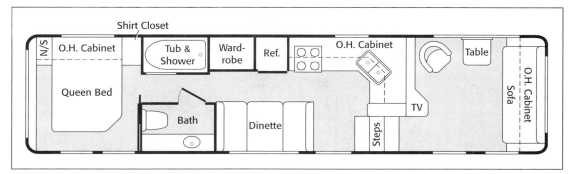

Figure 7.8 A floorplan offered by some fifth-wheel trailer manufacturers features the living room in the gooseneck area instead of the bedroom.

Travel Trailer Floorplans

Travel trailers don't fit quite so neatly into basic floorplans, but they have certain aspects to their floorplans that few manufacturers deviate from: The galley or the living room is rarely in the rear. The bedroom is not located in the center of the trailer; the closest

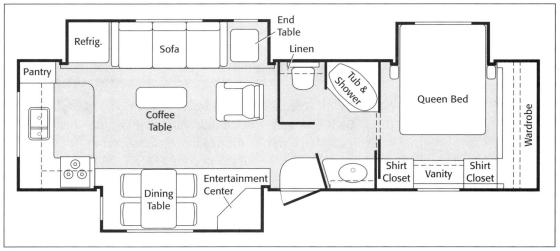

Figure 7.9 It's not uncommon to find fifth-wheel trailers with triple slideouts, one in the bedroom plus a slideout on both the street- and curb-side in the rear.

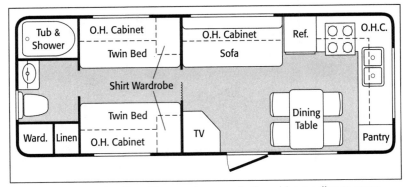

Figure 7.10 A travel trailer with a spacious rear bath and front galley. In some rear-bath models the galley is in the center and the living room is in the front.

it ever gets to the center is when the unit has a rear bath that runs the entire width of the trailer, then the bedroom is in front of the bath (Figure 7.10).

Two-bedroom models of travel trailers usually have one bedroom in the front and another in the rear. Like two-bedroom fifthwheels, the rear bedroom typically has bunk beds (Figure 7.11).

A slideout on a travel trailer usually contains a sofa and dining table and chairs (Figure 7.12).

Floorplan Variations

Nearly all RV manufacturers offer certain optional floorplan variations. Beds can be twin, double, queen, or bunks. Instead of a built-in dinette, a free-standing table and chairs may be an option. And two chairs may be substituted for a sofa.

STORAGE

A major concern of fulltimers is the amount of storage space in an RV; they necessarily need to have more items aboard than the average RVer on vacation.

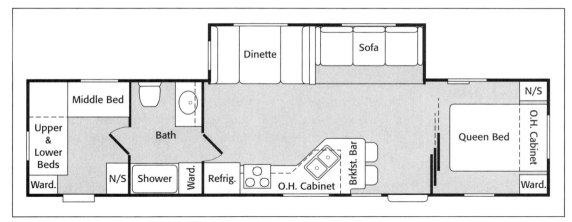

Figure 7.11 This two-bedroom floorplan includes a rear bedroom with three bunks instead of the more common two-bunk arrangement.

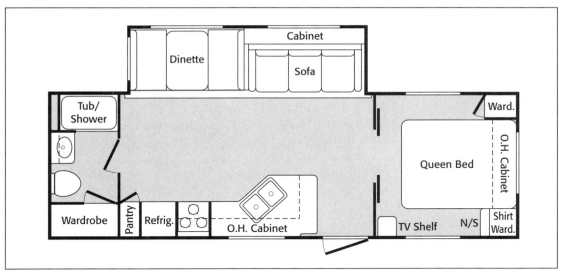

Figure 7.12 Slideouts containing the dining area and a sofa are available on some travel trailers.

The latest trend among builders is to make the interiors of RVs look more like house interiors. To achieve the spacious feeling of house rooms, however, they are sacrificing storage space. A wall that once may have been lined with cabinets is left bare. Deep cabinets have been replaced by shallow ones or, worse, open shelves that are virtually worthless for any sort of storage. Free-standing dining tables and chairs replace built-in dinettes so storage under the dinette seats is lost. Rarely is the area behind any free-standing furniture devoted to storage although space often exists for shallow cabinets there.

While all floorplans, even from different manufacturers, are much the same within each type of RV, the storage capabilities incorporated into similar types may be markedly different. Some manufacturers use all the space they can for built-in storage units, whereas others are decidedly unimaginative about where storage compartments can be installed. The quality of the unit seems to have no bearing on this; some luxury models have less storage room than some so-called budget units.

Size is also no indication of the storage facilities. We once compared a 29-foot travel trailer to the 23-footer we had at the time. The larger trailer had less overall storage space than our smaller one, and the storage space that existed was not well designed for what it was supposed to hold. We recently saw a 36-foot motorhome with less wardrobe space than our 29-foot trailer.

The RV you select should have enough wardrobes of the right height and width, and the galley must have room for all the appliances and kitchenware you need.

Storage space may not be what it seems. When looking at RVs, open every cabinet, compartment, and wardrobe to see what kind of storage area, if any, is in it. Many have little or no space in them because the area is taken up with plumbing, furnace ducts, fuse panels, or other equipment necessary for some of the RV's systems. If necessary, get down on your hands and knees to inspect some of these places.

Also check for usable storage facilities under dinette seats, bunks, beds, and under the sofa. Many beds have storage underneath them and a hinged bed platform so it can be lifted for convenient access. In some units the water tank is under the lift-up bed, leaving scant room to store anything. Motorhomes powered with a diesel engine nearly always have the engine in the rear beneath the bed. There is no under-bed storage in this type of motorhome.

Check outside storage compartments as well. Some of these are so small they aren't of much use.

To get an idea of whether you'll have enough storage space, it may be helpful to make notes or mentally picture where you might place your things. If a unit is otherwise suitable but shy of storage space, look for places where storage units can be added later.

Basement-model motorhomes and trailers with their huge storage areas under the floor could provide too much storage space. They may hold everything you would ever need, but consider how much weight would be added to the unit if such storage areas were packed full. As shown in Tables 6.3–6.6 in Chapter 6, "Selecting the Full-timing Rig," some units can't be loaded with a lot of cargo even if there is space for it.

BATHS

Check out a bathroom for size by going through the motions of all your normal bathroom activities. Sit on the toilet. Enough knee room? Is the toilet tissue accessible? Can you get up easily? This is a difficult maneuver in some baths. Stand in the shower (take off your shoes first). How's the elbow room? Can you stand up straight? Look in the mirrors. Is the lighting adequate? Open the medicine cabinet, if you can, while standing at the sink.

Some side baths are so small that a large person cannot comfortably use the facilities. Rear baths are generally fairly spacious. Odd though it may seem, this is one of the reasons we don't like them. Cleaning bathrooms is not something either of us likes to do, so the less there is of this room to clean, the better it suits us. What's more, the bath is the room in which we spend the least amount of time so we prefer to have it as small as practical, with the space devoted to other areas.

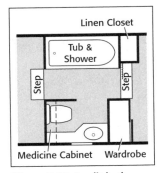

Figure 7.13 A split-bath arrangement such as this allows room for a large tub/shower.

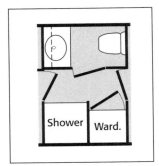

Figure 7.14 In this unit the door to the bedroom can't be left open without interfering with the wardrobe door, and the toilet-room door must be closed at all times so it won't block the passageway. Sliding doors on both the bedroom and the toilet-room would improve this arrangement.

If a rear bath has a window, and many do not, it's small and doesn't provide much ventilation—none at all to the rest of the unit if the bathroom door is closed, and most of us like to close off the bathroom even if it's not occupied.

A spacious split bath is found in many fifth-wheel trailers (Figure 7.13). Such baths are arranged either with the tub and toilet on one side or with the toilet and sink on one side and have a door at each end. One leads to the bedroom, the other to the galley/dining/living-room area. Obviously, no one can go from one room to the other if someone is using the bathroom and has the doors closed.

To avoid this problem some units have the toilet in a small room by itself that can be closed off from the rest of the bath (Figure 7.14). This can be a practical arrangement, but sometimes it's awkward because opening the bath door causes it to bang against another door, and it may be that the door can't be left open because it blocks a passageway. Hold on; didn't we just say that most of us prefer to keep the bath door shut when it's not occupied? Yes, we did. But if the separate room for the toilet has neither ducting from the air conditioner nor from the furnace (most don't), the door will have to be open sometimes to keep the room at a comfortable temperature.

Once in a while you'll find an enclosed toilet room with a small, opening window. This can be useful in hot weather, because if a window exists, it's even more unlikely that the room will have an air-conditioning duct.

With a good bath arrangement, the tub/shower in a fifth-wheel trailer can be close to the size of that in a fixed dwelling.

In many small trailers and motorhomes, the only provision for dining is either a dinette or a fold-up table with a sofa and, perhaps, a chair for seating. Room is available for both dining areas if the model has a bedside bath (Figure 7.15). This bath arrangement makes for cramped quarters, not only in the bathroom, but also in the bed area—an area that can't rightfully be called a bedroom because it's not really a room. It's merely a compartment with a bed in it and nothing else except maybe some overhead cabinets.

In a bedside bath, the shower stall is against the rear wall, with a solid partition between the shower and bed. The toilet is next to the shower stall, quite close, without much leg room for sitting. The sink is opposite the foot of the bed. A curtain or folding door on a curved track can be pulled around to close off the bath. When the curtain or door is in use, the only way out of the bed is though a small opening at the foot, which may be no wider than eighteen inches.

Side baths on large motorhomes and trailers may have an entrance from an aisle or hallway and another from the bedroom (Figure 7.16). Often a wardrobe is accessible from both the bedroom and the bath.

In large units it's not uncommon to find full-size showers with glass doors. This type of residential-size shower is a shower only, not a combination tub/shower.

In our fifth-wheel, one of the aspects of the floorplan we like is that no bathroom equipment is visible when entering from the outside (in some fifth-wheels, the toilet is in the sight line of anyone entering) and, even with the bath door open, very little of the bath can be seen from inside. A mirrored door can be seen by those seated on the street side, and only a sink corner is in view to those seated on the curb side. This is achieved because all the bath fixures are on one side—the street side. The toilet is between the tub and sink and set well back, next to the outside wall. The tub is behind a wall, and this wall is all that can be seen of the bath when entering from the outside (Figure 7.17).

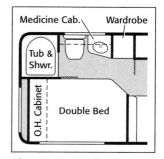

Figure 7.15 Small RVs may have a floorplan that includes a bedside bath.

BEDROOMS

All beds in full-timing RVs should have a mattress of the type found in other residences. The twin, double, and larger beds have this type, but the mattresses on other sleeping accommodations leave much to be desired. Foam is the material used for mattresses in cabover beds in Class C motorhomes and in bunks and convertible dinettes.

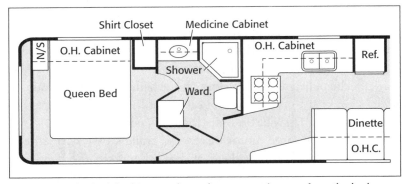

Figure 7.16 The bath in this motorhome has two entries, one from the bedroom and another in a passageway closer to the front of the motorhome. The wardrobe can be opened from both the bedroom and the bath.

Sleeping on foam isn't satisfactory for long. If it's the usual grade of foam used in RVs, after a few months of continual use it breaks down, compressing in the sections that support the most weight. When this happens, it provides very little support.

The cabover beds in Class Cs are queen-size or nearly so, but the mattress is usually in two sections. When not in use, one section is stored on top of the other at the front of the cabover section. The support for that section of the mattress slides under the two mattress sections to get it out of the way so there can be easy access from the cab to the living area.

Any foam mattress in sections, such as those in a cabover bunk and a convertible dinette, which is made up of both the seat and back cushions, can be uncomfortable for sleeping. Foam does not have much weight to it so it can easily shift out of place. Someone will end up sleeping, or trying to, on the crack or in the gap that forms between the pieces. The more the foam breaks down, the worse the problem becomes. If a convertible sofa is not of top quality, it may have lumps and ridges on the sleeping surface.

If you are considering a Class C for fulltiming in which the only bed is in the cabover section, you'll have to somehow climb into the bed every time you go to bed and every time you get up. At best this is a nuisance; at worst it could be a problem if your agility is impaired.

Ideally, no bed should have to be specially made up to be used. The best Class C for fulltiming should have a regular bed. A dinette should not have to be converted from a dining to a sleeping unit, and a convertible sofa should not have to be unfolded into a bed.

Making up a bed from scratch every night and unmaking it every morning is a tiresome chore. We talked with one fulltimer who had just purchased a new trailer. The feature she was most enthusiastic about was, as she put it, "my real bed." She was delighted that she would never again have to go through the morning and evening ritual of converting her sofa into a bed.

Fulltimers with children, however, may have to put up with the inconvenience of making up beds, unless they have an RV with two bedrooms.

Bed-making on a regular bed in an RV can be difficult unless the bed is accessible from two sides. Many trailers and motorhomes have island beds which makes the chore easier, but the island-bed arrangement cuts down on storage space. No overhead cabinets can be put on either side of the bed since they project into the walkway. If one side of a bed is against a wall, however, overhead cabinets can be installed and be out of the way.

This is a compromise that has to be lived with: either it will be somewhat difficult to make the bed, or it will be easy and some storage space will be lost.

Our fifth-wheel had an island bed, but we turned it sideways and put it in a corner (our reasons for doing this are explained in Chapter 9). Now that we can't walk around the bed to make it, we use a comforter as a bedspread. Its thickness allows it to be easily tossed over the sheets and blankets. It also hides any small wrinkles that may be in the bedclothes underneath.

A bedroom should have a door or curtain that can be closed for privacy. This is standard on most units.

Some bedside-bath models have storage compartments across the rear wall of the unit at the head of the bed. The only access to

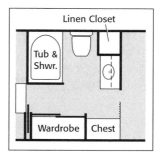

Figure 7.17 The bath in this fifth-wheel trailer provides privacy without sacrificing spaciousness.

this storage is by crawling across the length of the bed. If only little-used items could be stored in this area, it wouldn't be so inconvenient, but in more than one model like this, the only wardrobe in the unit is in this location. Any clothes that need to be hung on hangers would have to be kept there.

On some RV beds the mattress has one corner cut on an angle to provide sufficient walkway space (see the bedroom in Figure 7.8, page 183). When a mattress such as this needs to be replaced, the only choice is to replace it with another RV mattress. And often the mattresses used in trailers and motorhomes aren't the best quality. If the mattress hasn't the angled corner and is a standard size, another of better quality can be be substituted.

We replaced the mattress in our trailer with a Select-Comfort mattress. This is an air mattress, but it's nothing like the air mattresses found in sporting-goods stores. The Select-Comfort is the thickness of a regular mattress and covered with a luxurious, quilted fabric finished with welted edges. The mattress can be adjusted to the firmness you prefer. We have the dual-chamber model which allows each side of the mattress to be adjusted individually. Aside from being the best mattress we have ever slept on, a Select-Comfort has advantages for RVers. Being filled with air, it weighs less than other types of mattresses (we're in favor of anything that lightens the load we haul), and because of it's lightness, it takes less effort to raise our lift-up bed to access the storage area underneath.

Select-Comfort mattresses are available in all the standard sizes and even in a 48-inch width, which is the size of some bunks and small beds in RVs.

An interesting phenomenon occurs to RVers who have this mattress—one that those in fixed dwellings never experience. When you go up in altitude, the mattress gets harder, and when you come down, it becomes softer. After a trip with a change in altitude, you must have either a generator or inverter to provide the 120-volt AC electricity required for the compressor, or stay in a campground with an electrical hookup.

A Select-Comfort mattress is shipped unassembled but it's easy to put together and takes little time. A Select-Comfort store may be found in shopping centers in large cities. For the one nearest you or more information about the mattress contact: Select-Comfort, 6105 Trenton Lane North, Minneapolis, Minnesota 55442; (800) 831-1211.

THE LIVING-ROOM AND DINING AREAS

Many fulltimers do a lot of their living outdoors, but we can't spend all our time outside any more than we could when we were living in a fixed dwelling. There are bound to be rainy and cold days when lawn chairs or a picnic table can't be used, so a table and adequate seating inside the RV are necessary.

Every occupant of the RV should have a place with comfortable seating for dining; some dinettes seat only two adults comfortably. If the only dining table is one that can be pulled out in front of a sofa, try sitting at the table to see if the sofa is high enough in relation to it. Many sofa seats angle downward toward the back. It may be that you'll have to perch on the edge of the sofa, with your back unsupported, to reach the table easily.

In one 36-foot motorhome, we saw a rather makeshift sofa/table arrangement for dining when more than two people must be seated; the only other dining area in the unit is two stools at a galley counter.

When a free-standing table and chairs are in a slideout, the seating can be very cramped because the chairs are often limited in the distance they can be pulled out from under the table. If you are considering an RV with this arrangement, try out the seating to see if the chairs can be pulled out far enough for easy access, and check for knee room too; often there isn't much. Notice also how close any chair's legs are to the drop-off at the edge of the slideout. If they are near the edge, as most of them are, you'll have to be extra careful that the legs don't slip off when you're getting in or out of the chair.

All occupants should have a well-lighted place where they can be comfortable while reading, watching TV, engaging in hobby activities, and relaxing. This may be a chair, the sofa if it's comfortable enough for long-term sitting, or even a well-cushioned corner of a bed.

If any business work is done in the RV, a comfortable and uncramped place for this purpose should be available (see Chapter 11, "An RV Office for Working Fulltimers," for more information about work areas.)

Some RVs come equipped with a TV, and some have a special place for a TV with an electrical receptacle and a coaxial antenna connection. Whatever the case, check to see if the TV is located for easy viewing. In many motorhomes it is mounted close to the ceiling or three or four inches above the floor, which may be uncomfortable for long-term viewing. We have been in some units where the TV can be seen only by leaning far forward when sitting on the sofa or chairs. Those with bifocal or trifocal eyeglasses should check to see that they won't have to hold their heads at an uncomfortable angle when viewing. The TV can't usually be seen from the comfortable driver and passenger seats in a motorhome cockpit.

GALLEYS

Any RV large enough for comfortable fulltiming will have a galley with standard equipment: a sink, a stove, a refrigerator, and cabinets. What a lot of them don't have is an adequate amount of counter space. So counter space and adequate storage are the main things to look for when checking out a galley.

We have before us many beautiful, full-color brochures from leading motorhome and trailer manufacturers. They cover mid-size and large Class As, Class Cs, travel trailers, and fifth-wheels. The RVs range from top-of-the-line luxury models to modestly priced units. In nearly every model with a side or a split galley located more or less in the center of the unit, one feature is common to all—little counter space. What could have been additional counter space is taken up by the residential-size, double sinks that are standard in all the units.

In the galley photograph of one unit, two coffee mugs side by side take up the entire counter space. In another, a loaf of bread fills all the counter space. Another has nothing on the counter because, we presume, no item could be found to fit nicely in the three-inch-wide space that constitutes this RV's counter area (we know it measures three inches because it's no wider than the electric receptacle on the wall above the counter). Another, with what looks like about the same three-inch counter, is shown with a small dish of candy in the space. With such little counter area where can a toaster, coffeemaker, or other appliance be put? It's incongruous that in the big sink you can easily wash and drain the dishes used for cooking and serving dinner for six or eight, but there is no place to prepare such a meal. (In some units, meal preparation might be better done in the bathroom; there's more counter space there.)

A cover for one of the sinks is usually offered as a standard item of equipment. Achieving counter space by this means, however, is awkward, and is something we, as fulltimers, would not want to deal with every time we needed to use the sink. Where is the cover put when using the sink? Certainly not on the counter because the counter is not wide enough. On the floor? This is where one woman we know puts hers. Maybe you could swing around and put it on the dining table. However it is dealt with, it becomes a matter of "making do" every time a meal is prepared.

Had RV-sized sinks been used in these units rather than the residential size, from six to ten inches of counter space could have been gained. We should point out, however, that many trailers and motorhomes have little counter space even when RV sinks are used.

We realize manufacturers can't build exclusively for fulltimers. Their units must appeal to as broad a group of RV buyers as possible, but we can't imagine that having little or no counter space would be to anyone's liking.

If counter space is meager, check to see if a folding shelf exists or

"We can't imagine that having little or no counter space would be to anyone's liking."

can be installed at the end of the galley counter. A stove cover (which may be standard or an option) provides additional work space but, of course, can't be used if the stove is needed for cooking.

Some units have a pull-out cutting board, but it can't provide useful extra counter space unless it's the type that, when extended, rests on an open drawer. The other type has a decided downward slant when extended to its full length.

The counter space in a rear or front galley is more spacious than that in a side galley because the counter usually runs along a portion of the side wall as well as the front or rear wall. Even so, in many such units the counter space is surprisingly skimpy. The counter extending across the front or rear wall may be only about six inches deep—not wide enough to work on. We have seen some models where much of the counter can't be used because it involves stretching across the stove or sink to reach it.

The floorplans in RV brochures usually give a fairly accurate indication of the amount of counter space (Figures 7.18 and 7.19).

Residential-size sinks add to the weight of a unit since they are made of porcelain-coated heavy steel. This material is much heavier than the stainless steel used for RV-sized sinks.

Countertop Materials

In addition to heavy sinks, unnecessary weight is also added by many manufacturers who use ceramic tile or Corian for their countertops. At a recent RV show, we were surprised to discover that a small sink cover couldn't be removed by using the finger hole. One finger wouldn't do the job because the cover was made of Corian and very heavy. If sink covers are made of this material, most likely so is every countertop throughout the unit, and probably some table tops as well. Imagine how much weight is added with the use of this material. We're sure Corian is a fine material, but in an RV application, a lightweight plastic laminate is more suitable.

Stoves and Ovens

For years, standard galley equipment was a four-burner stove with an oven. When microwave ovens became popular they were included in the galley array as either standard or optional equipment. Soon after, some manufacturers decided that the only oven RVers should have is a microwave. They did away with the oven on the propane stove and installed only a three- or four-burner cooktop.

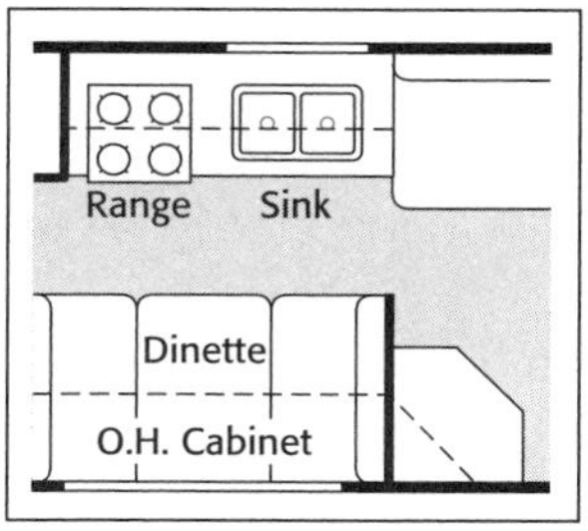

Be sure you can get the appliances you want for the type of cooking you do. Our trailer was equipped with a four-burner stove and oven and any other cooking arrangement wouldn't be satisfactory for us. We do some baking from scratch and occasionally use a packaged mix. Right now, as Jan is slaving away on the computer, Bill, who does nearly all the cooking in the Moeller household is preparing a roast for dinner. So, for our style of cooking, it's necessary to have a regular oven.

Our microwave oven, which we added a few months after we purchased the trailer, is used mainly for defrosting and reheating foods. It's very small, but adequate for our needs. A microwave/convection oven may be suitable for you if you need both types, but you'll need a source of 120-volt AC power to operate it.

If the cooktop is the three-burner type, two burners are at the rear and another, which may be a high-output burner, is centered between the two at the front. Although this burner has lots of space around it and can accommodate a large pan or skillet, we have heard that utensils much larger than the burner top shouldn't be used. The heat buildup can cause the stove knobs to become so hot they can't be touched. This happened to a friend of ours who burned her hand and had to use pliers to turn off the burner.

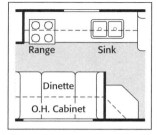

Figure 7.18 A check of this floorplan indicates skimpy counter space in the galley.

Figure 7.19 The space between the stove and sink shows that this galley has an adequate amount of counter space.

Galley Location

Because rear galleys are so popular, they are found in many RVs. We had to look long and hard for our trailer because we did not want a rear-galley model. In fact, we had to purchase our rear-living-room model without ever seeing one. Dealers just didn't stock them at the time we purchased ours.

Our reasons for not wanting a rear galley are many. One of them is the same reason we don't like rear baths; we don't spend a great amount of time in the galley, so we don't want this room to take up one of the best locations in the RV. Nearly all rear galleys have windows on three sides, but we would rather have this triple exposure in the living room. Often the best view is from the rear of a site, and we want to be able to enjoy it fully. When working in the galley, most people haven't the time to enjoy the view. It's just as well because nothing can be seen from the galley's usual narrow windows without bending down.

With a rear or front galley, the living room ends up in the center of the unit and the view from its windows are often of the RVs parked in the sites on each side.

Another objection we have to a front or rear galley has to do with traffic through the RV. We don't think we are unusual in that most of what we carry into our RV is food and kitchen supplies, and most of what we carry out is trash—food scraps, empty boxes, and other packaging. Since much of this goes into and comes out of the galley, it must be carried to a rear or front galley through the living room and across the carpet that may be in that area. We avoid this tracking-through because our galley is immediately inside the entry door.

The rear of a trailer is the most affected when going over railroad tracks, potholes, and any other types of bumps that may be encountered. The jarring and shaking that occurs can result in containers toppling over in cabinets and in the refrigerator, perhaps breaking and spilling the contents. Some slipping and sliding of cabinet contents may occur no matter what precautions are taken.

Although we slow down for bumps, we have had several experiences with items being affected by bumps just because they were in the rear. After one severe jolt, the rear-window shade jumped out of its bracket and fell off, the removable rear table removed itself from its brackets by itself, and books bounced out of bookcases. We prefer not to think about what messes we would have had to clean up if our galley had been in the rear.

The galley equipment and supplies; the refrigerator and its contents; the stove; the microwave oven; counters; and many cabinets filled with cooking utensils, appliances, and foods collectively constitute the heaviest "room" in an RV. Weight distribution is supposed to be a key factor in the initial planning of a unit, so any trailer with a rear galley *should* be designed and constructed to allow for the heavy weight aft. This being said, we still prefer to have a trailer where the area with the heaviest weight is concentrated over, or in front of, the axles.

While we're on the subject of weight, let's consider the slide-out pantry found in some galleys. Often this is a floor-to-ceiling unit. While it offers handy storage for bottles, canned goods, and cereal boxes, when it's well stocked it can add to the weight of your unit. A five-shelf pantry holds about thirty sixteen-ounce cans. Storing two-liter soft drink bottles in the pantry adds 4.8 pounds for a full bottle.

WINDOWS

As we mentioned earlier, we like windows and lots of them. We had a four-way exposure in our first full-timing trailer and we have it in the fifth-wheel trailer we have now. When we were shopping we found only a couple of manufacturers offering an optional front window. Since this was high on our list of wants, it figured prominently in our selection of the trailer we bought.

When we were shopping, fifth-wheel trailer models with a living room in the gooseneck had just been introduced. Then, nearly every model of this type had a front window. When we inquired about a front-bedroom model with a window we were repeatedly told that manufacturers didn't put them in because they leaked. Once we received this information when we were standing in a gooseneck-living room model with a window in the front. We asked the salesperson if the type of furniture used in the front room determined whether the window would leak. We sensed he didn't appreciate our attempt at humor.

Front windows are still a standard feature on travel trailers so there is no reason they shouldn't be on fifth-wheels too. It's true that a front window is more prone to leak than any other window since it receives the full force of the wind as the trailer is being towed, thus tending to work loose.

We had a leak in our travel trailer's front window, which we fixed, and we have had a minor leak in our fifth-wheel's front window, which we also fixed; this was years ago and it hasn't leaked since. We prefer to take our chances with leaks rather than do without a window. Another point: So much heat rises into the gooseneck area of a fifth-wheel we want as many windows as possible for ventilation in hot weather.

We aren't always in campgrounds with an electrical hookup, and we don't have a generator, so sometimes we can't use the air conditioner. Besides, we prefer fresh air and only use the air conditioner when it's extremely hot.

Many manufacturers install picture windows in their units in yet another effort to incorporate residential features. We think this is another installation best left for houses.

One of our objections to picture windows is that the opening portion is quite small in relation to the size of the window and provides little ventilation. Another objection we have to such windows has to do with privacy. When a picture window is in a house, which is likely set some distance back from the street or sidewalk, it's usually difficult for passers-by to look in. Not so in a campground where the sites are frequently close together.

Some units have a large window in the dining area. Since the table is visible, the food being eaten, the manner in which the table is set, and diners' legs are in view of anyone who walks by, or who is looking out from an adjacent unit.

Our trailer model was designed with dinette and living-room picture windows, but we persuaded the manufacturer to install regular three-louver opening windows in place of them.

Window Coverings

Certain types of window coverings may be an option. You may be able to choose between window shades, pleated shades, or miniblinds. Compared to blinds, window shades of good quality and the insulated type of pleated shades do a better job of insulation in both hot and cold weather. Blinds have no insulating effect at all and cannot be closed tightly enough to keep out drafts. Those with motorhomes are likely to have to put up with the rattling of blinds when they are traveling.

One of the reasons we find fulltiming attractive is that housecleaning is easy and takes little time. We want nothing in our RV that is diffcult to clean and take care of. In our opinion, miniblinds are mainly dust catchers. When we bought our trailer, we opted to purchase our own window coverings (good quality, room-darkening window shades) but the trailer arrived with a miniblind on the small galley window. We took it off immediately. It's bad enough to have to wipe dust from blinds; we didn't want to contend with cleaning even a small one that might have cooking grease on it.

COLOR SCHEMES

The colors used in RVs' interiors evolve and change according to what is currently popular in residences because RV manufacturers want their units to look as fashionable and up to date as possible.

But something many RV interior designers overlook is that they are dealing with an interior that is only about eight feet wide. In such a small area, a bold upholstery pattern can be overpowering, and the use of dark woods for the cabinetry, plus dark colors in the upholstery and carpeting, can make the interior seem gloomy and cramped. These impressions are intenisfied if there are few windows and inadequate interior lighting.

This is on our minds because we recently attended an RV show where we saw several of these overly-dark interiors. One unit had dark teal upholstery, medium-brown carpeting, brown-black walnut cabinetry, and not many interior lights. Because the entire rear wall was taken up by a ceiling-high entertainment center, there was no rear window to admit any light from that direction. We heard a woman who had been looking at the unit say to her companion, "Let's get out of here; it's depressing." We agreed with her. Dark, dimly lit living areas can be depressing whereas bright, light areas can have quite the opposite effect.

If the unit you select has a dark feeling to it because of the color of the cabinetry, you may want to select upholstery, draperies, and carpet colors in the light or medium shades that are usually offered. Color choices are a very personal thing and individual tastes vary widely, but we wouldn't ever opt for a predominantly brown color scheme if the woodwork is brown. We would prefer something in the cool colors of the blue and green spectrums to contrast with the warm wood tones of the cabinets and paneling.

We had no problem with an abundance of wood in our fifth-wheel trailer since all the walls are off-white, so we didn't have to be concerned with selecting a too-dark color scheme. We choose a scheme based on the upholstery we wanted. The only problem was that this scheme included carpet and draperies in mauve, a very fashionable color when we bought our trailer. Not only do we not like mauve, we didn't want such a trendy color in a unit which we intended to keep for many years. We knew that in time the mauve would look just as outdated as the chartreuses and oranges that were the fashionable colors in RVs years ago.

We were able to persuade the manufacturer to let us combine two color schemes so that a beige carpet and ivory drapes replaced the mauve ones.

It has long been known that the colors surrounding us affect our emotions. When only vacations and weekends are spent in an RV, interior colors aren't as important a factor as they are in a unit in which you live fulltime.

TRY BEFORE BUYING

Before purchasing an RV, try out anything that pulls out, up, and down, and that slides, swivels, and opens. A couple we met found that all nine windows in their fifth-wheel trailer would not open but didn't discover this until several weeks after they took delivery.

Pay attention to bedroom and, particularly, bath doors that may block passageways if they are left open. And on cabinets, see that the doors can be opened fully.

Check all hardware on cabinet doors, especially if you purchase a unit from the dealer's lot. Some units have cabinet hardware that is not very sturdy, and it may have been broken by other shoppers checking out cabinets.

AN OVERVIEW

Perhaps our outlook on fulltiming is different from others, but we are RVers first and fulltimers second. We think an RV that is a home should be outfitted and equipped like a home yet still embody all the desirable qualities of an RV: mobility, ease of maintenance inside and out, and coziness.

An RV should be one in which you can be comfortable, and one that allows you to go about the business of living—cooking, dining, showering or bathing, and relaxing—without any inconvenience. But we don't think it's necessary to achieve this comfort and convenience by incorporating residential features into the RV.

We've already discussed residential-size sinks with their heavy weight and large size. Other residential items that are now found in RVs are ceiling fans that don't allow much head clearance under an RV's low ceiling. Skylights are sometimes taking the place of more practical opening vents with an exhaust fan. Often when a skylight is substituted for an opening vent in the bath, it leaves the bath with no form of ventilation to the outside. If there must be skylights, they should be thermal-insulated and provided with a horizontal shade of some sort for blocking the light and sun.

Some residential items are not only impractical, but not at all suited for a movable house. A prime example of this is the huge, ceiling-high cabinet bank as wide as the unit that is in some trailers. What a job it would be to ready the contents of this for traveling! Wall lamps with glass globes are becoming increasingly common. Unless the screws holding the globes in place are continually checked for tightness they will eventually vibrate loose, then the globe will likely topple out and shatter. Chandeliers are found in some units. One woman told us she finally removed her chandelier after it had swung into a cabinet leaving dents and scratches. She said she couldn't anchor it securely enough to keep it from swinging while traveling.

For us, since we travel so much, we don't want to saddle ourselves with any of these items that require special attention prior to getting under way. No matter how long we have been sitting, we can be ready to go in about a half an hour and we want to keep it that way. We all have our own full-timing philosophy; keep yours in mind when shopping for an RV so you can purchase one that allows you to pursue the lifestyle you wish.

CHAPTER 8

Making Your RV More Livable

Although RVs are designed and built so that everything needed for basic living is in the unit when purchased, you can do some things to it to make it more livable.

PRIVACY CURTAINS

Some RVs have a sheer or loose-weave privacy curtain on certain windows, usually in the bedroom, and some have them throughout. They are useful in the close quarters of some campgrounds. The curtain admits light and air but, from the outside, the interior is not visible through it unless the inside lights are on.

Curtains of this type are useful and can enhance an RV's decor if the curtain fabric is a light tint of one of the colors in the upholstery or wall covering or in the neutral shades of white or beige.

Our trailer didn't come with privacy curtains, but we have added them to nearly all our windows. We wanted curtains that could be pulled when we were in a campground site without much privacy, but that could be pushed to the side of the window when not needed.

The curtains we selected are ready-made and a common, open-work, crocheted-type of cafe curtain. Without any alteration, the standard, 24-inch-long size fits all the windows except for the two-louver front window. For it, we simply cut off the top of the panel and rehemmed it. The curtains are hung on standard cafe-curtain rods.

We first put privacy curtains on only our three bedroom windows. Then we put one on the window by the dinette. Shortly after that we put them on all the remaining windows except for the small galley window. We like the way they look, they afford privacy when needed, and when pulled across a sunlit window they provide a pleasant, diffused light instead of the bright glare of the full sun.

PICTURES AND DECORATIVE ACCESSORIES

Pictures and displayed mementos contribute much to making living quarters homey. They can be photos of family, friends, pets, and special places you have visited. They may be paintings and drawings done by artists you admire, or be items you, family members, and friends have created.

Hanging Framed Accessories

Hanging framed items on RV walls is not as simple as on the walls of fixed dwellings. Frames must be firmly attached to the wall so they won't fall off or swing from side to side and mar the wall's finish when the RV is moving.

We use double-face mounting tape for attaching most objects to the walls. A picture frame with glass is heavy so enough tape must be used to hold it securely (directions for the amount needed are on the tape package). The quality of mounting tape varies considerably. We have learned that it's best to buy only name brands; the adhesive seems to be better and longer-lasting, and comes off easier should you want to remove the item.

The holding power of even the best mounting tape is limited; it seems to dry out eventually, so it's not wise to mount valuable breakables this way. Periodically inspect mounted items to see if they are still firmly attached to the wall.

Securing Accessories

Mounting tape can also be used to hold lightweight, decorative objects on shelves and counters if they are to remain in one spot. If you want to move the item occasionally, it can be held fairly securely with a small piece of florist's clay. The clay has just enough holding power to keep the item from shifting or sliding; however a little pressure releases it. The clay should not affect the finish of most RV materials, but it may leave a dull area or grease spot on some woods. Quake Wax, manufactured by Conservation Materials, Ltd., 1395 Greg Street, Suite 110, Sparks, Nevada 89431 (800) 733-5283, is an excellent product that won't harm wood finishes or painted surfaces, according to the manufacturer.

Dusting around semi-fixed objects can be a bother. Rather than attaching items so they will stay in place when under way, we have found convenient places to stow the few loose breakables we have. Putting them away is a routine part of our getting-ready-to-go procedure.

When it comes to photographs, if you have the right computer equipment you can scan photos and store them on a diskette for viewing on the computer. They won't add anything to the hominess of your RV, but you may be able to take along more pictures than you would without this type of "photo album."

BATHS

Although most RV baths have plenty of storage space they often don't have enough practical towel rods for even two people. It may be difficult for a couple with children to find adequate space for everyone's personal towels.

Towel Holders

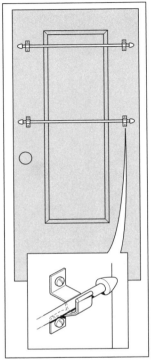

Figure 8.1 Cafe-curtain rods may be used for towel rods on a bath door.

Our first trailer came with just one towel rod large enough for just one bath towel. Because it was on the bottom of the medicine chest, which was mounted above the toilet, a large-size towel hung on this rod would have been in the way of anyone using the toilet.

The other towel holder was an impractical contraption built into a center panel on the bathroom door. It had three narrow rods that held a bath towel only if folded in thirds. We did not want to spend time carefully folding bath towels just to fit the rods, and we needed a place wide enough to spread towels to dry, so we replaced the holder with two brass cafe curtain rods (Figure 8.1).

Removing the built-in towel holder exposed raw, unfinished edges in the panel. To finish the edges we cut pieces of quarter-round molding to fit, mitered the ends, wrapped each piece with adhesive-backed covering in a wood-grain pattern that closely matched that of the door, and nailed them in.

To gain extra space for hanging hand towels and washcloths, we mounted another towel rod on the bottom of the medicine chest just behind the existing rod.

In our fifth-wheel trailer the only provision for towels was the before-mentioned single towel ring in an awkward location. A better location, the wall space adjacent to the shower, has a width sufficient for only one bath towel rod. Needing space for two towels, we bought a space-saving double rod, the type where one rod is in front of the other.

Towel rods can be mounted in the shower if care is taken to seal all screw holes so no moisture can enter.

Shower Supplies

The contrivances to hold shower supplies—built-in corner units and racks that hang from the shower head—are not suitable for use in an RV. Such holders are likely to spill their contents when the RV is moving and scratch the walls of the shower unless they are mounted so they can't move when under way.

It will be less of a nuisance if you keep shower supplies in a net bag with pockets. With a shower curtain hung by hooks, the bag is attached to a couple of the hooks. With a folding or sliding door, you can buy hooks suitable for hanging it over the door.

An Efficient and Usable Bathroom

It's important to us to have a bathroom where everything is convenient for use because we never use campground shower and toilet facilities.

Every time we want to shower we don't want to collect the toiletries, towel, shower thongs, clean clothes, and other needed paraphernalia and troop across the campground to a shower that may not be clean or is crowded. We don't want the concerns about whether we'll have privacy in the shower, and whether a bench or stool and plenty of hooks will be provided. We also don't want to be faced with the possibility of running out of hot water or a drain backing up. And we absolutely would not pay an extra fee to use a shower, as must be done at some campgrounds.

But the main reason for using our own bath is because our trailer is our home. When we lived in a fixed dwelling we didn't go to the back yard, next door, or across the street to use a bathroom or shower, and we won't do so now.

We are constantly amazed, though, at the number of RVers who use a campground shower instead of their own, especially those RVers who have units with suitable baths in them. We know of one full-timing couple with a large, luxurious trailer with a good-sized bath. They have a washer/dryer in their trailer so it's not necessary for them to go out to do their laundry yet they do go out to use the campground shower.

And last weekend we watched our campsite neighbors from a brand-new fifth-wheel the same size as ours trek, bathrobe-garbed, across the campground, to the showers on the far side.

TABLES AND CHAIRS

If you need extra work space or more chairs in your RV, folding tables and chairs may be used. Most folding furniture collapses into a slim, flat, easily stored unit.

Tables are available in many sizes and styles. Perhaps a card table can be used, or one of the many tables designed for outdoor use, or even one or more TV or snack tables. These usually come four to a set with a storage rack; give other RVers the tables you don't need and discard the rack if it presents a storage problem.

We purchased a folding table measuring 32 × 16 inches that has proved to be very practical. We can use it in several locations in our trailer and easily set it up when we need extra space. It's only 2½ inches wide when folded so it doesn't take up much storage space.

DOORS

Making your RV more livable may involve changing the way some doors open. If you are ordering an RV instead of buying a model from the dealer's lot, you may be able to specify how certain doors are to open. This requires some thought because you may not be aware of a problem until you are actually living in the unit.

We had such a problem with the door on a large galley cabinet on our travel trailer. When the door was open it was necessary to stoop to get under it, as it nearly closed off the galley walkway. We always had to be careful about being on the side that gave us access to the interior before we opened it.

We soon decided it was impossible to live with this awkward arrangement. We took off the door and turned it end for end so the hinges were on the opposite side. But the latch, which had been in the right bottom corner, was then in the upper left corner. We lived with it that way (we are both tall enough so we could reach the latch easily) because removing it would have exposed three screw holes that we didn't think we could patch satisfactorily. The previous hinge screw holes were plugged and were not too apparent when the door was closed.

When we ordered our fifth-wheel trailer we had some extra cabinets installed at the factory, and in our instructions we emphasized the way in which we wanted certain doors to open.

Fortunately, refrigerator doors are designed so they can be made to open either way. On our first trailer, the refrigerator door opened the wrong way but it was easily reversed.

Manufacturers should give a little more thought to the door problem, especially since some large RVs now have residential-type, solid doors with doorknobs in places where folding or sliding doors were used in the past. When such residential-type doors are used, they are often on models where access to the bath and the bedroom is from a narrow, curb-side hallway. We have looked at some of these units and have found, in many, that going from one place to another becomes an exercise in door juggling: One door can't be opened until another door is closed and both can't be left open at the same time. If your RV has any door complications, you may have to put up with them; there isn't much you can do about it.

Residential-type doors may prove to be impractical. Such doors fit into a frame with the hinges recessed into the frame, unlike some RV doors that have exposed hinges mounted on the wall, and, when closed, the door's edges extend over the door opening similar to cabinet doors. If there is any working of the RV's structural members, the door frame could become distorted, which could prevent the door from opening and closing properly. If we had uneven pressure on the stabilizing jacks we used on our 23-foot trailer, it distorted the frame just enough so that the opening and closing of the entrance door was affected.

On our fifth-wheel trailer, we had the factory omit a folding

If we had uneven pressure on the stabilizing jacks we used on our 23-foot trailer, it distorted the frame just enough so that the opening and closing of the entrance door was affected.

door between the bedroom and the bath because it took up too much space. For the infrequent times we want to close off the bedroom from the bath, we installed a floor-to-ceiling curtain on a sliding track. We made the curtain ourselves but we could have used one side of a pair of ready-made drapes. A fabric "door" could be a solution for certain awkward RV door problems.

OTHER MODIFICATIONS

In addition to the above modifications we removed the reading lights inexplicably installed above a small, open shelf in the middle of a bank of cabinets in both the living room and bedroom. Now, with the utterly useless light out of the way, we can use the shelf for storing paperback books.

Our trailer came with knobs for opening the windows. We replaced them with handles which we find to be easier and quicker to use.

The minor modifications described above constitute only a small part of what we have done in the way of modifications. The major modifications are described in the next chapter.

CHAPTER 9

Remodeling an Old or New RV

Although motorhomes and trailers are designed and built so everything needed for basic living is in the unit when purchased, alterations and additions can be made to almost any RV to make it more personalized and better suited for the uses of its occupants, especially since most manufacturers do little or no customizing.

In these days of high RV prices, it may also be practical to remodel a structurally sound preowned RV or an RV you may already own to make it more suitable for fulltiming. We have done considerable remodeling to both our full-timing trailers, but much more to the second one than the first. The reason for this is because new trailers fall far short of being suitable for our needs. In some previous chapters we've noted what we want in a trailer: plenty of opening windows, adequate storage space, and a relatively low unloaded vehicle weight, to name just three. While we wouldn't expect to find everything we want in a new unit, we can't find any new trailers with features even close to what we have with our present trailer. Until we do, we'll keep on remodeling and refurbishing the one we have.

On the following pages, along with general information, we describe some of the ways we modified both our full-timing trailers to make them better suited for us and our full-timing lifestyle. Perhaps you'll find these ideas, or variations of them, useful if you want to make alterations to your RV.

THE BIG THREE

Any older RV can look much newer if three major changes are made: new carpet, new upholstery, and new window treatments. If these improvements are done in contemporary colors, it will contribute greatly to a fresh, new look. You can also select colors you are comfortable with. An RVing friend of ours is presently shopping for a new motorhome but isn't having much luck in finding what he wants. He said, "None of them is the type where I can just kick back and relax." We know what he means; we wouldn't feel comfortable putting our feet up on the sofa, for example, in units decorated like a suite in an upscale hotel. We, like our friend, want an RV, not a traveling palace. He is seriously considering remodeling his old motorhome.

The Carpet

The carpet is often the first thing that catches the eye when entering an RV, especially if it is soiled, and it can become soiled quickly because it receives such concentrated use. If the RV is several years old, chances are that cleaning the carpet won't restore it to its former appearance, and it may also have worn spots. If this is the case, it should be replaced with new carpet.

Most new RVs in a size suitable for practical fulltiming have carpet as standard equipment. If not, you can install it. Carpet adds considerably to the hominess of an RV, and it also mutes sounds and provides a certain degree of insulation.

We have replaced the carpet in both our full-timing trailers. While it's not something we relish doing, it isn't too difficult. In each of our trailers we installed the carpet in sections. This made it easier to measure in the first place, and we didn't have one large, unwieldy piece to contend with when cutting. We also saved money because there would have been a lot of waste if the carpet had been cut from one piece.

To figure out how much carpet we needed, first we carefully measured the floor areas to be covered, then scaled down the figures so that one foot equaled a half-inch, and transferred them to graph paper. We cut the graph-paper plan into the predetermined sections so we could try them in various layouts on other sheets of graph paper we had marked to represent the standard twelve-foot and fifteen-foot carpet widths. This way we were able to determine exactly how much carpet was needed.

For carpeting our first trailer, we carefully cut templates from newspaper to use as patterns when cutting the carpet. The templates were placed on the carpet in the same way we had placed our scaled-down sections on the graph paper when we were determining the amount of carpet we would need. When carpeting our fifth-wheel trailer, we used the carpet we replaced as patterns.

The worst part of the recarpeting job in our fifth-wheel was removing the old carpet. The manufacturer of our trailer, like most manufacturers, installs carpet by putting it in as soon as the underflooring is in place. This means the carpet extends under the walls and floor cabinets. The only way to remove it is to cut it out, laboriously going along each wall and cabinet, and cutting as close as possible. The more accurately it's cut, the better the pattern you'll have. For cutting, we used a regular carpet-cutting tool and a small utility knife for cutting in tight corners. The job is easier if blades are frequently replaced, before they become dull.

The section for the living room and galley is about twelve feet long, and we were concerned about having a place we could lay out the new carpet to cut it. The paving in our site wasn't smooth enough, and it would have been impossible to cut such a large piece on the picnic table. We had stayed at this particular campground many times before, so when we asked the manager if he had a place

> *"The worst part of the recarpeting job in our fifth-wheel was removing the old carpet."*

where we could lay out the carpet he allowed us to use a maintenance shed. To make a clean surface on which to lay the carpet—there were a few grease spots on the floor and the new carpet would be laid face down for cutting—we got two refrigerator cartons from an appliance store and spread them on the floor. If we had been parked in a site with smooth concrete and intended to cut the carpet on this surface, we would have used such a cardboard base to keep the carpet clean and to preserve the sharpness of the knife blades by keeping them away from the concrete during the cutting.

We put a good-quality pad under the carpet; the "pad" installed by the manufacturer was merely ⅛-inch foam. We cut the pad first, then laid it in place in the trailer to see if any areas needed adjusting before we cut the carpet.

Although some people use tack strips or double-face tape for anchoring carpet, we used neither. The carpet fits around many pieces of furniture and other furniture is set on top of it so we thought (correctly as it turned out) this would be enough to hold it in place and keep it from shifting or wrinkling. In a few areas, such as on the sides of stairs, we anchored the carpet with tacks. We found that only ⅞-inch carpet tacks are long enough to provide holding power through the carpet and the thick pad.

Having the carpet unattached and in sections allows each section to be lifted or folded back so the floor underneath can be cleaned periodically. It's amazing how much sand and dirt sifts through the carpet no matter how careful we are about wiping our feet before entering.

In many RVs, the galley area isn't carpeted, and a vinyl floor covering or parquet is used instead. We had no hesitation about carpeting this area. Today's synthetics are easy to clean, and spots and spills are easily removed with a damp sponge. With carpet throughout, the entire floor can be cleaned with a vacuum; extra tools for mopping or sponging aren't necessary.

When we ordered our fifth-wheel trailer, we opted for a beige/gray carpet—the only neutral color offered—even though we didn't want such a light color. We were concerned that it would

> **"H**aving the carpet unattached and in sections allows each section to be lifted or folded back so the floor underneath can be cleaned periodically.**"**

be hard to keep looking clean and fresh. As it turned out, the color was an excellent choice. Even after a few years, it didn't look old because it had no obvious grayness as often occurs with carpets in non-neutral shades. The color proved to be so satisfactory, we took a piece of the old carpet with us while shopping for the new so we could match the colors.

Reupholstering

After a few years of use, upholstery in light colors takes on a grayness that eventually can't be removed. Darker colors have somewhat more longevity, but, no matter what the color, wear takes it's toll sooner or later and, when this happens, reupholstering should be done or new furniture should be purchased.

Unless you are very skillful, most reupholstering should be done by a professional. We successfully made some new zippered covers for the dinette in our first trailer, but it was fairly easy because the seats and back were rectangles.

When it came time to reupholster the pieces in our fifth-wheel trailer, we had a professional take care of the dinette cushions along with a sofa and chair. We decided to reupholster the sofa and chair because we couldn't find any ready-made furniture in the sizes and colors we needed.

In an older RV, not only the upholstery may need replacing; the foam on dinette seats and some convertible sofas that have received heavy use from sitting or sleeping may also need to be replaced. The upholsterer took care of replacing the foam in all the pieces we had reupholstered. At the same time we recovered the dinette cushions in our travel trailer we also replaced the foam.

If you need replacement foam for furniture used for sitting or sleeping, don't purchase the kind readily available in fabric stores or other retail outlets; it will break down within weeks of regular use. Long-lasting foam can be purchased from stores that specialize in foam, from foam manufacturers, and some upholstery shops (check the Yellow Pages under "Foam"). High-density foam is the type to use. It's more expensive initially but worth it because it lasts three or four times longer than other types. The outlets that sell foam also will cut it to size.

Window Treatments

New curtains or draperies for windows can be purchased, or you can make your own if you have a sewing machine.

Some ready-made curtains and fabric valances fit RV windows without any, or much, alteration, and much of the readily available curtain and drapery hardware can be used in RVs.

On some RVs, the window treatment consists of a fabric-covered "frame" (sometimes called a *surround*) on the top and each side of a window. The frame, usually held on by screws, can be removed and recovered. Or, if you don't like this treatment, the frame may be removed and replaced with curtains or draperies.

Our fifth-wheel trailer had a window treatment found in many RVs: wooden, fabric-covered valances and pleated draperies. In our latest remodeling, we redid all our windows, mainly because the valances were covered with the same fabric as the sofa, and we reupholstered the sofa with another fabric. We now have a ruffle valance of the same material as the gathered curtains.

The simple curtains were easy to make. They are merely rectangles with a pocket for a standard curtain rod in the top and are gathered by pushing the fabric to the ends of the rod. Easy-care poly/cotton fabric is used in both the bedroom and the dining/living room area. The colors are the same throughout, but the dining/living room area curtains are in a small checked pattern while the bedroom fabric has a pattern of larger squares. Since we have no need to close the curtains for privacy (we have window shades for this), the valance is made of matching fabrics and gathered in the center of the rod between the two side panels. So light won't come in above the curtains, we retained the top of the old valances, cut them down to match the curtain rod's projection, and reinstalled them at the top of the windows. Because we do sometimes pull the privacy curtains (described in Chapter 8), they are hung on a separate cafe-curtain rod behind the other rod. The window treatment in the dining/living room area is shown in Figures 9.8 and 9.9, on page 231.

COMFORT AND CONVENIENCE MODIFICATIONS

Although an RV may be basically suitable for your needs, you may find, as we did, that it can be improved by a little remodeling.

Beds

Beds that lift up to provide access to a storage space underneath are usually constructed of sturdy materials and supported sufficiently to prevent sagging. In our first full-timing trailer, the bed wasn't this type and the mattress support amounted to three slats. This wasn't adequate support for the mattress and wouldn't have provided us with the firmness we wanted.

To solve these two problems, we added a longitudinal support under the existing slats (Figure 9.1). A piece of ½-inch plywood, of a height to fit underneath the slats and the length of the bed, was set on edge under the slats along the center line of the bed. To hold it in position, the plywood was screwed to cleats on the floor and also to cleats on the slats. This reinforcement made the bed much more sturdy overall and supported the mattress suitably.

The modification also partitioned the area under the bed, making it a more practical storage area. Since one side of the storage area could be accessed only by lifting the mattress, items we used infrequently were kept there. Access to the other side was through two existing doors.

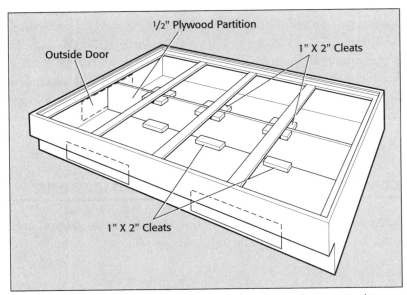

Figure 9.1 A fixed, vertical piece of plywood installed under the mattress slats not only prevents the mattress from sagging but creates a partitioned storage area.

Seating

In our travel trailer, the dinette-seat cushions rested on a series of metal bands that gave them so much springiness we found them uncomfortable to sit on. To make them firmer, we put a sheet of ½-inch plywood on top of the metal frame the bands were wrapped around. Because the frame had to be lifted for access to the storage area underneath, the plywood had to be anchored so it wouldn't slip out when the seats were lifted. To hold it in place, small holes were drilled at the back of the plywood so it could be lashed to the metal frame with thin rope.

If you want a recliner to replace other furniture, you may not be able to find one that will fit in your RV if you shop at a regular furniture store instead of a store that sells RV furniture. Most recliners for RV use are somewhat smaller than the residential recliners. No matter where you find a recliner, before purchasing, measure its extended dimensions carefully to find out if it will work in your RV. We once considered recliners but found we didn't have enough space to extend them. In order to install two recliners, a full-timing couple we know removed the sofa from a slideout, which provided enough space to install two large standard recliners side by side, with a small table between.

Table Space

As offered, the living room in our fifth-wheel trailer had no table at all. When we ordered the trailer, we wanted a table in the center of the rear wall of the trailer, between the sofa on the street side and the chair on the curb side, that could be used as an end table or extended for use as a dining table as an alternative to the dinette. We purchased such a table from our trailer manufacturer—a standard feature in one of the larger models—and installed it ourselves. We attached it to the wall with some unobtrusive hardware that allows us to completely remove the table if we wish (Figure 9.2). With this hardware, we found the table could slide from side to side as we were traveling or shift out of position if someone leaned against it. In order to prevent this, a small block of wood was attached to the underside of the table at the back at a 90-degree angle to the wall. A barrel bolt was installed on the block, which fit into a hole drilled in the wall and kept the table securely in place. The front end of the table was supported by a folding leg.

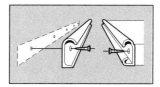

Figure 9.2 A table attached with this unobtrusive hardware is easily removed; slightly lifting the free end of the table releases the other end from the channel.

The dinette table in our fifth-wheel was the typical type set on two pedestals that could be removed if the dinette was converted into a bed. Since we didn't need to use the dinette as a bed, we wanted to eliminate the pedestals. We knew from previous experience that the pedestals were always in the way of our knees. When we ordered our trailer, we asked that the dinette table be shipped unmounted and that none of the pedestal hardware be installed. We attached the dinette table with the same type of hardware used for the rear table, and installed another a barrel bolt in the same manner to keep it from sliding. (We use past tense in describing these two installations because they don't exist anymore. We now have a better arrangement which we describe later in this chapter).

The Microwave Oven

Many manufacturers (the builder of our trailer among them) include a specially sized, prewired cabinet for a microwave oven and offer, as an option, an oven in a size that takes up all the space in the cabinet.

We don't use a microwave oven often enough to warrant having a large one (we didn't want to add the extra weight either), and we also couldn't do without all the storage space that would be lost with a large oven. Since large was the only size microwave oven the manufacturer of our trailer offered, we decided to purchase one in the size we wanted and install it ourselves .

In a factory installation, the oven is visible—not behind a cabinet door. We needed to install ours inside a cabinet (Figure 9.3), so we had to do some careful measuring to be sure the cabinet door would close and that there would be enough ventilation around the oven when it was in use. (Factory-installations have air vents on the top and bottom of the framework that holds the oven in place.) To provide for enough air circulation, we installed a short, pivoting arm that holds the cabinet door ajar when the oven is in use (Figure 9.4). Simply opening the cabinet door isn't an option because it extends so far into the walkway that it's an obstruction.

Water Faucets

If most people have a choice, they select a water faucet with a single control over the type with separate hot and cold knobs. While the single-control type is commonly found on galley sinks in RVs, the bath sinks often have the two-knob type. If this is the case in

Figure 9.3 This microwave oven takes up only a small portion of this cabinet. Note the foam strip on the cabinet to the left of the oven; this prevents the door from being scratched when it's wide open.

your RV, you can easily change the faucet to a single-control type as we did; it should fit into the existing holes on the sink, and little or no alteration to the pipes is necessary. The only adjusting we had to do was shorten the plastic pipe from the new faucet by simply cutting it with a knife. The built-in sliding stopper won't work on RV sinks so we removed it and put a small piece of clear mailing tape, which is waterproof, over the small hole at the back of the faucet that held the stopper control rod.

We had to do considerable searching to find the type of faucet we wanted: a lever instead of knob control, the faucet section parallel to the sink instead of being slanted, and with plenty of room between the end of the faucet and the back of the basin. Our reasons for wanting this type is because the knob type requires gripping the knob firmly to both turn on the water and adjust the

Figure 9.4 Instead of opening the cabinet door all the way for ventilation when the microwave oven is in use, thus blocking the walkway, a short, pivoting arm was installed to hold the cabinet door ajar.

Figure 9.5 A well-designed, single-lever faucet is installed on this bath sink.

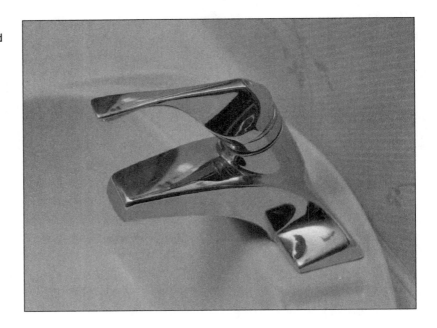

temperature, and reaching over the faucet to get to the knob means the faucet must be constantly wiped clean from dripping hands. The problems with a faucet that slants upward from the base, as we see it, is that water runs down toward the base—the part that's hardest to clean.

We finally found a single-control faucet that requires only a finger-touch to move the lever, which extends out to the end of the faucet (Figure 9.5). It would be a better design if the lever extended slightly beyond the faucet, but even as it is, it's easy to keep clean. The faucet is made by Eljer.

Some high-end RVs have a single-control faucet in the shower. We'd like to have one, but there isn't enough space behind the shower wall for the needed extra plumbing.

Aside from being easier to clean, we like a single-control faucet because it conserves water, which is especially useful when boondocking. There's no adjusting of knobs to get the right temperature, with the resultant water wastage. As the knob or lever on a single-control faucet is turned on, it can be instantly placed to achieve the desired temperature.

MAJOR REMODELING

We have gone through three remodelings with our fifth-wheel trailer (we made only minor modifications to our travel trailer). At this time the only areas we haven't altered are the bath and the galley, but they are satisfactory as is and we don't plan to change them.

All the remodelings were done to make the trailer more suitable for our individual needs as working fulltimers—to provide us with a comfortable and convenient place to live and work.

We started the first remodeling project the day after we took delivery of the trailer. Again, what we did may not apply to you, but it may give you some ideas when, or if, you decide to do any remodeling.

Preliminary Work

Before beginning a project, we draw accurate plans, including dimensions, of the front, side, and top view. We use cleats, in lengths of 1-inch × 1-inch and 1-inch × 2-inch wood, for anchoring upright pieces of wood to the floor and walls; for securing tops, such as a chest top; for supports for shelves; and for joining corners, except for a project that must support weight, we may use 2-inch × 2-inch cleats in some locations. These lengths of wood are included on the plans.

We calculate all measurements carefully, being sure to allow for the thickness of all the wood. If this critical measurement isn't included in the calculations, the project can't be assembled properly. Not allowing for wood thickness is a common mistake of those who haven't done much woodworking. If they have otherwise made careful measurements, it may require a bit of head scratching to figure out what went wrong. Remember: Measure twice, cut once.

Remodeling Project Number 1: A Computer Workplace

No dedicated office space existed in our trailer, so our first remodeling project was to arrange the bedroom to achieve a place for our office supplies along with a counter where we could do some simple paperwork and set up the computer and printer. Before ordering our trailer, we measured the bedroom in a similar unit on the dealer's lot. As with carpet, we made a plan on graph paper to be sure our idea would work and that everything would fit as planned.

The day after we took delivery, we started our project by moving the bed. Although the manufacturer of our trailer agreed to do certain customizing, when we asked to have the bed turned, they wanted no part of it. The sales manager did, however, send us a sheet of paneling so the sections of the bed frame we had to reconstruct would match the existing frame.

The bed, like the bed in many fifth-wheels, was an island-type with the head at the front of the trailer. We wanted to turn it so the head was against the curb-side wall, and one side as far toward the front of the trailer as possible. This we knew would be a complete rebuilding job and somewhat complicated because the bed is the type that lifts up for access to a storage area underneath. We had to be certain that when the bed was in its new position, it could be lifted without being obstructed by the overhead cabinets on the front wall and without interfering with the curtain rod on the front window.

Once the bed was relocated—it took about a day and a half to do the job—we placed one nightstand in the usual way at the side of the bed, parallel to it so the drawers can be pulled out in the normal manner. The other nightstand was turned 90 degrees so its back butts against the side of the other nightstand making an L-

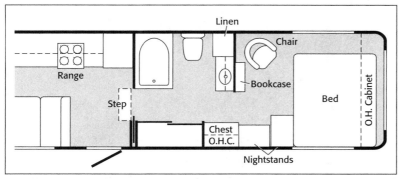

Figure 9.6 A rearrangement of the bedroom in the authors' fifth-wheel trailer resulted in space for a chair and a bookcase and allowed the nightstands to be placed so extra counter space was gained.

shaped counter. The drawer-side of the second nightstand is next to a chest in our bath/dressing room (Figure 9.6).

Since the drawers in the turned nightstand couldn't be used, they were removed, along with the supports. But in order to retain the storage in the nightstand, we made the top removable. It's held in place with cleats that fit into the inside opening (Figure 9.7). To access the now spacious storage area, the top is merely lifted off. For our purposes, this new storage area is better than what the drawers provided.

Above the chest in the bath/dressing room is a modified shirt wardrobe, which was offered as an option with our trailer. We wanted this storage unit for office supplies. At the factory, before it was installed, it was shortened so there would be enough space between the bottom of the supply cabinet and the chest top, which was to serve as a desk.

We installed shelves in the cabinet and partitioned them to hold our assortment of office supplies. On the bottom of the cabinet, we installed a single, 12-volt DC light fixture to provide illumination for the chest top.

The arrangement of the nightstands in conjunction with the chest top gave us nearly five feet of counter space—more than

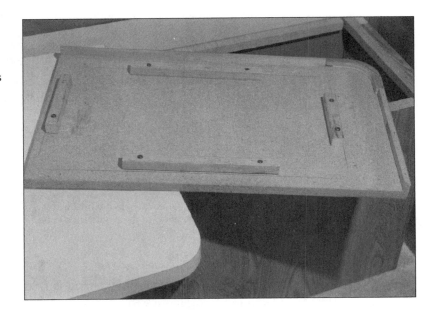

Figure 9.7 Converting a nightstand to a top-opening storage unit requires the top to be removable and cleats installed on the underside as shown. The cleats hold the top securely in place so it can't shift.

enough to set up our computer and printer, both of which are stored nearby.

Because there's no knee hole at the desk/counter we can't sit at it in the normal fashion. This is no problem because the area is used for little jobs that take just a few minutes such as writing a check or two and entering receipts, and the computer and printer are set up in this location when we have only a few sheets to print. (We have notebook computers so we can do our writing wherever we please, and when we have a lengthy print-out job, we may use one of the three other locations where we can set up the printer.) If we should want to sit down, we can use a small, folding stool we keep stored at the foot of the bed.

As a result of turning the bed, we gained extra space in the bedroom; now there's plenty of room for an upholstered chair and a bookcase. Our "upstairs" bed/sitting room/office is a great place for reading or doing computer work because plenty of light comes in the window next to the chair (we installed a 12-volt reading light on the wall above the chair for night-time use), and the bed, in close proximity to the chair, makes a handy footrest.

Remodeling Project Number 2: Adding Storage

Our next remodeling project wasn't nearly so complicated as the first because very little construction was involved.

The table we installed on the rear wall of the living room was replaced with a unit that served not only as an end table but also provided storage, and because the original-equipment chair wasn't comfortable, we also replaced it.

We weren't certain about what kind of a storage unit to use but we felt sure we could find a ready-made piece of residential furniture that would be satisfactory. We looked at many end tables and night tables but found nothing in the right size that afforded storage space. We even looked at toy chests, microwave oven carts, videocassette storage units, movable TV tables—just about anything that was small enough to fit and had built-in storage.

When we were on our way to the furniture department of yet another store, we passed a display of vanities in the bath department. Bingo! We knew instantly that this was what we'd been searching for. Here were ready-made units of the right width and height, with plenty of storage space, and even in a finish that matched the woodwork in the trailer. Never mind that a sink was supposed to fit on top; we knew we could engineer a top more appropriate for our uses.

We purchased a vanity with two doors and placed it where the rear table had been. In addition to two shelves, we installed a "floor" under the sink space. With the addition of a removable top we made from the table, a wide, deep bin was created. The top is held in place and lifts off similar to the nightstand top described earlier.

To fit next to the vanity in the rear curb-side corner, we purchased an upholstered office chair that didn't look too "officey." We needed one that would swivel so it could be turned and used at a fold-up table behind it, which was mounted on the rear wall. We constructed the fold-up table from the remainder of the table top and some of the leaves. When it was folded up it was held in place with two removable legs. Each leg was a one-inch dowel inserted into a furniture tip screwed to the underside, front edge of the table.

This incarnation lasted for quite a while, but we weren't entirely satisfied with the seating because we both wanted a place to stretch out. The sofa was fine, but the chair with a footstool wasn't comfortable enough. After a great deal of planning, we embarked on our most extensive remodeling project.

Remodeling Project Number 3: Altering the Dining/Living-room Area

This project involved altering by rearranging, removing, and rebuilding the entire dining/living-room area on the curb side of the trailer. Of the furniture we previously installed, only the vanity from Remodeling Project Number 2 was retained.

Figure 9.8 shows the arrangement before we started our most recent remodeling, and Figure 9.9 shows the results. The retained vanity is centered under the rear window in both.

Of the furniture that came with the trailer, only the console, a double-door floor cabinet measuring thirty-eight inches wide, fourteen inches deep, and thirty-two inches high, was kept. The console isn't visible in either Figure 9.8 or 9.9 but the TV, which is visible, is sitting on it. In Figure 9.8, the TV is sitting on the console top. In Figure 9.9, the TV is placed on a U-shelf that covers the satellite-dish receiver.

For this remodeling project, we removed the dinette and installed a counter in its place; moved the console about a foot forward of its previous location; installed a built-in settee in the rear, curb-side corner; and recarpeted the trailer from front to back. Although this can be described in a few words, it isn't the sort of pro-

Figure 9.8 The authors' living room and dining area as it was after Remodeling Project Number 2.

Figure 9.9 The authors' Remodeling Project Number 3 resulted in this arrangement of the living room and dining area. The major change was replacing the dinette with a counter.

ject you'd want to tackle unless you were staying put in one place for several weeks.

Before we began the project, we went over and over the plans trying to figure out where glitches might exist, how to best utilize the dinette cushions for the settee with minimum alterations, and how to do the whole project without losing any storage space. Careful planning is crucial because of the small space involved. Miscalculating in one area by as little as an inch can adversely affect another area.

Following is a description of how we handled the various sections of this project.

The Dining Area

Years ago we saw an RV with a counter for the dining area with storage cabinets underneath. We never forgot what we considered to be a very sensible arrangement, so we decided to modify our trailer this way (Figure 9.10).

The counter is a ready-made kitchen counter top, the type that can be purchased in nearly any home-supply store. A 6-foot length was the smallest we could find, about a foot longer than we needed. We considered shortening it ourselves, but decided it was worth the small cost for a professional to do it. Because the bathroom vanity we installed in Remodeling Project Number 2 worked out so well as a storage unit, we knew from the outset we would use two more vanities for the storage under the table and also to provide some of the support for the counter.

When we ate at the counter, we would be there for only a short time, but when we were doing computer work, we could sit there for hours. That's why we selected vanities in a width that would leave space for a knee hole between them where we could stretch out our legs and be more comfortable. One vanity, 24 inches wide, and another, 18 inches wide, serve the purpose.

Figure 9.10 Under the dining counter are two modified bathroom vanities, which provide storage space and some of the support for the counter.

When measuring vanities, we found that the 18-inch-width sizes are not as deep as the wider ones. We debated about whether to cut down the wider one or extend the shallower one by adding a piece of wood to the sides. As it turned out, we had to do neither, because we realized that we wouldn't be using both sides of each vanity. We planned to use the former dinette seat backs at each end of the counter, and they would take the place of one side for each vanity. We simply took the one unneeded side panel from the wider vanity and used it as the one side panel we needed for the smaller vanity.

A notch needed to be cut out of the vanities' sides so they would fit over the wheel well, to which the vanities would be partially anchored. After removing the dinette we discovered the original wheel-well covering was nothing but a flimsy piece of wood to which nothing could be anchored securely. We had no choice but to take time out from installing the vanities to rebuild the wheel well.

The counter covers the vanities where the sink is supposed to fit, so we couldn't access this space from the top as we can with the vanity in the living room. Since we couldn't have a lift-off top, we made the panel above the doors on each vanity removable, put in a shelf, and salvaged the otherwise unusable space. The panels are held in place by a barrel-friction catch on each side, and removed by pulling on the knob in the center of the panel.

At first, we looked for vanities that had a straight front, as opposed to the type that sloped outward at the top, but we couldn't find any of this style that were suitable. Now we're glad we couldn't find any; the slant-front style is the more practical because it provides more knee room when sitting at the counter.

Two dining table chairs provide the seating at the counter.

The long counter provides us with an excellent computer workstation with a good view out the window when we take a break from work, as well as when we have our meals there.

Friends of ours in the process of purchasing a new motorhome admired our counter arrangement and sought our advice about installing something similar in their unit. For the dining area they had a choice of a cantilevered table attached to the wall or a free-standing table. We pointed out that as long as they were going to change the area, if they opted for the free-standing table they wouldn't have to remove the other table from the wall and perhaps have a patching job to do. You might keep this in mind if you intend to alter a new unit; opt for furniture that's not built in, if you have a choice.

The Console

Moving the console forward about a foot may seem to be rather straightforward, but it proved to be otherwise. When the console was in its new position, we found it was no longer flush against the wall; the bottom of the console touched the wall, but, thanks to our manufacturer's sloppy construction, the top was a quarter of an inch away from the wall. In order to anchor it firmly it had to be flush, so we had no choice but to adjust the side by sawing some of it away. After we removed a thin, tapered, almost three-foot-long sliver from each side (the console has only three sides; the wall forms the fourth side) the console fit perfectly.

In the original arrangement, one panel of wood, finished on both sides, served as both the back of the console and the back of the dinette seat. We kept this arrangement but wanted a taller panel to hide the wires coming from the back of the TV and satellite-dish receiver. An extension of the desired height was cut from an unused section of the other dinette seat back. Matching holes were drilled in the top edge of panel and the bottom edge of the extension, 2-inch lengths of ¼-inch dowels were glued into the panel's holes, and then the extension was set on the dowels. To cover the joint, a thin strip of matching wood trim was attached with brads.

The original trim from the seat back was used to finish the top and sides. The trim is the type shaped like a wide, squatty T and attached with the descender of the T fitting into a groove in the wood. The seat back had this groove but the extension didn't. We thought we could cut the descender off and glue the trim to the extension, but we couldn't cut away enough of the descender for the trim to lay smooth. The only recourse was to cut a groove in the extension, which we did, laboriously, with a Dremel tool fitted with an engraving bit—the only bit small enough to do the job.

The Settee

We first envisioned the settee as one unit about five feet long, but as we went through various permutations of the planning, we came up with a better idea. The arrangement would be more versatile if we built in a shorter settee and achieved the length we wanted with a movable footstool on the end (Figure 9.11), so that's how we engineered it.

This allowed us to use, without altering, one set of seat and back dinette cushions for the seat and back of the new settee. A seat cushion from the other dinette set was altered for the top of the

Figure 9.11 The authors constructed this corner settee with a section that serves as a movable footstool. Storage space is under the settee and also in the footstool.

footstool, and a back cushion cut down for the end cushion of the settee. We salvaged enough material from the altered seat and back cushions to cover the base of the settee and the footstool. An upholsterer made the cushion alterations, but we stapled the fabric to the two bases.

Storage space is under the settee as it was on the dinette; the drop-lid that is the seat support lifts up for access, and there is also storage in the footstool, accessed by lifting off the top cushion and the lid underneath.

The footstool, being movable, can be used in front of the sofa, and either on the end, or in front of, the settee. We put gliders on the bottom so it slides easily, but not so easily that it shifts out of place during travel.

We needed a solid support for the end cushion of the settee since we often use it as a backrest when stretching out, and, without a support, the cushion would lean against the slanted back wall under the rear-window shelf. The folding table we installed in Remodeling Project Number 2 was used for this. It was cut to fit the rectangular area under the shelf. So we could use the space between the back wall and the support for storage, we turned the support into a door by putting a hinge on the bottom. Velcro tabs hold it shut. A small loop of webbing is used to pull the door open. As installed, the support is unobtrusive, and the storage area completely concealed.

Installing new carpet throughout completed this latest remodeling project.

Exterior Refurbishing

After we finished with Remodeling Project Number 3 inside, we tackled a project on the outside.

We have stone shields on both the front and rear windows, which were made of fiberglass in an aluminum frame. The trailer manufacturer's logo and some decorative striping were on the front shield, both of which were peeling and badly faded. We knew that removing everything on the surface would leave a lighter area underneath because we have seen other trailers on which this had been done. We didn't want this effect on ours because it would still look old and faded.

Our solution to the problem was to replace the fiberglass with Lexan. We thought it would give the trailer a newer look (it did), as well as providing visibility when the shield was down. When we overnight without unhitching, it's difficult to raise the front shield so, with the fiberglass, we had no way of seeing out. Although the rear shield is easy to raise, the Lexan served the same purpose; we didn't have to raise it to see out. To provide shade, which was another function of the fiberglass, we used Lexan in a smoke tint.

When we removed the fiberglass, we found it to be much thinner than we supposed, less than $\frac{1}{16}$ of an inch. Although it was supported in three places along its length, it rattled noisily when it was windy. The thickness of the Lexan is ³⁄₁₆ of an inch, and its rigidity has eliminated the rattling—another improvement.

Replacing the fiberglass with the Lexan was an easy job. The only tools needed were a drill, a screwdriver, and a rivet tool (the shields are constructed so the break in the frame is held together with a riveted plate). To avoid scratching the Lexan as we were installing it in the frame, we put towels on the picnic table and laid the shield on top of them, even though the Lexan had a protective paper covering (we didn't remove this covering until after the shield was installed on the trailer). Because we had to remove much of the protective paper on the other side in order to install the vertical supports, we covered the Lexan with a towel to prevent scratching.

Removing and reinstalling the stone shields was simple. Once the sliding arms (that hold the shield up) are unscrewed from the trailer, and a screw-stop removed from each end of the shield, it simply slides out. It's reinstalled by reversing the process.

Another problem we had with the exterior was peeling striping on the sides of the trailer. To keep the trailer from looking tacky, we wanted to replace it.

The wide striping band is composed of multi-width strips in two colors. Not all the strips were peeling, just those at the top of the band. We had a professional remove the peeling strips; we wanted to see how it was done so we could eventually remove the remaining stripping ourselves.

All it takes to get rid of the striping is heat. Point a hair dryer at what you want to remove and in a few seconds it lifts off. Mineral spirits clean up any sticky residue.

The sides of our trailer are made of extruded aluminum and, unlike the fiberglass of the stone shields, show no evidence of the former striping; the basic off-white color under the striping matches that of the unstriped portion.

We will eventually remove all the old striping and replace it with striping in more contemporary colors, but we'll probably leave the restriping to a professional.

"All it takes to get rid of the striping is heat.**"**

A PICNIC-TABLE WORKSHOP

Perhaps you are wondering how we accomplished all our remodeling projects, since we don't have a home-base with a workshop outfitted with woodworking tools and a work bench.

Our workshop is one available to most RVers—a picnic table. In fact, when we're about to start on a project, we seek out a campground with a picnic table in each site.

As for the tools, over the years we have winnowed down the great number we started out with to a few that are suitable for almost any job we want to tackle. All the woodworking projects described in this book (some are illustrated) have been done with these tools.

The main tool is a good-quality saber saw. Ours is a medium-priced saw because we need a feature not found on inexpensive models: a swiveling head so the blade can be set to cut in both the forward and back position, and also 90 degrees to the right and the left. This feature is necessary because occasionally holes have to be cut and other sawing done inside cabinets where there isn't much room to work. The saw has a variable-speed control, so it can be used with all types of blades, including smooth-sided finishing blades for a smooth cut, flush-cut blades, thin scrolling blades, and blades 3 and 4 inches long for cutting through thick wood. Some saw brands require special blades, but we purchased a saw that takes standard blades because we want to be able to go into any hardware store and find the replacement blades we need.

Another important tool is an electric drill with a selection of drill bits in sizes ranging from $\frac{1}{16}$ to $\frac{1}{2}$ inch, countersinks that drill pilot holes for #6, #8, and #10 screws, and a set of hole saws. We have a $\frac{3}{8}$-inch, variable speed, reversing drill and also a battery-powered drill. If you want only one drill, it should be the electric type because battery-powered drills are sometimes too large for doing work in cramped quarters. Other useful drill accessories are a right-angle attachment and a Portalign drill guide, which allows drilling holes with accuracy and alignment. The Portalign is like a portable drill press and breaks down into a small package so it's easy to store. We used this tool to make sure the dowel holes in the console back and extension on top of the back (described earlier in this chapter) were perfectly aligned. The Portalign is also useful if you need to drill a hole through the roof of your RV, as we did when we installed the roof mount for the satellite dish.

Along with an assortment of screwdrivers, we also have a battery-powered screwdriver with changeable tips. When you have a great many screws to remove or insert, this tool saves time and eliminates muscle cramps.

Our other major woodworking tools are: a 24-inch carpenter's square, an 8-inch try-and-miter square, an aluminum yardstick (for a straight edge), a 12-foot tape measure ¾-inch wide, two 8-inch pipe clamps, several small C-clamps, and a sanding block.

We would find it difficult to do our work without the sanding block (Figure 9.12). Many years ago a cabinetmaker introduced us to this useful, versatile, and very inexpensive tool. We've never seen a ready-made sanding block of this type, so we, like the cabinetmaker, made our own. It's nothing more than a 4 × 11³⁄₁₆-inch piece of ¾-inch plywood, with one end rounded off, and a hardwood wedge, which can be a 4-inch length of ¼ × ¾ screen mold (available in hemlock and oak in most home-supply stores), or you can whittle your own. To assemble the block, slip a standard 4 × 24-inch sanding belt over the plywood and insert the wedge—a gentle tap is usually all that's needed—between the belt loop and the plywood so the belt fits tightly and can't slip. To make insertion easier, taper one end of the wedge. We use 80-grit sanding belts for most of our work, but keep some 120-grit belts on hand for fine work.

Ready-made sanding blocks are available, but they are so short it's almost impossible to sand plywood edges to make them square. This job is easy to do with our homemade sanding block because of its length. Sand with the block parallel to the edge of the plywood. Use a light touch and check your work periodically with a square or by sighting down the edge. With practice you can straighten up terribly uneven cuts. The block can also be used for

lightly sanding edges of plywood to eliminate splinters; it's better and much faster than using an electric sander for this purpose.

Sometimes we have the lumberyard cut down a large sheet of plywood to sizes more manageable to work with on a picnic table, and as long as we're paying for someone else to do this job, we have the pieces cut to exactly the measurements we need.

For the cuts we make, the wood is laid on the picnic table with the finished side down (to avoid splinters on the good side when cutting), and, after carefully measuring with the tape measure, the cut lines drawn with a sharp pencil using the yardstick as a straight edge. We use the tape measure for measuring, not the yardstick or square, because the tape, having more increments, allows us to make more accurate measurements.

Before doing any sawing, we make sure the cut line is positioned so it's off the edge of the picnic table—we've seen many scarred tables where this precaution obviously wasn't taken.

For safety's sake, we use two pipe clamps to fasten the material tightly to the table so it won't slip. It's also easier to make an accurate cut if the material is firmly anchored. If possible, the cut should be made on the edge of the line in the part of the material you won't use. This way, any mistakes should end up in the scrap piece.

If you're learning to use a saber saw, it's a good idea to practice several cuts on scrap wood. It's best not to rush the cutting; go slow. If you veer off the mark, stop, go back, and start again. Even though an uneven edge can be corrected by using the sanding block, make the cut follow the side of the pencil line as close as possible.

A carpenter's square may not be exactly square, so we don't rely on it entirely for accuracy; if you should drop such a square, as we once did, it will be even more out of square and worthless except for use as a straight edge. The most accurate squaring is done with the smaller try-and-miter square. To check any square for accuracy, lay one side along the edge of a piece of plywood and, with a sharp pencil, draw a line along the portion of the square resting on the wood. Turn the square over and draw over the same line. If the square is accurate one line will be on top of the other; if not the lines will converge or separate, forming a long narrow V. If you get a variance in the lines and need to cut something exactly square, draw the same two lines on your work and make the cut in the center of the V.

An accurate try-and-miter square is useful in another way: it can be used for checking that the blade of a saber saw is perpendicular to the shoe. If not, adjust the shoe until it is. An improperly aligned saw blade can result in cuts that are not 90 degrees to the surface of the wood.

Another useful item we have is a Dremel rotary tool with a wide variety of attachments. It has served us well for projects it was not designed to do. We've used the small tool for drilling, grinding, routing, wire brushing, polishing, and carving. Once we had a new fifth-wheel hitch that was defective—the king-pin slot was not long enough to accommodate the pin so it would lock—and, not having a suitable grinding tool, we used the Dremel tool with a ⅜-inch grinding stone to enlarge the hole (actually it took six stones to complete the job). While the tool will do heavy-duty work, we keep extras of the attachments we use most often because they quickly wear out or break. The tool itself will eventually wear out if used for heavy-duty work—after thirty years we're on our fourth Dremel tool—but we don't mind replacing them. Considering all the jobs it does, it's relatively inexpensive (we recently bought one for $50), it's small and lightweight, and it eliminates the need for certain other larger tools.

Doing major work on a picnic table with a limited number of tools is not as easy or convenient as working in a well-outfitted workshop, but the jobs can be done.

Some of the remodeling we did to our trailer can also be done to a motorhome, but if you want to do extensive remodeling or re-building to a motorhome you may find the magazine *Bus Conversions* helpful. It contains articles written by RVers who have done major and minor remodeling projects to bus-type motorhomes. For subscription information contact: MAK Publishing, 3431 Cherry Avenue, Long Beach, California 90807; (562) 492-9394.

What makes an RV more livable is up to each individual, but, unless you have an RV custom-built to your specifications, there are many modifications that can be made to a stock RV to make it more suitable for full-time living.

CHAPTER 10

Storage

We all have more possessions than we need and we continually add to them because of wants, needs, fashions, and fads. We tend to hang onto items that should have been disposed of long ago. Fulltimers should avoid this constant accumulation of possessions, but many don't. Never mind that it's not practical to hang onto rarely used items. Never mind that every pound of weight increases fuel consumption. Never mind that the storage of all these items may make for cramped quarters. We must have our things.

Fortunately, an amazing amount of things can be stored in the average RV. It may require some thorough sorting and evaluation, but you'll probably be able to take most of what you want with you—within reason, of course.

Our experiences in solving storage problems may be of some benefit to you. Even though many of the items you have may be different from ours, all of us have clothing, cookware, toiletries, tools, food, supplies, and paperwork that is kept in the storage compartments of our RVs.

In addition to the usual day-to-day living necessities, we have an office in our trailer with all its attendant equipment, along with equipment needed for our writing and photography, including lots of reference material. Unless we wanted to live in an impossible clutter, early on we needed to achieve optimum space in every storage unit.

Although some of the storage ideas in this chapter originated with us, some are variations and adaptations from other people's ideas.

STORAGE IN A MOVABLE HOUSE

The prime consideration for RV storage is how items are affected when the RV is moving. All items must be stowed so that they won't break, fall, shift, or chafe when the RV is in motion. Also to be considered is the weight of everything stored in the RV and how the weight is distributed.

Storage for fulltiming is also different from storing items in an RV for vacation use. More things are needed—in our case everything we own goes with us—and they should be kept in some sort of order. Most of us can put up with a mess for a short-term vacation, but facing the inconvenience of disorganized storage every day—not being able to find what you want when you want it, having to continually search through items piled one on top of the other—is something that most of us don't want to live with for long.

Don't plan to move into an RV and immediately store everything in its proper place. It's not possible. It takes some weeks, maybe months, of living with your storage areas to determine exactly where the best and most practical places to keep things will be. Don't be discouraged if you can't fit in everything the way you want at first. As you live in your RV, solutions to storage problems will present themselves.

Rules for RV Loading and Weight Distribution

Here are a few general, but not hard-and-fast, rules about RV loading and weight distribution:

- Heavy items should be stored as close to the floor as possible.
- Numerous heavy items should not be located behind the rear axle; the ideal place for heavy objects or an assortment of objects that collectively weigh a lot is over an axle.
- The weight should be evenly distributed; no RV should be loaded so that it's obviously down in the rear or leaning to one side.
- If the full-timing RV is a trailer and the tongue weight is too light, it can be increased by storing heavy items forward of the axle, as close to the front of the trailer as possible.

Increasing Existing Storage Space

The capacity of almost every storage area can be increased by adding partitions or shelves or by compartmentalizing it with boxes, bins, and other containers. This should be done to large cabinets and compartments especially, so that items stored in them have little room to move, shift, or fall over when the RV is moving.

Partitions

On our 23-foot trailer, in the two large compartments that were accessible from both the outside and inside, we installed a partition in each so that two separate compartments were formed, one inside and the other outside. In the outside sections of the compartments we kept items used outside the trailer. The hitch equipment went into one compartment. Some of this equipment was likely to have had grease on certain parts of it—the socket ends of the equalizing bars for the weight-distributing hitch, for example, and the hitch itself—so we wanted to keep such items separate from others. The partitions performed this function as well as reducing the size of the compartments.

The partitions were cut to fit tightly, but, nevertheless, we caulked them around the edges so road dust would be confined to the outside sections. The snug, sealed partitions also aided in weatherproofing because they cut down on drafts. We noted a marked improvement in our cold-weather comfort after installing these separating partitions.

In our current trailer, the only outside compartment that opens directly to the inside is in the rear under the sofa. It's the only place for conveniently storing our leveling boards, the other outside compartment being too small. We didn't want the sometimes wet, often dirty, leveling boards to be inside the trailer next to the other items we intended to store under the sofa, so we partitioned this area too.

Perhaps partition doesn't accurately describe what we did, since we literally constructed a compartment (Figure 10.1). Before we

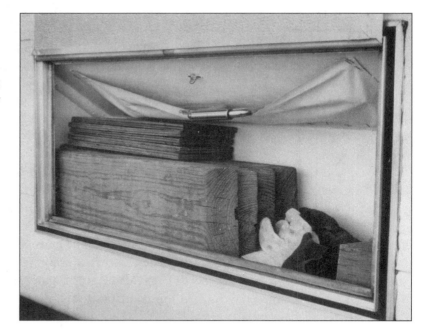

Figure 10.1 On the top of this specially constructed compartment for storing leveling boards is a vinyl pocket in which is kept the handle for the rear stabilizing jacks. The front of the pocket, shown unfastened, is held shut with a turn-button fastener.

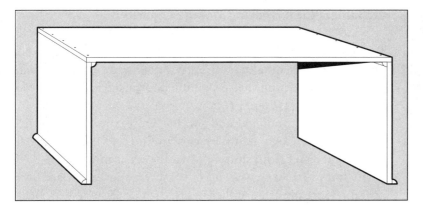

Figure 10.2 A U-shelf made of plywood and quarter-round molding is a useful device for adding an extra shelf in a cabinet. It can be movable or permanently anchored by inserting screws through the molding at the bottom of each side.

built it, we placed all our leveling boards and jack pads together in various arrangements to find which took up the least space, then built the compartment to that size. To keep out drafts we caulked every seam. This caulking also prevents bugs and spiders, which may be on the leveling boards, from getting inside the trailer.

The lengthwise reinforcement under the bed on our 23-foot trailer (described in Chapter 9, page 219) was designed and installed so that it would divide the underbed storage area into two sections.

Shelves

When we need a shelf in a cabinet with no wall to which it can be attached, we can sometimes purchase a suitable shelf, often the type made of vinyl-coated wire, but if we can't find one of the right size, we make our own (Figure 10.2). Such a U-shaped shelf can be easily and quickly constructed with a few tools and some ¼-, ⅜-, or ½-inch plywood. The thicker plywood should be used if heavy items will be set on the shelf. The shelves can be movable or fixed in place. Sometimes a box turned on its side with the opening toward the front makes a suitable shelf.

Figure 10.3 Boxes can be installed on cabinet doors for extra storage space. The box can be mounted securely with screws backed up with large washers.

Containers for Increasing Storage Capacity

To increase storage capacity in any location, large or small, boxes, bins, and other containers of appropriate size can be used. They can be set on existing shelves, on the floor inside cabinets, or hung on walls or doors (Figure 10.3).

If items are contained and not left loose, there is more usable space in a given area, items are easy to find and use, and no damage should result from shifting when the RV is moving.

All sorts of inexpensive plastic, wicker, and cardboard storage containers are available. Other items, such as wastebaskets, buckets, and dishpans, also lend themselves to this purpose. Use your imagination when looking for suitable storage containers; they can be found in places other than kitchen and closet departments. Try sporting goods, tool, hardware, baby, and toy departments. It was in a toy department that we found two small, rigid plastic suitcases that are just right for storing some of our power tools and accessories. They take up much less space than the regular cases for the tools.

If we can't find a container in the size we want, which often happens, we construct one by cutting down or altering an existing cardboard box. If the container will be located where it can be seen, we dress it up with an adhesive-backed, wood-grain, or plain- colored covering.

For large items that won't fit into an existing storage area and that must be taken in and out of their storage places frequently, such as our printer, we construct a special type of box. It's like any other box except that the top is a lid that lifts up and a side folds down for removal of the printer and folds up for storage (Figure 10.4 illustrates a box of this type we constructed to hold our printer).

The folding side, when up, is held in place by the lid. By lifting the lid, the side falls down and the printer is easily lifted out. When we had the older style printer which was longer and narrower, it too was kept in a box like this. In the place we stored it, it had to be on end. We constructed this box with the lid on the top and so that only about half the front side folded down. This still provided us with plenty of room to grasp the printer and pull it out.

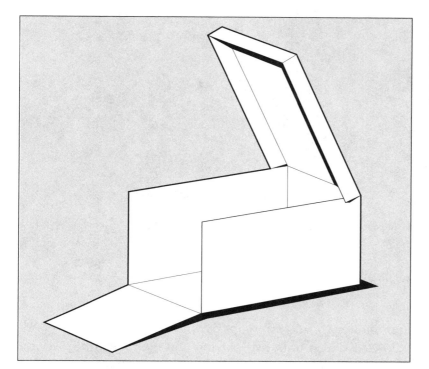

Figure 10.4 A bulky item, such as a printer, is easy to remove and put away if kept in a storage box with a lid that lifts and a side that folds down. Shown is the box used to store the authors' printer.

We make these boxes just large enough to hold the item, eliminating any extra space so the item can't shift around inside when we are traveling.

The printer box is visible, so we covered it with an ivory-color adhesive-back material close to the color of the trailer's walls.

Hooks

Various types and sizes of hooks can be used throughout an RV to provide extra storage. The inside of many of our outward-opening cabinet doors has one or more hooks on it. We use the hooks for storing items that would otherwise take up shelf space.

We increased the temporary storage space for rain-wet coats in

---

Figure 10.5 Hooks hung on the shower rod or in the shower itself are handy for hanging rainwear to dry.

our shower by adding hooks. We use one sturdy, clear plastic hook—designed to fit over the top of a door—that fits over the shower enclosure in the corner and another type that fits over the shower rod (Figure 10.5).

Since we have no place wide enough for a conveniently located hand-towel rod in the bath, we hang the towel on a plastic hook that is attached with mounting tape.

CLOTHING STORAGE

Fulltimers' clothing, which consists of casual wear and separates for the most part, only takes up about half the height of a full-length wardrobe, so the bottom of such a wardrobe can be adapted to provide other useful storage space.

In our previous trailer we had two long, deep wardrobes for clothing storage. We filled up every bit of the space under the hung clothing with bins and shelves (Figure 10.6).

Figure 10.6 In addition to clothing on hangers and folded clothing in the bins below, this wardrobe holds a table leaf extension and a folding chair.

We fitted one wardrobe with an L-shaped shelf that extended about halfway across the wardrobe a few inches below the bottom of the clothing hung above. Its vertical support formed a partitioned area which was further partitioned with a bin. These partitioned and sectioned-off storage areas held wearing apparel that did not need to be hung on hangers: underwear, socks, gloves, nightwear, caps, belts, and some knitted items. The stacking bins we used can be easily located in all sorts of retail outlets.

Under one wardrobe was a large, open space that would have held all our shoes and then some—but in a big, disorganized pile. The area was in a corner, and deep, making it an inconvenient place for storing shoes that we wore regularly. We added two full-width shelves to the space. When the shoes were lined up on the shelves, they were easy to see and reach. The doors to the shoe compartment opened outward and downward. On each door we mounted a fabric pocket, which we made specially to fit the doors. These convenient, roomy pockets were used for storing a pair of lightweight shoes or slippers.

The single, double-door wardrobe in our present 29-foot trailer was also adapted to maximize the storage space. Since we have a roomy chest of drawers in this trailer, we need to store only shoes and sweaters in the wardrobe, in addition to the clothes on hangers.

It was easy to figure out a shelf configuration for the left half of the wardrobe that would hold our sweaters, but storing all our shoes in the right half presented a problem. As in our smaller trailer, they would all fit in the area if they were just tossed in, but, as before, would end up being separated from their mates, and it would be a nuisance to root out shoes that happened to be on the bottom of the pile.

As we did with the leveling boards before building the compartment for them, we placed the shoes in various arrangements in the space to see which configuration accommodated the most pairs. We found that if the shoes were stood on end the greatest number of pairs could be stored in the most accessible way. In order to do this, we partitioned the right half of the wardrobe into four rows, each the width of one shoe, so the shoes would stay upright, and

put a panel on the front of the rows so the shoes wouldn't spill out.

Figure 10.7 shows the interior of the altered wardrobe. It doesn't show the half shelf on the back wall above the shoes. We had room there for a small shelf, so we installed one to hold hats, slippers, and other lightweight items. The top of the sweater compartment forms another shelf. Except for the top and left side of the sweater unit, which are plywood, the shelves are made of foam-core board (available at most craft supply stores) to save on weight; this material is sturdy enough to hold the weight of sweaters without sagging. The center dividers are loose and stay in place simply be-

Figure 10.8 This easy-to-make hanger can store several pairs of pants on a wardrobe door.

cause we made them to fit snugly. The shelves rest on cleats made of ¾-inch, quarter-round molding. Everything we built into the wardrobe is covered with a wood-grain, adhesive-backed material.

Bill has never liked pants hangers of any kind and does not want the inconvenience of storing pants on a regular hanger under another item of clothing. Long ago we devised a pant hanger that is easy to use and takes up little space; We used it in our house and in both our full-timing trailers (Figure 10.8).

Two strips of lath are attached vertically to the outer edges of a wide wardrobe door. A cup hook is installed on each side for holding the hanger part. Since our wardrobe doors aren't solid, as is the case in many RVs, the lath is necessary to provide a firm mount for the hooks. We used metal hooks because adhesive-backed, plastic hooks aren't strong enough for this purpose.

The hanger itself is a half-inch wooden dowel with a screw eye installed about ⅜ inch in from each of the ends. To attach the hanger, the eyes are slipped over the corresponding cup hooks. Each hanger can hold up to three pairs of pants.

The pants hanger is on the inside of one of the wardrobe's doors. On the inside of the other door, at both the top and in the middle, is a plastic strip with three hooks on it. The top hooks hold frequently used, long items such as robes, and the middle row is for lightweight windbreakers. Just inside the right door, high up on the wall, is a large hook for holding belts.

In this wardrobe, which measures 39 inches wide, 20 inches deep, and 64 inches high on the right side and 71 inches high on the left (the roof slopes upward), we store twenty-two shirts, seventeen pairs of pants (Jan hangs hers under her shirts), fourteen items of outerwear (rain parkas, sweatshirts, windbreakers, miscellaneous jackets and parkas for cool and cold weather), twelve sweaters, a half-dozen belts, two robes, and sixteen pairs of shoes. (We both have hard-to-fit feet and buy shoes when we find some that fit whether we need them or not. If we could find a pair when the need arose, we wouldn't have so many pairs to store.)

If there is no room in a drawer, on a shelf, or in a storage container to keep items of clothing folded and flat, they may take up less space if they are rolled. Knit polo shirts, for example, can be folded lengthwise down the middle, the sleeves folded in, then rolled up loosely, starting from the hem. If the garment is smoothed out as it is rolled, it will remain almost wrinkle-free. A rolled garment is easy to remove without disturbing other garments, something that can't be done too easily or neatly with a stack of folded garments. A bin in our old trailer that was used for storing polo shirts was too narrow to accommodate any folded shirts satisfactorily, but it held six rolled ones conveniently. Garments stored in drawers can sometimes be rolled to create extra space, and some sweaters may be rolled to fit into an odd corner.

Another storage option is to hang a shoe bag on a wardrobe door and use the pockets for small clothing items. They can even be used for shoes if the shoes don't put too much weight on the door.

Throw pillows with zippered covers can do double-duty if the stuffing is removed and replaced with clothing or linens: bulky sweaters, light- and medium-weight blankets, afghans, nightwear, swimsuits, or other seasonal items.

When we began fulltiming, we used wire clothes hangers which jumped off the rod in the rear wardrobe during travel. We changed to the thicker, plastic hangers and had no more problems. We have since learned from another fulltimer that if we had hung the wire hangers reversed they would not have fallen off. She also advised us to reverse rolls of toilet tissue and paper towels if they unwind when the RV is in motion.

Laundry

Where to store soiled clothes until laundry day seems to be a major problem for many fulltimers. Some, who have filled up all other practical storage areas with other things, keep soiled clothes in the shower. A few have doors in their RVs large enough and strong enough to hold a full laundry bag suspended by hooks. And some RVs have a built-in hamper, but most RVs have no specific or built-in place for laundry.

The general approach to the subject is that all soiled washables should be kept together in one place, usually in a bag. We have long since departed from this common concept and, in so doing, solved the problem of what to do with our laundry.

We keep our laundry in several different places. In our first trailer, resting on the top edges of a bin in each of our wardrobes, was a laundry box. We made these boxes so they fit exactly on top of the bins. They measured 10×18 inches and were 4 inches deep. (One of these laundry boxes can be seen in Figure 10.6, page 253, on the right, just under the hanging clothing.) Most small items of soiled clothing such as underwear and socks were dropped into these boxes. There was plenty of room for soiled hand towels, washcloths, and dish towels as well. On laundry day, we dumped the contents of the boxes into a laundry bag that was kept folded and stored in the bottom of one of the boxes.

In our present trailer, it's necessary to have a slightly different arrangement for the small items. At first we simply put the laundry bag in the cabinet under the bath sink where there was plenty of room for it even when full. To put the soiled items where they belonged, however, required four steps. The cabinet door had to be opened, the bag lifted out, opened, and put back in the cabinet. Our tendency was to ignore the bag and just toss the laundry into the cabinet. On laundry days we stuffed everything into the bag hoping we hadn't overlooked anything that may have landed among the other items stored in the cabinet. We corrected our lackadaisical laundry-collecting habits by hanging the bag, open, inside the cabinet (Figure 10.9). Two grommet holes were put in the bag and the holes go over two small hooks installed inside the cabinet near the top. Now, when we toss laundry into the cabinet it automatically goes into the maw of the laundry bag. On the door, hung on a hook, is a small drawstring pouch into which we put our extra quarters every few days so we'll have plenty for the washers and dryers.

When big items such as sheets and bath towels become soiled, we put them directly into the laundry basket, which we store in the large compartment under the gooseneck at the front of the trailer.

Other items of clothing that need to be washed, such as shirts

Figure 10.9 An easily accessible laundry bag is hung inside a cabinet.

and pants, are kept on their hangers, unless they are very soiled, until laundry day. Although we don't have so many clothes that we cannot remember which ones need to be laundered, the clean shirts are buttoned at the top and the soiled shirts, having been worn, are unbuttoned.

With this method we have no presorting to do; all the items in the bag and in the laundry basket are washed in hot water, and all the clothing from the hangers goes into machines set for permanent press. To keep things simple, when it comes to washable clothing, we buy only items that don't require special care when laundering so all of it can be washed at the same washer setting. Our system of keeping soiled clothes in different places may be worth trying if you have a laundry storage problem.

A laundry basket is a difficult item to stow in most RVs unless they are basement models or have a large compartment as ours does. With our previous travel trailer, the bed of our pickup truck was covered with a canopy, and we kept the laundry basket there. Many motorhomes don't have a large storage area like a pickup bed, but if an auxiliary vehicle is towed, perhaps a laundry basket can be kept in its trunk.

GALLEY STORAGE

If certain food items are stored improperly for traveling, they can make awful messes if their containers break and the contents spill out, so careful attention should be paid to galley storage.

Under-sink Storage

Almost all RVs have a large cabinet under the galley sink which can be made into a more efficient and practical storage area by compartmentalizing it. Most such cabinets have one shelf that, while dividing the area in half, still leaves each half with too large an area to conveniently and safely store items.

On this shelf in our under-sink cabinet we have a large plastic box in which we keep most of the foods that come in glass bottles and that don't need refrigeration, such as vinegar, cooking oil, olive oil, various cooking wines, corn syrup, and molasses. In the well-filled box, there is no excess space in which anything can tip over when the trailer is moving. The rest of the shelf is taken up by plastic canisters so the bottle box can't shift out of position.

If the bottle box and canisters had not filled up the cabinet, we would have used any extra space for storing rolls of paper towels. These make good fillers in almost any cabinet. They are light-weight, and the rolls can be stored vertically or horizontally.

On our previous trailer, on the floor of the under-sink cabinet, we installed a shelf shaped like a wide U under which we stored an electric skillet. The small space between the top of the U-shelf and the shelf above was just tall enough for storing baking pans. Next to the U-shelf were several small plastic baskets in which we kept potatoes, onions, apples, and the like. We kept some of our canned goods in this compartment in two separate boxes. In one, the cans were upright, in the other, on their sides. With this arrangement we achieved the maximum amount of storage in the existing space in the cabinet and in the boxes.

In our fifth-wheel trailer, the floor of the under-sink cabinet was on two levels. The back portion, about six inches above the floor, is the enclosed wheel well. Running along the entire width of the cabinet at the front was an exposed furnace duct.

We put in a false floor that rests on the wheel well and extends over the duct to the front of the cabinet. Although though this shortened the height of the lower portion of the cabinet by about 6 inches, the space provides better storage because we can now use the entire depth of the cabinet.

On one side of this cabinet, in the back corner, is a high-sided plastic box similar to the bottle box mentioned above, where we keep cleaning supplies we use frequently: glass and carpet cleaner, sponges and rags, all-purpose cleaner, and dusting spray. We use a box so the liquid items won't spill and also to keep all the cleaning supplies well separated from the canned goods we store in the other side of the cabinet. We don't use many canned goods so we don't need much space for storing them.

In this trailer we started out using the same boxes for cans we had in our other trailer, but we soon found a more efficient way of can storage. Four 1-inch × 1-inch wooden cleats were cut in a length equal to the cabinet's depth. They are nailed to the cabinet floor, running front to back, so they form three rows just as wide as a sixteen-ounce can—a little over three inches. The upright cans are lined up between the cleats. This prevents them from sliding from side to side as we travel, and the height of the cleats is just enough to keep the cans from falling over.

The drainpipe for the double sink extends horizontally for a distance across the cabinet, three-and-a half inches under the bottom of the sink. The area above the drainpipe was wasted space until we realized we could put a shelf there that would be just right for holding long, slim boxes of kitchen wraps and storage bags.

We made a shelf from a piece of Masonite cut to fit the area (Figure 10.10). The shelf rests on the horizontal length of drainpipe, which supports it on the front. The back of the shelf rests on a cleat mounted to the wall behind the sinks. Two screws through

"The area above the drainpipe was wasted space until we realized we could put a shelf there that would be just right for holding long, slim boxes of kitchen wraps and storage bags."

Figure 10.10 An otherwise useless space under the galley sink is turned into a storage area by the addition of a shelf.

the shelf into the cleat hold it securely in place. Not only have we increased our storage space by using this otherwise wasted space, we have an arrangement whereby the often-used products are easily visible and reachable.

One door of our under-sink cabinet holds a plastic wastebasket we use for a garbage container (Figure 10.11). Although we made the container removable—three holes in the back of the wastebasket fit over the heads of three screws in the door—it can be screwed directly onto the cabinet door; use washers under the screwheads in this case. Disposable bags are used to line the wastebasket. A bag of garbage can be heavy, so the wastebasket is supported by a small wooden shelf attached to the door with L-brackets. The positioning of the wastebasket on the door is important since there must be clearance all around so the door can be closed properly.

At the top of the other door is a vinyl-covered wire holder, which contains dishwashing liquid and sink cleanser. Instead of purchasing the wire holder designed for these items, which has sides so low that items could bounce out, we bought a holder that is designed for boxes of foil and kitchen wraps to be mounted horizontally under a shelf. We mounted it vertically on the door. The bottom, which is now a side in our installation, is about as high as the items kept in it; they can never fall out.

On the bottom half of this door is a holder for plastic lids for various storage and mixing bowls. (The bowls are in another location and stacked one inside the other to save space.) We constructed the holder from lightweight cardboard. It's merely a box, open on one end, with the front side cut down by half so the lids can be seen and grasped easily.

The under-sink storage space on some RVs comes equipped with roll-out, wire baskets. If yours does not have this feature and you want it, it may be possible to install your own. Often these types of baskets, which are found in home-improvement stores, are too deep or otherwise too large to fit into RV cabinets. Sometimes they can be made to fit if the track length is shortened.

If these residential-type baskets are unsuitable, a rolling storage container can be custom-made to fit just about any cabinet by using ball-bearing drawer slides, which come in various lengths, for the tracks. For an installation of this type, the drawer slides are mounted on the floor of the cabinet. A sheet of plywood should be attached on top of the slides as a base for the storage container that will be mounted on it. The container may be a wire basket; a plastic, openwork crate; a cardboard or plastic box; or one, two, or maybe three plastic wastebaskets mounted on the same piece of plywood. A barrel bolt or a hook and eye can be used to prevent the container from moving when the RV is under way.

Figure 10.11 A shelf was added to the door of an under-sink galley cabinet to hold a wastebasket.

Storage Containers

We rarely store any foods that come in bags and boxes in their original containers. Instead, we have plastic containers in many sizes and shapes into which we transfer these foods. After much trial and error we finally have a collection of plastic containers and canisters that fit into our galley cabinets with no wasted space.

By using our own containers we don't have to contend with such nuisances as cereal boxes that are too tall to fit on a shelf, rice and pasta packages that, once opened, cannot be resealed properly to avoid spilling, and foods in packages and boxes that would have to be piled helter-skelter on shelves.

Brown sugar, cocoa, baking soda, cornstarch, flour, sugar, rice, pasta, crackers, cereals, and other foods we use regularly each has its own special container. Cooking or mixing instructions, if needed, are cut from the original package and put into the container along with the food. A portion of a cereal's box with the name of the cereal on it is tucked into each cereal container.

With the containers all the cabinet space is used to the best advantage, the foods are handy, and they are kept fresher than they would be if the unused portions were stored in their original packages.

In our previous trailer, we had one long cabinet above the sink in which we stored dinnerware and glasses. To keep the contents from shifting when the trailer was moving, we made a shallow cardboard tray and anchored it in the middle of the cabinet with double-face mounting tape. The tray sectioned off the cabinet and was used to hold salt and pepper shakers, a toothpick holder, and juice glasses.

We use nonskid shelf lining (available at many retail outlets) in most of our cabinets which aids in keeping things in place.

Doors and Drawers

The inside of cabinet doors that open outward (instead of upward) can be used for storage. Our largest galley door contains measuring cups and spoons and pot holders (Figure 10.12). The measuring spoons are hung on finishing nails (the holes in the

Figure 10.12 A galley cabinet door is utilized for optimum storage space. The white notes (upper right) are commonly used cooking and measuring references.

spoon handles won't fit over nails with heads) driven in at a sharp angle. Our graduated measuring cups were hung on spring-clip cup hooks until we made a wooden holder for them. It's simply a 1-inch × 1-inch wooden cleat with recessed cutouts for the cup handles. A screw on each end holds it to the door.

We don't like to keep spice containers out in the open on a shelf because they may fall off during travel, and because they are hard to keep clean, especially when the shelf is in the galley. We keep our spices in a galley drawer that we have partitioned off so the spices are lined up in rows (Figure 10.13). Spice containers aren't designed to be stored this way, so, in order to identify the contents of each tin and jar, we had to label the tops of the containers.

When we use up a spice, we look for a replacement in a container that is short enough to fit in the drawer. If we can't find the spice in a suitable container, we transfer the new spice to the old container.

Figure 10. 13 To identify spices stored upright in a drawer, use either a permanent marker or labels on the lids to identify the contents of each container.

Cabinet Storage

Most of our pots, pans, and skillets are stacked one on top of the other. We store them with a piece of terry toweling between each to protect their inner and outer finishes. Otherwise, they would rub against one another when the trailer is moving. (Unless protected, a nonstick finish can be worn off in spots by this action.)

Two of our galley cabinets are higher on one end than the other because the high end is where the roof of our fifth-wheel begins its upslope to the bedroom. In one cabinet we store cookie sheets and baking pans on end on a wire shelf (Figure 10.14). The wire construction serves as a rack and helps hold the utensils upright because the handles on the ends of the cookie sheets and some of the baking pans fit between the wires. Mixing bowls are on the other end of the shelf and more baking pans fit beneath it.

The counterpart of this sloping cabinet on the other side of the trailer is where we store our small artificial Christmas tree. It's at

Figure 10.14 Baking pans are stored on end to take advantage of the upward slope of the cabinet.

the top of the cabinet and hanging on a slant to match the slope of the roof. Two slings of webbing cradle the tree. A grommet hole on each end of the slings fits over hooks on the back wall and just above the door at the front of the cabinet. To keep dust off, the tree is in a sealed plastic bag. Nothing else we own is practical to store in this odd, rather inaccessible place, but with the tree stored there, the entire cabinet area is utilized and the tree isn't taking up space somewhere else.

Under-Cabinet Storage

Appliances that mount under cabinets may work as space savers in some RVs. In some units, the manufacturer may mount a microwave oven or coffeemaker on the underside of a galley cabinet. If you want to mount such an appliance yourself, special care must be taken to anchor it securely enough so vibrations during travel, along with the weight of the appliance, won't cause the screws to work out. Unless the cabinets are solid wood this could be a problem. Whether the appliance is installed by the manufacturer or you, check periodically to see that the screws are tight.

Double-duty Galley Equipment

If your galley storage space is tight, analyze your cookware and appliances to see if you can eliminate some and put others to use in a variety of ways. Cakes can be baked in pans other than the size specified in recipes by increasing or decreasing the amount of baking times. A blender can be used for many food-processor operations, and a hand mixer can serve some of the purposes of a blender. We eventually got rid of the electric skillet we started out with. It took up lots of space, and we have another large skillet that we use on the stove that serves the same purpose.

Recipe Storage

We knew we would not have space in a trailer for all the recipe books we had in our house. We also realized that we use only a small number of the recipes in any book. To save space, we cut out our favorite recipes from all the books and pasted them on small loose-leaf sheets which fit easily into one binder (we don't have convenient space for a card file in the galley). The loose-leaf feature makes adding recipes easy. Our binder measures 9½ × 6 inches; a large binder won't fit conveniently in any of our galley cabinets, and it would take up too much counter space when open for use. The small binders can be found in many office-supply stores.

Those with the necessary computer equipment might scan or type recipes and store them in the computer.

Storage in the Refrigerator

The refrigerator should be considered a storage unit and items stored in it accordingly. Pack it to cut down on open space so items can't slide around or fall over, and so that there are plenty of chilled items to hold the cold, if you travel, as we do, with the refrigerator off (see Chapter 14, pages 386–387). When we are traveling in hot weather and don't have the refrigerator full, we fill the empty spaces with cans of soft drinks, either standing upright or on their sides. They are good "fillers," and they also retain the cold well.

In order to cool properly, air needs to circulate inside the refrigerator. If you've packed it full for travel, be sure to remove some of the items when you get to the campground.

Storage in the Microwave Oven

The microwave oven can double as a storage compartment if the items stored in it can't slide around. When we have a cake to stow for traveling and it won't fit into the refrigerator, we usually put it into the microwave oven where it rides safely. A stove oven is useful for storing such items as skillets and baking pans.

Storage for a Quick-Fix Tool Kit

One of our galley drawers is partitioned with drawer organizers, and in it we store flatware and cooking utensils, but another galley drawer, fitted with the same type of organizers, is used for an assortment of hand tools such as screwdrivers with various tips (every other screw on an RV seems to need a different type of screwdriver), regular and longnose pliers, diagonal cutters, a crescent wrench, a hand drill, a tack hammer, a small pry bar, a small socket-wrench set, a utility knife, tweezers, string, glue, and other small items that we use for minor repairs and simple installations.

Even in our smaller trailer, we had a galley drawer set aside for these tools. It's easy to take care of little repair jobs quickly if the tools are handy.

The other day we tightened a window handle as soon as we found it was loose, and many times we have tightened a loose knob on cabinets as soon as it was noticed. The crescent wrench came in handy for unscrewing a clogged water-faucet filter. With the pliers we bent in a bracket so a window shade with a penchant for falling off was held more securely. The flat-blade screwdriver is needed for prying off light-fixture covers when a bulb needs to be replaced. For the innumerable little repairs and fix-it jobs that need to be done on any RV, we don't have to go out of our way to pull out our large tool chests to find the proper tool.

BOOK STORAGE

Almost every RV has some space where extra storage units can be installed without disturbing or rearranging existing furniture or cabinets. In our previous trailer we needed more places to store books. Most RVers don't have to carry as many books as we do so they may not need special storage areas for them, but where we located our bookcases may give you ideas for adding extra storage units for items you carry.

To cut down on weight, we buy books in paperback editions whenever we can. Many of the books we read for pleasure are the small-size paperbacks. In our previous trailer, we had room on the end of a galley counter for a bookcase that would hold these paperbacks (Figure 10.15). (If the galley counter space had been skimpy in that trailer, the area would have been used for a fold-up counter extension.) The bookcase was in the entryway but, being only 4¾ inches deep, did not project into the walkway far enough to cause any problems.

The area on the end of the counter was tall enough to accommodate four shelves, but we chose to make an enclosed bin with a lid instead of a fourth (top) shelf. In it we kept small, frequently used items such as a flashlight, a ring with keys for the outside compartments, and a level.

The books needed to have something to keep them from falling out of the shelves when we were traveling. A hole was drilled in each side of the bookcase about three-quarters of the way up from the bottom of each shelf. Brass welding rods were bent to fit across the shelf and into the holes. The rod rested against the books and held them in. It was a simple matter to raise the rod to remove a book. The bookcase was made of plywood which we painted to match the brown trim on the cabinets. When we moved into our fifth-wheel trailer, we took the bookcase with us. It is now in our bedroom.

In our 23-footer, we put a similar, three-shelf bookcase for slightly larger paperbacks on the end of the vanity in the bedroom. We designed it to be movable and of typing-table height. When moved to the right it formed the end support for a fold-up typing table we installed. The table was mounted on the end of the vanity, and, when not in use, the bookcase was flush against it. Hooks and eyes kept the bookcase in place during travel.

In this trailer we added another bookcase behind the dinette. A top-opening storage compartment formed a shelf behind one of the dinette seat backs. The lid did not run the full length of the compartment, leaving just enough space for a small bookcase on the end. In this tight little corner, the bookcase height was limited to two shelves; any more would have interfered with the corner of the window valance. Small as it was, the bookcase held twelve books on each shelf. Still needing more storage space for books, we eventually added another bookcase, attached to the wall under the dinette table.

Our fifth-wheel trailer has plenty of cabinet space for books, but we don't store heavy, hardbound books in overhead cabinets; we prefer to keep heavy items in floor cabinets or other low storage areas. The overhead cabinets are considerably deeper than a standard bookshelf, and we found that no matter how neatly we lined up pa-

Figure 10.15 A bookcase for paperbacks is small enough to fit in several locations in many RVs.

perbacks in them, they slid out of place when we traveled. We solved this problem by putting rolls of paper towels along the back of the cabinets, effectively making the cabinets the right depth for books. Now the books stay in place because they have no space in which to slide around and they are at the front of the cabinet and easy to see.

We have a six-inch-wide shelf along the entire rear wall of our trailer under the window. There are eight inches of wall space from each corner to the edge of the window frame. We built two little cardboard boxes to fit on the shelf in each corner (Figure 10.16) and anchored them to the shelf with double-face mounting tape. These two small bookcases hold nineteen small books we use often, mainly reference books for birds, trees, wildflowers, and other nature-related subjects.

AUDIOCASSETTE STORAGE

We have a large collection of music audiocassettes and have always wanted a bookcase-like place to keep them. Finally, in our fifth-wheel, we have a storage place in which every one of our 288 tapes is visible and accessible—it's in the 4-foot high, slide-out pantry in

Figure 10.16 A bookcase for small books is tucked into each corner of a shelf that runs across the rear wall of the authors' trailer.

the galley (Figure 10.17). When we were shopping for a trailer, we hoped we could find one with a pantry of this sort because we had already figured out that a pantry, with considerable modifications, would be the perfect place for our tapes.

First, we built a plywood bookcase with Masonite shelves just wide enough and high enough for cassettes. Its overall size was determined by the existing pull-out frame that held the pantry's four wire baskets (which we removed). Merely mounting this tape case to the frame wouldn't have worked because the frame didn't slide out far enough so that we could see and remove tapes at the back.

Drawer slides were used on the existing pull-out frame to make, in effect, a double-distance pull-out. Two boards of ½-inch plywood were affixed to the frame, one a few inches down from the top of the frame, the other near where the bottom of the case would be when installed on the frame. After the drawer slides were attached to the boards, the case was installed on the slides. When pulled out all the way, no part of the case is in the cabinet so every tape is visible.

To pull out the frame, we put a U-shaped handle on the outside vertical member, and to pull the case out as far as it will go, we put a knob on the side of the case. To prevent sliding while traveling, a hook on the case fastens to an eye on the frame, and, in addition, the frame is locked, at the bottom, by the bunk latch that came with it. We retained the bottom pantry basket and use it for storing extra tape cases and other cassette accessories.

A small broom and a fly swatter hang from cup hooks in the narrow area on the inside wall of the compartment opposite the tape case. Since our tape case is technically in the galley, the inside of the compartment door has several cup hooks for hanging long kitchen utensils, such as spatulas and stirring spoons, that don't conveniently fit in a drawer.

Figure 10.17 A galley pantry has been modified into a storage unit for an extensive collection of audiocassettes.

OTHER STORAGE UNITS

There was a space on our 23-foot trailer only 7½ inches wide between the head of the bed and the wardrobe next to the bed. It was wasted space until we built a gun case to fit into it. It was just wide enough to hold a rifle and shotgun upright. This tall, slim container was the type described earlier in this chapter with a lift-up lid and a fold-down front for quick and easy access.

For both our trailers we have made small wastebaskets that can be tucked onto odd corners too small for a regular wastebasket. They are nothing more than cardboard boxes that fit exactly into their spaces. We cover the wastebaskets with an adhesive-backed covering that blends with the wall or the furniture next to the wastebasket. Such tiny wastebaskets scattered about are handy and unobtrusive.

CONSTRUCTING STORAGE UNITS

If a storage unit is to be made of wood, of course woodworking tools are needed and some carpentry skills as well. But you don't need to be a carpenter or have special tools to build some storage units. Often a cardboard box can be found in a suitable size or one can be altered to fit. The only tools needed are a utility knife, a straight edge to cut against, a ruler or tape for accurate measuring, a pencil or pen for drawing cut and fold lines, and clear mailing tape for joining seams.

The bookcase behind the dinette back on our smaller trailer was made from two, heavy, corrugated cardboard boxes. We found one box in just the size we needed for the bottom "shelf," and cut down another box to fit on top. The boxes were covered with an adhesive-backed, wood-grain covering. Many people thought they were made of wood.

Our gun case was first made from cardboard. It was the first time we used the folding-front design and the cardboard case was to be a prototype so see if it would work satisfactorily. It did. We used the cardboard case, also covered with a wood-grain material, for several years before we replaced it with a wooden case of the same design.

PERSONAL AND BUSINESS-PAPER STORAGE

Carrying around all the papers for your personal affairs and, perhaps, for your business is something the occasional RVer doesn't have to be concerned with, but fulltimers need to keep their papers with them in their RV. Motorhomes and trailers don't have room for standard file cabinets, and the usual storage areas in many RVs aren't suitable for conventional methods of storing papers.

Because we are conducting our business from our trailer and because much of the business is writing, we have an uncommon amount of papers to store. Early on, we had to find a way to store our papers in an organized, convenient way. After much trial and error we settled on using side-opening, pocket portfolios for storing most of the papers.

These portfolios, manufactured by Mead and Duo-Tang among others, are readily available at mass merchandisers and office-supply stores. We prefer the Duo-Tang brand because the pocket, which runs across the full, opened width of the portfolio, is stapled in the center; this keeps the contents of each side separate.

The pocket feature keeps everything in the portfolio secure. There's no chance of anything falling out of a pocket unless the portfolio should be turned upside down. The portfolios are large enough to hold an 8½ × 11-inch sheet of paper. They can be placed vertically in many RV cabinets or laid flat on a shelf.

The portfolios come in many colors and two styles, one with just the two pockets, the other with the pockets and a three-prong strip for inserting notebook paper. We use the prong type for an address book, and another for expense records. In separate, plain-pocket portfolios, we keep bills to be paid, letters to be answered, and stationery. Any correspondence waiting for an answer and any papers pertaining to something unresolved is put in a "pending" portfolio. We have a portfolio for storing statements and other documents from each of our bank and investment accounts and other separate portfolios for insurance and medical records.

It's especially important for fulltimers to keep warranties for all their products and equipment with them in their RVs. We use two portfolios for storing the papers—warranties, instructions, service-center locations—that come with so many items. One portfolio is for only the trailer and its original equipment; the other is devoted to other equipment, household items, and appliances. On each warranty we note the date the item was purchased. We periodically weed out any warranties that are no longer in effect.

Our papers and files were always difficult to work with and keep organized until we started using this type of RV-compatible portfolio system. You, too, may find these portfolios useful as a means of keeping your ordinary paper storage under control; however, valuable papers, such as titles, stock certificates, and the like would be safer if kept in a fireproof box.

OUTSIDE STORAGE

A problem with basement-model motorhomes and trailers is that in the cavernous compartments that run from one side of the unit to the other, what is stored in the center of the compartment may be hard to reach.

Sliding baskets, similar to those described earlier for use in under-sink galley cabinets, may be a solution to this problem. Some manufacturers' top-of-the-line units come with them already installed. If you install such a basket yourself to maximize space, you might arrange it so that the basket's location is in the center of the compartment but able to be slid out on the track toward the compartment door for easy accessibility to its contents.

If a sliding basket or a nonsliding storage container is used in a basement, it may end up being stowed far enough into the compartment so that it is beyond arm's reach. Something long with a hook on the end can be kept in the compartment so wanted items can be snagged and pulled within reach. A crowbar, a walking cane, or a telescoping boat hook—a regular boat hook may be too long to stow easily—may suffice for this.

We don't have basement compartments, but we have a hooking device for reaching items at the front of our pickup's bed so we don't have to climb into the truck. Our "snagger" is a ski pole (purchased at a Salvation Army store for less than a dollar) with a clothesline hook on its end. Since we don't use it to pull heavy items, we used duct tape to secure the hook to the end of the pole. If we needed the snagger for more heavy-duty work, we would attach the hook either with hose clamps or bolts.

The snagger is also useful for reaching items that blow or otherwise end up under the truck and trailer—a lug nut, for example, once rolled under the trailer—and for pushing and pulling low-hanging tree branches away from the side of our rig when maneuvering into some campsites.

As on many fifth-wheels, a large storage area is under the gooseneck on our trailer. This compartment is so cavernous that everything in it would soon be in an awful jumble if the items weren't organized. Nearly everything we keep in this compartment is in boxes. Storing odd-shaped items, or a collection of related small items in boxes, utilizes existing space to good advantage because the boxes can be stacked all the way to the top of the compartment if need be. Locating what is wanted is easy if the boxes are clearly labeled as to their contents.

> **"T**his compartment is so cavernous that everything in it would soon be in an awful jumble if the items weren't organized.**"**

STORAGE IN PICKUP BEDS

When we had a canopy on the bed of our pickup truck, we ringed the perimeter of the bed with built-in, top-opening plywood bins. These provided a great amount of storage. The bins on the sides were slightly wider than the wheel wells, and all were no higher than the top of the bed's sides.

Now, because our trailer hitch is in the bed, we have, at the front of the bed, a large, low-profile, steel storage box with a sliding cover that allows access from either side.

CONTAINMENT

The key to workable and convenient storage anywhere is containment. By this we mean keeping hard-to-store items in boxes or bags and all items of one kind together in one container (if the items are of a size that makes this feasible). For example, all our extra 12-volt interior and exterior light bulbs are kept in a box along with all extra flashlight bulbs. When any bulb burns out, we have to look in only one place for a replacement. Other examples: All fuses are kept in one box, as are all glues and sealants. Putting like items in boxes and bags makes them easy to find and use and maximizes storage space.

We have two water hoses of different lengths. Each one is kept in a bag so it cannot get loose and spread out in the compartment where both are stored.

Battery jumper cables are kept in a bag so they won't snake through the compartment where they are stored and interfere with other emergency automotive equipment kept in the same compartment.

Containment is especially useful when applied to collections of small items. In the bath we have a large, counter-to-ceiling cabinet at the side of the sink counter. We use part of this cabinet for holding toiletries and pharmaceutical items. On one of its walls we put a vinyl-covered, wire, double-shelf spice rack to hold items in small containers such as eyedrops.

Attached to the inside of the cabinet door is a plastic bin in which we keep many of the items we use every day: combs, razor, shaving lotion, deodorant and such.

FULLTIMING AND STORAGE

We have tried to arrange our storage so that it is just about as easy to stow items where they belong as to leave them unstowed; because of this our small RV is never messy. We have organized our storage so items are logically stored and easily accessible so we can find what we want when we want it. We are rarely irritated because we can't locate something or because it is too difficult to get out of its storage place.

Nothing can make a neatnik out of someone who isn't inclined that way, but if a little time is taken to work out efficient storage, fulltimers won't have to spend much of their time searching for items they need or becoming frustrated because they can't find them. Proper storage has the added advantage of not having to live amidst a constant mess. "A place for everything and everything in its place" is a good motto for fulltimers.

CHAPTER 11

An RV Office for Working Fulltimers

Today more and more fulltimers are finding ways to earn a living while they travel, and, for many of them, a computer, along with equipment used in conjunction with a computer, figure significantly in operating a business from an RV.

COMPUTER SELECTION

The selection of the type of computer, desktop or notebook (laptop) is largely a personal one. Some of our RVing friends who also write for a living tell us they can best do their work on a desktop model because of the larger screen and keyboard, but there are others, including us, who prefer the notebook type.

As far as we are concerned, the main disadvantages of a desktop model, and the main reasons we don't use one, are that it's so big it requires a large desk area for use, and before moving the RV it must either be removed and stored—for which another large space is needed—or left in place and secured so it won't move. We wouldn't be satisfied with leaving a computer set up all the time because it would always be a prominent focal point in the room. We do our work on a computer, and when we're done with the work, we don't want the computer dominating our environment, lest we feel as though we're still at the "office."

A notebook computer is so small that numerous storage places can be found for one in any RV suitable for fulltiming. We find it easy to store the four computers we have. (If you're wondering why we have four it's because we each need a computer and we have two old (very old) ones we still use because they are so uncomplicated and fast for word processing, which is mainly what we do, and we each have one newer model.)

Since a notebook computer can operate on internal battery power, it can be used anywhere, outdoors or indoors. You don't have to sit in one location to do your computer work. Jan is most comfortable doing her work sitting on the sofa with her legs stretched out with the computer on her lap. If she's been working for several hours and gets tired of sitting, she sometimes moves her computer to the galley counter and works standing up for a while. On occasion, we'll do some of our work in the truck as we are traveling.

Unquestionably, desktop computers have certain advantages, the main one being that their initial cost can be considerably less than notebooks and they can be upgraded and improved more easily and at lower cost. Desktop computers may also have more built-in features such as a CD-ROM, a larger hard drive, and more PCMCIA (Personal Computer Memory Card International Association), or PC-card, slots; however, a desktop and a new notebook computer are virtually the same otherwise.

New notebook computers, like new desktop computers, with 166-MHz Pentium MMX (multimedia exchange) technology, can be used for such business purposes as creating 3-D presentations or video-teleconferencing with business associates in far-flung locations. If you want to use your computer for entertainment, this technology allows you to show a movie with 3-D audio (from the CD-ROM) on the computer screen, and instantly view photographs from your digital still camera and movies from your camcorder.

COMPUTER STORAGE

If you look at manufacturers' brochures for new RVs, you're likely to find a number of them showing a computer—almost always a desktop model—set up for use in a special place designed for it, usually a desk or a desk-height shelf. What the photos don't show, and what isn't explained in the text, is if there is a way to anchor the computer in place for safe traveling or if there is a storage area in which it can be put while under way.

Some motorhomes have a computer station on the passenger-side of the cockpit—nothing more than a portion of the dashboard that slides out far enough to hold a computer so the passenger seat can be used while working. The brochure notes that the computer must be removed and stored in a safe place before traveling; evidently it's up to the owner to figure out where a safe place is.

None of the brochures we have seen shows a printer also set up, which may be because there isn't enough room for both a computer and printer in most of the stations. What's more, no close-by place where even a small printer can be stored is evident. Some working fulltimers may also need space near the computer for a telephone, a fax machine, a scanner, and other equipment.

What this boils down to is, if you want a workable computer station for your needs, you'll probably have to engineer it yourself.

We know of some fulltimers who have removed furniture from a slideout and installed the type of computer station that's available at many retail outlets, but most such stations need some modifications to make them suitable for an office that travels, especially if they have open shelves. And a means of anchoring the station itself, which can be heavy, must be devised.

You may be able to find residential furniture to serve as storage places for a computer and other equipment. Don't overlook top-opening furniture, such as a toy chest. It's often easier to get a good grip on a heavy item and lift it out rather than slide it out of a cabinet. The furniture may be able to do double-duty and serve as an

> **"**If you want a workable computer station for your needs, you'll probably have to engineer it yourself.**"**

end table or coffee table. We have seen attractive, top-opening, wicker chests large enough to hold a desktop computer.

When you're planning a computer station and find you're shy of desk space, give some consideration to increasing it with extensions attached to the desk that fold up or slide out. Don't forget to allow space for a comfortable chair. You may have to purchase one because many RV chairs are too low and/or uncomfortable for sitting at a desk.

Not long ago we saw a well-designed workstation/storage area for a notebook computer in, appropriately, an architect's motorhome. He altered his dinette table and turned it into a large, partitioned box about three inches deep. The table top was cut lengthwise down the middle and hinged so it can be folded back to expose the box underneath. The top folds back against itself and rests in an upright position on the far side of the table, with the folded part supporting the other half.

Inside the box, a notebook computer, a thin portable printer, a CD-ROM drive, and a flatbed scanner each fits neatly into its own cushioned compartment. The remaining space is taken up with other compartments, one of which contains the power supply and surge protector for all the equipment; other compartments, some of which have lids, hold small office supplies. Paper is stored in an overhead cabinet above the table. It takes only seconds to convert the dining table into a computer station, and vice versa. Having the table top in the dining position is all that's needed to ready the equipment for travel. From our point of view, the only disadvantage to this ingenious arrangement is that computer work must be done at the dinette, and most dinette seats don't provide comfortable sitting for long periods.

If a computer is stored during travel, it should be in a place with minimal bounce and vibration (probably not at the rear of the RV, especially if it's a trailer), and in a low spot so there's no danger of it falling out of a cabinet if the door should accidentally come open when the RV is moving, or toppling out when the cabinet door is purposely opened to remove it. The storage space should be tight enough so the computer can't slide. We store our computers, each in its own padded case, in a floor cabinet. The same care should be taken with storing printers, fax machines, and other delicate equipment.

If a desktop computer is always set up and not stored, it should be kept under a dust cover when not in use. Printers with ink cartridges must be stored in an upright position, not on end.

THE ALL-IMPORTANT TELEPHONE CONNECTION

Many fulltimers using computers for telecommunications have an obstacle—a big one—to overcome: the lack of a telephone in their RVs. There are ways to overcome this problem, but before we explain how to do so, let us digress to discuss the equipment needed for computer telecommunications.

Modems

In order to make data transmissions, such as sending and receiving E-mail, over a telephone line from your computer, it's necessary to have a modem (derived from MOdulator/DEModulator). The modem converts digital data from the computer into analog signals that can be sent over the analog telephone line to its destination, where another modem converts it back into digital form for the receiving computer (Exhibit 11.1).

The modem must be fast enough for today's speedy transmissions (Exhibit 11.2). A modem with a speed of 9.6kbps is the minimum needed for E-mail, and the minimum required by many Internet service providers (ISP) is 14.4kbps. The reason ISPs require this speed is so users won't tie up the lines for too long, thereby delaying access by other users.

The internal modems in older desktop computers may not be

EXHIBIT 11-1

Analog and Digital Technology

In order to explain the difference between analog and digital transmissions, let's start with a transmission we are all familiar with—human speech.

Speech is analog in nature. When a person speaks, the tongue and vocal chords create sound composed of changes in volume and frequency. When listeners hear the sound, their brains process it into speech.

Another type of analog transmission occurs when using a telephone. A microphone changes speech into an electrical current that varies continuously in strength and frequency to match the original sound input, and, later, a speaker converts the varying electrical current into sound. An analog transmission never changes in its basic form from beginning to end.

The language computers use is digital. Digital technology operates on the principle that all forms of data are in steps or units. A computer evaluates data in two conditions: high or low, on or off, 1 or 0. This system is familiarly known as a binary code; the word binary means having two distinct parts or components.

When the letter "A" is typed, it's represented by a series of ones and zeros: 01000001, to be precise. Each of these digits is a bit (derived from the words BInary and digiT), and any combination of eight of these digits constitutes a byte—a byte being each letter of the alphabet, each numeral from zero to nine, and all other individual characters on the computer keyboard. Most telephones are analog, so digital data must be converted to analog to be sent over telephone lines; a modem does this.

fast enough. With our old computers it took many minutes for transmissions that now take only a second or two. Depending on the computer's age, you may or may not be able to upgrade it with another modem, either internal or external.

Notebook computers can be upgraded only if they have a PC slot into which the card-shaped modem fits. If you intend to use a cellular phone for data transmission you'll need a modem that's cellular-ready or cellular-capable and one that matches your particular cellular phone (see pages 84–89).

If you must upgrade, a 28.8kbps or 33.6kbps modem is probably the best choice at the present time even though 56.6kbps modems are available. The 56.6kbps technology is going through growing pains and isn't compatible with many applications. Another complication is that two different 56.6kbps systems exist and the shakeout as to which will be the standard in the future hasn't yet occurred.

To make the telephone connection with a desktop or notebook computer with an internal modem, one end of a four-conductor telephone cord with RJ-11 plugs on each end is plugged into the computer's RJ-11 jack and the other end into the telephone jack. For notebooks with PC-card modems, the telephone cord is connected to the RJ-11 jack or other connector on the small cable attached to the modem. Using a 1-to-2 jack adapter in a wall-mounted telephone jack allows you to connect both a telephone and a computer to the same outlet.

The Portability Factor

Unless you are in a campground that offers telephone hookups, you'll have to use outside sources for data communications, and, of course, you'll need a portable computer—another reason notebook computers are so practical for RVers. Those with desktop computers, however, can have the convenience of portability without making the considerable expenditure for a notebook computer.

A handheld personal computer (HPC) will do the job. An HPC is just a smaller-than-notebook size computer with many of the features of its larger cousin: a keyboard; full-color or backlit black-image LCD screen; Windows CE, a program compatible with the Windows 95 program for desktop computers and notebooks; pocket editions of Microsoft's Word, Excel, and Internet Explorer; the capability to exchange files with other computers and to receive faxes and e-mail; and either an internal modem or PC card slot.

Even smaller, pocket-sized, personal digital assistants (PDAs), or palm-tops, as they are sometimes called, can perform some of the functions of an HPC, but have limitations because most of their operating systems are not compatible with Windows-equipped computers. Some PDAs have no keyboard; input is accomplished by writing on the screen with a stylus.

Because of their many features, HPCs cost more than PDAs. Although most cannot be connected to a printer, some can with the correct adapter (which often costs more than the computer).

We have found many telephone sites that don't even have space on which to set a notebook computer, so one of these smaller, hand-held units may be useful for certain notebook owners.

Finding a Telephone with the Right Connection

Locating a telephone with an RJ-ll jack that you are allowed to use is the next step. In a few campgrounds we've found public telephones with this jack available, sometimes with an adjacent table where the computer can be set.

Some campground managers will allow you to plug into the office telephone line if all you want to do is download e-mail, but you shouldn't expect this generosity to extend to any data transfer taking longer than a few minutes.

We couldn't use the office line at one campground, but the manager said we could tap into the telephone box outside on the corner of the building. This we did, both sitting on camp stools (the box being only about four feet above the ground), trying to juggle the computer and the acoustic couplers we were using then (more about this device later in this chapter) so as not to interfere with the connection; this was when our transmissions took many minutes. We got some strange looks from other RVers as they drove by.

Other alternatives for achieving a telephone connection are commercial sources such as Mail Boxes Etc. and Kinko's, which are found all over the country, and many other local businesses of the same type. Rates at any place are about the same: a nominal charge for e-mail communications and an hourly rate for both Internet use and renting a computer for doing work.

At many libraries you can access the Internet at no cost and some also allow you to send and receive e-mail.

Another choice is the so-called cybercafe. Here you can take care of your computer work and enjoy a snack at the same time. Most cybercafes are in large cities, so, for RVers, they may not be convenient for use.

A warning: Do not plug an analog modem (the type discussed earlier) into a digital phone system. Doing so will probably fry your modem because of the higher voltage on which digital systems operate. RVers, however, aren't likely to encounter digital telephone systems because they are found in many motel and hotel PBX systems and internal office telephone networks. Non-RV travelers often carry a special digital modem or a special connector/adapter to use with these systems. When in doubt about a system, ask what kind it is before using.

Acoustic Couplers

If an RJ-ll jack can't be located, data transfers can be done with an acoustic coupler—a device that fits over a telephone's handset and is connected to the computer modem. As long as the handset fits snugly into the coupler, transfers can be done from nearly any telephone, if there is adjacent space to set up both the coupler and the computer. Many travelers who stay in motels and hotels use acoustic couplers instead of a digital modem for compatibility with a digital telephone system.

A few years ago we were writing a self-syndicated, weekly newspaper column about RVing and sending columns to various papers on a regular basis. We used an acoustic coupler almost exclusively then, so we were on a continual quest for telephone locations where we could set up our equipment. We found the best locations at public telephone banks in large motels and hotels; usually a sizable shelf is under the telephone where equipment can be set and sometimes there are chairs at the telephones too. We also found spacious, quiet telephones in some hospitals but quickly learned that those too close to the radiology department resulted in our connection being zapped every time an X ray was made.

The coupler we used then was susceptible to outside interference, which could cause nothing but garbage to be sent or a complete disconnect, so we built a special foam-lined wooden box into which the coupler and handset were placed during transmission. The lid was designed to fit tightly to keep the coupler in close contact with the handset. After a preliminary scouting trip to locate a suitable telephone, we'd carry in a big bag containing the computer, the coupler in its box, a battery pack, and a stopwatch. The battery pack was necessary because of the long transmissions—we had some hour-long stints in those days—and the stopwatch let us know how much time remained for sending each column. With our equipment, four columns (the amount we usually sent at one time) of 750 words each (about 4,500 bytes) took ten minutes to transmit. Instead of standing around during these minutes, or sitting if we were lucky, we often read portions of a newspaper or a book, while glancing at the stopwatch periodically.

"**A**fter a preliminary scouting trip to locate a suitable telephone, we'd carry in a big bag containing the computer, the coupler in its box, a battery pack, and a stopwatch."

Data Transmissions with a Cellular Phone

It's perfectly feasible to send data transmissions with a cellular phone as long as you're willing to pay the price; charges are usually the same as for voice calls. But data transmissions are very fast so air time charges may be comparatively less.

All you need is an analog cellular phone capable of sending data (not all can), a computer with a fax/modem compatible with the phone, a cellular-connection interface, also known as a data transfer box, (available from your cellular provider) for connecting the computer to the phone, and a compatible connecting cable.

The Cellular Connection by Motorola is available for use with regular modems and fax machines. It provides a dial tone, ringer voltage, auto-dial/auto-answer, and a RJ-11 jack so the modem or a fax machine can be plugged in.

Digital cellular phones handle data transmissions differently than analog cellular phones. Since they operate on several different and noncompatible technologies, some can handle data transmissions and some cannot. Those that can require special computer modems and connecting cables to connect the phone to the computer.

Bill Higby, a cellular expert at Cellular One in Albany, Oregon, gave some good advice: Purchase the phone and all items used in conjunction with your phone for data transmission—connection boxes and cables—at the same time from the phone provider. Then, when you're ready to buy a modem, check the specifications on the modem you are considering to make sure it's compatible with the phone and its equipment. Often modems are compatible but the connecting cables are not.

If your provider should be unable to give you the information, you may be able to find what you need on the World-Wide Web at: www.wow-com.com.

New methods of sending data are in development which will require special modems.

"When you're ready to buy a modem, check the specifications on the modem you are considering to make sure it's compatible with the phone and its equipment."

Cellular phones are available combined with a PDA, a modem, and a small screen for viewing messages. Along with voice communications, these so-called "smart" phones can also transmit data.

While using a cellular phone with a computer while traveling, it's best to be stopped instead of moving because the hand-off from one cell to another as you move may be interpreted as a disconnect. Interference can also destroy data transmission by missing small pieces of data or causing a disconnect.

Satellite Telephone Service

To the traveling fulltimer, satellite service can provide instant communications no matter where you are. The only dead spots for satellite phones are places where the phone's antenna hasn't a clear path to the satellite, such as if you were in a tunnel, under a dense tree, or surrounded by high buildings.

Computer connections are easy to make, and since satellite systems are digital, communications are high speed and free of interference except when it's raining or snowing heavily.

Right now satellite service is too expensive for most people. Phone prices begin at about $3,500 and can be as high as $5,000; monthly charges run around $85. In the near future, perhaps by the time you read this, phone prices are expected to drop and eventually may be about 10 percent of the present cost, with monthly charges similar to cellular charges. Perhaps, in the future, satellite phones will also be reduced in size and weight. Now the phone and the antenna fit in a carrying case about the size of a small suitcase that weighs about twenty-seven pounds.

If you were to purchase a satellite phone, you have to decide whether to buy one serviced by a satellite system that is in geostationary earth orbit (GEO), or low earth orbit (LEO), or medium earth orbit (MEO). See Exhibit. 11.3.

Antennas for phones using GEO satellites are about the size of a chessboard. The phone can't be used while traveling because the an-

GEO Satellites

GEO satellites travel in an orbit 22,300 miles above the earth, in the same direction and at the same speed as the earth's rotational speed so, in effect, the satellite remains stationary above a given spot on the earth's surface. Most TV, weather, military, and some telephone satellites are the GEO type.

Being so far from the earth's surface, radio signals from a caller must make a 44,600-mile round trip from the caller's phone to the satellite and back down to the gateway, or base station. This requires a powerful transmitter.

GEO satellites are so high in altitude their individual signals cover a large section of the earth's surface, so only four or six satellites of this type are needed to cover the entire globe.

LEO Satellites

LEO satellites are placed in orbit at altitudes of a few hundred to a thousand miles. A planned array of sixty-six satellites will cover the entire surface of the earth as they travel around it.

LEO satellites require smaller, less powerful transmitters than the GEO type.

MEO Satellites

MEO satellites will be in orbit at altitudes around 6,000 to 7,000 miles. Six to twenty satellites will provide global coverage.

---

tenna must be set up and aimed at the satellite's location, just like satellite TV. For this reason, such a phone may not be practical for traveling fulltimers. Because GEO satellites are so high, the signal from them has a quarter-second delay, which can be noticeable when making a call. GEO satellite systems are also the most expensive.

Smaller, less powerful transmitters are needed with LEO satellites, so small, whip-type antennas of the type now on cellular phones are adequate. Since LEO satellites are moving at high speed, one call is handled by a satellite for about 15 minutes then handed off to the next satellite passing overhead, much the same as cellular calls are handed off from one cell to another as you travel.

Although MEO satellites are not in use at this writing, this system will figure in future satellite phone selection. An advantage of the MEO satellite system is that a single satellite will be in a caller's range for about one hour, so frequent hand-offs to another satellite won't be necessary.

Connections to a satellite phone for data transfer are the same as for cellular phones although a special modem may be needed.

WHAT DOES THE FUTURE HOLD?

As far as mobile communicating is concerned, the future, with all sorts of benefits that may be of use to fulltimers on the move, may be as close as next week or years away.

Some of the new satellite phones will be dual-mode, which means they can be used for both cellular and satellite communications, and tri-mode, which provides service from the satellite as well as both analog and digital cellular networks and switches from cellular to satellite when the caller passes out of range of a cell.

OTHER COMMUNICATION EQUIPMENT

Pagers

A pager may be useful for RVers who need to have people get in touch with them at low cost.

Most pagers suffer from the same coverage problems as cellular phones, although satellite paging service is available. Some new units are actually cellular phones with a built-in pager, and they may have a keyboard and a PC-like display screen.

You can select a tone-only pager, which simply emits a tone to let you know you are to call your service carrier for a message, or a pager that sounds the tone and then gives you a voice message. Another type displays a numeric phone number or numeric code on a screen, and yet another type, an alphanumeric pager, displays both messages and phone numbers.

Two-way pagers allow transmitting and receiving text and numeric phone numbers; some have voice capability for short messages.

While pagers don't have the capacity for long messages that regular e-mail has, they are an alternative and some fulltimers may find a pager is all that's needed.

Often cellular-phone and pager service can be combined with landline long-distance telephone service and accessing the Internet.

One pager, called a satellite communicator, is slightly larger than a hand-held cellular phone. Via satellite, and at a relatively reasonable price, its integrated global positioning system (GPS) receiver provides you with your exact location anywhere on the face of the earth, as well as allowing two-way e-mail communicating.

Fax Machines

As long as you have some sort of telephone connection, you can use a fax machine. Although many computers have the capability of sending faxes, the material must be typed or scanned before it can be sent. With a dedicated fax machine, no preliminary work needs to be done. Simply insert the material and send it.

Multifunction Computer Printers

A multifunction computer printer is a useful tool if work volume justifies the cost. One unit, along with the printer, also serves as a fax machine, a copier, and a scanner. Finding a place to store this rather large, bulky machine in an RV may be a problem.

E-mail and the Internet

E-mail and the Internet, or Information Superhighway, as it's often called, are available to computer-owning fulltimers as long as they have a telephone connection and a service provider. E-mail allows you to send and receive messages in a fast, dependable fashion, and on the Internet, you can locate information on nearly anything you want and infinitely more information on what you don't want.

One type of e-mail and Internet provider is a nationwide on-line service, such as America Online (the largest), CompuServe, and Prodigy. Some charge a monthly base rate to which is added an hourly charge beyond a stipulated number of free hours; others charge a flat monthly rate.

E-mail is also available from Internet service providers, companies whose primary function is to provide telephone access to the Internet, but along with access they also provide subscribers with e-mail capability. Since ISPs are small, no-frills operations with nothing to offer but service, monthly rates can be very attractive, especially since there are no extra charges above the monthly rate. You can locate ISPs by looking in the Yellow Pages under the "Internet Products and Services" heading.

There is a monetary aspect to signing up with an ISP that traveling fulltimers should consider: When you obtain your service from a local ISP, and don't remain in the area, most likely you'll have to make a long-distance call each time you want to access the Internet and pay the long-distance charges for as long as you're logged on; very few ISPs have toll-free numbers.

ISPs have an advantage over the nationwide providers when it comes to selecting your e-mail address. Because ISPs are local, they don't have thousands of subscribers so there's a better chance of getting the address you want.

Before you can access the Internet—a physical "superhighway" connecting a global network of computers—and consequently the World-Wide Web, the information source, you need a Web browser. The most popular browsers are Mosaic, Internet Explorer,

> **"S**ince ISPs are small, no-frills operations with nothing to offer but service, monthly rates can be very attractive.**"**

and Netscape Navigator. A browser is provided at no extra charge when you sign up with an on-line service or an ISP. If you don't like the provided browser, other browsers can be downloaded free, or you can purchase Web browsers at computer stores.

If you want only e-mail service, you can use an e-mail provider such as Juno Online Services, HoTMaiL, or NetAddress. Everybody can afford the service because it's absolutely free. Along with your e-mail, however, you'll receive advertisements, because selling ads is how the services make their money.

Juno is the largest of the free e-mail providers. Logging on to send and receive e-mail can be done anywhere in the country because Juno has 400 local-access telephone numbers and a toll-free number to use if no local access is available.

To obtain the Juno software, which is also free, call (800) 654-5866, or get a copy of the software from someone who has it (Jan's sister gave it to us). It's perfectly legal to pass around this software. In fact, the company encourages this sort of dissemination. The software can also be requested on the Juno Web site: http://www.juno.com.

HoTMaiL and NetAddress are World-Wide-Web-based providers. You need no special software for the services but you do need a Web browser and their Web addresses, which are: http://www.hotmail.com and http://netaddress.usa.net.

You must have certain equipment to access e-mail: a computer with a 386 or later processor, 16MB (megabytes) of RAM, Windows 3.1 or Windows 95, and a modem with a speed of at least 9.6kbps. Macintosh users need Mac O/S 7.1 or greater and at least 8MB of RAM, but they should have a 68030 or better processor. Right now these are the minimum requirements but, like so much computer-oriented technology, they may change. In the future it may be necessary to use newer computers with Pentium II processors and modems with speeds of 28.8kbps or higher.

Set up your RV office with only the equipment needed for your work. If you have an old computer that's satisfactory for what you do, there's no need to invest in a newer model. And as for the telephone connections, which all of us seem to need once in a while, choose the type that provides you with the greatest convenience while fitting into your budget.

If your traveling business involves a computer and telecommunications, you'll find lots of tips to make your work easier in two books, both written by June Langhoff, *The Business Traveler's Survival Guide: How to Get Work Done While on the Road,* and *Telecom Made Easy.* They may be ordered from the publisher: Aegis Publishing Group, Ltd., 796 Aquidneck Avenue, Newport, Rhode Island 02842; (401) 849-4200 or (800) 828-6961. World Wide Web address: www.aegisbooks.com

CHAPTER 12

Electronic Entertainment and Information

Fulltimers in their RVs can enjoy the same quality of electronic audio and visual programming as they did when living in a fixed dwelling, if they want to. When some people begin fulltiming, however, they want to divorce themselves from the world and what's going on in it. This is their privilege, but any fulltimer who travels at all needs to have some way of receiving reliable weather reports, at the very least.

WEATHER REPORTS AND TRAVEL INFORMATION

The best weather reports, short of those broadcast by the National Oceanographic and Atmospheric Administration (NOAA) on special weather radio stations (see pages 315–316) are on TV. The forecasts usually include detailed statewide coverage and a brief summary of weather throughout the country. A map of the lower forty-eight states is often displayed with visuals depicting storm patterns and the direction in which they are moving, giving you advance information that may affect your travel plans. Radio reports are usually brief, localized, and not of much value to someone who is passing through an area.

We have often put weather information to good use. Once we selected a certain town for a mail drop, not knowing the only campground in town was a very expensive one. Our mail had not arrived when we got to the town so we had no choice but to stay at the campground until it came. On the midday TV news we heard that a major winter storm was headed our way and was expected to reach us the next day. The forecasters weren't sure whether we would receive rain or snow, but warned viewers to be prepared for the worst. We didn't want to spend any more time than necessary in the high-priced campground, as we would have had to do if several inches of snow fell, and we could not go on, since we'd be heading into the storm.

We scouted around and found a mobile-home park twenty miles away with much lower rates. Next day, after we picked up our mail, we hitched up early to make our short run before the weather deteriorated. It had begun to rain lightly as we were getting ready to go. Our neighbor asked us if we knew what the weather was farther north. He couldn't get any weather on his FM radio and, until we told him, knew nothing of the winter-storm watches and warnings in effect.

We were settled in the mobile-home park just as the rain began to fall heavily. We don't know what happened to our fellow traveler, but we heard that more than a foot of snow fell in the area where he was headed.

Another time, within hours of reaching a major city, while listening to the radio as we were driving, we heard that the portion of the interstate on which we would be traveling was closed because of a construction accident and wouldn't be open until late in the day.

Any sort of communications receiver, AM/FM radio, TV, and even a citizen's band radio (CB) can be useful to RVers for receiving weather reports and travel information.

TELEVISION

A TV for your RV can be as large as you wish as long as there is a place to keep it for comfortable, convenient viewing, and a safe place to store it while traveling.

Those who boondock may want a TV that operates on both AC and DC. A color TV operating on 12-volt DC power can draw nearly three times as many amps as a black-and-white TV. If this is a concern, shop around to find a TV with minimum consumption because amperage draw varies from brand to brand. Small TVs, both color and black-and-white, require less 12-volt power to operate than larger ones.

We have a 9-inch color TV and a 5-inch black-and-white TV; both are AC/DC models. The color TV draws 4.75 amps, and although we enjoy color TV, sometimes we don't use it when we're without an electric hookup because of the high-amperage draw; instead we use the black-and-white TV because it draws only 0.78 amp.

Motorhomes factory-equipped with an AC-only TV usually have a small inverter just for the TV so it can be used when on battery power.

A 9-inch TV is the smallest size available with a remote control.

TV Antennas

No matter how good the TV, it won't receive a good picture without a proper antenna. Rarely is the built-in antenna on the TV itself satisfactory.

TV antennas come in several different styles, all of which are one of two types: directional or omnidirectional.

Directional antennas receive stations from only one direction and must be rotated and aimed at each station's antenna. Omnidirectional antennas, which are usually circular or boomerang shaped, receive stations from all directions at the same time. This type is sometimes used on motorhomes so passengers can watch TV while traveling.

The reception from both directional and omnidirectional antennas is good; however, an omnidirectional antenna's range is between 30 and 40 miles, whereas a directional antenna can bring in stations up to 100 miles away.

Traveling fulltimers will find themselves in many different areas where TV reception ranges from excellent to marginal, so a directional, roof-mounted antenna is the best choice.

Figure 12.1 With a coupler-splitter, one antenna can feed two TVs.

Some RVs may have a provision for the TV in only one place, with the antenna wiring routed to the antenna outlet there. If this is not where you want your TV located, or if you want to use it in other locations, proper antenna wiring will have to be routed to each other location for decent reception.

Most newer RVs have 75-ohm coaxial cable installed for TVs and antennas, so when adding to the TV/antenna system, for good reception use the best quality 75-ohm cable.

A coupler-splitter may be useful (Figure 12.1). This device allows one antenna to feed two TVs or two signal sources, such as cable service and an antenna, to one TV.

While traveling, many fulltimers must store their TV in a different place than where it's located for viewing. For connecting and disconnecting, screw-on and push-on F-connectors can be used (Figure 12.2). The push-on type is the easiest to handle and can be put to good use on connections that are disconnected frequently. The screw-on type should be used for more permanent connections.

TV Amplifiers

Most newer RVs have a built-in antenna amplifier (Figure 12.3), but if yours doesn't, one should be installed.

An amplifier greatly increases the signal strength, or gain, of an antenna in receiving the weak signals that exist in fringe areas.

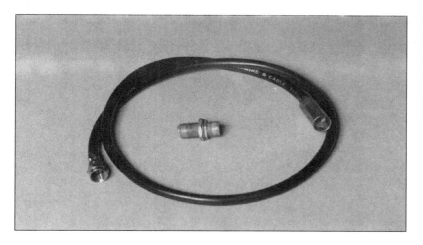

Figure 12.2 A length of coaxial cable is shown with a screw-on F-connector on one end (left) and a push-on F-connector on the other end (right). A barrel connector (center) is used to connect two coaxial cables together.

It's best to have an amplifier with an on-off switch because the amplifier may not be needed when close to a local station; in fact, using an amplifier in this situation may overload the signal and result in poor picture quality.

Some amplifiers have an LED pilot light to let you know when they are on. Since the 12-volt amperage draw is milliamps, it won't have much effect on the batteries if the amplifier were left on all

Figure 12.3 An antenna amplifier improves picture quality in fringe areas. Shown is an amplifier with an on-off switch and a 12-volt receptacle. (Courtesy Winegard Company)

the time; but current flows through the amplifier which, like any-thing electric, can short out, so the amplifier should be turned off when not in use.

Amplifiers are susceptible to static charges from lightning dur-ing electrical storms. In order to avoid damage from lightning, lower the antenna and turn off the TV and amplifier in severe elec-trical storms.

Some TV antennas have a built-in amplifier. It can be protected from damage in electrical storms by installing a switch (if it does-n't have one) on the 12-volt wire that runs to the amplifier so it can be turned off. If the built-in amplifier was damaged, the entire antenna would have to be replaced.

Damage from lightning is quite a common occurrence. It does not have to be a direct hit; the static present in the air from a dis-tant electrical storm is sometimes enough to cause damage.

Cable TV

Many private campgrounds have cable TV hookups for their guests. The fee for this is often included in the overnight rate, or there may be an extra charge of a dollar or two. Most times what you get for your money is real cable TV with a selection of many channels. But in some campgrounds located where TV reception is poor or nonexistent, unless a high antenna is used, the cable may be nothing more than a hookup to the campground's master an-tenna providing the stations the antenna is capable of picking up or the stations subscribed to.

Except for some TVs with screens smaller than 9 inches, all TVs are cable ready or cable compatible. If you want to use one of these small TVs with cable and receive the full range of cable channels, be sure to purchase one designated cable ready (most are now).

When an extension is necessary to reach the campground's cable connection, the extension may be furnished by the camp-ground; you may be asked to leave a deposit if you use it. We carry our own extensions, a 25- and a 45-footer, which can be connected to each other on the rare occasions when one or the other won't reach. They are 75-ohm coaxial cable, so they're compatible with all cable TV connections.

Unless you have a new RV, nearly all of which have a built-in exterior cable connection, you'll have to route the cable through a window, door, or exterior compartment.

Satellite TV

Few products have captured the fancy of RVers like the 18-inch diameter satellite TV dishes. As soon as they were introduced, they sprouted on RVs everywhere. A month after the dishes were on the market, we were in a campground along with twelve RVs equipped with a dish. After quizzing some of the owners about the Direct Satellite System (DSS) and receiving nothing but positive comments, we bought a dish shortly thereafter. If you ask us about our satisfaction with the system, we, too, would have nothing but positive comments. For information about the workings of a satellite system, see Exhibit 12.1.

The cost of satellite systems has been steadily dropping, and now some are no more expensive than a new TV—a few hundred dollars. When you buy a system, you'll get the dish, a receiver, and a remote control. A separate installation kit is offered, but it's for installing the dish on a building and not needed for RV installation.

Because the dish is so portable and easy to set up, fulltimers who return to a home base regularly can use one dish, set it up when they are at the home base, then remove it and take it with them for use on their RV. (In this case, the installation kit may be needed.)

Installing a Satellite TV System

Two basic options exist for installing the satellite dish; it may be portable or permanently mounted, usually on the roof of the RV.

Some RV roof-mounted satellite antennas are automatic. A

12-volt DC motor drive coupled with a controller, or positioner, automatically raises the dish, aims it, and lowers it for traveling.

The most sophisticated, and most expensive, automatic system is designed for motorhomes so passengers may view TV while under way. The dish, enclosed in a fiberglass pod to protect it against wind, can lock on and track the satellite as the motorhome is moving. The manufacturer, Datron/Transco (200 West Los Angeles Avenue, Simi Valley, California 93065; (800) 287-5052 or (805) 584-1717) offers a built-in dish option of Skycell satellite telephone reception, which provides the capability to send and receive faxes, E-mail, and access on-line information services.

Nonautomatic roof-mounted systems are manually controlled units that work in much the same way as does a regular roof-mounted TV antenna: An elevating crank on the ceiling of the RV is turned to raise and lower the dish.

The size of the DSS receiver is too large to fit inside the typical RV cabinet, so a place for it will have to be found where it is well ventilated, and, for convenience, where it can be operated with the remote control.

We built one of our U-shaped shelves to fit over the receiver—allowing room for ventilation—which sits on the console described in Chapter 9, page 230. The TV's location is on the U-shelf, atop a swivel so we can turn it for viewing from nearly anywhere in the trailer (this arrangement is partly visible in Figure 9.9, page 231).

The receiver operates on only 120-volt AC power, so for viewing when you're without an electrical hookup, a generator or inverter must be used. Our receiver is rated at 34 watts or 0.28 amp. When operating on our 600-watt inverter, it draws 3.11 amps.

Aligning the Dish

Aligning the dish with the satellite is not difficult. The procedure varies with the type of mount, but the basics are the same. With our roof mount, we must first use a compass outside the trailer, taking a bearing to find the direction, in degrees, the trailer is headed. Inside the trailer, on the mount, a movable compass ring, marked off in degrees, is adjusted to match the compass bearing.

The next steps are universal for all DSS users: The TV and receiver are turned on and the dish-pointing option selected from the main menu. You have two choices for aligning the dish: your latitude and longitude or your zip code. We always use the zip-code option (since our zip code is always changing, we have purchased a small zip-code directory). Using the number keys on the remote control, the zip code is entered and appears on the screen. The next screen shows the degrees of both the elevation and the azimuth angle (a compass bearing, in degrees, in a clockwise direction from north) to which the dish must be set. For example, with our present zip code of 95360, the elevation is 41 degrees and the azimuth angle 134 degrees.

On our mount and most other nonautomatic mounts, the elevation is adjusted by turning a crank. There is no precise way of knowing where any degree of elevation is, but after adjusting the dish a few times, you'll learn how many turns of the crank put you in the ballpark. We start our elevation adjusting with the dish in its most upright position, so our adjusting is achieved by cranking it down. When you are in the northern states, the elevation needed makes the dish nearly upright, but as you move south you'll find it will become lower, little by little.

To obtain the azimuth angle with our mount, the dish is rotated until a pointer aligns with the azimuth angle (134 degrees in our example) on the compass ring.

Once the dish is adjusted for elevation and azimuth angle, the signal-meter option is selected on the dish-pointing menu. If the dish is not properly aligned with the satellite, a beeping sound is heard; a continuous tone indicates proper alignment. The strength of the signal is shown on the TV screen. Fine tuning, by turning the dish slightly, can achieve maximum signal strength.

Correcting improper alignment is done by moving the dish slightly to one side, and, if the signal still isn't received, then moving it slightly to the other side. Sometimes the elevation may also need minor adjustment. It takes only a few setups to get the hang of positioning the dish. We can usually align it in a couple of minutes.

Portable mounts may be either ready-made or homemade. Some of the manufactured portable mounts are tripods; others are clamps designed to hold the dish to a roof ladder. A portable unit by Winegard includes the dish fastened to a wide, circular base containing a built-in compass and level (Figure 12.4).

We have seen many homemade mounts in a variety of designs, some ingenious, some simple, depending on the inventiveness and needs of the owner. The simplest arrangement of all is just to attach the dish to a picnic table with a C-clamp.

> *It takes only a few setups to get the hang of positioning the dish. We can usually align it in a couple of minutes.*

Figure 12.4 This portable satellite dish has a level and compass incorporated into the base. (Courtesy Winegard Company)

If your dish is portable without any built-in features on the mount, you'll find it useful to have a good compass—the type used by hikers—a torpedo level, and a hand-held signal-strength meter (some RV-supply stores carry these meters). The compass is used to determine the azimuth angle for aiming the dish. The level is needed to make sure the post on which the dish is mounted is exactly vertical to the ground in all directions. Since you'll be working outside when setting up the dish where you may not be able to see the TV or hear the beeping and continuous tone, the signal-strength meter serves to indicate when the dish is aligned with the satellite.

The coaxial cable used for DSS installations must be the RG-6 type instead of the more commonly used RG-59, which has too much signal loss for the weak satellite signals. For the best reception, you may find it necessary to do some rewiring in your RV.

Selecting a Satellite System and Obtaining the Service

Judging from the dishes we see, the type we have, the direct satellite system (DSS), is the most popular with RVers although two other systems with small dishes are available: Primestar and the Dish Network. We know of no mounts, portable or permanent, for RV application with the Dish Network or Primestar dishes.

All you need to do to obtain satellite service is to call the company of the system you select, choose the package you want, and provide a billing address.

DSS receivers are designed to be connected to a telephone line so users can have the convenience of remote-control selection of pay-per-view movies and sports events. If you don't have an installed telephone line, you can have the same services, but you must go to a telephone to order your selections from the provider, sometimes at higher cost. Without a telephone connection, you will be denied access to NFL football and other sports packages because of blackout requirements.

The broadcast times on the program menu is set for the time zone of your billing address. As you travel you'll have to calculate when programs are broadcast in your area.

DSS programming is available from DirecTV and USSB (U.S. Satellite Broadcasting); Primestar and The Dish Network each has its own programming. We selected DirecTV because of its wide variety: fifteen channels devoted exclusively to movies from the 1930s to the present; thirty-nine channels for news, information, and variety; numerous channels for sports; and thirty audio-only channels providing just about any type of music you can think of. USSB programming includes eighteen channels, mainly with movies from the 1980s to the present, and four variety channels. You can subscribe to either DirecTV or USSB, or both.

At this time you can't receive local stations from a satellite system. For the times when we want national news but are out of the range of stations we can pick up with our regular TV antenna, we subscribe to an extra low-cost package that gives us ABC, CBS,

NBC, Fox, and PBS, each broadcasting from different places around the country—PBS comes from Denver, for example.

You can select what you wish to view from the on-screen menu, but we find it much easier to use the *Satellite Direct* guide. This magazine contains all the listings for both DirecTV and USSB. It's available by subscription, or it can be purchased from many places where magazines are sold. At first, we had a subscription but often we were without the current month's issue until our mail caught up with us. Even though it's slightly more expensive, we now buy a copy each month. We often find the guide in supermarkets and Wal-Marts.

Problems with a Satellite System

The problems with a satellite system are few and mainly caused by the weather. Wind can shake or vibrate the dish enough to cause temporary breakup of the signal. Depending on the dish's orientation, steady strong winds may cause so much interference the picture disappears. Tripod-mounted dishes seem to be less affected by wind than a roof-mounted dish, perhaps because it's lower down and may be sheltered by the RV, or a building.

Heavy rain and snow causes the signal to be lost, as does a buildup of snow on the dish. If the RV is in the path of microwave transmissions from telephone or television towers or near motors or electrical equipment that can cause interference (your own microwave oven, perhaps), a poor picture may result.

In order to acquire a strong signal, you must have direct line-of-sight to the satellite. If buildings, leaf-covered trees, or nearby high ground are in the path of the satellite, no signal can be received. With a portable dish, you may be able to move it to a position nearby where the signal can be received; if it's roof-mounted, this may not be possible.

Once, when we planned a week's stay at a certain wooded campground, we set up the dish before we unhitched because we suspected we would have a problem getting the satellite signal. We moved the trailer—just slightly—three times before we got the dish out of the way of the trees. Although we're pretty good at sizing up sites as to their signal availability, we'd have fewer problems and find more suitable sites if we had a portable dish.

Satellite TV offers superior reception when compared to both cable and reception with a regular antenna. The images are always sharp, there are no color shifts between channels, no snow, and no ghosts.

VCRs AND VCPs

A welcome adjunct to an RV's TV system may be a videocassette recorder (VCR), or a unit without the recording capability, a videocassette player (VCP).

VCRs are available only in 120-volt AC models, but VCPs operate on both AC and 12-volt DC power. On 12-volt operation, a VCP draws little amperage. VCRs are usually too large to fit in typical RV cabinets, but the generally smaller VCPs might fit.

In our installation, the VCP is wired to a coaxial switch installed in the cable between the roof antenna and the TV so we can either switch to the antenna for TV viewing or the VCP. Most VCRs have a coaxial jack on the back for connecting the TV antenna to the recorder, thereby routing the signal from the antenna though the VCR, eliminating the need for a switch. If the antenna is connected to the VCR, it can be damaged along with the TV during electrical storms.

On some RVs, mostly motorhomes, a VCR is offered as a built-in option. It's usually placed in a cabinet on either side of a built-in TV or in the same cabinet as the TV. Having a VCR built in and factory installed eliminates any concerns about where to install one yourself.

Some small TVs have a built-in VCR or VCP and may be AC/DC models. These compact, combination units are usually lightweight enough to be easily lifted from a counter for storage on the floor during travel.

STEREOS AND AUDIO PLAYERS

Automotive stereos and small stereos specifically designed for RV use (usually installed by the RV manufacturer) are the types most commonly found in RVs. They often include a cassette or compact disc (CD) player. The stereo itself may be an option, but many RVs come equipped with the wiring for a stereo, an external antenna, and maybe two or four speakers.

If good sound reproduction is important to you, particular attention should be paid to the brand of stereo offered by the manufacturer; sometimes they aren't top-quality units and, if offered as optional equipment, it may be better to purchase your own. If speakers are included as standard items, they too may be unsuitable for good reproduction. We replaced all four of our standard speakers with better-quality speakers.

An RV's metal outer skin or metal frame acts as a shield against radio waves, so an external antenna is needed for optimum radio reception. An external antenna provides good local reception on AM and FM and some distance reception on FM, particularly if the radio has a built-in distance amplifier.

Automotive stereos, which are small and operate on 12-volt DC power, are ideal for RV use. Unless the RV has a solid-state charger with a built-in electromagnetic interference (EMI), or hum, filter, the 12-volt connections should be made directly to the battery, bypassing the fuse panel, twisting the two wires as they are run. Many chargers lack a filtering system and cause a hum in the radio, especially on the AM frequencies.

Portable AM/FM stereo-cassette or CD players with speakers attached have a built-in antenna, so poor reception results in fringe areas when used inside the RV.

The amperage of 12-volt automotive stereo-cassette and CD players ranges from about ½-amp to as much as 8 amps on some of the high-wattage units. The amperage draw increases in proportion to volume increases. An equalizer with a booster can add as much as 6 amps more. When you're without shore power, merely listening to the radio or playing cassettes or CDs can cause quite a drain on the battery, which can be a problem in motorhomes where the stereo is often wired to the starting battery instead of the house batteries. We have met several motorhomers who haven't considered this, and found themselves without engine starting power.

The latest wrinkle in automotive stereos is satellite reception. The digital audio radio service (DARS) uses two GEO satellites (see Exhibit 11.3, page 293) to broadcast signals and provides fifty channels of CD-quality music, news, weather, and sports programming. The antenna is the size of a silver dollar and can be mounted on the windshield or rear window.

Special DARS radios are available as well as a conversion adapter that's inserted into an existing car stereo's cassette or CD player; no wiring is necessary. The stereo can be used for local programming simply by removing the adapter. The monthly cost for the service is about $10. The radios and adapters are available from some large electronic-appliance stores.

HAM RADIOS

Full-timing hams can easily use and store their equipment in an RV because most ham radio equipment operates from either built-in batteries or a 12-volt DC power supply and takes up little space. The necessary special antennas can be permanently installed, or extremely long antennas can be set up for use, then dismantled and stored on the roof of the RV or in another convenient place for travel.

Hams can communicate with each other over vast distances with their equipment—even around the world, and ham radios can be linked to computers and other sophisticated equipment.

To become a ham-radio operator requires special training and licensing, but acquiring the skills and knowledge needed are within the capabilities of nearly everyone. Knowledge of Morse code was once a requirement for all classes of ham licenses, but now a technician license class exists that does not require code.

If you are interested in learning more about ham radio, contact any ham operator or the American Radio Relay League, Incorporated, 225 Main Street, Newington, Connecticut 06111. Books on ham radio are available at Radio Shack and electronic-supply stores.

Bill communicates on the two-meter band with other hams as we travel around the country. Using a network of two-meter wavelength repeaters, he has talked to other hams over 200 miles away. Networks of these repeaters are linked together across the country. Because the high wattage of ham transceivers reaches far beyond the range of cellular phones, a two-meter transceiver can sometimes be useful in an emergency.

By participating in various networks, or nets, ham radio operators can enjoy long-range, direct communications with other operators who have similar interests.

RVing hams may wish to check out the Good Sam RV Radio Net and the Wally Byam Caravan Club International RV Service Net. See Exhibit 12.2 for broadcast schedules and frequencies.

WEATHER AND CB RADIOS

A weather radio that receives nothing but the aforementioned NOAA broadcasts is useful, but it can't pick up the signal from the transmitter when the station is more than fifty miles away. Weather radio reception is better in nonmountainous areas because of the nature of the VHF radio waves, which are line of sight.

NOAA broadcasts also can be received on scanner radios that receive a variety of other broadcasts, such as police, fire, marine, and aircraft communications. A scanner requires a special external antenna for RV use.

A CB radio can be a comfort and convenience for traveling full-timers. With a CB you can ask for and receive information about road conditions from your fellow travelers. When you're on the road, other CBers can alert you to problems with your rig you may not be aware of: perhaps a tire going flat, or a raised TV antenna, or smoke or water coming from under your RV. Most RVers use Channel 13 for communicating from rig to rig; truckers use Channel 19 (see Exhibit 12.2).

One of a CB's important uses is for obtaining help in an emergency. The highway patrol monitors Channel 9 for this purpose. A CB also is handy when traveling in a group or caravan for communicating among the RVs.

Many portable CBs simply plug into a cigarette-lighter socket. An antenna with a magnetic base can be set on the roof of a vehicle's cab and removed for safekeeping, or the antenna and the CB can be permanently mounted. No special license is needed to operate a CB.

USEFUL COMPUTER PROGRAMS FOR TRAVELERS

Instead of collecting maps and poring over them to find the best routes for trips, you may want to let your computer do your planning. Travel planning software (we use Rand McNally's Tripmaker and Streetfinder) provides you with detailed itineraries and large- and small-scale maps of your route. A typical itinerary contains all the highway numbers on the route, mileage and traveling time for each leg, direction of travel, and can include, among other things, fuel consumption, refueling stops, and how much your fuel expenditure will be.

EXHIBIT 12.2

Ham Radio Networks

Days	Area	Times/Zones	Frequencies
Wally Byam Caravan Club International RV Service Net			
Daily	Eastern and Central U.S. and Canada	7–9 AM/ET*	7.233.3 MHz
Mon.–Fri.	U.S., Canada, and Mexico	Noon–1 PM/ET	14.308.0 MHz
Mon.–Fri.	U.S., Canada, and Mexico	5–6 PM/ET	14.308.0 MHz
Mon.–Fri.	Central U.S.	5–5:30 PM/CT*	3.918.0 MHz
Mon.–Fri.	Rocky Mountain	6–8 AM/MT*	7.263.0 MHz
Mon.–Fri.	Pacific Coast	8–10 AM/PT*	7.268.5 MHz
Good Sam RV Radio Net			
Mon.–Fri.	U.S., Canada, and Mexico	7 PM/CT	7.284 MHz
Mon. & Thu.	U.S., Canada, and Mexico	8 AM/CT	7.123.0 MHz
Sat.-Sun.	U.S., Canada, and Mexico	7 PM/CT	7.284 MHz

*ET: Eastern Time Zone; CT: Central Time Zone; MT: Mountain Time Zone; PT: Pacific Time Zone.

As far as we know, no software of this type contains an extensive campground database, but some programs may include campgrounds in state and national parks.

If your travel destinations include cities, you may find a city-map program useful. It provides a map of the city with a route of the best way to get to the desired address. Certain programs even show detailed images of buildings along the streets.

Some programs include a global positioning system (GPS) receiver that plugs into a notebook computer and displays a city map showing the exact position of your vehicle as you travel through the streets.

Similar systems that display data on a small, computer-like screen installed on the dashboard of a vehicle are available. Some high-end motorhomes are equipped with this on-board navigation system.

For those who do much traveling on interstates, aids such as the Road Whiz Ultra Interstate Travel Guide and the Otis RV Navigator may be useful. These hand-held units provide all sorts of information of interest to travelers, such as mileage to and locations of services including campgrounds. The information is displayed on a tiny screen above a small keyboard. These units are available at some RV-supply stores.

CHAPTER 13

Electricity and Electrical Equipment

The pleasures, comforts, and conveniences of an RV would not exist without electricity, so from the fulltimer's point of view, the RV's electrical systems are most important.

In fixed dwellings the power is there when needed, and using it rarely involves anything more complicated than turning on a switch or plugging in an appliance. But the power for an RV can't exist unless the occupant sees to it that it's operative. Since most RV systems depend on electricity for their operation, RVers should have a basic understanding of how an RV's electrical systems work. Often the quality of electric service depends greatly on how fulltimers use their electrical systems, whether in a campground with an electrical hookup or in a primitive campground with no hookups. The safety of your RV and its occupants is also affected by how electricity is treated.

RV electrical systems aren't complicated. Merely understanding how they function will enable you to solve many simple problems, should they arise.

All modern RVs have a 120-volt alternating current (AC) electrical system—the standard type found in fixed dwellings—and a 12-volt direct current (DC) system. The 120-volt AC system receives its power from a campground hookup or other external source, which is called shore power. The 12-volt DC system is powered by the RV's batteries.

THE 120-VOLT AC SYSTEM

A modern RV's 120-volt AC system consists of an external power cable, a master switch, a switch/circuit breaker for each circuit, several 120-volt AC wall receptacles, and a built-in battery charger (some manufacturers call this a power converter and in older units this was known as a converter/charger). The charger performs two functions: It converts 120-volt AC current to 12-volt DC power, and it supplies a charge to the batteries, if needed.

The AC electricity can be used to run most RV refrigerators and this system is needed for the operation of air conditioners and other 120-volt AC equipment, such as TVs, toasters, coffeemakers, microwave ovens, and electric heaters.

120-Volt AC Electric Accessories

Figure 13.1 Three different types of 15-amp male/ 30-amp female adapters

Adapters and Extension Cords

Some extra accessories are needed in order to use an RV's 120-volt AC system with the various outlets found in campgrounds across the country. Most of the accessories aren't expensive. Used RVs may already have much of the equipment.

Most RVs are equipped with a three-prong, 30-amp plug on the external 120-volt AC power cable, but not all campgrounds have outlets to accommodate this plug; some have only 15-amp service (it may be mistakenly called 20-amp service). For this, a 15-amp male/30-amp female adapter is needed (Figure 13.1).

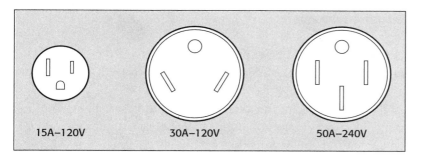

Figure 13.2 These are the three most common receptacles found in campground electric boxes. A box may contain one, two, or, sometimes, all three receptacles.

15A–120V

30A–120V

50A–240V

Some motorhomes and large fifth-wheel trailers have 4-prong, 50-amp plugs. Other adapters are needed to connect such units to 15- and 30-amp outlets. Fifty-amp service is 240-volts AC instead of 120-volts and consists of two separate 120-volt circuits. Adapters used with these plugs combine the two 120-volt circuits into one 120-volt circuit, so when an adapter is used, this single circuit should not be overloaded. In Figure 13.2 the three types of the most common campground outlet configurations are shown.

A heavy-duty extension cord designated 10/3 (containing three 10-gauge wires) in a 25- or 50-foot length should be part of your electrical equipment. Such cords are available with either 30- or 15-amp connectors.

When a 15-amp extension is used in a 30-amp outlet, a 30-amp male/15-amp female adapter is needed (Figure 13.3).

A 10/3 extension is needed to avoid voltage drop in case the extension is used when running high-wattage appliances such as an air conditioner and an electric heater, although some loss in voltage occurs when long extensions are used no matter what the wire gauge. The longer the extension, the greater the drop; however, less voltage drop occurs with a heavy-gauge wire than with a light-gauge wire of the same length. For this reason, never use an extension cord unless absolutely necessary and, if you have extension cords in various lengths, use the shortest one possible.

Figure 13.3 A 30-amp male/15-amp female adapter is needed for some hookups.

Circuit Analyzers

Figure 13.4 A circuit analyzer is used to check the wiring in electric circuits. Two different models are shown.

No fulltimer should be without a circuit analyzer (Figure 13.4) so campground electric outlets can be checked to see if they are suitable for use.

When plugged in, the analyzer's three indicator lights are illuminated in various combinations that show either a proper circuit, any of several aberrations that may be in the circuit, or, when no indicators are lit, no power. An explanation of the light combinations is on the analyzer housing.

After plugging the RV's shore-power cable into a 120-volt AC outlet, check the electric service with the circuit analyzer by plugging it into a 120-volt receptacle in the RV. (We plug our analyzer into a receptacle on the underside of a galley cabinet; in this location we can see it through the galley window and can check it without going inside. When we are getting ready to leave a campground, we plug in the analyzer so it's in place, ready for use, when we arrive at the next campground.) The analyzer can be plugged directly into the campground's electrical outlet prior to connecting the shore-power cable. In the shore-power-cable compartment, we have an extra analyzer we use for this if we suspect there is no electricity at a site.

Analyzers have a 15-amp male-prong configuration so a 30-amp male/15-amp female adapter is needed for checking 30-amp outlets. An analyzer, even with adapters, isn't useful for checking a 50-amp outlet because it carries 240-volt service. To check 50-amp outlets, put the analyzer in the RV's interior receptacles. Try the analyzer in several receptacles to be sure you are getting a reading of both the 120-volt circuits in the 240-volt system.

After the analyzer is plugged in, note which of the analyzer's three lights are on, and check them against the explanation on the analyzer housing. Most times, no problem exists (see warning). If there is a problem, you should report it to the campground manager and move to another site.

Sometimes we arrive at a campground and find no one on duty; at one, we stayed for a week and never saw the manager or owner. In such situations, if the analyzer shows either reversed polarity or an ungrounded outlet, and for some reason we don't want to move to another site, or another site isn't available, we have devised ways to correct these two situations.

Correcting Reversed Polarity   While a reversed polarity condition can't hurt you physically, it can cause damage to electrical equipment such as TVs, VCRs, and computers. That's why one prong of the two-prong plugs on some electrical equipment is wider or has a flared end; the plug can be inserted in only one way thus assuring the proper polarity. This plug affords no protection if reversed polarity exists in the circuit, however.

Reversed polarity usually occurs with 15-amp outlets that are incorrectly wired. It can be corrected on such outlets simply by turning over a two-prong plug and reinserting it so the prongs are opposite the way they were before. This can't be done with a 15-amp male/30-amp female adapter because the 15-amp end of the adapter has a grounding pin in addition to the two prongs (the grounding pin on some of the adapters can be seen in Figure 13.1, page 320). The plug can't be reversed because, in the upside down position, there is no hole to accommodate the grounding pin.

To achieve the configuration allowing the plug to be reversed, a grounding adapter, a two-prong-to-three-prong type with a grounding tab must be used (Figure 13.5). (If the two-prong side of the adapter is polarized, that is, one of the prongs being wider than the other, the wide prong can be filed down so it can be turned over and inserted.) When a grounding adapter is used, the plug has no grounding provision, so a ground wire should be attached to the plug and fastened to something metal that provides a ground, such as a water faucet, the metal conduit from the outlet box, or the box itself. Whatever is used for a ground must be metal and be set into the earth.

Figure 13.5 A two-prong-to-three-prong grounding adapter is seen here.

Figure 13.6 A grounding adapter modified to include a ground wire.

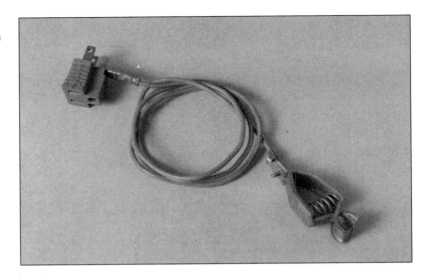

We modified a grounding adapter to include a ground wire (Figure 13.6). On one end of a 3-foot length of 12-gauge wire is a ¼-inch, female, crimp-type connector, which is attached to the grounding tab on the adapter. On the other end of the wire is an alligator clip, which makes it easy to attach the wire to a pipe or outlet box.

Reversed polarity doesn't often occur in a 30-amp outlet, but if it does, the following sequence of adapters achieves the proper polarity: A 30-amp male/15-amp female adapter in the outlet with the grounding adapter plugged into the 15-amp end of the adapter, and, plugged into the grounding adapter, a 15-amp male/30-amp female adapter to which the shore-power cable is connected.

Once all the corrections for reversed polarity have been made, check again with the circuit analyzer to make sure the circuit is now correct.

Correcting Ungrounded Circuits The danger to you with an ungrounded circuit is if you happened to be using a piece of electrical equipment with a metal case and a short occurred. You could

get a shock from touching the metal. Because of this, all circuits should be grounded, if possible.

When we encounter an ungrounded 15-amp outlet, we use our modified grounding adapter but, not needing to reverse the polarity, insert the adapter in the normal manner and hook up the ground wire as described previously.

For 30-amp, ungrounded outlets, which are also rather uncommon, we use a slightly different grounding wire. It, too, has an alligator clip on one end but on the other end is a crimp-type, ¼-inch ring connector. The opening in the connector slips over the grounding pin of the 30-amp plug (Figure 13.7).

Achieving a ground by attaching a ground wire is easy, but it's not an ideal ground; it merely affords some degree of protection, and it's better than no ground at all.

AC Voltmeters

It's useful to know and monitor how much voltage is received from a campground electrical hookup. Voltage can be easily checked with a plug-in, 120-volt voltmeter, or a panel voltmeter (Figure 13.8) can

Figure 13.8 A voltmeter, either the plug-in type or a panel meter (above) should be used to monitor voltage.

be installed in the RV. A voltmeter can also be used to check voltage from other AC sources such as a generator and inverter.

It's amazing how often campground voltage is less than satisfactory. Low voltage can cause certain electrical equipment to overheat, and it can harm or result in the malfunctioning of some equipment, especially electronic items such as microwave ovens, TVs, and computers, and the compressor in older air conditioners. None of this equipment should be operated on less than 100 volts. If some high-amperage electrical equipment is used in a low-voltage situation, keep in mind that it lowers the voltage even more.

We once noticed the picture on our TV was shrinking in size. A check of the AC voltage with a voltmeter indicated the trailer was receiving only 90 volts. On many other occasions we have noticed the lights seemed dimmer than usual. When this happens, a voltage check usually shows the voltage is low. This situation occurs when the charger isn't getting enough voltage to operate properly, and the lights are running off the RV's batteries instead of the charger.

In many campgrounds low voltage occurs when too many RVers are using too much electric equipment at the same time, especially air conditioners and electric heaters. Often when this occurs it's because the campground is inadequately wired. When a notice is posted at a campground that no air conditioners or heaters are allowed, it's usually because the wiring won't stand such loads.

If a campground has old or inadequate wiring, a campsite at the far end of a campground or on the end of a row of sites may have the lowest voltage. It's important to be aware of this if a long-term stay is planned at such a campground.

AC Power Indicator

When we are plugged into shore power we want to know when we are, or are not, receiving power. We use a tiny neon nightlight for this—the type with the light incorporated into the plug casing, not the type with a replaceable bulb. The one we use is made by GE, model number GE#E3960-02D.

The nightlight is kept permanently plugged into a receptacle visible from all parts of the trailer. A glance at the light lets us know whether the 120-volt power is on or off. If it flickers, it's an indication that the voltage is low.

Surge Protectors

Electronic equipment is very sensitive to voltage surges (spikes). Surges can originate from the local power plant and also be generated by electric storms when lightning strikes power lines. To guard against spikes, a surge protector can be used. The unit senses a momentary voltage overload in the circuit and either absorbs the extra voltage or burns out, much in the same way a fuse does. Many surge protectors have one or two lights that indicate the unit is functioning properly and that a good ground is present; surge protectors afford no protection when used on an ungrounded circuit.

We have installed surge protectors on our microwave oven and

TV receptacles and on the receptacles where we use our computer equipment. The surge protector we purchased for the TV is a special type that not only protects against spikes in the AC power line but grounds the coaxial antenna cable as well.

While surge protectors are not lightning arresters, they offer some protection from lightning. Before we used surge protectors we once had a blown picture tube on our TV from a nearby lightning strike and, on another occasion, burned out an antenna amplifier during an electrical storm.

Usually the price of a surge protector indicates its quality; the higher-priced units offer the best protection. For computers, purchase a protector with a clamping voltage as low as 140 volts.

One type of surge protector is designed to be used in the campground outlet; the shore-power cable is plugged into the protector. Another type is a surge arrester, which is wired into the AC system of some high-end RVs.

Ground Fault Circuit Interrupters

A ground fault circuit interrupter (GFCI) is a device incorporated into a 120-volt AC outlet to prevent electrical shock. It senses when an unsafe condition is present and deactivates the outlet so no current flows through it. It's reactivated by a reset button or switch. Most newer RVs have a GFCI in a bathroom outlet and, perhaps, in the galley, and may have another on the patio outlet. If your RV has no GFCI outlets, or you want to install additional GFCIs, it is simple to do; the only tool needed is a screwdriver. A GFCI is incorporated into some of the surge protectors for use in campground outlets.

GFCIs can create some interesting situations. On our 23-foot trailer, the bathroom outlet, which was a GFCI type, was wired into the same circuit as the outside patio outlet. Bill found that he could not use his electric razor in the bathroom outlet as long as it was raining heavily outside.

Lately we have encountered a more universal problem with GFCIs. The electrical code in some states requires that GFCIs be installed in the electric outlets in campgrounds.

After having a problem with the GFCI tripping as soon as we plugged in at many different campgrounds, we finally figured out what causes this to happen. We have a transfer switch that automatically switches over to inverter power when shore-power isn't being used. During this switchover, the two contacts on the relay don't make contact at exactly the same instant and therefore cause the GFCI to trip.

We have since found that many RVers are having the same problem, especially motorhomers who, if they have a generator, have a switch between it and the shore-power. But a built-in charger with a switch can trip a GFCI, and even a circuit analyzer plugged into an outlet is sometimes enough to make a GFCI trip.

In discussions with numerous campground managers we've been asked if we knew a way to overcome the problem. There is a way, but it involves defeating the purpose for which the GFCI was installed. A GFCI can properly perform its function only if there is a good ground connection between an RV and the site's electrical outlet. Remove the ground and the GFCI won't trip.

The ground can be eliminated by using the grounding adapter mentioned before; the attached ground wire is not used in this application. With a 30-amp outlet, plug a 30-amp male/15-amp female adapter into the outlet, and to this, plug in the grounding adapter in the normal manner. Attach a 15-amp male/30-amp female adapter to the plug of the shore-power cable, and plug it into the grounding adapter. Always check this arrangement with a circuit analyzer to be sure that in eliminating the ground, you haven't created a reverse polarity situation.

A question may come to your mind: Since the GFCI was installed for my protection, isn't it dangerous to defeat it? It's no more dangerous than it is to use an AC generator or an inverter when you're boondocking. What type of ground do you have then? Without an electrical hookup, the only ground is provided by the

> **"A** GFCI can properly perform its function only if there is a good ground connection between an RV and the site's electrical outlet.**"**

ground wire in an RV's AC system that is attached to the chassis of the RV. When you use the grounding adapter to defeat the ground in the site's electrical hookup, even though you're hooked up, the chassis becomes the ground.

Wait a minute. Didn't you just say that with an ungrounded outlet a ground connection should be established? Yes, we did. But if you encounter this particular situation, you'll have to decide if you want to have electricity, which is included in the fee you paid for the campsite, or do without.

GFCIs are being installed in campground outlets to protect tenters who may use electrical appliances when it's damp or rainy. This is fine for tenters, who don't have GFCI-equipped tents, but not for RVers who are site occupants by a large majority. In our opinion, GFCIs do not belong on campground outlets, except, perhaps, in a special section set aside exclusively for tenters. The only logical place for GFCIs is in, or on, the RV where they can do some good yet not cause problems.

Amp Ratings and Overloaded Circuits

Many RVers have a cavalier attitude about using a campground electrical hookup; it's there to be used so they plug in and think no more about it until a problem develops. Many don't realize that, unlike a house which has many circuits, a 15- or 30-amp campground electrical hookup is just one circuit; consequently, many RVers' electrical problems stem from overloading this one circuit. Such problems can be avoided if amperage is considered when using an electric hookup.

The amp rating of an electrical connector (a plug and the wire it is joined to) designates the maximum amount of amps (current) it is designed to carry. For example, no more than a 30-amp load should be put on a 30-amp connector, and a 15-amp connector should never carry more than 15 amps. Incidentally, these ratings are for intermittent use; neither connector should carry a constant load of the full 15 or 30 amps. The full load should be used for only short intervals.

To determine the total number of amps being used, the amperage rating of electrical equipment must be known. The wattage or amperage rating is imprinted on most electric equipment and appliances. If only the wattage is listed, the amperage can be calculated by dividing the wattage by the voltage. For example, a 900-watt toaster has a rating of 7.5 amps: 900 divided by 120 (volts) equals 7.5.

Using Table 13.1, some quick mental calculation proves, for example, that a microwave oven, an electric heater, and a hair dryer can't all be running at the same time on one 15-amp circuit. The least that will happen is that the circuit breaker will trip, or if

TABLE 13.1
Common Wattage and Amperage of Selected AC RV Appliances

Item	Watts	Amps
Color TV, 9-inch	60	0.50
Color TV, 13-inch	70	0.58
Satellite receiver, 18-inch dish	34	0.30
Refrigerator, automatic electric/gas (running on 120 volts)	300	2.50
Built-in charger, 45-amp	620	5.17
Coffee maker	900	7.50
Microwave oven, 450-watt*	960	8.00
Microwave oven, 750-watt*	1,500	12.50
Hair dryer	1,200	10.00
Electric heater	1,500	12.50
Air conditioner, 13,500 Btu	1,630	13.60
Computer, desktop	100	0.83
Computer, notebook (operating with AC adapter)	90	0.75
Printer	240	2.00
VCR	90	0.75
Vacuum cleaner, hand-type	240	2.00
Drill, ⅜-inch	350	2.91

*Given wattage of microwaves is cooking wattage only; in operation wattage increases to about twice the amount of given wattage: 450 watts = 960 watts or 8 amps; 750 watts = 1,500 watts or 12.5 amps.

fused, the fuse will blow. The worst circumstance would be that the connector or outlet would char or melt, ruining one or the other or both. For safety's sake, some simple calculating should always be done to avoid overloading your campground outlet.

One winter in a campground in Oregon, we were in a site next to another fulltimer who overloaded a circuit and ended up with an extension cord burned through in two places. He was using a single, interior-type, 16-gauge (rated at 10 amps), two-wire extension cord to run two, 1,500-watt (12.5-amp) electric heaters. We found out later he had also burned out the electric meter and had to pay for its replacement.

We buy electric heaters rated at either a maximum of 1,200 watts (10 amps) or that have a 1,200-watt setting. This wattage provides plenty of heat and allows for the use of a TV and other low-wattage equipment at the same time the heater is being used on a 15-amp circuit.

THE 12-VOLT DC SYSTEM

The 12-volt DC system, the primary electrical system in modern RVs, consists of the batteries that are used to power the interior and exterior lights, the water pump, the furnace, and a fuse panel or circuit-breaker panel.

Some RVs are equipped with refrigerators that can be operated on 12-volt current, and may have certain other items, such as a built-in stereo, that run off the 12-volt system.

With the installation of 12-volt outlets, an AC/DC TV and other 12-volt appliances and equipment—VCRs, fans, vacuum cleaners, soldering irons, and even certain computers—can be operated from the RV's batteries.

On travel trailers the batteries are often mounted on the A-frame or in a compartment at the front of the trailer. Fifth-wheel trailers usually have the batteries installed under the gooseneck or in a side compartment which should be, but may not be, near the front of the trailer.

Motorhomes generally have one or two batteries for starting the engine and for other automotive functions and a separate house battery or a bank of two or more house batteries.

Familiarize yourself with the fuse panel in your RV. If each circuit is not identified as to what it services, you may want to label them yourself. Pull one fuse (or switch off one circuit breaker), then turn on all lights and try the water pump and other 12-volt accessories. Anything that does not work is on that circuit. Repeat the process for each circuit.

If your RV has a fuse panel, always keep a supply of spare fuses on hand.

Battery Types

Motorhomes have two types of batteries: the deep-cycle type for house use and another known as the SLI (for starting, lights, ignition) type for automotive functions; trailers have only house batteries.

SLI batteries, usually the type that require no maintenance, are effective only when constantly kept in a fully charged condition, as they are by the alternator when the engine is running. SLI batteries should not be used as house batteries because they are not designed to have a large percentage of their capacity drained before they are recharged.

A deep-cycle battery is the only type suitable for RV house use. Before purchasing any battery, check to see that it is specifically labeled for RV use or for RV/marine use. Although most deep-cycle batteries are the wet-cell type, which require periodic addition of water, some deep-cycle batteries are the no-maintenance type.

We recently replaced our wet-cell, deep-cycle batteries with gel-cell batteries. This type of battery is sealed, doesn't require ventilation or maintenance, and is superior to other deep-cycle batteries when it comes to the charging capabilities. They are supposed to last longer (some manufacturers claim a ten-year longevity), but we don't know about that yet since we have had ours for only four years. We hope the claims are true, because gel-cell batteries cost about three times as much as other types.

If your fulltiming includes staying at primitive campgrounds and camping in other places without an electrical hookup, your RV should be equipped with at least two batteries, but if you plan on staying only in places with an electrical hookup it's possible to get by with just one.

Battery Sizes

Popular RV battery sizes are shown in Table 13.2. Although Group 22 batteries are available, this classification has been omitted because they haven't a large enough capacity for practical boondocking. Higher-rated batteries than the ones shown can be purchased, but, because of their physical size, it may not be possible to install them in some RVs. Six-volt golf-cart batteries are one type of higher-rated, larger-sized batteries. These batteries in the 220-

TABLE 13.2
RV Battery Sizes

Group	Cold-cranking Amp Averages	Reserve Capacity Averages (minutes)	Amp-hour Averages
4D*	775–1314	250–285	150–190
8D*	920–1050	350–430	221
24*	500–520	120–130	70–85
27*	570–635	150–165	90–110
29	675		110–117
GC-2**	575–1150	345–350	208–225
T-105***	no rating	419	217
T-125***	no rating	477	235

  *Gel-cell batteries also available in this size
  **6-volt batteries
***6-volt batteries made by Trojan

amp-hour size are usually the same size as a Group 24 battery except for being about two inches taller.

Usually the A-frame-mounted battery tray on a travel trailer accommodates only two Group 24 batteries, but the tray can be modified to hold two of the slightly larger Group 27 batteries.

Batteries carry a rating for their cold-cranking amps, which relates to the battery's ability to start an engine at a certain ambient temperature. For house batteries this is a useless rating. In order to purchase a proper house battery, some indication of the amp-hour (Ah) rating or the reserve capacity is needed. Each house battery in a two-battery bank should have a reserve capacity of at least 120 to 130 minutes, or 75 amp-hours. Amp-hour ratings are based on the so-called 20-hour rate: A battery is discharged at a specific amp rate that allows the voltage to drop to 10.5 volts in 20 hours. For example, a battery discharged at a rate of 5 amps for 20 hours is a 100-amp-hour battery.

If the reserve capacity of a battery is known but the amp-hour rating is not, this rating can be roughly calculated by multiplying the reserve capacity figure by a factor of 0.63.

Table 13.3 shows how many hours a typical battery will operate under different amp loads. The figures in the table indicate the useful life of a battery under a constant load, but in most normal use, loads are applied intermittently rather than constantly so both batteries listed would last longer than indicated. Note how rapidly battery capacity diminishes as the load increases.

TABLE 13.3
Rates of Battery Discharge to 50% of Capacity*

Group	2.5 Amp load	5.0 Amp load	10.0 Amp load	15.0 Amp load
24	17.0 hr	7.25 hr	3.1 hr	1.9 hr
27	21.0	9.00	3.9	2.4

*Discharge under a constant load

As a battery is discharged, the voltage decreases. When the voltage drops to 11.8 volts, much electrical equipment will cease to operate. Many batteries, when discharged to below 50 percent of capacity, reach this voltage.

Ideally, all batteries in a bank should be of the same size and age and from the same manufacturer.

Battery Maintenance

To achieve the best service from batteries, keep the terminals clean and, if the wet-cell type, see that the water is at the proper level. A little petroleum jelly or dielectric tune-up grease (available at auto-parts stores) on the terminals helps prevent corrosion.

If corrosion should occur, it can be dissolved with a baking-soda solution. Put a teaspoon of baking soda into a 3½-ounce paper cup and fill the cup with water. Bend the edge of the cup to form a V-shaped spout and the solution can be poured directly onto the terminal. Keep the cell caps on while cleaning the terminals so none of the soda solution can get into the cells.

Only distilled water should be used when adding fluid to the cells. When we had wet-cell batteries, we always kept a container of this water on hand in case we needed it when we were far from where it could be obtained.

Battery Discharging and Recharging

Determining the Rate of Discharge

When an RV is operating on its 12-volt DC system, it's useful to know how much 12-volt equipment can be used, and how much the batteries will be discharged by using such equipment. This can be calculated by adding together the amp rating of each electrical item used, then multiplying this total by the number of hours each will be run in a given period.

Table 13.4 includes examples of the hourly amperage draw of common 12-volt DC items. During an evening an average full-timer may use two lights continuously for four hours and the color TV for three hours, resulting in a total of 21.6 amp-hours:

Two lights @ 1.2 amps = 2.4 amps × 4 hours =   9.6 Ah
One color TV @ 4 amps × 3 hours =   12.0 Ah
                                        Total 21.6 Ah

The water pump, which is used to supply water to the faucets and for toilet flushing, would most likely be used at times during the evening. The water pump draws 8 amps if it runs continuously for an hour, but it's not used continuously, so the cumulative number of amps used is generally small. Another 2 amp-hours may be added to allow for water pump usage and other lights that may be used intermittently, bringing the evening's total usage to 23.6 amp-hours.

To carry this example further: If the batteries are discharged 23.6 amp-hours in an evening's use, 28.3 amp-hours—1.2 amps for every amp-hour used—must be restored to the batteries to recharge them. The more a battery is discharged, the longer it takes to recharge it. Lengthy recharge times may be impractical for those who camp for extended periods without an electrical hookup. To avoid a long charging time, it's advantageous to recharge the batteries often and as quickly as possible.

In the preceding example, if the battery bank's total capacity is

TABLE 13.4
Typical Hourly Amperage Draw of 12-Volt DC RV Equipment

Item	Amps
TV, color, 9-inch	4.0
TV, black and white, 9-inch	1.5 to 2
TV, black and white (late model), 5-inch	0.8
Light, incandescent ceiling	1.2
Light, single fluorescent	0.7
Furnace, 31,000 Btu	8.2

150 amp-hours (two 75-amp-hour batteries wired in parallel), only 15 percent of the batteries' capacity would have been used. If you had one battery of a 55-amp-hour capacity, the usage would have depleted that battery's capacity by 42.9 percent. Having large-capacity batteries allows you to live comfortably for longer periods of time before recharging is needed.

The foregoing recharging rates and amperage-draw calculations are theoretical because many factors—battery age, ambient temperature, and others—make it impossible to calculate the recharging time or discharge level accurately.

To be on the safe side, batteries should be discharged no more than 50 percent of their rated capacity, even though some batteries, in certain circumstances, can be discharged to 60 to 80 percent of their rated capacities.

Phantom Loads

The amperage draw of the so-called "phantom" loads existing in many RVs must be included in any battery discharge calculations. Many RVers are unaware of phantom loads because some are concealed, or they are simply overlooked as a source of amperage draw.

Phantom loads are present in illuminated switches, built-in monitoring meters, clocks, the memory in stereos (which requires power even when the unit is turned off), gas detectors, motion lights, and the refrigerator if it's an automatic model. The electronic brain of our automatic refrigerator consumes .74 amp per hour of 12-volt DC power whether it's running on 120-volt AC or on propane. The clock and memory of our stereo and gas detector each require about .025 amp per hour. These phantom loads add up to 0.79 amp per hour or a whopping 18.96 amp-hours per day. We have known of RVers who have left their rigs without an electrical hookup for a day or two and returned to find their batteries dead because of the continual amperage draw of phantom loads.

Battery Charging

As long as house batteries can be kept charged, fulltimers are free to go anywhere they want and enjoy all the comforts and conveniences of home without having to depend on an electrical hookup. Lots of fulltimers want to go off into the wilds and camp but are apprehensive about doing so. What holds them back, usually, is the concern about keeping their RV's house batteries charged during a period of boondock camping.

Nowadays there are plenty of efficient ways to recharge batteries, and, if an RV is properly equipped, there need be no worries about camping without hookups. We truly enjoy this sort of camping; cutting the umbilical cords of hookups seems to impart a greater sense of full-timing freedom. We like the feeling of being miles away from towns, traffic, and crowds in a primitive camping place, yet being able to have all the modern conveniences.

Principles of Battery Charging

To have a satisfactory battery-charging system, the principles of battery charging should be understood. Some people mistakenly believe that amperage is what charges a battery, and the higher the amperage the better. It's true that high amperage charges a battery more rapidly than low amperage, but amperage determines the speed at which the batteries charge; it's the voltage that actually charges a battery. (All methods of charging have a limit as to the amount of amps at which they can charge, hence the reference to amperage in the ratings of chargers.)

When a discharged battery is connected to a voltage source with a voltage higher than the voltage of the battery, current (amperage) flows from the higher voltage to the lower voltage. The greater the difference in voltage, the faster the current flows. This can be likened to water in a pipe, flowing downhill from a high container to a lower container; the higher the hill, the faster the flow.

A fully charged battery at rest (with no load on it) should have a reading of 12.7 volts, and a discharged battery, 11.8 volts. You'll notice the difference between being fully charged and discharged is not much—only 0.9 volt.

Most battery chargers provide between 13.5 and 14.5 volts to effect a charge. This voltage, being higher than the voltage of a fully-charged battery, allows current to flow to the battery and thereby recharges it.

A fast charge can be obtained from a charging source that puts out from 14.0 to 14.5 volts. A voltage of 13.3 to 13.8 volts is considered to be a slow charging rate or a trickle charge on the lower side.

As mentioned earlier, the greater the difference in voltage between the charging source and the battery, the faster the current flows into the battery. But during the charging process, the difference in voltage between the charging source and the battery is constantly decreasing and, as a result, the charging rate continually slows.

Battery-Charging Methods

At present, there are two methods for charging batteries, the so-called "tapered" charging and multistage charging.

Tapered charging has been in use for years. With this method, a constant voltage is used to achieve charging. As a battery is discharged, its voltage drops to the level of the discharged battery's capacity. For example, if a battery is discharged to 12.3 volts and the charger voltage is 14.4 volts, a large amount of current will flow, up to the maximum output of the charger. As the battery voltage rises, the charger delivers less current to the battery. When the battery reaches the charge voltage, the battery is considered to be charged. While this method is a good one, and recommended by battery manufacturers, it takes many hours for recharging.

Multistage charging is a newer, more efficient method of charging. The first stage of the two-stage charging cycle uses a constant amperage output that doesn't taper off until the battery voltage reaches the charger voltage; then the second stage kicks in and the voltage is allowed to remain constant and the amperage tapers off, as it does in the tapered system.

Here's a comparison of the two methods: If a 30-amp tapered charger is used, the charger delivers 30 amps for a short time, perhaps for about ten or fifteen minutes, until the battery's voltage starts to rise, at which time the amperage rapidly drops to about 10 amps. The amperage continues to drop until, after several hours, the battery reaches a full charge. By contrast, a multistage charger delivers the full 30 amps of the charge until the voltage reaches the charge level, then tops off the battery with the second stage until the battery is fully charged. Obviously, applying a constant 30 amps for an hour or more charges faster than applying 30 amps for fifteen minutes or so.

Measuring Battery Charge

Table 13.5 shows the different levels of battery charge as measured by two different methods. The old and still preferred method is to use a hydrometer to determine the amount of sulfuric acid in the electrolyte liquid in the battery. This provides a reading of the specific gravity of the solution.

Another, easier method is to use a good-quality digital multimeter or a voltmeter (discussed on pages 353–356), which indicates the state of charge by reading the voltage of the battery.

Alternators and Alternator Charging

When moving on after camping without hookups, the engine alternator (which uses the tapered charging method) in a motorhome or a tow vehicle acts as a battery charger for the house batteries. The primary function of an engine alternator, however, is to charge the SLI battery. This is what an alternator is designed

TABLE 13.5
State of Charge of Battery By Specific Gravity and Voltage

State-of-Charge Percentage	Battery Voltage	Specific Gravity
100	12.7	1.27
75	12.5	1.25
50	12.3	1.19
25	12.1	1.15
Discharged	11.8	1.12

to do, and it performs this operation efficiently; when the engine is started, the alternator puts out a voltage high enough to quickly recharge the battery.

But with deep-cycle house batteries, which may be discharged as much as 50 percent after a night's usage, most original-equipment alternators with their tapered-charging method take six hours or more for recharging, and even this may not be enough to bring the batteries to full strength. The reason for this is because, as the voltage of the battery increases during charging, the amperage flow from the alternator decreases until it reaches about 5 amps or so. At this rate it can take many hours of charging to bring batteries to 100 percent of capacity.

The use of 12-volt DC equipment such as an automotive air conditioner and headlights during travel increases charging time because some of the current flow, which would otherwise go to the batteries, is diverted to the 12-volt equipment.

The charging rate is directly affected by the engine's rpm so running at a higher speed charges batteries more quickly than when the engine is at idle speed.

If you have a motorhome with an automatic energy selecting (AES), or three-way, refrigerator (this type isn't installed in trailers), and you intend to operate it on 12-volt DC power while traveling, you may need to install a high-output alternator. Operating on 12 volts, the refrigerator draws as much as 25 to 30 amps and an original-equipment alternator may not provide enough current to run the refrigerator along with other equipment.

Installing Adequate Wiring

Motorhomes are wired at the factory and have the equipment for battery charging built in. But the trailer dealer is often the one who installs the tow vehicle's house-battery charging wiring.

Motorhomes are generally wired to automotive standards so the wiring should be adequate. But trailer owners have to be responsible for seeing to it that suitable wiring is installed on their rig; dealers or service technicians may not do it on their own. It costs a little more to have the proper gauge wire used in battery-charging installations but it's worth it.

Wire gauges are designated by number. The higher numbers denote the lightest wire: 8-gauge wire is heavier than 14-gauge wire, for instance. The lighter the wire and the longer its run, the more the voltage drops. If voltage drops too much in a charging line, the batteries won't charge at all.

The run from the alternator to the trailer electrical connector cable (our own abbreviation for this is TECC) outlet is long enough so that wire no lighter than 8-gauge should ever be used. Any lighter-gauge wire won't provide adequate battery charging.

Table 13.6 shows how wire size and length affect charging. The voltage drop is figured for 25 feet, which is about the distance from the alternator in a full-size, standard cab, pickup-truck tow vehicle to trailer batteries located at the front of a trailer. Wire size should also be determined by the size of the alternator. For example, a 120-amp alternator should be wired with a minimum of 4-gauge wire for a run of 10 feet or under. Longer runs require 2-gauge wire. Table 13.7 lists the "ampacity" (current-carrying capacity expressed in amps) of different wire sizes.

TABLE 13.6
Voltage Drop for Different Wire Sizes and Charging Rates

Alternator Charge Rate (in amps)	Wire Size Gauge (AWG)*	Voltage Drop over 25 Feet (volts)	Voltage Loss Effect at Alternator Maximum Charge Rate of 14.5 Volts** (volts)
20	14	1.28	13.21***
	12	0.80	13.69
	10	0.50	13.99
	8	0.32	14.17
	6	0.20	14.29
	4	0.12	14.37
30	14	1.93	12.56***
	12	1.21	13.28***
	10	0.76	13.73
	8	0.48	14.01
	6	0.30	14.19
	4	0.18	14.49
50	14	3.21	11.28***
	12	2.02	12.47***
	10	1.27	13.22***
	8	0.80	13.70
	6	0.50	13.99
	4	0.31	14.18
75	8	1.20	13.30***
	6	0.75	13.75
	4	0.47	14.03
	2	0.29	14.21
	1	0.23	14.27
100	6	1.00	13.50***
	4	0.63	13.87
	2	0.39	14.11
	1	0.31	14.18
	0	0.25	14.25
125	4	0.79	13.70
	2	0.50	14.00
	1	0.40	14.10
	0	0.31	14.18

*American Wire Gauge
**Alternator output may vary.
***Insufficient voltage for fast battery charging

If the house batteries in a motorhome are in the engine compartment, therefore close to the alternator, alternator-to-battery voltage drop is not critical, but if the house batteries are in another location, voltage drop must be a consideration.

Service personnel at RV dealers, auto-parts store clerks, and auto mechanics can't always be relied upon to give good wiring advice. Once when we were trying to purchase some 8-gauge wire, an RV service manager said we didn't need such heavy wire; any size would charge the battery.

When we bought our 23-foot trailer the dealer installed the necessary wiring, and used 14-gauge wire. With the engine running and the TECC hooked up, the 65-amp alternator in our then tow vehicle delivered only 13.5 volts at the trailer batteries, which provided a charging rate of a mere 7 to 10 amps. After a short while, we replaced the inadequate wire with heavier 8-gauge wire and doubled the charging rate—an improvement but not entirely satisfactory because the full alternator voltage wasn't being delivered to the battery.

Eventually we upgraded again and now we have a 4-gauge charging line. With the 125-amp alternator in our present truck, full alternator voltage is received at the batteries and charging time is reduced significantly.

The charge line is made of twin-wire welding cable with plug-in connectors for the hookup between the trailer and the truck. It's long enough so it can be plugged in without the trailer being hitched up. It's installed so that the original charge line is bypassed, but it has been left in place so when we are driving with the batteries fully charged, they will remain topped off.

Changing to heavy-gauge wiring will be in vain if the ground connections between the trailer and tow vehicle are poor. They must be the equivalent of the same wiring that's installed on the positive side of the battery. Often these ground connections are inadequately wired or ignored. On many rigs, the chassis provides the ground, or return negative side, of the system, but don't rely on

TABLE 13.7
"Ampacity" of Different Wire Sizes*

Wire size (AWG)**	Amperage Capacity
18	6
16	8
14	15
12	20
10	30
8	55
6	75
4	95
2	130
1	150
0	170

*For general reference only
**American Wire Gauge

a chassis ground; instead run a separate ground wire to the truck's battery ground or the starter ground.

Isolators

An isolator electrically separates the SLI battery from the house batteries and prevents the SLI battery from being discharged along with the house batteries, thus eliminating the possibility of not having enough power left to start the engine. An isolator also facilitates proper charging of dissimilar batteries. For instance, the engine and coach batteries are usually dissimilar in size, type, capacity, and each accepts a charge differently.

Because both the engine and house batteries in a motorhome are connected together in a common system, most motorhomes are equipped with an isolator unless they have a dual-output alternator, in which case an isolator is not necessary.

Tow vehicles are usually disconnected from trailers when the rig is parked so the battery systems are separated. As long as the rig is disconnected, there's no danger of engine batteries becoming discharged so an isolator is not really necessary, but those without an isolator in the tow vehicle should make sure the TECC is disconnected when parked for overnight or longer.

Isolators are available in different amperage sizes. The isolator should be a higher amp rating than the alternator; for example, a 120-amp alternator should be coupled with a 150-amp isolator.

Other Methods of Battery Charging

When without an electrical hookup, aside from the alternator, RV batteries can be charged by a built-in or portable generator, and by solar panels. When electricity is available, the built-in charger takes care of keeping the battery charged, and a portable, automotive-type battery charger can also be used.

Built-in Chargers

A built-in charger changes the 120-volt AC power from an electrical hookup into a 12-volt DC power source. When using shore power, all the RV's 12-volt equipment can be used without discharging the batteries. If the batteries are down for any reason, the charger recharges them.

Older chargers with an output of around 13.5 volts are primarily for providing 12-volt power. Their battery-charging capabilities are limited because they charge at a rate of only 5 to 7 amps. At this low rate, if you have been without an electric hookup for two or three days and the batteries are considerably discharged, it takes many hours for a recharge.

Recent developments in charger design have resulted in both ta-

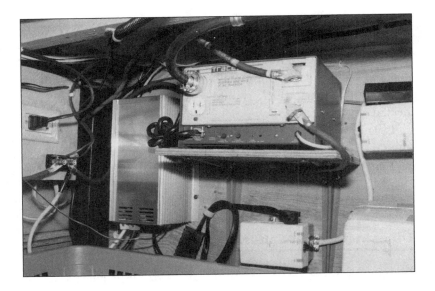

Figure 13.9 The authors' 45-amp charger (left) and 600-watt inverter (right). The two small white boxes are circuit breakers.

pered- and multistage charging units that operate at 14.0 to 14.5 volts and charge at a 40- to 75- amp rate, and these can be found in many newer RVs (Figure 13.9).

Generators

Many motorhomes are equipped with a built-in generator and larger trailers often have a special compartment where a generator can be installed. If no compartment is large enough or otherwise unsuitable for adding a generator, a portable generator can be used. Generators have outputs ranging from 400 watts to 17,000 watts, and are powered by either gasoline, diesel fuel, or propane.

The main purpose of a generator is to provide 120-volt AC power, but many generators have a DC outlet that can be used for charging batteries. The charging rate of most of these generators is only 7 to 10 amps. This is not nearly enough for practical charging, but if the generator's 120-volt output is utilized with a high-amperage built-in charger, faster, more efficient charging can take place. A generator with a wattage that's too low, however, can't be used in this manner; it must have a high enough rating to handle the amperage load of the charger on a continuous, not intermittent, basis. For this application, portable generators should have at least a 1,000-watt rating.

Solar Panels

One of the best methods of battery charging is with solar panels. A solar panel's photovoltaic cells collect light from the sun and convert it into electrical energy. This charging process is a good one and the only fuel needed is sunlight, and it's free.

Solar panels are available in a variety of sizes ranging from small, one panel, low-voltage, trickle-charge units that deliver 0.2 amp at full power to large 120-watt panels that charge at 7.5 amps maximum. The small, self-regulated (unadjustable) panels usually deliver enough amperage to compensate for the battery drain of phantom loads when the RV is left unattended for a length of time, but this type of panel cannot be used for recharging deep-cycle batteries. For this, larger panels are needed along with a regulator so the charging process can be controlled.

We installed solar panels to improve our charging system so we could boondock-camp for longer periods. While our efforts to upgrade our alternator charging paid off, we were still plagued with not being able to fully charge the batteries from the alternator without running the engine for four or five hours (which we never did, by the way—we were careful not to discharge the batteries too much).

We first installed a solar system composed of two 48-watt panels and a regulator, and later added another panel of the same size for a total of 144 watts. Under ideal conditions, the three panels charge about 9 amps at a 14-volt rate until the batteries reach full-charge voltage. Then the regulator shuts off the current flow until the battery voltage drops to 13.2 volts, when it again allows current to flow.

This is the ideal way to charge batteries—at a constant full amperage until the batteries are fully charged. (For our gel-cell batteries the set-point on the regulator is 14 volts, but it can be set to 14.5 volts for wet-cell batteries.)

It takes little light for the panels to start charging. In the morning, with the sun just barely over the horizon, the panels begin charging at an amp or so. The charging rate increases as the sun rises toward its zenith. Even on cloudy days the panels charge at a reasonable rate. A big advantage of solar charging is that during the day, amps drawn from the battery for normal usage are replaced almost instantly, so these amps don't have to be replaced later as would be necessary with other methods of charging.

One of the best features of solar charging is that it's quiet. We, and our camping neighbors, if any, aren't bothered by the noise of a generator or an engine running when the batteries are being charged.

Another good feature is that a solar system requires hardly any maintenance. Once the system is installed, the maintenance consists of wiping dust from the panels or cleaning them with window cleaner when they are dirty.

Selecting and Installing a Solar System To find out how many panels you need, simply add together the amp draw of all 12-volt items that would ordinarily be used in an average twenty-four-hour period (see Table 13.4, page 337, for the amp draw of some common 12-volt items). The total amp draw indicates how many panels are needed to restore what has been drawn from the batteries. For example, a 33-cell, 48-watt panel charges about 15 amps in the winter with full sunlight and 24 amps in the summer because of the longer days. A good rule of thumb is to figure one 48-watt panel for each 105 amp-hours in the system, or one watt of panel output for every two amp-hours of battery capacity.

Installing panels on most RVs is easy. Each panel is mounted on the RV's roof with eight screws (Figure 13.10). Our greatest concern with the installation was that a hole might need to be drilled

Figure 13.10 Seen here is the authors' solar-panel installation with wiring routed through a holding-tank vent. Not shown is a recently-added third panel, placed at a 90-degree angle to the other panels and to the right of the roof vent (lower left.).

in the roof in order to route the two-conductor wire to the regulator. This proved not to be a problem because we were able to use an existing hole in the roof; the wires were fed down a nearby holding-tank vent pipe. Inside the trailer, a hole was drilled in the vent pipe just below the ceiling. The wires were pulled though, connected to the regulator—which had been previously installed, then another pair of wires was routed to the batteries. The complete installation took about two hours.

A holding-tank vent pipe was the best wire access for our installation, but a refrigerator roof vent may also be used as an alternative to drilling a hole in the roof.

Solar-Panel Regulators We opted for a regulator with a two-scale meter that gives both the battery voltage (its condition) and the amp-charging rate (Figure 13.11). The regulator has a blocking diode to prevent reverse current flow; a phenomenon that occurs when panels draw current from the batteries after dark. The regulator has adjustable set-points for both the high and low voltages so the panels can be adjusted to turn on or off at any desired voltage level.

As a safety precaution, we installed a 25-amp fuse in the positive wire going to the battery.

Figure 13.11 The authors' solar panel regulator is mounted so it can be easily monitored. (Underneath the regulator is a remote switch for the inverter.)

Our regulator model has a separate terminal for a trickle charge line that can be used on motorhomes for topping off the engine-starting battery.

An RVer we know put his solar panels to use in an unusual way when the alternator belt in his motorhome broke while on a trip. He used his solar panels to generate the electricity needed to run the engine, and he was able to drive home and make the repair.

For detailed information about solar systems consult *RVer's Guide to Solar Battery Charging* by Noel and Barbara Kirkby. It may be ordered from RV Solar Electric, 14415 North 73rd Street, Scottsdale, Arizona 85260; (602) 443-8520 or (800) 999-8520.

Battery Conservation

When relying on an RV's 12-volt DC system for electricity, battery conservation should be paramount. No lights should be on unless they are being used and, if possible, limit usage to one or two lights at a time. Turning off the TV unless someone is watching it, using exterior lights only as long as needed, and giving up long, leisurely showers are additional ways to conserve battery power.

Another way we conserve power is to reduce phantom loads. We have installed a switch on our stereo to turn off the power to the clock and the pre-set button memory. We have two TVs and sometimes use the 12-volt DC black-and-white model when on battery power; it draws less than half the amps of the AC/DC color TV when used in the DC mode.

Monitoring and Measuring Equipment

Those who boondock need an accurate method of checking the state of charge in the batteries, and in any camping situation a way of monitoring and checking out the electrical systems is useful. This can be done with simple multimeters, sophisticated panel meters, and monitor panels.

Multimeters

A multimeter is a most versatile instrument for checking batteries as well as for troubleshooting AC and DC electrical systems and equipment. A simple, analog, needle-type multimeter incorporating all the functions needed by the average RVer can be purchased for less than $20. Sophisticated, digital multimeters with many functions are considerably more expensive (Figure 13.12).

Multimeters are easy to use but, unfortunately, there seems to be no simple way for the beginner to learn to use one. Instructions for multimeters aren't usually basic enough for beginners and many are poorly written and organized.

We use a multimeter as a backup for our other meters on both 12-volt DC and 120-volt AC electrical systems, especially when checking voltage. We have made special test leads with 12- volt and 120-volt plugs for convenient, safe use. By using a multimeter,

Figure 13.12 A multimeter with a digital readout provides the most accurate measurements.

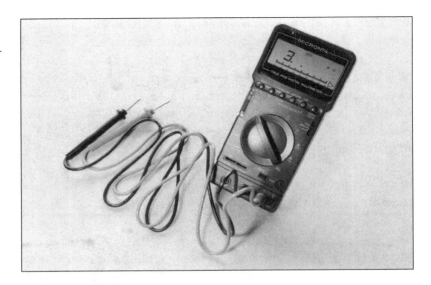

we've been able to save time and money by locating and solving electrical problems that otherwise may have needed the attention of an outside service person.

Analog multimeters are good for checking AC voltage and troubleshooting campground outlets. They can be used to check the presence of DC voltage, but the scale is not expanded enough for accurate battery monitoring.

Digital multimeters provide highly accurate readings of both AC and DC voltages and can be read from an AC or DC outlet or directly from the battery.

Monitor Panels and Battery Meters

An RV's built-in monitor panel usually includes a battery-condition meter on which the level of charge is indicated by a simple meter with no markings or a series of three or four lights; either type is worthless and should not be relied on.

A voltmeter is much better for monitoring batteries and, for this purpose, is the minimum equipment you should have. A voltmeter can indicate the battery state-of-charge, problems with the charging system, and problems that may be developing with the battery.

A panel voltmeter can be installed or a good quality multimeter can be used as a portable voltmeter. Either should be the digital type with a readout to two decimal places if possible, but you may be able to find a panel voltmeter with one decimal place only; two-decimal place multimeters are common. The reason for needing a two-decimal-place meter is because of the difference between a fully charged battery and a completely discharged battery being 0.9 volts. A two-decimal-place readout provides 90 measuring increments whereas a one-decimal-point readout has only 9 increments. An instrument with more increments indicates faster up and down changes in voltage, thereby providing the most information and more accurately measures the higher voltage used when charging.

For more accuracy when reading battery voltage, always read the voltage after the battery has rested for at least fifteen minutes with no discharge or charge applied.

Some high-end RVs may have a factory-installed battery-monitoring system. If you don't have this in your unit, you can install your own system as we did.

Just after we purchased our fifth-wheel trailer, we installed a monitor panel that incorporates a voltmeter and also has a provision for two separate current measurements. It's wired so different functions can be monitored individually. We can check on the amperage draw of the inverter as well as any item of 12-volt equipment in the RV's system. A readout of the charging rate can be obtained for all charging systems: built-in charger, inverter in its battery-charging mode, solar panels, and the tow vehicle's alternator when the TECC is connected and the engine is running.

We recently added an amp-hour meter to our monitoring system (had this type of meter been available years ago, we might have installed it and not the monitor panel). This meter shows how many amp-hours have been consumed since the batteries were last charged. This function is very useful when boondocking. At a glance we can check how many amp-hours the batteries are down—and modify our usage if necessary—and during charging,

> **"F**or more accuracy when reading battery voltage, always read the voltage after the battery has rested for at least fifteen minutes . . .**"**

Figure 13.13 From left to right, the authors' amp-hour meter showing the batteries have been discharged 13.4 amp-hours, a switch for changing from the inverter to the charger, and a monitor panel showing the batteries are being charged at 28.5 amps. The switch is on the inverter setting so the charger of the inverter is doing the charging. (The previously-described voltmeter is underneath.)

when the batteries are completely recharged. The meter also includes an ammeter for measuring loads and charging and a two-decimal-place voltmeter for checking battery voltage. Among many other features it also lets us know how many hours the batteries will last at the present rate of discharge and records the deepest depth of discharge the batteries have experienced.

All our monitoring equipment is installed on the side of the vanity in the bath (Figure 13.13). Here they are unobtrusive yet easy to see, and it's a short run for the wiring to the batteries.

12-Volt DC Outlets

Cigarette-lighter plugs and sockets are what the RV industry uses as 12-volt electrical connections. We have never liked these connectors because after some use, they often don't make good contact. Our first 12-volt TV, equipped with a such a plug, required a delicate touch and much fiddling to coax it into working. Aside from being inefficient, we think these lighter sockets are unsightly and the plugs are cumbersome, unwieldy, and always in the way when storing the 12-volt item. But most important, we think they are a potential safety hazard. A child may be curious about the large opening on the socket and stick something into it. If anything metal were inserted into the socket, an arc can occur when the center contact is shorted out to the sides of the socket. The metal can become red-hot instantly and cause a severe burn to the hand holding it.

We ceased using cigarette-lighter connectors for our 12-volt items after our experience with that first TV and switched to connectors that look like a smaller version of the standard 120-volt AC outlets and two-prong plugs (Figure 13.14). They are unobtrusive and small enough to be installed nearly anywhere (Figure 13.15). Most large electronic-supply stores carry this type of connector.

Figure 13.14 The authors use these 12-volt plugs and outlets to replace cigarette-lighter installations.

The connectors are rated at 7.5 amps, which is adequate for most 12-volt items. The plugs have one prong larger than the other for proper polarization, an important feature because many DC items won't work unless the polarity is correct.

Replacing the lighter plug with the two-prong plug is easy. Sim-

Figure 13.15 A 12-volt outlet has been installed next to a 120-volt outlet in the bath of the authors' trailer.

ply cut off the lighter plug and solder on the other, but before making the cut, determine which of the 12-volt item's wires is attached to the spring-loaded pin of the lighter plug. This is the positive wire and it must be soldered to the wide prong of the two-prong plug.

Any 12-volt item that has a fuse incorporated into its lighter plug can be converted to the two-prong connector by wiring a fuse holder in the positive wire at the plug.

120-Volt AC Power Without a Hookup

Both generators and inverters provide 120-volt AC power. A generator operates on fuel, just like an automotive engine, but an inverter uses the house batteries to power it.

AC Generators

A generator is the most common provider of 120-volt AC power when an RV is not hooked up to shore power. Aside from charging the batteries as previously discussed, generators of the proper wattage can be used independently of shore power to operate just about any 120-volt AC electric item such as microwave ovens, TVs, electric tools and appliances, and air conditioners.

Large generators are designed for heavy loads, such as air conditioners and it's not cost-effective to use them for light loads, such as a TV, or intermittent loads such as an electric drill. When operating, generators deliver their full wattage rating, and, with a light load, little power is used for the fuel expended. The life of the generator will be prolonged if it's used to carry proper loads.

One of the biggest drawbacks of a generator is the noise it creates when it is running. Some campgrounds, even some with no hookups, have regulations prohibiting generator use or restrictions on the times a generator may be used. A generator can also add hundreds of pounds to an RV's weight.

If a portable gasoline generator is used and extra fuel is carried for it, it must be kept in an approved container. State laws vary as to the type of containers that can be used, and some states require gasoline containers to be carried outside the vehicle.

The nuisance of carrying extra fuel for a generator can be eliminated with a propane generator; this type can be connected to the RV's existing propane system.

Inverters

An inverter converts 12-volt DC battery power into 120-volt AC power. It uses battery power to do so—a good deal of battery power. Even so, with judicious usage, inverters can be a valuable accessory for the fulltimer. Unlike a generator, an operating inverter is completely silent.

Inverters are best used for short term, 120-volt AC convenience loads, such as running appliances and electric tools that aren't normally run for long periods. Long-term operation can seriously deplete the batteries.

A simple type of inverter produces unregulated AC voltage and can be used to run motors such as those on electric drills and shavers. The voltage can vary and become excessively high so they should not be used for electronic equipment such as TVs and VCRs unless the inverter has a frequency control, which is found on some models. When operating, simple inverters draw the full amperage load at which they are rated, thus creating considerable drain on the batteries.

Solid-state inverters are the most efficient of all and have many built-in automatic features that protect against overload, overheating, and low battery voltage, any of which will shut down the unit. Unlike other inverters that operate at maximum power at all times, solid-state inverters have a search mode so the current and voltage are shut down until a load is on line, then the unit is activated and delivers just enough current to run the item being used.

A rough estimate of battery consumption is: For every amp of AC power produced, 10 amps will be drawn from the battery. To calculate the amperage draw, divide the wattage of the item to be used by 12, and multiply the result by the amount of time used, converting the time into the decimal equivalent of an hour. As an example, we'll use a 1,200-watt appliance: 1,200 (watts) divided by 12 equals 100 (the amp draw if used for one hour). We're going to use the appliance for only fifteen minutes, or 0.25 of an hour: 0.25 multiplied by 100 equals 25, so 25 amp-hours would be used. For a more accurate calculation, multiply the amp-hours (25) by an efficiency factor of 1.1 because inverters operate at about only 90 percent efficiency. This brings the total amp-draw to 27.5 amps.

In the search mode, solid-state inverters can remain on continuously providing constant AC power availability, because in this mode they draw only a minuscule .022 to .06 amp (.5 to 1.5 amp-hours in twenty-four hours). Remote-control switches are available so the inverter can be turned on and off from a convenient location.

Some inverter models have a built-in battery charger with ranges from 25 to 100 amps, along with a transfer switch (relay), so if AC power fails or is turned off, the inverter switches to battery power automatically. When shore power returns, the inverter switches off and the battery charger begins to recharge the batteries.

Considerable rewiring of the RV's AC system may be necessary for this transfer-switch utilization. The inverter must be wired into the RV's system between the shore-power line and the main circuit-breaker panel. The air conditioner, an AC water heater, and other high-amperage items should be removed from the system and provided with their own circuit-breaker panel because running such items from an inverter is impractical. Figure 13.16 is a schematic for such an installation according to manufacturers' recommendations.

Because we wanted a 120-volt AC power source when boondocking, mainly for our printer (the computers can operate on internal batteries or from a 12-volt DC source), we purchased a solid-state inverter when we got our solar panels. Since these inverters are available in 200- to 3,000-watt models, we had to determine the size we needed. The amperage of the printer is low enough for a 200-watter to easily handle, but we figured as long as we were going to buy and install an inverter, it might as well be of a size suitable for running many of our other 120-volt items so we could use them while boondocking.

We made our selection based on the amperages for the AC equipment we intended to use and purchased a 600-watt model with a built-in 25-amp battery charger. This is an ideal wattage for our battery bank of two Group 27 105-amp-hour batteries (higher-wattage inverters require more batteries with higher amp-hour ratings). Being small and lightweight, it was much easier to install than a higher-wattage unit. The inverter installation is shown in Figure 13.9 on page 348.

The 600-watt unit has proven to be more than adequate. About the only equipment we have that can't be run from it is the air

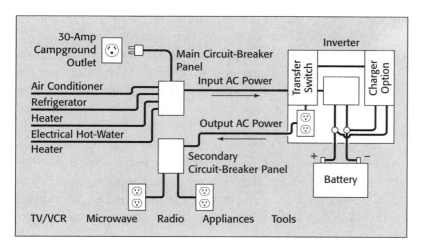

Figure 13.16 A wiring diagram for transfer-switch utilization as recommended by inverter manufacturers.

conditioner and an electric heater. We can't use our 450-watt microwave oven for long when boondocking, but we can use it for about a minute or two without any problem.

An Inverter Wiring Plan We devised a wiring scheme that allowed us to install the inverter so that the built-in transfer switch is not used, but so the inverter still functions automatically when it is turned on (Figure 13.17).

A 30-amp, AC, double-pole, double-throw relay is installed in the shore-power line before the circuit-breaker panel. One input comes from the shore-power line and the other from the inverter's AC outlet. The output is connected to the circuit-breaker panel. The exciter-coil circuit comes from the shore-power side. With this wiring arrangement, when we want to use the inverter, we make sure the air conditioner is off at the main breaker panel, and we set the refrigerator to operate on propane.

When the shore power is off, the relay automatically switches to the incoming inverter current. It's not necessary to physically plug in the inverter.

If an inverter has its battery charger or a built-in charger plugged into the AC line when the inverter is in operation, the inverter will burn out. To prevent this from happening by accident, we installed a special AC circuit with an outlet for plugging in either the built-in charger or the inverter's battery-charger. This circuit is wired into the shore-power cable ahead of the relay. When current comes through the power cable, the current reaches the charging equipment, and when the power is off, the charging equipment is automatically disconnected. The circuit is protected by its own 15-amp circuit breaker.

For safety's sake, it's a good idea to install a fuse in the 12-volt DC positive cable from the inverter to the battery. We use a 100-amp fuse, which is the right size to protect our inverter (Figure 13.18), and another fuse of 100 amps or more on the ground side of the 12-volt system where the batteries are connected to the chassis (Figure 13.19).

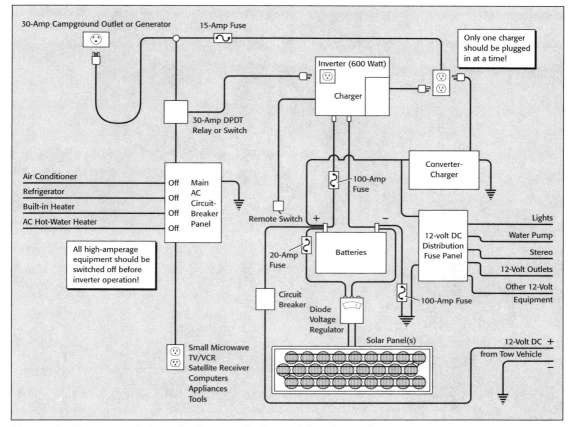

Figure 13.17 The authors' wiring plan bypasses the inverter's built-in transfer switch but still allows the inverter to function automatically.

We use the inverter more than we ever expected. It works efficiently with the printer, because, in the search mode, it draws no appreciable amperage except when the printer is actually in use. Once when we were without an electrical hookup, we discovered a bolt had sheared off on the trailer's front jacks. The only way to repair it was to drill out the broken bolt. It was easy to do using an electric drill powered by the inverter.

An inverter and a solar system are good partners. When we stop

Figure 13.18 To protect the authors' inverter circuit, a 100-amp fuse is installed in the 12-volt DC positive cable from the inverter to the battery.

Figure 13.19 A 100-amp fuse is installed between the battery-ground cable and the chassis.

traveling to prepare lunch, we often have a sandwich conveniently heated in the microwave. By the time we are ready to get under way again, the solar panels have usually recharged the batteries.

TROUBLE-FREE ELECTRICAL SYSTEMS

We have gone to considerable lengths to have efficient 12-volt DC and 120-volt AC electrical systems in our RV. This has added immeasurably to our fulltiming enjoyment, not only when we are in campgrounds with electrical hookups, but especially when boondocking.

Those who don't want, or don't have, systems as elaborate as ours can still have virtually trouble-free electric systems if these few basics are implemented:

- Carry the needed adapters and extensions.
- Always check the campground outlet with a circuit analyzer.
- Don't operate sensitive AC equipment on low voltage.
- Don't overload AC circuits.
- Have batteries of a suitable capacity for your needs.

- Practice battery conservation when without a hookup.
- Be aware of both AC and DC phantom loads.
- Use heavy-gauge wire for rapid, efficient battery charging.

For more detailed and expanded information about RV electrical systems, you may want our book, *RV Electrical Systems, a Basic Guide to Troubleshooting, Repair, and Improvement,* published by Ragged Mountain Press, Camden, Maine. It may be found at your local bookstore or ordered from TAB Books, (800) 822-8158.

CHAPTER 14

Water, Sewage, and Propane

Water and propane systems are rather simple; either they work or they don't, and most of the time they do. They are relatively trouble- and maintenance-free. If the water pump is defective, it can be replaced. If the propane regulator doesn't work, a new one can be installed. Loose connections in either the water or propane system may cause leaks, but these are easily corrected. In our previous trailer, a loose wire made the water pump inoperative; it was fixed in minutes.

With used RVs, problems in the gas or water system may arise because of certain unknowns, such as the amount of wear the water pump has received or the condition of the propane-carrying lines and hoses. It may not be possible to determine how long either system has been out of operation, which sometimes can cause more problems than using a system continuously. Once any problems occurring from disuse or abuse are corrected, however, full-timers can use their RVs' systems with confidence.

THE WATER SYSTEM

RVs can receive an unlimited supply of water from their taps when hooked up to an external water connection. Water is also available from the internal water tank.

Both water supplies work on pressure. The pressure when using the internal tank is provided by the RV's 12-volt water pump; the external pressure is that of the city water system.

Either system routes water to the water-heater tank. As long as water pressure is available, the water-heater tank will be replenished whenever necessary, and as long as the heater is lit (or in operation on electricity, if it's a dual system), hot water is available.

Water from either the internal tank or the city water supply is used to flush the toilet.

The internal water system starts at the fill pipe, which is connected to the water tank. A 12-volt pump draws water from the tank and maintains pressure in the lines at all times. A check valve stops any backward flow of water. After the check valve, water lines run to the taps, toilet, and water heater.

The external, or city water, part of the system is simply a screw-in hose attachment with another check valve, which is coupled to the city water system with a hose. The external system also has a check valve and uses the same piping as the internal system.

Only one system should be in use at a time. Even though the check valves prevent pressure from one system from flowing into the other, the water pump may be damaged with dual usage, although this is rare.

Water-System Accessories

Hoses

The water hose should be the type specifically designated for drinking (potable) water. Any other type of hose may impart an objectionable taste to the water or, perhaps, taint it in other ways. Hoses for potable water are usually white.

The hoses are sold in lengths of 10, 25, and 50 feet. In your travels you are bound to find some situations requiring a 50-foot length, but, for ease in handling, two 25-foot lengths can be used.

A drinking-water hose may be either round or flat. We have never liked a round hose because, when in use, it rarely lies flat and its coils loop along and above the ground and present a tripping hazard to anyone walking in the vicinity. Because of the tendency to coil, it's difficult to drain after use. And when coiled for storage it takes up a fair amount of space.

We use a flat hose, but not the type that self-stores on its own reel: Before a reel hose can be used, all of its length must be unwound from the reel, which requires more time and effort than readying the other types of hoses. We have talked with several RVers who have had difficulties when rewinding the hose; kinking is sometimes a problem, and if the built-in squeegee doesn't work properly, all the hose won't fit on the reel. A hose on a reel, however, takes up less storage space than any other type.

The flat hose we have is made of the same type of material as the round hoses. We like it because it's easy to drain, and it can quickly be folded for storage and unfolded for use.

The brand of hose we use, Flat-Line, may be found in some hardware and farm-supply stores, and we understand that the manufacturer, Anchor-Swan, expects them to be in RV-supply stores soon. To find the location of your nearest dealer, call (800) 848-8707.

We have two lengths of hose that total 50 feet, and each length is kept in its own bag. A net bag with a drawstring top, such as the type citrus fruit comes in, makes an ideal storage bag. Before storing, we screw the ends of each hose length together; it makes storage easier, and keeps out dirt and insects.

Pressure Regulator

The water system in a recreational vehicle is designed to operate at a maximum pressure of about 40 to 45 pounds per square inch (psi). The city water pressure in some places may be as high as 125 psi. Too much pressure coming into the RV's system can make the toilet leak around its base and may cause pipes to crack or split. One RVer told us that the hose to his shower head once ruptured when he was hooked up to high-pressure water.

A water regulator, a simple, inexpensive device, should be used whenever hooking up to city water since there is no way of knowing what the pressure is. The regulator reduces high pressure to a safe level for the RV's system.

Use the regulator at the faucet, not at the RV; this protects the hose from bursting from too-high pressure. (High-pressure hoses, usually copper colored, should not be affected by high pressure, but being made of a very stiff material, they are extremely difficult to handle and store.) In spite of the use of water regulators, high pressure eventually will cause problems with hoses and fittings.

It's easy to forget the regulator when leaving the campsite, but it's unlikely that the hose would be forgotten. So the regulator won't be left behind, fasten it to the hose with a wrench so it's tight enough to require a good deal of force to unscrew it, then always attach the regulator to the faucet so it's just finger tight. This way, the regulator should stay on the end of the hose when it's disconnected.

Water Thief

A device called a *water thief* is necessary for filling the water tank from a faucet that does not have a threaded hose connection. The water thief has a rubber sleeve on one end and a regular hose fitting on the other. The tight-fitting sleeve goes over the faucet, and the other end is connected to the hose.

Unthreaded faucets are usually found in public campgrounds where individual sites don't have water hookups. Such faucets are unthreaded to discourage people from hooking up to them long term. Use a water thief for only long enough to fill jugs or the RV's tank; don't use it to hook up to a communal water source.

Other Water-System Accessories

When a hose is connected to the RV's city water inlet or inserted into a fill pipe, the hose tends to kink at the point where it begins its vertical drop. To eliminate the kink and also prolong hose life, a connector with a 90-degree elbow can be used. It can be screwed directly to the city water inlet, but for filling the tank, purchase a separate spout to attach to the elbow. The spout fits easily into the fill pipe, unlike most hose nozzles.

Fulltimers should also have a Y-valve to use when one faucet serves two campsites—in case your neighbor doesn't have one.

If the water tank needs to be filled when no water faucet is nearby, it's often a messy, wasteful job when doing the filling with a water jug. The spout may not be long enough to fit securely into the fill pipe, consequently much of the water may spill. This problem can be solved by using a funnel with a long, flexible nozzle that fits deeply into the fill pipe (Figure 14.1). So it doesn't have to be a two-person job, the funnel can be held upright by means of an S-hook on a length of string attached to a window or anything the hook can be attached to above the water intake. The funnel should be used for only potable water and kept clean by storing it in a plastic bag between uses. Funnels of this type can be found at auto-parts stores.

Figure 14.1 On some RVs, a funnel arrangement as shown makes adding water easier when using a water jug to fill the tank.

WATER QUALITY

One of the greatest concerns for many traveling fulltimers is the quality of the water that goes into their RV.

Different parts of the country have different kinds of water: hard, soft, sulfurous or metallic tasting, cloudy, foamy, or crystal clear. In a few localized areas the water may be downright unsafe. If so, nothing can be done except use bottled water or move on to another place. Most other water quality problems can be taken care of by using a water filter.

Sanitizing a New RV's Water System

Before using the water tank and lines on new RVs, they should be sanitized according to the manufacturer's instructions. If no instructions are available, the following procedure can be used:

1. Half-fill the tank with water.
2. Through the fill spout, pour in ¼ cup of chlorine bleach for each 15 gallons of tank capacity. Never pour straight chlorine into the fill spout; always dilute it with water.
3. Fill the tank to capacity.
4. Open all faucets until the water flows steadily from them; then close them.
5. Leave the bleach in the tank for three hours.
6. Drain the system and flush it by using the tank drain and faucets.
7. To remove any remaining chlorine taste and odor, dissolve ½ cup of baking soda in 1 gallon of very hot water, making sure all the baking soda is dissolved.
8. Pour the solution into the tank and let it stand for 8 to 10 hours or overnight.
9. Use the faucets and tank drain to drain the tank, then flush the system twice with fresh water.

Sanitizing a Used RV's Water System

If you purchase a used RV, you have no way of determining the condition of the tank or how long it has been standing, full or empty. Either may cause the water to have a bad taste or foster bacteria growth.

On an RV whose water system is suspect, the procedure for sanitizing the tank is slightly different from that of sanitizing the system on a new unit:

1. For each 10 gallons the tank holds, put 4 teaspoonfuls of dishwashing detergent into the tank.
2. Fill the tank.
3. Open every tap in the RV and run the soapy water through until the tank is empty.
4. Refill the tank with clear water.
5. Drain the tank by running the water through all the faucets.
6. Put a strong chlorine mixture in the tank: ⅔ cup of chlorine bleach for each 10 gallons of water. Again, dilute the chlorine in water before pouring into the fill pipe.
7. Open each faucet individually and allow water to run through it until a chlorine smell is detected. Repeat at hourly intervals until the chlorine smell is immediately evident when the faucet is opened; it may take several hours of repeating the procedure for this to happen.
8. When the smell can be immediately detected, empty the tank by running the chlorinated water through the faucets.
9. Flush the system with fresh water until no chlorine taste remains, or use the baking soda solution mentioned on page 372.

Any cleaning and purifying procedure is time consuming, but should be done when warranted.

Unlike many RVers, we use the water from our tank—our internal system—all the time. Rarely do we hook up to a water faucet for longer than it takes to fill the tank. By using the tank water regularly, the water never sits long enough to become stale, or for bacteria and algae to grow, so it's always ready for use when we boondock.

Because what is in the tank is our sole water supply, we are careful about the water we put into it. Before filling the tank we run some water through the campground faucet to get rid of rust or other matter that may have accumulated in the pipe. Often we run some water into a glass to see if it's foamy, cloudy, colored, or clear, or if it has an abundance of particles such as sand or those mysterious black flecks that we often encounter.

We also taste the water. If it has a disagreeable taste we won't use it. Sulfur water, which is often found in many southern states, smells awful as it comes from a faucet, but aeration usually removes the odor. Fortunately, movement of the RV provides plenty of aeration.

Water Filters

No matter how the water checks out, we always use a filter whenever we fill the water tank, and we would use the filter if we were using city water instead of the tank. Some RVers use two filters of this type for double filtration.

We install the filter at the campground faucet, which protects the hose as well as the RV's water tank from impurities. A three-foot length of hose is attached to the faucet, then to the filter, so the filter can rest on the ground. For storage, both ends of the short hose are screwed to the filter openings. We started this practice of screwing the hose ends together one time after finding several earwigs in the inlet side of the filter.

Most water filters come with pipe fittings. For use with a hose, hose fittings have to be added.

Although the type of filter we use can be permanently installed in a water line, we have not done this for two reasons: First, to have filtered water at both the bathroom and kitchen sinks, we would need two separate filters and each would take up valuable storage space. We could get by with one filter installed near the water pump, but to change the filter cartridge would be inconvenient since items stored in the water-pump compartment would have to be removed to gain access to the filter. Second, we want the filtering process to take place outside the tank so impurities never enter it.

Water filters are available in different sizes and can be purchased from hardware and RV-supply stores, and other outlets. We have a small filter because it's easier to store and the cartridges are inexpensive (larger ones cost about three times as much). We have had to replace filters after just a couple of uses in two different campgrounds that had a high iron content in their water, and, in another place, we got only one usage from a filter because it became completely plugged with sand during one filling of the tank. Normally, however, a filter lasts for several months of tank fillings.

Water Purifiers

A water filter is not the same as a water purifier. A filter removes sand and other particles from the water and improves the taste to some degree. Some types of water purifiers provide the cleanest, purest water because they perform not only the functions of the filters but also remove bacteria and disease-causing viruses and micro-organisms. Such units generally cost hundreds of dollars. Other purifiers, which are still pricey, don't treat water quite as thoroughly.

For RV use there are certain drawbacks to using a water purifier: Some require 120-volt AC electricity for operation; some require high water pressure which means that they won't work with the pressure provided by the RV's water pump; most are large units that don't lend themselves to convenient placement in an RV; most are slow-acting as they process the water; and certain units require several gallons of water to produce one gallon of purified water, so a considerable amount of water is wasted.

It would be impractical to install two water purifiers in an RV, so only one faucet, probably the one in the galley, would dispense potable water. In this case, brushing teeth, and drinking water from the bath faucet would be done with unpurified water. It would also be impractical to install the purifier so it served all faucets, therefore processing shower and dishwashing water. If you are thinking about installing a purifier, do some investigating to find the purifier that best suits your purpose because your expenditure will be considerable.

Fulltimers who do much traveling should purchase a brand of filter or purifier for which cartridges and supplies are easily obtained.

WATER CONSERVATION

Water conservation is a way of life with us, not only because we don't hook up to city water and want to avoid having to refill the tank every other day or so, but also because we spend a lot of time in places without hookups and any potable water source. When we are being reasonably conservative, the 60-gallons in our tank lasts about five days. When really conserving we can push it to seven days—including some showers, albeit skimpy, but certainly better than none at all.

Lots of water is wasted when adjusting a two-knob shower faucet to the right temperature. We predetermined the knob placement for the mixture that provides the temperature we like and then marked each of the knobs with a thin strip of colored tape at that point. We put two more strips of tape at intervals on each knob to indicate the position where the water flow increases. By using these settings we can obtain the right mixture instantly, and there's never any doubt about the direction the knobs must be turned.

For a conservative shower we adjust the push-button valve on the shower head to just a trickle for wetting down and turn off the water completely while soaping. We allow a little bigger trickle for rinsing. (Jan thinks she may hold the world's record for the least amount of water ever used for a shower.)

We use the same method for washing hands and faces. The tap is never left running during the entire operation.

We also conserve water when dishwashing by using a dishpan instead of one side of the double sink to hold the wash water. Our dishpan is usually the largest pan or bowl we used for preparing the meal. Since a skillet is too shallow to be a satisfactory dishpan and too large to fit inside a bowl or pan for washing, we wash it last by pouring the water from the dishpan into it. For rinsing, we set a washed bowl or pan filled with hot water in the sink, and dip other items into it. To complete the conservation cycle, we reserve this water for rinsing the sink itself after cleaning it. Before washing, we clean off all food residue from the dishes with a spatula or paper towel. Having nearly clean dishes to begin with means less water is needed to wash them. It keeps drains from clogging as well, since food particles and grease aren't flushed down.

In our present trailer the water heater is located close to both the galley and the bath sinks. In many RVs, especially those with rear galleys, the run from the heater to one sink or the other can be quite long. This was the arrangement on our previous trailer; the water heater was much closer to the bath than the galley. When we were making an extra-concentrated effort to save water, we drew hot water for galley use from the bathroom tap. Even though the heater was in close proximity to the bath, some three cups of water had to be run before it became hot. We didn't waste these three cupfuls; they were collected in a pan or bowl and saved for other uses. We only resorted to such measures when water was not readily available and when we stayed in the same dry area for some time.

WATER HEATERS

Most water heaters in recreational vehicles have either a 6-, 8-, or 10-gallon capacity. The water heater may be the type that operates on propane, or a combination type that operates on both propane and electricity.

The propane models operate on the same principle as a residential unit: the pilot light is lit and the thermostat set to the temperature desired. Some propane heaters have an automatic pilot light, but with others the pilot light must be manually lit with an igniting device—a spark gun or flame lighter.

The propane is ignited in another type of propane water heater by a 12-volt DC-powered electronic ignition, controlled by a remote switch inside the RV. There is no pilot light. When water temperature drops to a certain level the propane burner is automatically ignited.

Combination-type heaters have both an electric heating element and a gas burner and may be operated on 120-volt AC power or propane, or for extra fast recovery, the gas and electric modes can be used together. The electric heating element in 6-gallon tanks is rated at 1,000 watts, and in the 10-gallon tanks, at 1,500 watts. When the electricity is heating the water, the amperage drawn may be too high to operate safely from a 15-amp outlet, particularly when operating in combination with other high-amperage equipment. Some RVers often overlook the water heater as a source of electrical overload problems.

All water heater compartments have some sort of ventilation to dissipate heat, usually a grill in the compartment cover, but high winds can enter through the grill and blow out the pilot light. The flame can be protected from the wind by attaching a shield over the grill. A shield can be made from heavy aluminum foil held in place with duct tape. Don't seal off the grill entirely. Rather, loosely arch the foil across the grill, and tape down only the top and bottom edges and the edge facing the wind direction.

We used a foil shield for many years but, no matter what type of tape we used, it always took some of the door paint off when we removed the shield. We finally hit upon the idea of making a permanent shield from sheet metal (Figure 14.2). A sheet-metal shop cut and bent the shield. It's attached over the grill with screws.

When the thermostat on our heater is set at its lowest position, the water is hotter than it needs to be so in warm weather, we use only the pilot light for heating the water in our six-gallon tank (the control-knob is set to the "pilot" position instead of the "on" position). The water isn't overly hot but certainly sufficient for washing and showering; in fact, we always need a little cold water in the mix.

If all the heated water is used at one time, the pilot alone takes quite a while to heat another tankful of water. But when we take our usual conservative showers we find six gallons to be plenty of hot water—even if each of us showers one right after the other.

Those who hook up to city water may not be as conservative, and a 6-gallon-capacity tank probably wouldn't provide enough hot water for two close-together showers. The burner would be needed to quickly heat the tank water.

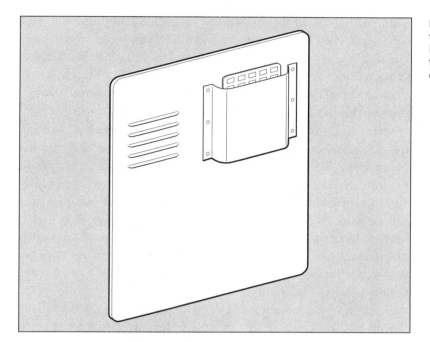

One of the main reasons we use only the pilot is to spare us, and our neighbors, from the blowtorch noise of the burner. We started this practice just after we moved into our 23-footer. The water heater was located under the bed, and the noisy burner going on during the night disturbed our sleep.

HOLDING TANKS

Just as RVers are responsible for hooking up their electricity, so are they responsible for getting rid of their sewage. Emptying the holding tanks is something none of us enjoys, but it must be done. Modern RVs are designed so that the chore can be done quickly and easily.

Holding tanks can be emptied into a sewer hookup at the site in campgrounds, or at dump stations, which are found in many private parks even if all sites have sewer hookups. Some states have free dump stations in highway rest areas; they can also be found at some service stations. Some city parks may have a dump station even if the park has no campground; and some municipalities provide dump stations.

Often a dump station has two water sources, one for flushing the dump area and the other, a few feet away, is potable water for filling tanks. Signs generally indicate which is which. Often a hose of some type is on the dump section's water source. If a hose is also attached to the drinking water faucet, we won't use it for filling our tank. We use our own hose, as we have no way of knowing how sanitary the drinking water hose is. We spray the faucet with disinfectant before attaching our hose, and to avoid contamination we are careful not to let the ends of the hose touch the ground in any dump station vicinity.

A few years back, we were in a small campground without water faucets at the sites. The only potable water outlet was adjacent to the dump station. The manager provided one long drinking-water hose that reached to all sites, so those who were staying for a few days didn't have to move their rigs to fill their water tanks. When we ran out of water, we found that our hose wasn't long enough to reach our site so we went over to get the campground hose, which happened to be inside a trailer that was parked at the dump station. This aroused our suspicions. When we asked the occupant of the trailer about the water hose, she said we could have it as soon as she was done flushing out her holding tank. From the door, we could see the hose in the toilet. "I'll have to wash it off first," she said. We told her not to bother. We wouldn't think of filling our water tanks from a hose that had been in a toilet.

Shortly thereafter in another campground, we saw a neighbor rinsing the end of his sewer hose by sticking the water faucet into it. He didn't seem to be taking any precautions about not touching the faucet with the sewer hose. We rarely rinse our sewer hose at the water faucet, but if we do, we hold the sewer hose well below

"We use our own hose, as we have no way of knowing how sanitary the [campground's] drinking water hose is."

the faucet so there is no chance of them touching each other. We avoid splashing water so nothing undesirable splatters on the faucet end or handle, or on the ground in the vicinity.

We have seen messes at dump stations caused by dimwits who haven't the intelligence to figure out that a sewer hose should always be used when dumping. Such people park their RV close to the dump station apron, take the cap off their holding tank pipe, and open the valves. This invariably spills the sewage over a good portion of the dumping area.

Although most RVers are careful when disposing of holding-tank contents, there are too many careless and downright stupid people who are clearly not concerned about cleanliness and sanitation, and who have no consideration for others who may come in contact with the filth they have left behind.

When we must empty the holding tanks, only one of us handles the dumping operation. We have a pair of loose-fitting rubber gloves to wear when handling the sewer hose. If it's necessary to fill the water tank at the dump station, hands are washed with soap and water before touching the water hose.

On the few occasions when we want to thoroughly flush out the black-water holding tank and a dump station hose is not available or not long enough, we use our regular hose with a special nozzle for only this purpose. It's pointed, with a small orifice, and delivers a strong, narrow steam of water. We never put the hose into the toilet but hold the hose above it and direct the water stream into it. When the job is finished, the nozzle and the end of the hose are washed off with water, then wiped with undiluted chlorine bleach, and rinsed again with water.

A special hose attachment for flushing holding tanks, a long wand that can be inserted into the toilet, can be purchased. The wand delivers a jet spray that can be aimed into the corners of the holding tank where waste often collects.

When parked in a site for several days, it's a good idea to keep the black-water valve closed and empty the tank every three or four days. This allows some liquid to accumulate in the tank so

> **"W**e have seen messes at dump stations caused by dimwits who haven't the intelligence to figure out that a sewer hose should always be used when dumping.**"**

when it's dumped the liquid washes away paper and solids. If the black-water tank valve is left open all the time, the tank may need to be specially flushed out periodically.

When emptying the tanks, empty the black-water tank first and then use the contents of the gray-water tank to flush the sewer hose.

SEWER ACCESSORIES

Fulltimers should carry a variety of sewer fittings and adapters. Once in a while we find it necessary to use a coupler that reduces the diameter of the sewer hose, or a curved 45-degree hose adapter. We carry 20 feet of sewer hose in two 10-foot sections. For joining them together we prefer the threaded type of fitting that can be screwed in. One hose is a semi-rigid type that can be collapsed to about six feet. The other is the more flexible type that collapses to about a third of its extended length. We like the semi-rigid type because it lasts for years.

We have never felt the need for any device to support the sewer hose so that it runs on a slant into the sewer connection, although if the sewer hose is hooked up and used on a continual basis, such a support may be useful. There are several supports on the market, but the sewer hose affixed to a slanted two-by-four provides the same results.

Some public campgrounds have a catchment for gray water at each site. These gray water dumps aren't regular sewer hookups, and it may be awkward (and may be prohibited) to use the sewer hose for dumping the gray water. For this situation it's useful to have a holding-tank pipe cap with a fitting for a regular water hose. A length of hose for gray water use (never to be used for drinking water) can be attached to the cap and easily directed into the gray water receptacle. We have a length of green hose for this purpose so it won't be mistaken for our white drinking-water hose, and it's kept in a different compartment than the drinking-water hose.

The most flexible sewer hoses are made of fairly thin plastic and don't last long, so if this type of hose is used, a new hose periodically has to be attached to the adapter that fits on the holding tank drain. Unless the adapter is a screw-in type, this is not easy to do; as soon as one side of the hose is slipped on, the other side pops off. Pouring hot water on the end of the hose to be attached causes the hose to expand and become more flexible, thus easier to work with.

PLUMBING AND COLD WEATHER

Many recreational vehicles are being built with an enclosed under-body and with the heating ducts routed to the holding and water tanks and water lines. RVs of this type rarely have any freeze-ups in cold weather. Our previous trailer did not have this feature, so we needed to take certain precautions in below-freezing temperatures.

When we were not hooked up to a sewer, we put some an-tifreeze in both the holding tanks every other day or so. Depending on the temperature, we used anywhere from a half a cup to one cup for each of the 40-gallon tanks we had. The antifreeze was not so much to keep the tanks from freezing (this wouldn't have hap-pened unless it was very cold for a sustained period of time) as it was to keep the drain open and the valves unfrozen.

Once we were caught with our tanks antifreezeless in a sudden cold spell. The drain and valves froze solid. We eventually thawed them by leaving a heating pad tied around the drain for several hours, and periodically giving the valves sustained blasts of hot air from a hair dryer.

When it's very cold outside, the water lines inside the RV can freeze if they don't receive enough heat. Keeping cabinet doors ajar on all areas through which the water lines are routed usually keeps them warm enough to prevent freezing.

To avoid having the water hose freeze in cold weather is another reason we use water from the internal tank rather than hooking up to city water. In many campgrounds located in cold-weather areas, each site's water faucet is protected by insulation or wrapped with heat tape to keep it from freezing, but the hose attached to it, being full of water and exposed to the air, will freeze if not protected as well. The hose can be wrapped with heat tape and covered with insulation, but this is a nuisance unless you are staying put in one place for some time. Some fulltimers have a special heat-tape-wrapped hose they use in only cold weather. For such a hose to be effective, a layer of insulating material must cover the heat tape, and the shortest length hose possible should be used, being just long enough to reach from the faucet to the RV's water connection. In extremely cold weather the hose may still freeze.

A heat tape also can be wrapped around the holding tanks' valve and drain assembly to keep it from freezing. When driving in cold weather, the vehicle's speed has the effect of lowering the air temperature and this can cause drains and valves to freeze if antifreeze is not used in the holding tanks.

PROPANE

Propane, or LP- (for liquid-petroleum) gas, is so easy and convenient to use that many of us tend to forget it is potentially very dangerous. Improperly or carelessly used, it can cause devastating explosions and fires. Although common sense will prevent these disasters, everyone who uses the substance should be aware of the potential.

The most common problem RVers have with propane, if they have any at all, is leaks. Every person living in the RV should know that gas leaks must never be investigated with any type of open flame, yet never a year goes by that we don't hear of someone using this method, invariably with dire results.

If a leak is suspected, check it by brushing a soapy solution on the questionable joints. Bubbles appear if a leak exists.

If you smell gas when entering an RV, never turn on or use anything that will cause an electrical spark or flame until all the windows and doors have been opened and the gas has dissipated. Propane is heavier than air so it settles to the lowest point in the RV. Since the water pump is usually located at a low point, it's especially important not to use the water pump if propane odor is detected.

Never sleep with all windows tightly shut when any unvented propane equipment, such as a catalytic heater, is being used since it depletes the oxygen. Opening a window an inch or two is all that is necessary to replenish the oxygen.

A gas detector can be installed that will warn of a leak by emitting a high-pitched tone.

Filling Propane Cylinders

Propane cylinders are filled either by weight, or by volume, depending on which part of the country you are in. They are designed to be only 80-percent filled with liquid gas and should never be filled beyond this level. Although a cylinder holds more gas, it's dangerous to fill it to more than 80-percent capacity. As of September 1, 1997, Department of Transportation (DOT) cylinders on new RVs must be equipped with a stop-fill valve to prevent overfilling.

If you have cylinders older than this, the operator should control how much gas is put in to avoid overfilling. Before filling, the operator should open the cylinder's 80-percent bleeder valve by loosening it with a screwdriver. The cylinder should then be filled just until liquid propane vents from the valve, which usually occurs either when the scale indicates the proper weight is reached or the meter registers the proper gallonage. At that point, the supply of gas to the cylinder should be shut off. The cylinder is then filled to the right level.

Those responsible for filling propane cylinders should be instructed in the proper methods, but when the gas is purchased from other than a bulk dealer there's a good chance of encountering operators who know next to nothing about the operation. RVers should always oversee the operation to make sure their cylinders are properly filled. More than once, we've used one of our screwdrivers to open the 80-percent valve because the operator was unaware it existed.

Cylinders also have a relief valve. Any time excessive pressure builds up in a cylinder the relief valve automatically releases the pressure. Pressure increases can occur in extremely hot weather because heat causes expansion within the cylinder, so especially in hot weather, cylinders should never be overfilled.

A propane cylinder should not be transported in a position other than the one in which it is used: Upright cylinders should be carried upright and horizontal cylinders should be transported in a horizontal position. Empty or full, cylinders should not be allowed to roll around or be tipped over. A plug must be in the valve for cylinder transportation in some states.

The preceding information applies mainly to those with trailers; most motorhomes have a built-in tank which can be filled only by driving the motorhome to the supplier or having the supplier come to the motorhome. And, of course, a motorhome's unremovable tank can't be weighed so it must be filled by volume.

Use of Propane While Traveling

Many fulltimers travel with their refrigerators and water heaters operating, but we always turn off the propane supply at the cylinders before we get under way because we don't need it. The items in our freezer never defrost even in the hot weather—not even ice cream, and the interior of the refrigerator stays at a safely cold temperature for several hours. Maybe it's because our refrigerator is well-insulated and has doors with a good seal (we always give them an extra push to be sure they are firmly shut before we start traveling). But perhaps the main reason we have no problems with retaining cold in the refrigerator when it's off is because of our traveling habits. We almost never travel 200 miles in a day; a 100 miles, or less, is more usual for us, so the refrigerator is never off for very many hours. In hot weather we keep the refrigerator well packed—empty space doesn't retain cold but chilled items do—and we try to avoid opening the refrigerator door during the trip.

We also always have enough residual hot water in the tank to take care of our needs for the short times we are traveling.

Because propane equipment requires a flame to operate, all such equipment must be turned off when the rig is in a filling station. If we did use propane-fueled items while traveling, we would make sure they were turned off before we were anywhere near the pumps. Some RVers, however, find it too much of a bother to turn off and then relight propane equipment—in spite of the great inherent danger. We hope we'll never encounter them in a station where we're refueling.

According to law, the propane must be shut off before traveling through tunnels and boarding ferries.

Fulltimers' Propane Usage

When we aren't using propane for heating, one seven-gallon (30 pound) cylinder lasts a month or more. If we are using the furnace when temperatures are in the twenties or lower, one such cylinder lasts about a week.

Since we have two cylinders, we often don't refill a cylinder immediately after it runs out unless we are staying put for a while. Why should we haul around the weight of a full propane cylinder if we don't need it? So we won't forget to refill the empty cylinder before the other cylinder becomes empty, we keep a record of the date when the cylinder ran out. Because we know our average usage (you'll learn yours after a few months of living in your RV) it's easy to determine when we need to refill.

Care of the Propane System

Fulltimers use propane several times a day for one thing or another. This constant use is better for a propane system than the occasional use and extended layup periods a vacation RV's propane system receives.

When preparing cylinders for a long layup, air may be inadvertently introduced into the cylinders. They have to be purged before they can be used again.

A gas appliance with intake and exhaust ports may require major servicing if insects decide to use the ports as nesting places when the appliance is out of operation. Evidently they are attracted to the odor-causing chemical that is added to the gas.

CHAPTER 15

Climate Control

As a fulltimer, you'll be able to control the climate in which you live simply by moving your home to a place where the weather is cooler or warmer. But no matter where you go, you may still experience some hot weather in the summer, and wintering in the South can sometimes be chilly, even cold, so having methods of heating and cooling your RV are important.

Climate-control equipment should always be kept in operating condition in case of unseasonable weather. One year at the end of summer, we had an early cold wave with nighttime temperatures in the low twenties. We didn't have to do anything to ready the furnace for use other than turn it on.

INSULATION

Fulltimers who intend to spend any time in cold climates should have an RV suitably insulated for such weather. All RVs are insulated, but the amount and quality of the insulation vary widely. Carefully reading manufacturers' brochures may provide an indication of how well a unit is insulated. Manufacturers that are proud of the way their units withstand cold weather may provide a cutaway illustration showing how the insulation is installed. In some brochures, the subject isn't even mentioned. One trailer manufacturer promotes an optional cold-weather package that makes the trailer safe and comfortable to live in at −30°F. If an RV is needed for cold-weather living, be sure it has adequate insulation.

Block Styrofoam and residential-type fiberglass batting are the most prevalent types of insulation used in RVs. Block foam is used in most motorhomes; trailers may have either or a combination of both. In addition, both motorhomes and trailers may have other insulating materials.

Even if you don't intend to spend time in a climate where insulation is needed for warmth, remember that good insulation helps to keep an RV cooler in hot weather too. It also serves to deaden outside noises.

HEATING

Heating an RV can be accomplished by using the built-in furnace and gas and electric heaters.

Furnaces

The built-in heating system in most RVs is much like that in residences in one respect: All you need to do for heat is to turn on the furnace and set the thermostat to the desired temperature.

Most RVs are equipped with a propane-fueled, forced-air, thermostat-controlled furnace with heating ducts and outlets throughout the interior. A few luxury motorhomes have a heating system in which a small electric pump circulates heated water through pipes around the perimeter of the interior. Both operate on 12-volt DC power.

In nearly all cases, the Btu (British thermal unit) output of the furnace is sufficient for the size of the RV in which it is installed. Our 31,000-Btu-output furnace is capable of keeping our 29-foot trailer shirtsleeve-warm when the temperature is well below freezing.

Furnaces are relatively trouble free if they are kept clean. Dust on the furnace unit should be vacuumed away periodically. Duct registers that can be closed are useful for keeping dust out of ducts in seasons when the furnace is not being used. If you don't have this type of register in your RV, they can be purchased at RV-supply stores for easy self-installation. In addition to closing completely, this type of register has adjustable dampers for regulating heat flow.

If the furnace blower or thermostat does not operate, a fuse may be blown. When the thermostat is turned up high enough to kick on the burner but does not, the contacts in the thermostat may be pitted. A multimeter can be used to troubleshoot most electrical problems connected with the furnace and thermostat.

Nothing should be stored on top of the furnace ducts if they are made of flexible tubing, and no items that could puncture or tear the ducts should touch them. If the ducts are squashed, the air cannot flow freely through them, and any sort of an opening, even a pinhole, destroys some of the heating efficiency. Sharp angles in the ducts' routing also reduce heat flow. If the duct is not stretched out smoothly when it's installed, this too affects the amount of air that goes through it.

In our previous trailer, we had one duct that ran across the end of a storage compartment under the bed. To avoid damaging it when items were being removed and replaced in the compartment, we enclosed the duct in its own little compartment by putting up a simple partition.

Forced-air furnace blowers draw between 3 and 8 amps, depending on the size of the furnace and its age; later models are the most efficient. Prolonged use of the furnace on battery power can seriously drain the batteries even though the blower operates intermittently.

Catalytic Heaters

We use a catalytic heater for the times when we we're boondocking and don't want to expend battery power to run the furnace, and when we want to conserve propane by not using the furnace when we have an electric hookup.

Catalytic heaters are available in three sizes with Btu outputs

ranging from 2,800 to 7,600. Two models with the higher outputs
have automatic ignition and are thermostat controlled. The automatic ignition operates on 12-volt DC power and requires 5.1
amps for starting, .7 amp for reignition, and .2 amp once in operation. Thermostatically controlled catalytic heaters are not recommended for use in elevations above 5,000 feet.

Some states have regulations prohibiting the installation of catalytic heaters in RVs. You may be able to purchase such a heater in
these states, but no one in the state can install it for you.

Catalytic heaters are simple and quiet, there is no flame when
operating, and they have no fan or any other moving parts. Since
the heater has no provision for circulating air, it should be installed as close to the floor as practical to take advantage of the
natural rise of heated air.

In our fifth-wheel, we started out with a 5,800-Btu model, but it
heated the 29-foot trailer too well; on the lowest heat setting, the
trailer was often too warm. We eventually switched to a 2,800-Btu
model, which, we have found, is enough to keep the trailer comfortably warm in temperatures slightly below freezing. We kept the larger
heater to use when we happen to be in extra-cold temperatures, and
we have used it a few times. We put it to good use two years ago when
we were in Branson, Missouri. It was in January and we experienced
a week of below-zero temperatures—unusual, the locals said. Unusual or not, we had to endure it, but we were quite comfortable.

When a catalytic heater is put in an RV, a common location is
on the end of a galley counter. In our 23-foot trailer, we put ours
in a more central location—in the walkway between the galley and
the side bath, on the outside wall of the bath—so more of the
trailer would benefit from its heat.

In our fifth-wheel trailer, we have the heater mounted on the
wall that divides the "upstairs" from the "downstairs," facing the
galley and the living room. Since heat rises, the bath and bedroom
upstairs receive plenty of heat.

We didn't have a suitable space for wall-mounting the larger-
output heater, which is also physically larger, so we turned it into a

free-standing unit by installing the optional legs. So it could be moved and turned to face the direction we wanted, a custom-fabricated, 6-foot extension hose was used for the gas line.

A tee was installed in the refrigerator's gas line for the gas supply. In our trailer, this line runs through the storage compartment under the bath floor next to the upstairs/downstairs dividing wall. A copper tube extends from the tee through the wall to the left of the steps to the bath area. The tubing terminates in a flared fitting with a plug. Although the plug itself would probably be enough to prevent gas leaking, as an extra safety measure a petcock was installed in the tubing, out of sight behind the wall. Although the installation was designed for the larger heater, it turned out to be in just the right location for the smaller heater.

It may seem that with this installation it would be a nuisance to use the heater, but it's not. The petcock is easily reached by opening the trap door to the storage compartment .

On any heat setting a catalytic heater can make adjacent surfaces quite warm. In our travel trailer, the heater faced a row of drawers in the galley counter. To protect the counter from the heat, a dishtowel was hung from the top drawer. On the rare occasions when the heater was on its highest setting, a long sheet of foil was hung from the drawer to reflect the heat.

When we were using the larger heater in our fifth-wheel, keeping heat way from adjacent surfaces wasn't quite as critical because of the way the heater faced, but we thought the heater would be more efficient if the heat could be directed. We came up with the idea of using movable doors for this purpose. For just a few dollars, a sheet-metal shop fabricated a door for each side of the heater from heavy-gauge aluminum, bent to conform to the angled, wire-grill front. Each door was attached to a side of the heater with two hinges held on with pop rivets. When closed, the doors cover the grill and self-store by fitting snugly against it. For channeling heat, the doors can be opened to any position desired. The doors worked out so well we had another set made and installed them on our wall-mounted heater (Figure 15.1).

> **"O**n any heat setting a catalytic heater can make adjacent surfaces quite warm.**"**

Figure 15.1 The authors designed and installed some accessories for their catalytic heater. The doors serve to direct the heat, as does the metal shield behind, but the primary function of the shield is to keep heat away from the wall.

As with other heaters, dust should be kept from a catalytic heater by covering it when not in use. Slip-on covers are available from outlets where the heaters are sold.

Electric Heaters

An electric heater can be used for interior heating in cool weather, but it won't do a satisfactory job alone when the temperature is much below freezing.

When an electric heater is used, not only do the external power cord and outlet have to be of an amperage-rating high enough to withstand the wattage of the heater, but so does any extension cord used with the heater inside the RV.

As a safety practice, we are never absent from the trailer with an electric heater running, even for as little as half an hour, unless we are within sight of it. Even with the proper cords and outlets, fires can occur from a malfunctioning heater. An electric heater should be set well away from any combustibles and placed so no papers or other flammable materials can fall onto or into it.

It's important to keep electric heaters clean, too. When used regularly in the confines of an RV, dust accumulates quickly. The dust on the case and grill can be vacuumed off, but the heater must be dismantled in order to thoroughly clean the fan blades and motor. A clean heater operates more quietly, efficiently, and safely than one with a heavy dust buildup.

While lots of heaters on the market are small enough for convenient use and storage in RVs, it may take some searching to find one that has a 1,200-watt setting or a maximum rating of this wattage. Many heaters are rated at 1,500 watts, but this wattage is not safe to use with 15-amp electrical hookups while other 120-volt items are being used.

Most electric ceramic heaters, however, have a thermostat that can be adjusted to settings ranging from 350 to 1,500 watts. The brand we have provides plenty of heat at the lower settings.

A true ceramic heater has a ceramic disk or block nearly as large as the heater case. Expect to pay upwards of $70 for a heater of this type. Many heaters with much lower prices are advertised as being ceramic. We've never been able to figure out what in these heaters is ceramic, but it certainly isn't part of the heating element.

CONDENSATION

When it's cold outside and an RV is being heated by any means, condensation can form and it can be a nuisance. The cooking, bathing, even the breathing of the RV's occupants all create moisture, and since the moisture in an RV is relatively confined, it becomes concentrated and can turn into water droplets. These collect on windows and roof vents, walls and ceilings in the galley when cooking, and in the bath when showering. Wall areas adjacent to studs may develop condensation if the unit has an aluminum frame.

Larger RVs have fewer condensation problems than smaller units because any moisture generated has more room in which to disperse. For example, much less condensation develops in our 29-footer than in our previous 23-foot trailer.

Condensation can be reduced somewhat by slightly opening the bath roof vent (if your RV has one) when showering, and by operating the range-hood fan when cooking. Teakettles and pans of water should not be allowed to boil and steam for any length of time.

Sometimes when condensation forms in enclosed, unventilated storage compartments it encourages mildew growth. We had such condensation problems in our 23-footer, especially in locations where the morning sun struck the outside of the trailer after a cold night. The warmth of the sun created condensation in the still-cold compartment. We stopped the condensation in the worst problem area, the bottom corner of the rear wardrobe, by lining the corner with ½-inch thick panels of Styrofoam.

In our present trailer, we stopped condensation from forming on the back wall of our wardrobe by covering the wall with sheets of ¼-inch-thick foam-core board.

Leaving storage compartment doors open during cold nights so the compartments can receive heat from the furnace or other heaters can alleviate condensation.

STORM WINDOWS

For prolonged stays in cold weather, storm windows are useful. They can reduce propane consumption if the furnace is being used, and they eliminate condensation on windows. RVs with double-paned windows, however, don't need separate storm windows.

A common type of storm window found on trailers is a large piece of glass mounted in a rigid frame that fits over the screen. Some are held in place by turn tabs; others fit into a channel on the regular window frame. Unless the storm window is a tight fit, drafts can enter all around the frame. Drafts can be eliminated by putting weatherstripping on the edges of the storm window, or, less desirable, by taping it on all sides.

A major problem with large, rigid storm windows is that they are difficult to store in the rig when not in use, although they may fit in the storage compartments of some basement-model RVs. If stored anywhere in the RV, they need to be protected so they won't become cracked or broken during travel.

The vinyl storm-window kits for residential use sold in hardware and home-improvement stores can be adapted for use on some RV windows. Read the instructions carefully before purchasing to see if there are any glitches that may prevent use on your windows.

One type of vinyl storm window is simply taped to the window frame. Another type (the type we use) has a two-section channel to hold the vinyl in place. One section of the channel is attached to the window frame with mounting tape (the tape is on this part of the channel when purchased). The cut-to-fit vinyl is placed over the window and the channel, and the other channel section is snapped into the mounted section.

Vinyl storm windows affect visibility only slightly. If care is taken with removal and storage, they may be able to be reused. The channel is not removed; it remains in place on the window.

Storm windows can't be put over motorhome windshields or on driver and passenger side windows, so considerable heat loss will occur in this area unless the motorhome is equipped with an insulating curtain that can be pulled across the cockpit windows.

Roof vents and skylights should have their own "storm windows" to reduce the considerable heat loss and to eliminate annoying dripping condensation. Clear vinyl (found in hardware, fabric, and variety stores), cut to size and taped to the vent frame with

"The vinyl storm-window kits for residential use sold in hardware and home-improvement stores can be adapted for use on some RV windows.**"**

clear, waterproof tape, will do the job and not block out light from translucent and transparent vents.

Ready-made covers are also available. One type is made of flexible, opaque vinyl and affixed to the vent frame with snaps. Another type is a square of thin, rigid, opaque plastic held in place with a bracket screwed into each corner of the frame. Neither of these covers is held tightly against the frame so they won't completely stop condensation from forming but they do stop the dripping.

We purchased one of the rigid types for the bedroom vent, which we use year-round. In cold weather it prevents condensation from dripping onto the bed and us, it blocks out early morning light and campground lights at night, and, in the summer, it keeps out the sun. The bracket is designed so the cover can be placed on two different levels. When we want the vent open but also want light-blocking, the cover is put in the lower position, which holds it slightly away from the vent and allows air to circulate through the vent.

If it's necessary to use tape for any sealing, try to find a tape that leaves no residue when removed. Some may not leave a residue when applied for a short time; however, if left in place for several months, they may leave a difficult-to-clean gummy mess. Rubbing alcohol or a spray lubricant such as WD-40 may clean it up, but first test the surface in an inconspicuous place to make sure the product won't harm it. Sometimes a piece of fresh mailing tape firmly pressed onto the residue, then quickly lifted off, removes residue, but it may take several pieces of tape and quite a bit of time to finish the job.

COLD-WEATHER SITUATIONS

When staying in cold weather for an extended period of time, the RV should have some type of skirting around it. This prevents wind from swirling around underneath the RV and provides a certain amount of insulation so the unit, especially the floor, is warmer and there is less chance of anything freezing.

Skirts can be flexible vinyl or tarp material attached to the unit with tape or snaps and the bottom edge weighted with bricks, stones, or logs to keep it from blowing around. Rigid vinyl and aluminum skirts can also be used. A fellow RVer who planned to spend one winter in Montana cut composition-board panels that fit snugly under and around his trailer and installed a thick layer of insulation under the entire floor.

Insulated drapes and good-quality window shades of heavy-weight vinyl do much to keep out cold and cut down on drafts from windows.

Throw rugs, small carpet pieces, or anything else that fits along the bottom of the door will prevent drafts from that area.

One winter when we were living in our 23-footer, we taped an oversize vinyl panel inside each of our exterior compartments, making the interior of the trailer near these compartments warmer and less drafty. One side and the bottom of each panel was left loose so we could easily get at the items stored in the compartment. If we hadn't needed frequent access to these compartments, we would have run tape all around the outside of the compartment door to seal it off completely. Exterior compartment doors and the entry door are usually weatherstripped at the factory, but, if not, you can add weatherstripping easily.

In cold weather you may find yourself sealed into your RV by iced-over doors, as we did once after an ice storm. We remembered reading about another RVer to whom this had happened and tried his trick—using a hair dryer to de-ice the door. It worked. We also discovered that a hair dryer is useful for thawing other frozen equipment and plumbing.

An often-overlooked cold-air entry point is the range-hood vent opening. It's a large opening, and when facing into a strong wind creates a considerable draft. If you wish to seal this opening but be able to unseal it when cooking, seal it off on the inside by covering the filter screen on the range hood itself with a piece of foil. Remove the filter-screen, wrap a piece of foil around it, and put it back in place. The foil can be easily removed when using the

> *"In cold weather you may find yourself sealed into your RV by iced-over doors, as we did once after an ice storm."*

exhaust fan. You can also tape a piece of foil across the filter screen, but tape only the opposite ends. To use the fan, loosen the tape on one end so one side of the foil drops down.

COOLING

The ability to travel and live comfortably in an RV in hot weather is made possible by fans, opening windows, awnings, and air conditioners.

Air Conditioners

Most fulltimers want an air conditioner for hot-weather use. A roof-mounted air conditioner, or two if the RV is large, is the most common arrangement, but some RVs are equipped with central air-conditioning units located in a compartment inside the RV.

Like furnaces, air conditioners require little maintenance other than cleaning. For cooling efficiency, periodically rinse the filter (located behind the grill) with water. While the grill is off, remove any dust that is visible inside the unit. Seasonally remove the outside cover from the evaporator on the roof to clean out road dust, leaves, and insect nests.

It's important to know the amperage rating of your air conditioner; most draw from 11 to 13 amps. It may not be possible to use the large unit on a 15-amp circuit. If you are careful about your amperage load, you can get away with using a smaller air conditioner and certain other low-wattage electrical equipment at the same time on a 15-amp circuit.

When we use our air conditioner on a 15-amp circuit, we operate the refrigerator on gas and resort to our solar panels for our 12-volt needs so the only load on the AC circuit is the air conditioner.

A common problem with air conditioners is not in the unit itself but in the campground's electrical hookup, which may have voltage too low to operate the air conditioner properly. Air conditioners require a specific amount of voltage for the high momentary surge needed to start the compressor. If the voltage does not meet this requirement, the compressor may not start; it may just hum.

Most new air conditioners have an overload device that shuts down the compressor when it becomes overheated, which is usually the result of low voltage. The overload resets itself in a few minutes, allowing the compressor to run again. If the compressor goes on and off, check the voltage first before assuming there is something wrong with the air conditioner.

Long-term use of an air conditioner on voltage that is marginal—not quite low enough to trip the overload device—may cause premature compressor failure.

At times there may be enough voltage to start the compressor, but during the several hours the air conditioner may be running, a low-voltage situation develops. For example, this can occur if the campground is not properly wired and your neighbors turn on their air conditioners or use other high-wattage electrical equipment. Monitor the voltage with a voltmeter to be on the safe side.

You can cause a low-voltage situation in your RV yourself if you need to use an extension cord to reach the campground hookup, and the extension is of inadequate wire-gauge. Any extension used for running an air conditioner or an electric heater should be 10/3 wire.

As long as air conditioners are regularly operated with the proper voltage, the compressor itself should not be damaged. So many fail-safe devices are built into today's air conditioners that compressor blowout is rare. If a service person diagnoses blowout as your problem, it would be a good idea to get a second opinion before authorizing replacement of the compressor, the cost of which is just about half that of a new air conditioner.

If the air conditioner runs normally but does not cool, the problem may be a leak. It will have to be tracked down, fixed, and then the air conditioner recharged with refrigerant.

If the circuit breaker trips repeatedly each time the air conditioner is turned on, it's an indication that an electrical or mechanical problem exists.

Many brands of roof air conditioners can be equipped with a

heating element, most of which draw 16 amps and should not be used on a 15-amp circuit. Another factor to be weighed when considering this option is that the air conditioner's location is on the ceiling—the worst place for any kind of a heater. Since hot air rises, the floor area, where it's needed, won't receive much heat. The air conditioner's blower moves the hot air around, but it can't direct it to where it's really needed.

Fans

If air does not circulate well in an RV, a fan can help move it along. It does not have to be one that operates on 120 volts AC. Several styles of 12-volt DC fans are available. Some are designed to be permanently installed and others are portable and can be used wherever a 12-volt outlet is available.

A 12-volt fan draws about the same number of amps as does a 12-volt light bulb, making it practical to use when boondocking.

A small, 12-volt fan would be a welcome addition to the cab-over bed area on a Class C motorhome. It can be put to good use even when 120-volt power is available since most 120-volt fans are too large for that particular area.

A roof-vent fan can move lots of air through an RV if its the type on which the blade area nearly fills the entire opening of the vent. This sort of fan was offered as an option on our trailer so we had one installed in the bedroom vent. It has proven to be an excellent accessory. We use it to remove hot air from the trailer, especially in hot weather when we return to a closed-up trailer after being away. With all other vents and windows closed, a rear window is opened so air is pulled through the entire trailer, and in just a few minutes the hot air is sucked out.

We prefer natural ventilation to air conditioning, especially when we are sleeping. With the fan on the lowest of its three speeds, and the window at the head of the bed open, a gentle, cool breeze wafts over us. The fan has a thermostat so it can be adjusted to shut off or come on at a desired temperature. We have a Fan-Tastic Vent Fan (similar fans are made by Maxxair Vent Corporation), and a feature we like is that the blades are made of clear plastic so they don't block the light from the vent.

It takes little amperage to run these vent fans, so they can be used to great advantage when boondocking, when electricity may not be available for running an air conditioner.

Windows

Tinted window glass is standard or an option on some RVs. The darker windows definitely keep a unit cooler in the summer—and also in the winter. When some warmth from the sun is wanted, tinted glass blocks much of it out.

Reflective adhesive-backed sheeting on windows is another way to keep out sun, but unless most of your time is spent in a hot climate—where temperatures are around 100°F for long periods—this sheeting should not be needed.

Another cooling option are sheer or open-weave privacy curtains, which diffuse sunlight but admit air.

In hot weather, heavy window shades block a good deal of heat from entering, just as they prevent cold air from entering in cold weather. When we are traveling in hot weather, we often pull all the shades, so no matter in which direction we travel no sun can enter. When we arrive at our destination we often find the temperature inside the trailer to be five to seven degrees cooler than the outside temperature.

Awnings

Another useful RV accessory is a full-length awning, which will keep the RV cooler inside, with or without the air conditioner operating, and provide shade outside. Some RV's have a full-length awning on the curb side and individual awnings on windows on other sides. On trailers, the rear and front windows, if they have either, may have stone shields (sometimes called rock guards) on them, which serve as awnings when raised.

It's not always possible to park so that one awning will keep the sun off all day. A full-length awning can also be placed on the street side of a unit, but since large awnings are heavy, the added weight of a second awning may make this impractical.

On trailers, one of the supports of a full-length awning may have to be located over a window. If the window is nonopening it presents no problem, but if the window opens outward, it can't be opened until the awning support is lowered.

HOT-WEATHER SITE SELECTION

Where and how the RV is parked can make a difference in keeping it cool. If the campground has trees, try to park in a place that's shaded in the afternoon, the hottest part of the day. If shade isn't available, a site where the afternoon sun won't hit the RV broadside—unless you have an awning that can shade it—is desirable. We sometimes try to select a site where the door faces north, so it will be in the shade all day, and we can have it open without the sun streaming in.

Other factors need to be considered in site selection: We sometimes received some heat bounceback and unpleasant, glaring reflected light when we were parked close to a white building. If possible, park where there is good air circulation. If buildings block the wind, you may find your site hot because little breeze can reach it.

Incidentally, the refrigerator functions better in hot weather if the RV is parked so that the side the refrigerator is on is shaded or away from the full intensity of the sun.

A point about RVs that most people, including manufacturers, don't give much thought to: An RV with a dark-colored exterior will absorb more heat and thus be more difficult to cool than white or light-colored RVs.

CHAPTER 16

Rig Maintenance: Inside and Out

As far as we are concerned, ease of maintenance is one of the real joys of fulltiming. If you are used to keeping up a house and yard, you may actually feel somewhat guilty about how little maintenance you'll have with your RV. It's almost as if you are getting away with something. Enjoy. The guilt soon goes away with the realization that little maintenance is just another of the benefits of this way of life. After a while, when you see some poor individuals mowing their lawns, you may chortle smugly to yourself and wonder why they haven't seen the light and taken up your free and easy lifestyle.

Except for jobs requiring specialized equipment, fulltimers can perform nearly all general maintenance and many repairs if they want to. Some fulltimers who don't have to watch what they spend don't have to be do-it-yourselfers, but if you are on a limited budget, doing your own maintenance and repairs can save you a great deal.

Another advantage to doing your own work is that you will make sure things are done right because it's in your best interest to do so. You will care, because what you are working on is your property.

Of course, not all mechanics and service people are careless or incompetent, but often you never know until the work is done. They may leave out a part. They may not tighten all fastenings properly or be careful about keeping dirt and foreign objects from items on which they are working. If they cannot fix what needs to be repaired, they may not admit it but charge for the "work" done anyway.

Whether or not you do your work yourself, you should understand how all the systems in your RV function. The benefit of knowing about your RV is that you can make an intelligent judgment about what work needs to be done or if it needs to done at all. Informative articles about RV systems appear regularly in *Trailer Life* and *MotorHome* magazines, and more detailed information about maintenance and care can be found in the new edition of the *RV Repair & Maintenance Manual, Third Edition,* by Bob Livingston (order from Trailer Life Books, 64 Inverness Drive East, Englewood, Colorado 80112; (800) 766-1674). Owner's manuals are also a good source of information.

For your own protection, don't be like the motorhomer we met who said he didn't want to know how anything worked (after we had just helped him solve a problem with his electrical hookup). "I just want to push a button or flick a switch and have it work," he said. Don't we all wish it were as simple as that?

If a problem crops up with a piece of equipment on our trailer, we may call the manufacturer for advice. We often find out what is causing the problem, and how we can fix it, or have it fixed. A telephone call is cheap compared with any repair bill, and many manufacturers have a toll-free number. The number to call is usually in the owner's manual or on the instruction or warranty sheet.

On one occasion our refrigerator cooled only intermittently when operating on electricity. We called the manufacturer, and the consumer-service representative described two possible causes of the problem and how to correct each. Both proved easy to do, and we managed to fix the refrigerator ourselves.

If a service person tells us we need an expensive repair, we usually call the manufacturer for a second opinion.

It's a good idea to periodically inspect all areas that may need maintenance. This keeps you aware of what's going on and allows you to take care of problems before they require major work.

HOUSECLEANING TOOLS

Most fulltimers rely on a vacuum cleaner for their main interior cleaning tool. Some manufacturers offer built-in vacuum systems with their units . When we inquired about having this option on our trailer, the salesman advised against it. He said a satisfactory amount of suction would not be available in the outlets farthest away from the vacuum motor. We decided against a built-in vacuum, but not for that reason (we don't know if he was right or wrong); we found the motor, hose, and accessories for a built-in vacuum took up more space than a portable vacuum.

A vacuum cleaner with upholstery, dusting, and crevice tools is particularly useful for cleaning an RV's small areas, odd corners, and storage compartments.

We use a 120-volt AC vacuum cleaner exclusively because the 12-volt models we have tried take longer to clean, aren't powerful enough to do a good job, and may not have many, or any, attachments.

We've noticed that some RVers keep their vacuum in an outside compartment. If we kept ours outside, we are sure we wouldn't use it as often as we should.

A carpet sweeper can be used instead of a vacuum cleaner when 120-volt AC power is not available.

We have room for a standard-size, long-handled broom, but if we didn't, we would carry a whisk broom for those jobs when only a broom will do.

In addition to the normal cleaning tools and supplies, we save old toothbrushes to use for jobs such as cleaning stove knobs, stubborn spots on our textured window shades and walls, around sink faucets, and along counter edgings.

DUSTING

When living full time in a recreational vehicle, dust collects quickly. It's always in the air and it has to settle somewhere. In an RV it doesn't have much area in which to dissipate. And a certain amount of road dust will enter even the best-sealed RV. Although dusting needs to be done frequently, there is much less of it to do in an RV.

Since window and door screens are on the inside of most RV windows, they collect their share of dust. Whenever we dust with the vacuum instead of a dust cloth, we always use the dusting tool to go over all the screens, including those in the roof vents. As long as we are at it, we dust all grillwork: the furnace compartment covering, furnace duct registers, the air conditioner grill, the back, sides, and top of the television. We would dust miniblinds this way if we had them (or purchase a special vacuum tool just for miniblinds). A vacuum dusting tool is the only way to clean such items easily and thoroughly.

CARPETING, DRAPERY, AND UPHOLSTERY CARE

As a result of concentrated use, carpeting becomes soiled more quickly in an RV than it would in a larger area. Eventually, vacuuming alone won't remove the soil; the carpeting needs to be cleaned by another method. Most carpeting in newer RVs is stain resistant and soil can be cleaned off with a damp sponge. When more thorough cleaning is needed, we don't use a detergent carpet cleaner as this leaves a soapy residue that seems to attract dirt. We use either Woolite or Scotchguard foam carpet cleaner, and even these sparingly. Unless all the foam is removed by repeated rinsing, this too will attract dirt.

In some large RVs, there is room enough to maneuver a steam cleaner or shampooer, which could be used for a badly soiled or dingy-looking carpet.

Carpet needs to be replaced when it becomes so soiled that no method of cleaning restores its brightness. In smaller RVs this may be every few years. In larger units, where the traffic is not as concentrated, carpeting lasts longer.

Much dirt, mud, and sand can be kept from the carpeting by having a door mat both inside and outside the door. Inexpensive carpet samples or throw rugs can be used for this purpose. We use carpet samples that cost a dollar or two, and when they are soiled beyond the stage where cleaning with a damp sponge is not enough, we throw them away and buy new ones.

To give us another foot-wiping place, we have carpeted the fold-down door steps. We can't use ready-made vinyl-loop mats (the kind that are attached with an adhesive strip or springs) because they are too thick to allow our steps to fold. After some experimenting we found the best way to attach the carpeting on our steps is with wire. The ends of a length of wire are pushed down through the carpet and through the perforations in the metal step, then pulled tightly so the wire is semi-buried in the carpet nap. To secure it, the ends of the wire are twisted firmly together under the step.

When we travel, we may stop several times along the way to shop, refuel, or have lunch. The trailer may be parked in a place where oil and grease are on the ground, such as in service stations and highway rest areas, or where it's wet from rain.

To avoid soiling the carpet if we enter the trailer, prior to a day's run, we always put a vinyl runner in the entryway that extends from the door across the width of the trailer (Figure 16.1). Vinyl runners such as these are sold by the foot in hardware and home-improvement stores. We keep the runner handy in the entryway, rolled up and stored in one of our fold-down-front boxes. The entire front on this box drops down when the lid is raised, so the rolled-up vinyl can easily be removed and replaced. The box fits tidily into a space next to the door. So it would be unobtrusive, we covered it with an adhesive-backed material in a color close to that of the wall.

Upholstery and draperies should be cleaned according to the instructions in your owner's manual—maybe. The owner's manual for our previous trailer said the draperies should be dry cleaned. When we took them to the cleaner we were told dry cleaning would ruin them; they should be washed. A second opinion

> **"To** avoid soiling the carpet if we enter the trailer, prior to a day's run, we always put a vinyl runner in the entryway that extends from the door across the width of the trailer.**"**

Figure 16.1 Before traveling, the authors put a vinyl runner on the floor by the entry door. When not in use, the rolled-up runner is stored in the box shown.

agreed with the first. We crossed our fingers and washed the draperies. They cleaned up beautifully. Most owner's manuals are written to cover all RV models of a particular manufacturer, so the manual may not deal specifically with a variation you may have in your particular RV. Check with professionals when in doubt.

We often give the draperies a light going-over with the vacuum dusting tool and use the vacuum upholstery tool for regular cleaning of upholstered items (and sometimes for the carpet in places where the rug tool won't fit). Our upholstery is stain resistant as is the upholstery in most RVs. Like the carpet, it needs only wiping with a damp sponge to remove most spots and soil.

We clean the seats of upholstered pieces about every other month. The furniture receives so much concentrated use that if we didn't clean it regularly, the seats would eventually become slightly grayer than the rest of the upholstery.

To remove stains and stubborn grime from just about any surface, including cloth, we often spot clean with Simple Green liquid cleaner, diluted or undiluted according to the intensity and type of the stain or soil. Unless we have used Simple Green on a surface before, we always test it in an unobtrusive spot first.

BATH MAINTENANCE

Most RV bath fixtures are plastic or fiberglass which means they shouldn't be scrubbed with harsh, abrasive cleansers, which will scratch the surface. Even repeated scouring with mild cleansers can roughen the surfaces of plastic fixtures.

A liquid cleanser such as Soft Scrub works well when a little abrasiveness is needed. Window cleaner makes fixture surfaces sparkle. We especially like it for cleaning the shower walls; it easily removes dried water spots and leaves the walls streak-free. We also use a soap-scum remover periodically in the shower and on the faucet. We do this before taking a shower so we can take care of rinsing the cleaned surfaces with water (as the directions recommend) before we step out.

Whether or not we have used the soap-scum remover, we always wipe dry the walls in the shower after use. Our shower/tub is one molded unit with walls about five feet tall. If you have just a shower basin with a caulk or molding seal around the edges, check often to see if it is sealed tightly all around. If not, water can seep down behind it and cause mildew to form or wooden structural members to rot.

Our toilet has a good seal on it; nevertheless we frequently use a deodorizer. We haven't the space to store a large bottle of liquid deodorizer in the bath, and don't want the concern of spillage, so we use the tablet type and put in extra tablets in hot weather, when holding tanks are their most odoriferous.

CARING FOR WOODWORK
AND WALL COVERINGS

Cabinets in recreational vehicles may be wood or a vinyl-covered wood look-alike. Both have an easy-care finish that can be wiped with a damp cloth to remove soil. A spray dusting/cleaning product usually removes finger smudges and leaves a shiny finish. A spray-on product such as 303 Protectant can restore the luster to vinyl-covered surfaces.

Because some of our galley cabinets pick up a film of cooking grease, we clean them every couple of months or when needed with a grease-removing, liquid spray cleaner. We use the cleaner sparingly and wipe the cleaned surface with a damp cloth or sponge, then dry it with a soft cloth. Never use large amounts of water or liquid cleaner when cleaning wood or imitation wood finishes. Consult your owner's manual for recommendations about cleaning these surfaces in your RV.

Vinyl wall coverings also can be cleaned with a liquid spray cleaner. Sometimes where the molding on a counter top meets a textured wall covering, a dingy, gray buildup occurs in the textured finish because of repeated counter wipings. We use liquid cleaner on a toothbrush to scrub out the buildup from the little indentations in the texture. The toothbrush bristles are tiny enough to clean between the bumps and ridges of the texture. If the liquid cleaner doesn't do the job, we resort to Soft Scrub on a toothbrush, rubbing gently to avoid removing any of the wall covering's finish.

An RV's ceilings stay clean for a long time if the occupants don't smoke and if the range-hood fan is used regularly when cooking. Dishwashing detergent or a liquid cleaner removes soil and film from many ceiling finishes. When using any liquid above your head, take care to shield your eyes from drops and mist. Fabric ceilings, which are found in some RVs, can be cleaned with a vacuum upholstery tool or, if badly soiled, with upholstery shampoo.

ROOF-VENT MAINTENANCE

Roof-vent covers and their screens collect a lot of dirt and dust. Bathroom-vent covers may accumulate mildew. Most screens can be removed for cleaning by undoing a few screws in the frame (and unscrewing the fan switch on the bathroom vent.) Squirt the screen with liquid cleaner, then go over the entire screen with a brush (a toothbrush is good for this) to loosen dirt. Rinse under a faucet and shake dry. The cleaning and rinsing is better done outside so spatters from the brush won't make another mess to be cleaned up, and rinsing is easier under an outside faucet than in a sink.

The vent covers can be cleaned with a window or liquid cleaner. A toothbrush is useful for cleaning around the vent hinges, support, and in corners.

While cleaning the vents, check the weatherstrip gasket. Reattach it if it has come loose. Sometimes the gasket can be pressed back into place, or it may need to be reglued.

CLEANING SUPPLIES

We rarely do a major housecleaning of the entire trailer at one time. Instead we do little jobs every now and then as necessary so we don't have to devote a lot of time just to cleaning (this is high on our list of least-liked chores). To make this spot- and area-cleaning easy, we have all the cleaning supplies we use regularly in places where they are readily accessible. We keep a box of supplies in both a galley cabinet and a bath cabinet. It may seem unnecessary to have two sets of cleaning supplies only twelve feet away from each other, but we find that we get jobs done more quickly if supplies are right at hand.

We don't have room for a roll of paper towels in the bath, but we made a small, narrow, cardboard box to hold towels cut in quarters. The box is affixed to the inside of the cabinet door where the cleaning supplies are kept. The small squares are just the right size for most cleaning jobs in the bath where towels would be used instead of a sponge.

DEALING WITH ODORS

Cooking odors don't have room to disperse in an RV as they do in a house, and tend to linger. We have entered some RVs and had our nostrils assailed with stale cooking odors. We don't want a smelly trailer, so we use a room deodorizer all the time. It's a small, solid type that we keep in a corner where it's out of sight but centrally located so it takes care of the entire trailer. If we cook bacon or some other food that leaves a strong odor, we give the trailer a spritz with a spray deodorizer in the same fragrance as the solid.

PEST CONTROL

Some RVs without an enclosed underbody may have gaps around plumbing pipes where the pipes enter through the floor. Any such opening can be the entryway for all sorts of pests, large and small, from ants and roaches to rats.

In our 23-footer, we had a charming little field mouse as a house guest for a couple of days. It came in through a small gap next to the shower drainpipe. We sealed the hole by packing steel wool around the pipe and wrapping duct tape over the area to hold it in.

Another way rodents can enter is by crawling up the shore-power cable. Figure 16.2 illustrates a simple device that can be made from sheet metal to prevent rodents from gaining entry by this route.

Close all outside compartments when you cannot observe them; we once saw a stray cat jump into an open one.

If screens have holes, flies and mosquitoes will find their way in through them. If you have a screen hole, you can place a piece of tape over it or stuff a wad of tissue in it temporarily, but the screen should be patched with another piece of screen or replaced as soon as possible.

Most people who have traveled in the South know about the precautions that must be taken to keep from being overrun by roaches. For those who have not spent time in the southern states or Mexico, here are a few facts: The cleanliness of your RV has nothing to do with keeping roaches away; they are just as happy living in a clean place as a dirty one. Any roach that gets in may deposit eggs somewhere or eggs may be brought in from outside, often in the folds of paper bags and under the labels on cans and jars. Any carton that is glued should be suspect as a roach hideout or egg depository; roaches like to eat glue. Groceries should be thoroughly inspected before they are taken inside.

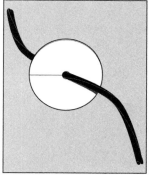

Figure 16.2 This device can be installed on the shore-power cable to keep mice from entering the RV. It's simply a circular piece of sheet metal about 6 inches in diameter with a hole in the center, just large enough to accommodate the cable, and a slit on one side, for easy attachment to the cable.

Kill any roach the moment you see it, if you can. Some southern roaches are nearly two inches long—easy to see but difficult to kill unless whacked with a heavy object. We found a hammer to be a good weapon for dispatching these monster pests. If a roach is too fleet-footed for you and runs into a confined area where it can't be reached with a roach bludgeon, use a spray insecticide to kill it. Don't let it get away or you may have scores of roaches to deal with soon. When spraying, be sure there is adequate ventilation, and thoroughly wash any items the spray lands on, especially kitchen-ware items.

As careful as we were, we were not entirely successful in keeping roaches out of our RV when we were in the South. Luckily, we've never been overrun with roaches—we've been invaded by only one or two at a time—so we've never needed the services of a professional exterminator, the only way of eliminating a severe roach infestation.

Unpleasant as it is, keep roaches in mind when buying a used RV in the South. One of our friends found that he acquired a bumper crop of roaches along with the used trailer he purchased.

EXTERIOR CLEANING

The exterior finish on motorhomes and trailers usually stays new-looking for years with little care other than an occasional cleaning.

If you prefer to wash your unit when it's time for cleaning, you may not be able to do so because vehicle washing is not allowed at many campgrounds. There are good reasons for this:

- Water is scarce and must be conserved in many arid areas of the country.
- Some people use much more water than they need, resulting in sites covered with unsightly piles of suds and puddles of water.
- Water may be plentiful but expensive; the campground operator may not be able to afford having guests use water for vehicle washing.
- The operators of luxury vacation and resort RV parks, or the operators of any campgrounds for that matter, simply may not want to have any sort of maintenance work done on their premises.

Some towns have do-it-yourself recreational vehicle washes, similar to car washes. They have bays tall enough to accommodate trailers and motorhomes and a catwalk so the top and roof of an RV can be reached. Truck washes are also large enough to accommodate trailers and motorhomes.

We used to clean our trailer with water (when there were no campground regulations forbidding it), usually by working from a bucket for the washing, using the hose adjusted to a trickle for rinsing, and cleaning only a small section at a time. But now we rarely use water for exterior cleaning. When we were cleaning the windows one day, some of the window cleaner was accidentally sprayed on the painted finish of the trailer and as we wiped it off, we found it cleaned superbly. We experimented with more and more of the trailer and in very little time, one entire side, including the windows, which were what we had set out to clean, was spick-and-span.

Now we clean the trailer almost exclusively with this waterless method. Because it's so simple and easy to do, we don't put off what used to be a dreary chore: We would first change into old clothes because we knew we'd get wet and messy. Then we would string the hose around the campsite and collect buckets and brushes, cleaner, rags, and a ladder (taking the time to assemble all the equipment needed for washing often caused us to delay the job). Having gone to the trouble of collecting all the needed equipment, we felt we had to do the whole trailer. With our tall, 29-footer, that's a tiring job even with both of us working at it. Our final chore was to put all the cleaning equipment away.

Using window cleaner is so much simpler. To do the job, all that is needed is a spray bottle of window cleaner and a handful of paper towels (we tear them in half). A plastic grocery bag for holding the towels hangs from one wrist. When a towel becomes soiled it's wadded up and dropped into the bag where it finds its way to the bottom underneath the clean towels. It's easy to work out of the wide mouth of the bag, and it keeps the towels from blowing if it's windy.

If the exterior surface is dusty, as much dust as possible is gently wiped off with dry paper towels; if a liquid is applied to dust, the muddy streaking it creates is a mess that requires extra effort and materials to clean.

We like this method of cleaning because we can start or stop the job whenever we want. We never allow the trailer to become really dirty, so a cleaned area doesn't contrast noticeably with the uncleaned sections.

Once, at a truck stop, Bill went in to make some phone calls; Jan whipped out the window cleaner—a container of which is stored in both the galley and the bath—and a few towels and cleaned a portion of the trailer while she was waiting. We finished the job later when we arrived at our destination.

Window cleaner may remove black streaks if they haven't been neglected for too long. On our trailer, we sometimes get short, black streaks emanating from the lower corners of the windows that window cleaner won't remove. For these, a damp sponge with

> **"O**nce, at a truck stop, Bill went in to make some phone calls; Jan whipped out the window cleaner . . . and a few towels and cleaned a portion of the trailer while she was waiting.**"**

a minuscule drop of Soft Scrub (from an unshaken bottle, so less of the abrasive material is present) is gently rubbed on the streak, which removes it instantly. The area is wiped with a clean, damp sponge (the other end of the same sponge the Soft Scrub is on can be used) so no residue remains. We also have had good luck using a gel cleaner for such streaks; there's no abrasive in the gel products.

About eight ounces of window cleaner is all that's needed to clean our trailer and its windows, and maybe forty paper-towel halves. We've never figured it out, but we suspect the cost is probably about the same, or less than, using a special RV cleaner.

Our trailer has a painted, extruded aluminum exterior on which the window cleaner works very well. We assume it would be just as effective on units with fiberglass exteriors.

Where lots of bugs have met their doom on the front of the trailer, we sometimes use water from a bucket to soften the carcasses, then scrub with a net-covered sponge to remove them. We also occasionally use the type of tar and bug remover that requires no water rinse.

A toothbrush is useful for spot-cleaning a pebbled surface, the type found on the lower front of some trailers. When rinsing a pebbled surface flood it with water—a well-saturated sponge will do the trick—to flush away the grime from the small crevices.

LEAKPROOFING THE RV

Leaks inside the RV most likely come from a roof seam or from around a window. All potential leak sources should be checked regularly and sealed if needed. Look for cracks in roof seams, voids in the window sealant, and, harder to see, hairline-width places along the edges of the sealant where it has come loose. Inspect these areas carefully for tiny holes where seepage into the walls can occur. Leaks such as these may not be apparent until much damage has been done.

Owners of RVs with laminate sides must be extra careful about roof leaks. If leaks aren't caught early, they can cause delamination, which is an expensive repair. If delamination from leaks occurs while under warranty, you may have to pay for the repair yourself if you haven't done the maintenance as outlined in the owner's manual.

On many trailer windows, leakproofing can be done with a putty strip (available in rolls at RV-supply stores). After removing and cleaning the window frame, a strip of new putty is laid around the window opening. Then the window frame is set back in place and screwed down. Mineral spirits should be used to remove old putty residue and for cleaning tools and hands.

Putty shrinks eventually. If shrinkage or voids are found around the edges of a window, the putty should be replaced. If a leak is noticed inside the RV, new putty may eliminate it. Before going to the trouble of removing and rebedding a window, make doubly sure the sealant is the problem; check the screws in the window frame to see if any are loose. If so, tightening them may stop the leak. When we removed the trim on our windows to see if dirt had collected behind it and was causing the black streaks at the corners we mentioned earlier, we found many loose screws in each window. Instead of just tightening the screws, we removed them and coated them with caulking before being reinserted; this method makes them leakproof.

Silicone caulk is often used for sealing on RVs. It must be removed before new caulking can be applied—often a difficult job. Sometimes the bulk of it can be sliced off with a sharp knife and any remaining bits scraped off with a knife or flat screwdriver blade, or rubbed off with a finger using a lot of pressure.

We tried some silicone caulk remover. It softened the caulk, and we were able to remove it, but it also softened the paint under the caulk. When we wiped off the caulk, the paint came with it leaving bare metal.

Silicone caulk seems to attract road grime and turns black. A swipe or two with some tar remover on a rag removes such grime and diesel soot.

"Silicone caulk seems to attract road grime and turns black.**"**

VEHICLE AND ENGINE MAINTENANCE

Automotive engines are becoming more and more sophisticated and complex. Special equipment is often needed for diagnosing and fixing problems. Unless working on engines is your hobby, most engine troubles are best taken care of by a qualified mechanic. You can do most routine servicing if you want to and if you are in a campground where vehicle servicing is allowed.

Any engine or transmission that has to pull a heavy load, whether in a motorhome or tow vehicle, needs to have basic servicing done more frequently than vehicles that don't do heavy-duty work. The owner's manual contains a service maintenance schedule. Tow vehicles have two servicing schedules: one for use when towing, the other for regular use. Follow the schedules for oil changes, transmission-fluid changes, filter replacement, brake servicing, and the like; otherwise, serious mechanical problems may result that may make the vehicle unsafe to drive. Proper maintenance makes any vehicle last longer.

Trailers should have the wheel bearings cleaned, inspected, and repacked according to manufacturer's instructions and the brakes checked at regular intervals.

Changing oil and transmission fluid are two of the most important maintenance procedures for fulltimers who put a lot of miles on their rigs. We remind ourselves when these jobs are due by putting two, small, pressure-sensitive labels on the inside back wall of the glove box where they are easily seen every time it's opened. One is labeled "oil," the other, "transmission." Each has the date of the last servicing and the mileage at which the next servicing is due. (Because we have a diesel and a clean fuel filter is necessary for optimum performance, we have a fuel-filter-change reminder label also.)

In a spiral notebook, we keep a record of all fluid changes, as well as when any oil is added between oil changes and when servicing of any type is done.

Unless engine batteries are the no-maintenance type, water should be added as needed. When under the hood checking the battery, give the fan belts the once-over. Look for cracks and check them for tightness. House batteries should be checked regularly as well unless they are the no-maintenance type.

Any trailer hitch ball, whether on a trailer or on a tow dolly, should be well greased. On a travel-trailer hitch, lubricate any part of the hitch equipment that works against a metal surface, except for the slide bar on a sway control, which must never be lubricated.

Trailerists should check the suspension system often. Look for wear on spring hangers and elongation of bolt holes in the hangers and on the shackles.

The area where the pin box fits on a fifth-wheel hitch needs periodic lubrication unless a non-lube disk that slips over the pin is used.

Electrical connections between a tow vehicle and trailer or between a motorhome and a tow dolly or an auxiliary vehicle should be sprayed regularly with a moisture-removing compound such as WD-40.

It's a good idea to check out running lights each time before the RV is moved. If one does not work and the bulb is not burned out or improperly seated, the bulb may not be making proper contact. Remove the bulb and spray some WD-40 in the socket. If that doesn't solve the problem, try cleaning the contact points with emery cloth.

TIRES

Often overlooked when it comes to basic maintenance are the tires. Since all RVs put heavy loads on their tires, it's most important that they be inflated to the proper pressure. Check them frequently, when they are cold.

When a trailer or motorhome is parked for some time in one place, the tires should be covered to protect them from the sun, which can cause deterioration. Anything can be used that will keep the sun off. Some RVers merely stand a piece of plywood next to the tires. Ready-made snap-on or slip-on tire covers can be purchased.

A tire that blows out can cause a lot of damage to an RV. All tires should be replaced before they become dangerously worn.

All RV tires, including trailer tires, should be balanced.

MAINTENANCE AND REPAIR EQUIPMENT

Earlier we mentioned keeping an assortment of tools handy inside the RV for doing simple maintenance and fix-it jobs.

When it comes to storage, tools shouldn't be buried so it's a problem getting to them, or jobs may be left undone or let go too long if tools aren't accessible.

The tools and spare equipment you need depend on the amount of work you do yourself and where you travel. A trip along the Alaska Highway, for example, requires more such items than travel over interstate highways in populated areas.

RVers should keep extra automotive fluids on hand: oil and transmission and brake fluids. Don't store opened containers of brake fluid. Moisture from the atmosphere can enter the container and may cause brake problems if used. Buy the smallest size container of brake fluid and don't open it until needed.

If a water filter is used, keep extra cartridges on hand.

The more flexible type of sewer hose never lasts long and it can't be used if there is a rip in it, so a spare hose is handy. The spare can be used when an extension is needed to reach a sewer connection.

CHAPTER 17

Campgrounds

Finding a place to park the rig seems to be one of the most worrisome aspects of fulltiming for many of those about to embark on the lifestyle. The basis for this statement is because of the numerous times people have asked us, "How do you find a place to stay?" This shouldn't be a concern for anyone; not only are there plenty of campgrounds throughout the country open in all seasons, there are numerous publications to aid in finding those to suit your needs and budget.

HOW TO FIND A CAMPGROUND

Locating campgrounds is easy. Several different campground directories can be purchased at bookstores (usually in the travel section), newsstands, and RV-supply stores, and ordered directly from the publishers.

Directories that contain listings for all states and also Canada and Mexico are the annually published *Trailer Life Directory for Campgrounds, RV Parks & Services* and *Woodall's Campground Directory.* Both may be found in the preceding outlets or can be ordered by mail. For the Trailer Life directory: Trailer Life Books, 64 Inverness Drive East, Englewood, Colorado 80112; (800) 766-1674.

For Woodall's: 13975 West Polo Drive, Lake Forest, Illinois 60045; (800) 323-9076.

In addition to its all-state directory, which is a thick book, Woodall's also publishes separate directories for eastern and western states. Since these are about half the thickness of the all-state directory, we usually purchase the smaller versions. It costs just a few dollars more than buying the one directory, but it's worth it for the convenience when referring to the directory and storing it.

Bookstores and newsstands are good sources for campground directories about the local area.

The American Automobile Association (AAA) has several regional campground directories available to members. The AAA directories have many listings of public campgrounds, in addition to listings of private campgrounds meeting AAA criteria.

Many states also issue their own camping guides. They are free and available at welcome centers on interstate highways, local visitor centers, and chamber of commerce offices. We also look for brochures for individual campgrounds in these places; some may have a discount coupon.

Directories typically list all types of campgrounds, from those that are primitive with no hookups to resorts with every sort of facility an RVer could want. Nearly all contain specific travel directions for reaching each campground, along with information about the number of sites, what hookups are available, whether the campground is open all year or seasonally, and the fee charged (Figure 17.1).

Most list the time limit, if one exists, that an RV can occupy the site, maximum size of RV that can be accommodated, and services available at the campground: laundry, pay telephone, propane, groceries, and the like. Some include the altitude.

The Trailer Life and Woodall's directories both rate campgrounds—Trailer Life with a number system, Woodall's with stars. The Trailer Life directory is unique in that it has a rating for the campground's visual appeal. When this rating was introduced, we didn't think it would be of much use to us, but we have found it to

How to Read a Campground Listing

Each listing gives you advance information such as the exact location of the campground, its rates, and the completeness of its facilities. This example is from the *Trailer Life Directory*, which carries a full explanation of all its symbols and details.

Location on map. Check for the proximity of campground. Is another one closer?

Elevation. High elevation may mean a long, steep (gas-burning) climb.

Good Sam Club. The Good Sam Park symbol means that Good Sam Club members save 10 percent on camping fees if they pay in cash.

Season. Avoid an unnecessary drive; be sure the campground is open. Rates may be lower during "shoulder" seasons, in this case, April and November.

Access. Good access roads mean saving wear and tear in getting there.

Directions. Precise directions save you a telephone call and searching time. If the campground is just off an interstate, it might be more expensive than another farther from the highway. If its a remote campground, save backtracking by picking up supplies in advance.

Regulations. In this case, if you have a pet, you know not to waste a trip to this campground.

Site description. You can save an unnecessary trip if the sites are unsuitable for your needs. The availability of shaded sites may mean less air-conditioning time. Note also the availability of hookups. If you don't need them, compare the number of available sites to the number of hookup sites. If some sites do not have hookups, you can probably save money by requesting such a site.

Facilities. Evaluate your needs of the moment; if you need some simple groceries, or need to fill your LP tanks, the availability of such services can save you a side trip.

Recreation. If the campground seems to have enough to interest every member of the

FORESTVILLE – **A4** *Springtown*

✗ **VIEWLINE RV RESORT** (Priv) 55+. Elev 2895 ft. Apr 15 to Nov 1. LOSF. Fair gravel access rd. From Jct of I-80 & exit 46 (SR-447), N 5 mi on SR-447 to Elm Ave, W 1.5 mi (L). Good paved/gravel interior rds. No pets, 25 tent sites, 10 rental units. **SITES** (150 total spaces.) Avail: 75 paved, 25 grass, 50 dirt, patios, no slide-outs, mostly shaded, 75 pull-thrus (30 x 55), back-ins (20 x 35), big rig sites, 14 day max stay, some side-by-side hookups, 110 W, 100 S, 110 E (30/50 amps), city water, modem hu/site, cable TV. **FAC** Restrooms & showers, dump, security, public phone, laundry, groceries, firewood, ltd RV supplies, LP gas, food service.. **REC** Clear Lake: freshwater fishing, tackle, swimming, boating: ramp, dock, marina, rental. Pool, spa, adult room, shuffleboard, horseshoes, rec hall, game room, planned activities, playground, rec field. Last year's rates: $14 to $23.50, V,M,D no reservations, viewline@rv.com (818) 555-4908
✔ **TL: 7/8.5/8**
See ad this page & web ad
camping.tl.com/campgrounds/viewline/

family, you'll undoubtedly save on day trips away from the campground. If there's a boat ramp, you'll save the launch fees you'd pay elsewhere.

Rate guidelines. Rates listed in the *Trailer Life Directory* are for two adults, including additional fees such as cable TV, air conditioning, and heating. These are always just guidelines, but useful for comparisons with other campgrounds. If you like, enjoy the "float" period that charging allows; note that charge cards are accepted.

Ratings. These are just as important as the rates. The ratings tell you what you're getting for your money, the completeness of the facilities, the condition of the restrooms, and also the campground's visual appeal and environmental quality.

Advertising. The presence of an advertisement can be useful; an ad may supply additional information, such as a map that just might determine your choice of campground.

Figure 17.1 A campground directory provides RVers with the information needed to aid them in the selection of places to stay.

Figure 17.2 These familiar signs found on interstate and other highways direct RVers to campgrounds and dump stations.

be helpful; it often influences us when we are trying to chose between several campgrounds in an area. The Trailer Life directory is also the only one that lets RVers know whether a campground's sites can accommodate slideouts and rates a campground's laundry facilities for cleanliness. Campgrounds that are Good Sam Parks are indicated in the Trailer Life directory—useful for members of the Good Sam Club because they receive a 10 percent discount on the daily rate.

Some directories contain a map of each state that shows the towns where campgrounds are located. State directories generally arrange their listings by areas or counties.

We use many directories because we have found that not all campgrounds are listed in any one directory, and we usually purchase new editions annually, so we'll have current information.

The familiar blue signs with a white trailer seen on all interstates and many other highways have arrows beneath them indicating the way to campgrounds (Figure 17.2). These signs should not be used exclusively to find campgrounds. You have no information about the campground and how far away it is. Often we can correlate the sign with a listing in a campground directory, but on a few occasions, we have seen this sign and found no listing in any of our directories. In this case, if we have the time, we check it out in case we may want to stay there at some future date.

Many road maps indicate public campgrounds, but few provide any more information than just a symbol designating the location. Relying on a map alone for finding a campground isn't practical. Locations are sometimes imprecise, and you have no way of knowing in advance whether the campground is suitable for the length or type of your RV.

If you must stay in an area where no campgrounds are listed in your sources, perhaps one can be found in the Yellow Pages of the local telephone directory. Look under the headings: Campgrounds, Recreational Vehicle Parks, Trailer Parks, and Mobile Home Parks.

Military RV, Camping & Recreation Areas Around the World is a directory of Fam-camps—campgrounds open to any active duty or retired member of the armed forces, civilian Department of Defense employee, and dependents and family members. It may be purchased from: Military Living Publications, P.O. Box 2347, Falls Church, Virginia 22042-0347; (703) 237-0203.

TYPES OF CAMPGROUNDS

A great diversity of campgrounds is available for RVers, from those in the hearts of cities to those off the beaten path in the back country. They may be private or public. Some are under the administration of the federal government: those in national parks and national forests, on Bureau of Land Management (BLM) lands, and at Corps of Engineers (COE) projects.

Nearly every state has a park system, and many of the parks have campgrounds. Some county parks have camping areas. All across the country, from the smallest hamlet to good-size towns, you'll find city parks with camping facilities. Campgrounds are maintained by some paper, lumber, and power companies, and camping may be available at fairgrounds.

Although the contiguous forty-eight states have an abundance of campgrounds, there are areas in certain states where camping facilities are some distance apart.

Membership campgrounds may not always be conveniently located for fulltimers. All too often they are heavily clustered in vacation areas and almost nonexistent in other places. Some membership campground associations don't have facilities in all states.

Campground Rates and Facilities

The highest campground rates are found in resort towns, vacation areas, and at RV parks in and around large cities. Rates are higher in campgrounds with such amenities as swimming pools—heated or not—saunas, tennis courts, and golf courses.

Private Campgrounds

"Rates at many campgrounds on old highways that have been bypassed by the interstates are some of the best camping bargains.**"**

Some private campgrounds have a flat fee that includes all hookups while some have one base fee and an additional, separate charge for each hookup: electricity, water, and sewer. If you elect to have no sewer hookup in one of these places, there may or may not be a charge if you use the campground's dump station. We have stayed at several campgrounds where the base fee plus the dumping fee was higher than the charge for full hookups.

In some campgrounds, the rate with or without hookups does not include the use of the showers. There may be an extra charge for shower usage; some showers have a coin-operated meter. Many campgrounds impose a charge of one or two dollars per day if an electric heater or air conditioner is used. If the campground offers cable television, it may cost an extra dollar or two if you wish to use it, although we have noticed that this charge is now often included in the regular rate.

One fact about private campgrounds has few exceptions: Any campground adjacent to an interstate highway costs more than a comparable one that is not so conveniently located for the traveler. If you want to save money, find a campground a distance away from the interstate. Rates at many campgrounds on old highways that have been bypassed by interstates are some of the best camping bargains.

We have stayed at campgrounds on interstate highways many times, and we have observed that some of the people running the campgrounds seem to be rather cold and impersonal, giving the impression that they are interested in only taking our money. We'll give them the benefit of the doubt and assume this attitude occurs because so many of their customers are transients who pull off the highway late in the day and are gone early next morning, and those registering the campers are so busy that they have no time to establish any personal rapport with their customers. Nevertheless, we don't feel welcome or at home in many such campgrounds, and we rarely return to them a second time. Aside from the high rates charged, a campground next to an interstate highway is noisy. This is a fact with no exceptions.

Off-season rates aren't often found unless the campground is located in a popular vacation area or in the Sunbelt.

We are of the opinion that any time the cost for a campsite approaches that of a motel room—any motel room—it is overpriced. After all, room-cleaning service is not provided with any campsite as it is in a motel. What's more, a motel never charges extra for using heat or air conditioning, as is the practice at many campgrounds, regardless of how high the base rate is. And most motels have a phone in the room for the use of their guests, and impose no extra charge for cable TV, which often includes some extra-cost channels not in the basic cable package.

No matter where you stay, you should get what you pay for. With electricity, often you don't. Any time we are charged a high rate—around $20— for a campsite that does not have 30-amp service, we feel we are being ripped off.

In a campground where the electric hookup is fused instead of being equipped with a circuit breaker (there are still plenty of these around), some misguided campground operators fuse a 15-amp circuit with a 30-amp fuse and claim you are getting 30-amp service. All you are getting is cheated. In such a situation, electrical equipment drawing the full load of 30 amps can be used for only a short time, perhaps only half an hour, before your plug and the site's outlet begins to burn. If you have to use a 15-amp plug in any outlet without an adapter, it's not 30-amp service no matter what amperage fuse is used in the circuit.

Cable and satellite TV are something else that may not be what you think you are paying for. If the cable outlet is merely a connection to the campground's antenna, providing the usual local programming, you may not want to spend any extra for it.

Facilities may not always be as listed in a directory. Once in October, we stayed in a campground with a posted notice informing guests that the main bathhouse, which contained the showers, was closed for the season. Not only was there no place for showers, but the only toilet facilities were two unheated, portable toilets. We don't use campground bathrooms or showers, but if we did, we would have been angry, after pulling in, to find the campground's

> **"C**able and satellite TV are something else that may not be what you think you are paying for.**"**

facilities were far short of what was listed in our directory. Some directory listings do contain the phrase: "Limited facilities in winter," but no indication of when "winter" begins.

We have noticed, too, that rates are rarely lowered when the swimming pool and other recreation facilities are closed for the season. It's wishful thinking, but we would like to receive lower rates if we did not use the campground's bathhouse, pool, or any other convenience and recreation facility provided. Once, at a campground in a small Nebraska town, the manager deducted two dollars from the daily rate because we told her, when she asked, that we use our own bath facilities.

Inquire about weekly rates even if you plan to stay in a campground for as little as four days, and check the monthly rate if you'll be staying only two weeks.

We have found numerous campgrounds where the rate for a few days equaled or exceeded the weekly rate, and the monthly rate was just a little more than that for two weeks. Since we have a loose schedule and don't usually have to be any place at a certain time, we have often stayed over to take advantage of these types of rates. If, for some reason, we want to leave before the period we have paid for expires, we may still be money ahead, or at least break even on what we would have paid with a daily rate. Years ago, a campground operator quoted us a very low weekly rate, but admonished us that we would have to stay the entire week in order to receive it.

Aside from saving money, there may be another advantage in paying for a longer period than you plan on staying: If the weather is bad when you intend to leave, you can stay over without any extra charge. This has worked to our advantage several times.

When we are undecided about whether we want to stay longer than overnight, we sometimes ask if the overnight rate can be applied to a weekly rate; this can be done in many places, but there are those where it can't. Before staying long-term, we sometimes prefer to spend one night to see if we have noisy neighbors and to determine if the campground may otherwise be unsatisfactory.

Often the lowest weekly or monthly rates are found in mobile-home parks.

We try to avoid campgrounds with a charge for each individual hookup. Almost without exception, they seem to be the most expensive campgrounds. We prefer to seek out small, out-of-the-way places with a reasonable, flat rate. There is a campground like this on the Oregon Coast. The owner is an RVer himself. He told us that it irritates him when he pulls into a campground and finds he has to pay extra for everything. So he charges one flat, very reasonable rate that includes cable TV.

The campground rate is low because no recreation and bath facilities are provided—RVs must be self-contained to stay there—and, unlike some others in the area, it's not on the ocean front. When we stay at this campground, an ocean view is not important to us. As fulltimers, we know we'll be parked in other places with an ocean view. Every single place we stay does not need to have a glorious panoramic view. In this campground we are satisfied, for the time we spend there, with a grassy site surrounded by tall conifers, with the ocean less than a quarter of a mile away.

We once stayed in another campground in the same section of the Oregon coast across the road from the ocean. It was years ago, and we paid the then-high rate of $10 for electricity only. Our assigned site had the laundry on one side and another RV, quite close, on the other. Our view from the front was a metal storage shed; from the back we saw the rear of a restaurant. As a contrast, later in the year in Montana, we stayed at another campground with a $10 rate, but this included full hookups, a wide site, use of the pool, and a breathtaking view of mountains in every direction.

Public Campgrounds

Many state parks have a day-use charge in addition to the camping fee. In some states, the day-use charge need not be paid if the user has purchased an annual permit. One year we saved quite a bit by buying annual permits for parks in three different states. In a few states, residents of the state pay one rate for using the state facilities; nonresidents pay more. Some states issue passes for seniors entitling them to reduced rates in state-park campgrounds.

If you intend to visit federally administered places such as national parks, purchasing a Golden Eagle or Golden Age Passport can save you money on entrance fees.

The Golden Age Passport is available to anyone sixty-two years of age or older. The one-time cost is $10. The passport allows free entry to any facility where a fee is charged and also a 50 percent discount on camping fees.

A Golden Eagle Passport, for those under age sixty-two, is good for a year and costs $50. It entitles a family or carload to free admission to any national park, monument, and recreation area but no camping discounts.

A Golden Access Passport, for blind and permanently disabled persons of any age, is free and has the same benefits as the Golden Age Passport.

Most campgrounds in national parks have no hookups. State parks' facilities range from primitive to full hookups. If a city or county park has any facilities, it may be only electricity. Sometimes water is at the site; if not, a central water supply is usually available. The most primitive campgrounds may have toilets of some sort and may have a drinking water source as well.

The rates for camping in national parks have gone up like campground rates everywhere. In some, the rates almost equal the rates in private campgrounds with full hookups. What you have to decide is whether the rate is acceptable for the beauty, quiet, and away-from-it-all ambiance that can be found in many of these campgrounds.

Camping in some state parks is not a bargain either, as it once was. The rate in some state parks for sites with or without hookups exceeds that of private campgrounds with hookups in the same area. The daily rate may be fairly low, but a daily entrance fee (we know of one that is $6) may boost it considerably. While many state parks are beautiful, some aren't. A few years ago, we entered a state park and found what we considered to be a high rate. Only electricity was included at the site. Except for being well maintained, the park was not appealing. It was neither beautiful, nor quiet, nor away by itself; it was merely a large, treeless, grassy area next to a highway just outside a town. We went on to another campground.

CAMPGROUND SITE SELECTION

We prefer to select our own campsite, but often this isn't possible. Sites are assigned in many private campgrounds and in some public parks during peak seasons. Sometimes we are allowed to select a site from a chart. When this happens, we try to take a look at the site before signing up for it.

The features we look for first are whether the site is long enough for our rig, if there is enough room for maneuvering into the site, and whether there are any low, overhanging tree branches. We have stayed in many well-maintained private campgrounds in which the operators overlook trimming back tree branches that could interfere with parking, not clear the roof of tall RVs, or obstruct a satellite dish or TV antenna when it's raised. We also check for branches on the side extending into the site.

We look at how level the site is. We're not overly picky about having our trailer exactly level, yet we find we need to use leveling boards in about two-thirds of the sites in which we stay. This is no problem because we have several leveling boards we can use singly or together for different leveling situations. We've come across a few sites (mostly in public campgrounds) in which it was impossible to level our trailer as much as necessary. Unless the RV is equipped with automatic levelers, all fulltimers should carry leveling equipment.

We check to see if the site slopes upward or downward. If the back of a site inclines downward, it may not be possible to raise either a travel or fifth-wheel trailer high enough to release it from the hitch, or, if it can be unhitched, lower it enough to level the unit. If a site is higher in back than in front, the front of a trailer or motorhome may not be able to be raised high enough for leveling.

CAMPGROUND HAZARDS

When selecting a site or a campground, consider how rain, snow, and ice may affect getting in and getting out. Once a tractor had to pull our rig out of a muddy site; another time our campsite was over a tiny grassy knoll that had become so wet and slippery from rain that the truck couldn't pull the trailer over it. Grass, for all its desirable qualities, can be a nuisance to RVers. We have had so many problems with slick, wet grass that we look askance at any grassy site that isn't perfectly level.

Sometimes an uphill or downhill campground entrance presents a problem in wet weather, and a steep, loosely graveled incline can sometimes cause slipping.

We are careful about staying too near streams and rivers when flooding may be a danger. We once intended to stay for a few days in a municipal park in a small Nebraska town. We parked in a site about 100 feet away from the river that curved around the campground area. A 10-foot high bank was behind our trailer and atop the bank, on another level, was a large, roofed pavilion. While we were registering, the manager volunteered the information that at one time flood waters reached the roof of the pavilion. During the night it rained heavily in our area and farther west. By morning, the river had risen about a foot to bank level and during the night it crept toward the campsites. Next morning, water was only about 20 feet from our trailer so we figured it was time to get out of there. We later read in the local newspaper that the water in the park rose enough so that about half the trailer would have been submerged had we remained there.

Another time in Georgia, we pulled into a county park and took a site overlooking the river, about twenty feet above the water. It had been raining for several days in the area, and when we registered we asked if there was any chance that the campground could be flooded. We were assured that this had never happened. After setting up, we left to run some errands. When we came back the river had risen considerably. We kept picking markers—branches and rocks— to watch to gauge the amount of rise. All night long we checked periodically as one marker after another disappeared under water. Late the next day the river finally stopped rising when its level was about six feet below our site, so we didn't have to leave.

Since the waters in both these campgrounds rose slowly, there was no danger of flash flooding; had there been, we wouldn't have stayed at either place. We greatly respect what the forces of nature can do, and many of the campsites we select are chosen on the basis of what nature may have in store for us.

Before we were fully accustomed to the whimsicalities of Mother Nature, we were once given a site immediately in front of a steep hill, on which several trees of various sizes were growing. One of them, about eight inches in diameter, was right behind and slightly above the trailer. When we arrived at the campground, it was misting. Soon it was raining heavily and the wind began to blow. By next morning the ground was saturated. The wind was gusting so strongly that we could see the ground over the roots of "our" tree heaving as the tree swayed back and forth. It looked as if it could topple onto the trailer at any minute, so we moved to a safer site. The tree stayed where it belonged, but we slept better knowing it wasn't above us.

We are careful about parking under trees with dead branches that could blow down in high winds, but once we were in a campground where tall cottonwoods arched over every site. The wind was blowing strongly one morning as we were having breakfast. We were startled by a loud report as if a gun had been fired. The noise brought us and our neighbors outside to see what had happened. A branch about three inches in diameter and five feet long had hurtled down and, spear-like, had pierced the top of a fiberglass cover on the pickup truck in the adjoining site.

We cast a wary eye at overhead electrical lines, too; they can

"We greatly respect what the forces of nature can do, and many of the campsites we select are chosen on the basis of what nature may have in store for us."

blow down. And electric wires nearby often create interference, which affects television reception. Trees around a site can cause ghosts in TV pictures and prevent satellite TV reception.

In hot weather, we like to have some shade (being careful about the trees we park under, of course), but in cool weather we would rather not be under trees in order to receive some warmth from the sun. Once we were parked in a beautiful site in a dense forest with trees so thick the sun never shone on the campsite. They made the trailer so dark that we had to use the interior lights during the day—a concern because we had no electrical hookup.

You may want to avoid parking directly under campground lights if you don't have a way of blocking out light from your sleeping quarters.

If you use campground shower facilities, it's a good idea to inspect them before registering, especially if you intend to stay for a few days or weeks.

Many campgrounds in national forests can't accommodate large RVs—large meaning those over sixteen or twenty-two feet in length. Some campground directories include site limitations in their listings, but some do not. Even with a short-length limitation, it may be that one or two sites in such campgrounds are suitable for a larger than specified RV, but it may not; or others may already have occupied the larger sites, if they exist.

When we want to stay in an unfamiliar national forest campground, we generally scout it out on foot before taking our rig into it. On many occasions we have found campsites that would have been suitable for the trailer, but the roads leading to them were so poor that we didn't want to risk taking the trailer over them.

TRAVELING WITHOUT CAMPGROUND RESERVATIONS

In all our years of fulltiming, we have made reservations at campgrounds perhaps three or four times. Reservations aren't usually necessary for us because we don't travel many miles in a day—usually arriving in the early afternoon. If your habits are different from ours, you may need to smooth your way with advance reservations to be sure you'll have a place to stay.

Know the reservation policy of any campground at which you reserve a site: How long will the site be held? How much of a deposit is needed to hold a space? Will the deposit be fully refunded if you have to cancel? Many disputes have arisen because of the lack of understanding about reservation policies.

Another reason we don't often need reservations is that we don't normally travel in tourist seasons to crowded campgrounds where reservations are advised.

We are never found in a popular vacation area such as Yellowstone National Park during the busy season. When we visit the park, we do so in June and October. Yes, there is a chance of encountering bad weather—ten inches of snow in June once, and six inches in October another time—but our trailer is suited for camping in all climates so we were comfortable and we enjoyed seeing the white-mantled park while driving on roads nearly clear of traffic.

On long holiday weekends, and often on any weekend, especially in the summer, we hole up in a private campground in a town and stay out of parks and recreation areas. Aside from the admittedly selfish reason of wanting to have places all to ourselves as much as possible, we have another reason for traveling, or not traveling, as we do: Since we are free to come and go as we choose, it's fairer to let time-limited vacationers have the sites we may otherwise occupy. Parks are overcrowded as it is in peak vacation periods. Why should we add to the overcrowding—and the long lines at the dump station?

In the northern states, in April through June and in the months of September and October, travelers are unlikely to encounter blizzards and extremely cold temperatures. Any snow that falls usually disappears quickly in these months, except in the higher elevations.

We cherish experiences we have had during the off-season: The campground at Monument Valley, Arizona, is on a high bluff. The

> **"O**n long holiday weekends, and often on any weekend, especially in the summer, we hole up in a private campground in a town and stay out of parks and recreation areas.**"**

valley, with its incredible rock formations, falls away at the very edge of some of the campsites. Once, in March, we were the only people in the campground. We watched the shadows lengthen across the valley as the sun set. That night the stars sparkled with a not-often-seen brilliance; there were no intruding, artificial lights for miles. At dawn the huge, orange sun rose through a purple mist. All the grandeur of Monument Valley was ours alone.

A public park near a very small town in Alabama is about a mile outside the city limits. The campground is nestled among wooded, grassy hills, and our campsite was just a few yards from a small lake. During our week's stay one January, we discovered that visitors to the park were few and far between. Most days and nights we had the place to ourselves. The attendant came to unlock the park gate at seven o'clock in the morning and locked up at eight o'clock in the evening. No one could get in to disturb us in "our" park. The trees were still bare, the better to see the birds: a pileated woodpecker, brown creepers, Carolina chickadees, and purple finches, among others. We saw twenty-three different species of birds without moving from the campsite. Regularly, midmorning and late afternoon, a large flock of bluebirds came to feed around our trailer. There we found our first wildflower of the year, an early spring beauty, blooming in a sheltered place.

One October, our trailer was parked in a private campground located on a secluded cove on the Maine coast. A broad sweep of lawn sprinkled with tall pines led to the rocky shore. No one else came into the campground during our stay. We didn't have to share the lovely Indian summer days with anyone but the friendly couple who ran the campground. Not being pressured with the rush of business, they were relaxed and free to chat.

We could go on and on, but these experiences illustrate some of the reasons why we prefer camping in popular tourist areas offseason. You could become hooked on it too. It's fascinating to be in a place where no noises other than the sound of nature surround you. And it's delightful to be off by yourself now and then in a world that's becoming ever more crowded.

CAMPING IN NONCAMPGROUNDS

RVers can park in a variety of places that are not campgrounds, although in many of them stays of only a few hours or overnight are allowed.

Rest Areas

Overnight camping without restrictions is permitted in only a few states' highway rest areas. Many have limitations on the time you can park in the rest area—eight, twelve, or eighteen hours are common—so, in effect, overnighting can be done without breaking the rules. Some have signs posted warning:

No Camping Allowed, or
No Overnight Camping allowed.

Officials don't seem to have a common definition of camping, but it often means that no tents are to be set up in the area. Those sleeping in their RVs are no different than truck drivers who often use rest areas when they sleep. If truck drivers can do it, RVers should be able to do the same thing in the same place. Don't take our word for it, though. What is allowed or not allowed as far as RVers are concerned depends in large part on how the law enforcement officers on duty interpret the regulations and how lenient they are.

In years past we have overnighted at rest areas, but now we would think twice about doing so. These days, rest areas, especially at night, can be hangouts for those who are up to no good. If it were necessary for us to spend the night in a rest area, we would never step outside the trailer during the night.

Truck Stops

Truck stops were once the exclusive province of truckers, but nowadays they are anxious to have RVers' business, so much so that campgrounds are an adjunct to some truck stops.

At truck stops without a campground, the RV parking policy, and whether or not there is a charge, varies. We always inquire about the policy before parking.

Unless the parking lot is very large we wouldn't want to park overnight because we might be taking up a trucker's space, and we wouldn't sleep well, what with the comings and goings of the noisy rigs at all hours, and the nonstop roaring of the collective cooling engines on refrigerator trucks.

Other Overnight Camping Sites

Overnighting is sometimes allowed at restaurants and service stations with large parking areas. Always ask permission of the manager before doing so. If you park, of course, you should patronize the establishment; eat a meal in the restaurant, or buy fuel from the service station.

We once needed to take a sunset photograph of a certain location. The only campgrounds in the area were many miles from where we would take our shot, and we did not relish a long drive back to one of them after dark. In a nearby town we asked and received permission to stay overnight in the large parking lot of an auto-parts store.

An elderly lady loner we know prefers not to unhitch her trailer for overnight when she is just traveling through an area. Being on a tight budget, she has to watch what she spends. She frequently stays overnight in small-town shopping-center parking lots but first always checks with the manager of the main store to find out if it's allowed.

If we intended to overnight in a shopping center, we would try to park in a well-lighted section of the lot, and, as in a highway rest area, we wouldn't leave the RV at night after the stores were closed.

As we travel around the country, we notice more and more shopping centers with signs posted prohibiting overnight parking, but we have also seen RVs obviously parked for an overnight stay in such places. We wouldn't park where it was specifically forbidden. We want a good night's sleep; we don't want to risk being rousted out of bed by someone ordering us to move on, or writing out a citation, or both.

During your travels, if you plan on living in your RV while parking overnight or for a few days in the driveway or on the grounds of a friend's or relative's house, ask your host to find out if any local ordinances prohibit this. Some localities won't allow RVs to be parked anyplace where they are visible. Some permit RV parking, but the unit cannot be lived in. These local regulations vary widely, so if you are preparing for an extended visit, know the facts before you make firm plans.

COLD-WEATHER CAMPING

Cold-weather camping without hookups should not be attempted unless your rig is equipped for it, which means more than just having proper insulation. The RV should be equipped with a dependable, adequate source of heat, reliable batteries with enough amperage for your needs and a way of charging them, full propane tanks, enough extra food in case you become snowed in, plenty of warm clothing, and some way of receiving weather reports.

Some Cold-Weather Camping Hints

Following are a few hints for comfortable and safe cold-weather camping (some are a recap of points mentioned in earlier chapters):

- Bear in mind that batteries become more difficult to recharge as the temperature drops.
- Keep snow cleared from the refrigerator roof vent as well as the furnace intake and exhaust ports, should it accumulate to such a depth.
- The campsite should be sheltered from all winds as much as possible, but especially north winds. Sheltering trees, however, can blow over in heavy winter winds and branches can break off when weighted with snow or ice.
- Carry chains or have suitable tires on any engine-driven vehicles.
- Keep antifreeze in holding tanks so drains won't freeze.
- Connect the water hose to the outside faucet only if the hose is well insulated. Otherwise, use water from the internal tank and fill it as needed.
- A blow dryer is useful for thawing frozen drains and iced-over doors and slideouts. If no electricity is available, keep a can of deicer handy; it can be used on outside compartment and vehicle doors as well.
- Make sure all outside compartment doors are weathertight.
- If an electric heater is used, be sure the electrical hookup has a receptacle of an adequate-amperage size.
- Open a window slightly when heating the RV with any type of propane or solid-fuel heater.
- Keep lower cabinet doors ajar so water lines won't freeze.
- Keep the RV warmer with suitable window coverings.
- Insulate the underside of the RV by putting skirting around it, or if you are in a snowy area, pile up snow around the RV.
- If cold-weather camping is done regularly, select an RV with the holding tanks in a heated compartment.

- Before leaving to winter-camp in an isolated place, let someone know where you'll be and when you plan to return.

Camping in the winter is becoming a popular pastime. Many campgrounds in the Snowbelt are open year round and cater to cold-weather campers by offering heated swimming pools, saunas, ice skating, snowmobiling, skiing, ice fishing, and just about any other wintertime recreation you can think of.

CAMPING ETIQUETTE

No matter where you camp, observe not only the campground's rules but general good manners as well:

- Keep your site clean and free of clutter. The people who pile all sorts of belongings under their units don't have to look at the unsightly mess, but others do.
- Clean up after pets and don't let them run loose, no matter how well behaved they are. If your dog barks or whines when it's left alone, don't leave it alone.
- Don't make any extra work for the campground operators; they have their hands full with normal maintenance.
- Turn off exterior lights when they aren't needed, especially at night so your neighbor's sleep won't be disturbed.
- Don't leave a mess in the shower, laundry room, or at the dump station.
- Always leave a good impression, especially if you are a full-timer, so all of us pursuing this lifestyle will be welcome wherever we go.

CHAPTER 18

Setting Up and Breaking Camp

I f you have been primarily a vacation RVer before becoming a fulltimer, you won't have had too much opportunity to develop systems for getting under way easily and for setting up a campsite quickly and efficiently. As you begin fulltiming and traveling, you'll develop certain procedures that will soon become second nature to you.

Usually the procedures involved with getting ready to travel, hitching, unhitching, and securing the RV in a campsite are a mutual effort with us, but we seem to be in the minority. With many couples, all too often these tasks are left to the men. We think fulltiming is much more satisfying if there is complete cooperation between partners. One person should not always perform certain duties exclusively.

Look at it this way: What if your partner were out of commission or unavailable? Whom could you call on to do his or her work? If you both know how to do everything, you can do it all on your own if need be. A lot of satisfaction and self-confidence comes from knowing you are capable of handling your rig's procedures by yourself.

USING CHECKLISTS

RVers can't simply pull out of a campsite to begin a day's run without making certain preparations both inside and outside to ready the RV for travel.

So we won't forget anything that needs to be done we use two checklists, one for preparations inside, and another for what needs to be done outside (Figure 18.1). Each item on each list appears more or less in the order in which it should be done. On the outside list we include every step of the hitching procedure no matter how basic. After the hitching is done, we glance at the list to be sure nothing has been forgotten.

It's useful to have some sort of a checklist. No matter how good your memory, there will be times when other things are on your mind or you are distracted and something may be overlooked. We often see RVs on the highway with the TV antenna up or the doorsteps down. On two occasions we have noticed rigs about to pull away from the campsite with the water hose still attached.

Exhibits 18.1 and 18.2 and may give you some ideas about items to include on your inside and outside checklists. These lists can be expanded to include preparations peculiar to your RV and its type

Figure 18.1 A portion of the checklist the authors use for breaking-camp preparations that are done outside. The actual list contains twenty-three items.

Rear jacks	✔										
Kingpin jack	✔										
Jack handle	✔										
Kingpin lock	✔										
Water heater	✔										
Propane off	✔										
Holding tanks	✔										
Sewer cap	✔										

and whether you're traveling with children and pets. Those with motorhomes will have certain procedures different from trailerists.

We also have a very short checklist that we use when we stop and have lunch in the trailer. This list reminds us to close the propane cylinders, shut any windows and roof vents that were opened, secure the refrigerator door, turn off the radio, turn off the lights and the water-pump switch, and remove the wheel chock (if used).

We produce our checklists on the computer and print out

EXHIBIT 18.1
Interior Pre-Travel Checklist

❏ All windows and roof vents should be closed, unless you prefer to have some air enter the interior while traveling.
❏ The TV antenna must be lowered and the TV, if not built in, secured so it won't fall or be bounced around. If the TV is set on the floor in the center or at the front of the RV, not in the rear, it should ride well. A roof-mounted satellite dish must be lowered and a portable dish stowed. The receiver, if not permanently mounted, must be stowed.
❏ Unless you intend to have the refrigerator operating while under way, turn it off. Lock the door if it has a lock; if not, be sure the doors are shut tightly.
❏ If the furnace has been on, turn it off and the thermostat down. If an electric heater has been used it should be turned off, unplugged, and stowed.
❏ Put all loose items away. Anything that can slide off should not be left on counters and tables. We have a fruit bowl that is stowed in one side of the double sink when we are traveling; two small house plants go in the other side. A teakettle that usually sits on the stove can be put in the sink for traveling; we have space for ours in an overhead cabinet. A few loose items that we keep on a shelf at the back of the trailer are put away in a cabinet above the shelf. The bedroom clock is put into a cabinet.
❏ Be sure the water-pump switch is off. Most manufacturers recommend turning it off while the RV is in motion so water sloshing in the tank won't cause the pump to cycle.
❏ Turn off the water heater if you have an inside-controlled electric-ignition type.
❏ If the RV has two doors, lock the one that is not being used while breaking camp.
❏ Secure any sliding and hinged doors.

copies whenever we need them. Traveling as much as we do, we use up the squares on a list quickly.

If you don't have a computer, graph paper can be used for checklists—the kind with one-quarter inch squares is best—or notebook paper suffices if a few vertical lines are ruled to form the check-off boxes. You may want to make a master copy and make photocopies from it.

Many of the items on our list are pretty basic, but we include them all. Using the list takes only seconds and we never have to worry about forgetting anything.

The checklist idea won't work unless the list is convenient for use as you go about breaking camp. We store ours, along with a pencil, in a small plastic envelope taped to the inside of a galley cabinet door. For use, we lay the list on the counter beneath. In this location, almost opposite the entry door, we don't have to go out of the way to use it.

EXHIBIT 18.2
Exterior Pre-Travel Checklist

❏ Put away any items stored under the rig.
❏ Disconnect the TV cable if hooked up to the campground's cable jack.
❏ Roll up awnings.
❏ Depending on the hookups at the site, fill the water tank and empty the holding tanks if necessary. Put away the water hose and sewer hose and any loose sewer fittings used.
❏ Turn off the water heater if it's not controlled from inside.
❏ If the RV is connected to an electrical hookup, disconnect and store the shore-power cable and any adapters used.
❏ Turn off the propane supply unless needed for the refrigerator.
❏ On a trailer, lower and secure the stone shield(s).
❏ Retract or remove stabilizing jacks and wheel chocks or blocks, unless you have a trailer and want the chocks to remain in place during the hitching procedure.
❏ When there is no longer need to go inside, secure the steps and lock the door.

More Checking

Once the trailer is hitched, before pulling out of the site, we make sure that all equipment we have used in the hitching process is put away and all outside compartments are locked. We both take a final walkaround, making a visual check to see that everything has been done.

Next, one of us goes to the rear of the trailer to check out the lights as the other one activates—in the same order each time—left- and right-turn indicators, the truck-brake lights, the trailer-brake lights (by using the manual override lever on the controller), the running lights, and the emergency blinkers.

If we have used leveling boards, we remove any wheel chocks still in place, then pull the trailer forward, remove the boards, and put them and the chocks in their storage compartment.

Before we leave the campground, we check the trailer brakes to see that they are working properly.

An outside doormat is the only item we keep outside the trailer, and since it's included on our checklist, there isn't much chance of its being left behind. If we habitually kept such items as folding chairs or a barbecue grill outside, we would incorporate them on our checklists.

HITCHING AND UNHITCHING

Many fulltimers look upon hitching and unhitching as a distasteful chore. It shouldn't be. Establishing a routine for the procedure makes the job easier, and you'll soon find shortcuts to make the work go quickly.

A travel trailer, a fifth-wheel, and an auxiliary vehicle towed on a dolly behind a motorhome all require different hitching routines. A fifth-wheel trailer is easier to hitch than a travel trailer. A tow dolly can be maneuvered by hand somewhat, so if it's lined up properly, it isn't too difficult to attach to the motorhome.

Hitching a travel trailer is somewhat more complicated than the others because of the weight-distributing hitch, the type that should be used on all but the smallest trailers.

The system we devised for hitching our travel trailer may be of use to others who have travel trailers:

After we secured the inside of the trailer and did everything outside, including placing all the hitch paraphernalia—spring bars, sway control—under the A-frame, we were ready to hitch up. The hitch itself was removed from its compartment (we kept it stored it in a trailer compartment so we didn't have to carry its considerable weight around with us in the truck when the trailer was parked) and inserted it in the receiver. The trailer A-frame was raised, if needed.

One of us backed up the truck while the other, standing beside the A-frame, gave mostly hand signals and sometimes verbal directions for positioning the hitch correctly under the coupler.

For positioning the ball exactly under the coupler, one person was stationed to the left of the A-frame so he or she would be visible in the driver-side mirror. The other maneuvered the tow vehicle. The driver lined up the tow vehicle as straight as possible with the trailer. The person at the A-frame imagined that the hitch bar, on which the ball is mounted, was an arrow that must be pointed directly at the coupler. If the "arrow" pointed to the right of the coupler, the driver was instructed to turn the wheels about halfway to the left. If it pointed to the left of the coupler, the wheels would be turned to the right. Then the driver was signaled to come back slowly until the "arrow" pointed at the coupler, then to stop.

At this point, the driver was told to straighten out the wheels, then slowly back the vehicle. If the wheels were straight, and the driver backed straight, the proper alignment would be made. If not, the driver was again directed to stop before backing all the way and make a minor correction of the wheels in the needed direction. Then, again, the driver backed the tow vehicle until the "arrow" pointed at the coupler, straightened out the wheels once more, and continued the backing. Sometimes we had to go through this routine several times. Even so, it takes longer to read about it than it does to execute the maneuvers.

During this procedure, the person at the A-frame gave indications, as necessary, with hands or fingers as to the distance remaining between the ball and the coupler. The driver should not try to second-guess the direction-giver by looking in the rearview or the passenger-side mirror. Instead, the driver's attention should be focused solely on the driver-side mirror and the person visible therein, and nowhere else.

If one person miscalculates, the other just does what has to be done for correction without creating a scene. No doubt we have all witnessed some of the dreadful arguing that goes on between some couples during hitching up. There really is no excuse for such behavior. Keep calm and take your time. Fulltimers don't have to be in a hurry.

(Bill miscalculated once. He signaled with his thumb and forefinger that Jan was to come back a quarter of an inch when in fact the distance was only three-sixteenths of an inch. We're just funnin', but in truth, we perfected this system to such a degree that we could understand how much to move back when the distance was a mere fraction of an inch.)

Once the ball is under the coupler but too far to one side or the other, it can be shifted slightly sideways while the tow vehicle is stationary: Turn the wheels of the tow vehicle to the right or left, and the ball moves one way or the other. With the truck we had then, the position of the ball could be shifted as much as an inch either way with this maneuver. The amount of lateral shift varies from vehicle to vehicle, depending on the distance from the rear axle to the ball; the greater the distance, the more the shift.

Sometimes the coupler slides over the ball but can't be latched. Merely shifting the stationary tow vehicle into neutral (from reverse where it has been since backing up) often creates enough of a movement to permit latching. If it doesn't, then shift into drive. That almost always does the trick.

After the hitch was connected to the coupler, we stationed ourselves on each side of the A-frame, each attaching the safety chain and the equalizer bar on his or her side. One person put on the sway control; the other attached the breakaway lanyard and electrical connection. As one cranked up the A-frame jack, the other removed the boards from beneath it.

Unhitching was done in reverse order.

A trailer-A-frame jack should always rest on something solid so it won't sink into the ground. In a level site, we used two blocks of wood under the jack with a combined height of about five inches. Each was about a foot long so when used together they wouldn't teeter or shift. If the back of the site is higher than the front, more boards may be needed to raise the A-frame high enough for fore-and-aft leveling. When more than two boards are used, they should be crossed, with the bottom board running fore and aft, to eliminate the tendency for the stack to roll. If the back of the site is lower than the front, only one board may be needed.

If you have to hitch up by yourself all or most of the time, you may want to have one of the several types of hitching aids available. These can be found in RV-supply stores, or they may be advertised in *Trailer Life* magazine.

Without a hitching aid, perhaps a method we used on occasion may be helpful: Put a piece of 4-inch-long, ¾-inch-wide tape (use a dark color so it's easy to see) vertically in the center of the trailer (this is just above the propane cylinders on most travel trailers). The tape should be aligned directly behind the coupler. Put an identical piece of tape on the rear window of the tow vehicle (or rear canopy window) directly in line with the hitch ball.

Position the tow vehicle squarely in front of the trailer. (This procedure won't work if the tow vehicle must be brought in at an angle.) Back up, using the rearview mirror to keep the two pieces of tape lined up, until the hitch is about two feet from the coupler. Get out and note the distance remaining between the ball and the coupler. Get back behind the wheel, leaving the door partially open. Find a spot on the ground that is in line with your eye and the back edge of the door. From this spot, locate another spot on the ground that is approximately the same distance as from the ball to the coupler. (Both spots can be marked with a twig or stone.) Back up until the door edge is even with the second spot. The ball should then be in position. If it's off laterally, move it by turning the steering wheel in the tow vehicle, as previously described.

When it takes considerable effort to hook or unhook spring bars, it's probably because the A-frame, coupled with the hitch, isn't high enough. To avoid straining your back, raise the A-frame with the tongue jack.

To help remember how many links of the spring-bar chain to take up, put a ring of tape or paint on the link immediately before the positioning link (the one that goes over the hook or into the slot on the tongue bracket). Any marking on the positioning link itself will soon wear off. If any great amount of weight is shifted in the coach at some future time, the positioning link may be a different one.

With a weight-distributing hitch, it's necessary that the tension on the spring bars be such that both the tow vehicle and trailer are parallel to the ground when hitched. The coupled hitch should neither sag nor be elevated.

On occasions when the tow vehicle is tilted sideways—in relation to the trailer after the trailer is leveled in the site—the hitch ball may not release easily from the coupler. Having someone stand on the hitch or rear bumper of the tow vehicle usually adds enough weight to pop it loose. Once, though, we had to use a crowbar to pry the two apart.

In the same circumstances, it can be difficult to snap up the spring bars when hitching. It may be necessary to pull the trailer a few feet ahead, off its leveling boards, so it's on the same plane as the tow vehicle, before the spring bars can be engaged.

Hitching with the tow vehicle angled should present no problem, although, in this situation, we found something that may have

> **"H**aving someone stand on the hitch or rear bumper of the tow vehicle usually adds enough weight to pop it loose.**"**

been peculiar to our rig: When the trailer was hitched and ready to go with the truck on an angle, we could not latch the canopy door until the truck was straightened out. Evidently, the spring bars distorted the truck frame just enough so that the door would not close properly.

Fifth-wheel Trailer Hitching

Hitching a fifth-wheel trailer is much easier than hitching a travel trailer and if you can drive, you should be able to do it by yourself with ease. Everything you need to see, the hitch assembly and the kingpin on the trailer that must engage it, are visible in the rearview mirror and through the rear window of the truck.

To make it even easier, we put a very visible guide on the hitch plate: Two pieces of white tape on the front of the hitch, one on each side of the slot (Figure 18.2). For the best alignment while backing, the driver shouldn't turn around to look at the hitch because then it's viewed at an angle; use the rearview mirror. The tape guides are especially useful when hitching up at an angle.

Figure 18.2 On some fifth-wheel hitches, the slot isn't visible to the driver. If so, white tape on the front of the hitch plate can serve as guides for lining up the kingpin with the slot. Shown is the driver's view through the rearview mirror. The two white guides are just visible on the top edge of the white area across the bottom of the mirror. The white area is a storage box.

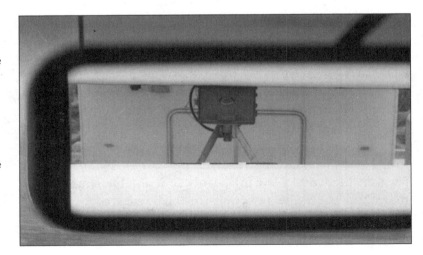

With our fifth-wheel, we still work together while hitching only because it's quicker and it saves the driver from having to get in and out of the cab so much.

One person is at the front of the trailer and takes care of raising or lowering the front, while the other opens the jaws of the hitch on the way to the cab of the truck. As the driver is backing, the person at the trailer makes any needed height adjustment so the kingpin will engage the jaws. The driver can tell when the hitch is latched because it's usually accompanied by a loud clunk. When this is heard, the driver shifts into a forward gear and applies just enough throttle to put forward pressure on the hitch. This securely latches the kingpin into the hitch, and the action pushes the lever to the position where the safety pin can be inserted.

After the driver has done this and applies the truck brakes, the person at the front of the trailer ducks under the gooseneck to double-check that the jaws are closed, plugs in the trailer electrical connector cable, shuts the tailgate, and begins to raise the front jacks. Meanwhile the driver leaves the truck and puts the safety pin in the hitch lever and attaches the breakaway lanyard.

Not all hitches function exactly like ours, but the basic principles of hitching are the same with all fifth-wheel hitches.

We are always extra careful about checking to see that the jaws are closed. We have seen many fifth-wheels whose owners evidently aren't so particular. Their trailers are the ones with dents in the underside of the gooseneck. Such dents usually occur when the kingpin pulls free of the jaws when the truck is moved and the trailer drops onto the sides of the pickup's bed.

Before we bought a hitch with a plate that tilted both front to back and side to side, we once found ourselves in a site where the level was such that the truck was too low on one side, making it impossible to engage the kingpin. We got out of the predicament by putting some leveling boards under the truck's rear wheel on the low side.

It's not necessary to unhitch a trailer every time you stop overnight if the rig is parked on a level surface. With travel trailers,

> **"**It's not necessary to unhitch a trailer every time you stop overnight if the rig is parked on a level surface.**"**

however, it's a good idea to lower the tongue jack, release the spring bars, and chock the wheels. When staying hitched with the fifth-wheel, we lower the front jacks just enough to take most of the tongue weight off the truck. If the trailer needs some slight fore-and-aft leveling, the front can be raised just a little by using the front jacks. If the front needs to be lowered, this can be done by putting leveling boards under the trailer wheels on both sides.

LEVELING

After moving the trailer into a site, the first thing to do before un-hitching is to check its level.

The primary reason for leveling any RV is so the absorption-type refrigerator will work properly, although recent refrigerator models are much more tolerant of off-level conditions than older ones.

The secondary reason for being on the level, as far as we are concerned, is that we don't want to live on an angle and have cabinet doors swinging shut when we want them to remain open and sleep in a bed that isn't level.

Leveling doesn't have to be a chore. It's not difficult if you can see and use the level easily, if you carry an assortment of leveling boards so the RV can be set straight in any of the variety of site configurations you'll encounter, and if you develop a leveling routine.

As with other RV procedures, the more times you level a unit, the more adept you'll become at judging just how much it needs to be propped up, and the process will go quickly.

Since the level of the RV should be determined by the refrigerator, to establish a norm, just after we purchased our trailer, we set the level in the freezer and leveled the trailer from side to side and fore and aft. Once it was as level as we could make it, a short length of one-by-two wood was nailed to a partition just inside the entry door, aligned so that when the level is set on it, the bubble is exactly centered (Figure 18.3). The door sill agrees with the fore and aft level of the refrigerator, so the level is placed on the sill for lev-

eling in this direction. In order for it to be handy for use, the level is stored immediately inside the door in the box we use for the vinyl runner described on page 409.

Types of Levels and Leveling Equipment

For accurate positioning a dependable level is needed. We tried several levels that mounted on the outside of the RV but found none that were satisfactory. Two levels must be mounted on the unit so it can be leveled from both side to side and fore and aft. The levels that are stuck on with adhesive can shift in hot weather, although they would stay in place if they were screwed in.

We eventually went back to using a 9-inch torpedo level, the same level we had always used to double-check the other levels. We find the torpedo level to be easier to see and interpret, and its bubble movement is quick; it doesn't have the inertia of some of the other levels we experimented with.

We carry several leveling boards in different heights: six ½-inch boards (plywood) and four 1½-inch boards (two by eights). All are wide enough and long enough to fit comfortably under one tire, yet short enough so they can be inserted between the wheels.

Any leveling board an inch or more in thickness should have a 45-degree bevel on one end so a tire doesn't have to roll over a sharp edge as it moves up onto the board. A bevel on both ends is convenient.

We are used to working with the blocks and can level our trailer quickly with them, but some fulltimers may want to purchase a set of levelers. A set of the tapered-ramp type eliminates the need for carrying boards of different sizes. The RV is simply driven onto the ramp and stopped when it has gone far enough up the incline to make it level. Such levels often come with a set of wheel chocks, which are necessary because the wheels are on an incline.

Often we have been able to level the trailer simply by backing up or moving forward slightly in the site. This, too, is something that comes after a little practice.

With either type of trailer, it's a simple matter to level it fore and aft by raising or lowering the tongue jack on a travel trailer or the front jacks on a fifth-wheel.

We haven't arranged our level placement for the driver's convenience. We've found the leveling procedure goes faster if the driver stays put while the other person checks the side-to-side level, and either signals that the level is okay, or places leveling boards where needed, then motions the driver to move onto the boards and signals to stop when the tires are situated properly. This way the driver doesn't have to get in and out; the person who is out can do the running around.

Unless a motorhome is equipped with an automatic leveling system, the leveling will have to be done with boards. Side leveling is no more difficult than with a trailer except that boards usually have to be placed on the low side under both the front and back wheels. Fore-and-aft leveling, however, presents more of a problem because there is no way of simply adjusting a jack to achieve the proper level.

If a motorhome needs longitudinal leveling, boards have to be put under both wheels, in the front or back, once the side leveling is taken care of. It may be that boards of different heights are under three wheels of a motorhome. Boards used for leveling a motorhome from the front and back should be of combinations that total six inches of height. In some sites the front or rear wheels on a motorhome have to be propped up this high to make it level. Motorhomers probably will develop a knack for estimating the height needed to achieve level, but doing the actual leveling always takes some time to accomplish.

STABILIZING THE RV

We use jacks for the same reason we level the RV: comfort. We don't want a bouncy, unstable, springy home, but we've seen some RVers who don't bother with jacks.

When jacks are used, don't make the mistake of using stabilizing jacks—the common aluminum stacker jacks—for leveling; they aren't designed for this purpose. It would be extremely difficult and dangerous to try to raise the weight of the RV with the jack's tiny handle.

Certain jacks are designed to level as well as stabilize. Some RVs may be equipped with this type of jack, or they may be offered as optional equipment. Permanently mounted to the RV's frame, they are hinged and fold up under the bottom of the RV when not in use. Ours are this type but we've never been successful in using them for leveling; it takes too much muscle.

For safety, jacks should always be placed under chassis frame members.

In some instances, one end of a travel trailer is so low that a stacker jack with its threaded screw stem inserted won't fit, even if the stem is at its lowest point. Here's how we used to handle such situations when inserting a back jack:

1. Remove the stem (the jack can be used without it).
2. Place the base of the jack under the trailer.
3. Slide the jack along the desired frame member until it be-

comes snug. If there is no point where it is snug against the frame member, put the jack base on a board to raise it up.

4. Lower the A-frame two turns or give a short burst to an electric jack; this raises the rear of the trailer.
5. Push the jack back until it is again snug.
6. Raise the A-frame the same number of turns it was lowered to maintain the fore and aft level already established.
7. Check the jack to see that it's tight. If not, lower the A-frame two turns again.
8. Move the jack farther back or prop it up a little more. Then raise the A-frame again.

To place a jack base under the front, in step 4 raise the A-frame before lowering it.

Some permanently installed crank-down jacks can't be used effectively when the RV is too low to the ground. They give the best support when each jack is positioned at a 45-degree angle, at least. If the RV is high off the ground, blocks should be put under the jacks to achieve this angle.

Large motorhomes don't need stabilizing as much as trailers and small motorhomes because they have stiffer springs; they are less affected by people moving around in them.

Although it's not really needed, we often use a kingpin jack for extra stability. If nothing else, it cuts down on shake at the front of the trailer in high winds.

CHOCKING

It isn't absolutely necessary to chock the RV's wheels if the site is perfectly level, but in an off-level site we always feel more secure with the wheels chocked. It's so much a part of our setting-up routine, and so easy, that we do it regularly. That way, we never have to remember to chock the wheels if the site is off level.

We once used the triangular type of chock that rests on the ground next to the wheel, but some years ago we switched to the type that fits vertically between the tandem wheels (Figure 18.4). En route, when we have to park the trailer on a slope, perhaps when we stop for lunch or park in a lot to do some shopping, we always use the chock.

A wheel chock can be anything that has enough height to prevent the tires from rolling over it: a block of wood, a brick, a boulder, a tree branch, a log, or any of the manufactured chocks.

Figure 18-4 An easy-to-use wheel chock that fits vertically between tandem wheels can be secured with a bicycle lock.

AIDS FOR OUTSIDE WORK

For most outside work that includes hitching and unhitching, we wear work gloves. Sometimes the leveling boards are muddy and unpleasant to handle without gloves; and when it's cold, gloves make it easier to work with cold metal.

We also have an 18-inch square of ½-inch plywood that we use when we have to kneel down to do a task. It keeps our clothes clean when the ground is wet or muddy and is easy on the knees if we are working on gravel and concrete.

UTILITY HOOKUPS

As mentioned before, we always use a circuit analyzer before we hook up the electricity. Each time we break camp, one of the things we do (it's on our checklist) is plug the analyzer into the electric receptacle over the galley counter. It's visible through the window, which is on the street side, as is the shore-power cable. After we arrive at the next campground and plug in the shore power, a glance in the window lets us know the state of the circuit.

We keep another analyzer in the compartment with the shore-power cable in case we need to check the electricity before pulling into a site. We often do this in places where the campground manager or attendant is not on duty to inform us about sites where there may be a problem with electrical service or where the electric outlet looks old, burned, or otherwise suspect. Before we started this practice, there were a few times when we had parked in sites that were difficult to maneuver into and then found that no electricity was available.

When we have a sewer hookup, we don't leave the drains on the holding tanks open. Some liquid must be allowed to accumulate along with the solids in the black-water holding tank so it will drain better. If we are spending some time in one campground, we empty the tanks only every three or four days. Whenever we empty them, the black-water tank is emptied first. After it's drained, the accumulated gray water is run through the hose to flush it out.

There were a number of reasons mentioned in Chapter 14, "Water, Sewage, and Propane," why we never hook up to the city water. Here's another important one: We want to eliminate the possibility of the trailer being flooded with water.

We've been parked next to several trailers and noticed water dripping from the underbody—a sure sign that water is leaking inside the unit. If the owners were at home, we called it to their attention. If they were absent, we took it upon ourselves to turn off the water, and either left a note on the door or informed the campground manager about what we had done. If we did hook up to city water, we would make it a habit to turn off the water at the outside faucet before leaving the trailer for any extended period.

KEYS

Not long ago we saw the couple in the site next to us preparing to leave. They had a motorhome and were towing an auxiliary vehicle. They were about to put the car on the tow dolly, but the keys to the car, of which there was apparently only one set, couldn't be located. Quite an argument took place with each accusing the other of having misplaced the keys. We couldn't avoid hearing the goings-on because our windows were open and the sites were close together. The keys were finally located.

This story is used to make the point that every adult occupant of an RV should have a complete set of keys for everything connected with the RV. We each have our own set that we always carry with us, and we go a step further and have a third complete set of keys that we keep in the trailer. If one of us should lose a set, the third set can be used until duplicates are made.

CHAPTER 19

Driving and Handling Practices

Some people approach RV traveling as they do airplane travel; that is, trying to reach their destination as quickly as possible. This is not, and should not be, what fulltiming is about. Traveling itself constitutes much of the fun in this vagabond lifestyle.

For full-timing couples, the traveling should be a partnership. Truly rewarding and successful fulltiming comes from each partner knowing every aspect of operating and handling the rig.

TAKE IT EASY

Most people would probably agree that driving on crowded highways for long periods of time is not fun. No one would choose to take up highway driving as a recreational pursuit, and we are sure no one becomes a fulltimer with the idea of spending most of the time behind the wheel of his or her rig.

Nothing turns off people to traveling more than too much traveling. Driving back and forth across the country as fast as you can is not only tiring but quickly becomes boring.

Of course, driving is a large part of RV traveling, but there are ways to make it more fun and less of a drudgery—and at the same time safer: Simply don't go too far or too fast. There's no reason to be in a hurry. For fulltimers, one cliché is especially true: Today is the first day of the rest of your life. Why speed through it on succeeding days?

We can't imagine many situations that would require a fulltimer to drive 500-mile days, or 400-mile days, or 300-mile days, or even 200-mile days. If you feel you must drive many miles to reach your destination, either allow more time for the trip or choose a closer destination. Our attitude is, if we have to drive long distances day after day, we might as well get a job driving an 18-wheeler and make some money at it.

Our day's runs are usually under 100 miles; if they exceed that amount, they rarely reach 200 miles. Many have been only 20 or 30 miles. Once we went just 3 miles—to another more appealing campground on the shore of a large lake.

Short trips are easier on both people and equipment. After a long spell at the wheel, your reactions may not be as quick as they should be; you may become drowsy and find it difficult to be as attentive as necessary. Even if you and your partner share the driving chore equally, long driving days are tiring. A bonus of making the day's run short is that it enables you to avoid night driving and night arrivals.

Our short runs allow us to leave late in the morning, after the rush-hour traffic, and to arrive at campgrounds before they fill up. We have plenty of time to stop along the way for sightseeing, shopping, and lunch. We can even delay our departure until after lunch if we desire. One of the greatest benefits of short trips is not having to drive fast to make miles.

If you do have long runs, several stops should be made during the day. It's good for you and good for your rig. It's refreshing to get out, stretch, walk around, and relax by concentrating on something other than the highway and traffic. Tires last longer if they are given a chance to cool down occasionally, and stopping provides an opportunity for making a visual inspection of tires and walking around the rig and looking under it to see that everything is in order.

TAKE IT SLOW

The speed at which you drive your rig affects its safety and your physical well-being. If you want the stress of battling for your space on the highways at the maximum speed limit, go ahead. We would ask you to wave at us as you whiz by, but you won't have time for any such pleasantries; you'll be concentrating too much on the road.

Our experience has taught us that on interstate and four-lane highways, a good speed when towing the trailer is ten miles under the maximum speed limit or if there is a truck speed limit, at that speed or slightly lower. Our attitude about truck drivers is that they are people on the job, and we don't want to be responsible for impeding or interfering with their work.

Driving slower than the maximum has many advantages:

- Everyone who wants to travel at the speed limit can easily pass us.
- Since we don't keep up with the pack, we are never caught in dangerous boxes with other vehicles close ahead, behind, and beside us. Traffic disperses from around us, leaving plenty of space.
- We rarely have to switch lanes for passing because everyone is passing us.
- The time needed for slowing down or coming to a complete stop is less—something that must always be considered when driving an RV rig.
- It allows a little more time to react in critical situations.
- It increases the amount of miles you get from each gallon of fuel. Cutting speed by as little as ten miles an hour can result in a significant reduction in fuel consumption.
- When moving slower than the rest of the pack there is even time enough to enjoy the scenery.

When we are on a two-lane highway, we travel at our usual under-the-speed-limit rate if we aren't holding up others behind us. When those behind have no opportunity for passing, we travel at the speed limit but look for a place where we can pull off onto the shoulder or other safe place to let traffic get around us. Our normal practice is to cut our speed when another vehicle is passing us on a two-lane highway to enable the passing vehicle to get around us more quickly.

We don't like drivers who follow too closely behind, so we give them every opportunity to pass by signaling our intentions by tapping the brakes, edging over to the right as far as we can, then slowing down so they won't have to speed around us.

NO SCHEDULE
IS THE BEST SCHEDULE

The hazards of too-rigid preplanning are many. No one can know in advance what lies ahead each day. A schedule may be upset by traffic jams, bad weather, or detours. When a delay occurs, most schedule-makers feel they have to make up the time they have lost. The result may be that they drive too fast or too long, creating a great deal of stress for themselves in the process. Those that set schedules aren't in the best humor when they can't keep to the schedule.

Our preplanning involves nothing more than deciding to be out of the cold weather in the winter and the hot weather in the summer. Even such loose planning does not always work out for us, however. We often end up spending time in places where the climate is less than ideal because we have found something we think is worth staying around for, regardless of the weather.

When people ask us where we'll be next month or next week, we can never give them a definite answer; we simply don't know. If we think we know where we will be at some future date, we still won't tell anyone about it—not anymore, that is; we may change our minds.

A few years ago we decided to go quite far south for the winter months. We met a friendly couple in a campground as we were on our way and found we were bound for the same area. Once they got there, the other couple planned to stay in that area for several months; we didn't know how long we would end up staying once we got there.

We agreed to look up the couple when we arrived. Our new-found friends were traveling much faster than we were (it seems as if everybody travels faster than we do) and left early next morning. As we were heading south late in the morning, we changed our minds about where we wanted to spend the winter, and went back to the campground where we had stayed the night before. The rate was reasonable, it was in an area we liked, and far enough south so that any winter storms would not be too severe. It would also be a base from which we could explore the surrounding countryside, which was of considerable interest to us.

We eventually moved a little farther south—we don't like to spend months at a time in one place—but we never got as far into the Sunbelt as we had "planned," and, of course, never rendezvoused with the friendly couple either.

Leaving a campground and then returning within hours was somewhat unusual, even for us. Normally, we would decide to stay over before we were on the road. We are more likely to change our plans about where we are going in the middle of our driving day. We may stop sooner, or go on for a few more miles than we planned. Then again, we may take off onto a beckoning route in a different direction.

Once, we stopped for lunch in a remote rest area on a little-used highway. It was on a high hill overlooking a beautiful valley. We decided to spend the night there, since we found no restrictions on camping overnight.

Our loose scheduling doesn't mean that we are irresponsible or undependable. We are just taking advantage of one of the greatest features of fulltiming: the ability to go where and when we please. After years of having nothing but time-restricted vacations, it's a wonderful feeling to know that we don't have to be in a certain place on a specified date, a freedom we enjoy immensely.

"After years of having nothing but time-restricted vacations, it's a wonderful feeling to know that we don't have to be in a certain place on a specified date, a freedom we enjoy immensely."

AVOIDING CROWDED HIGHWAYS

When we have a choice, we much prefer taking roads that are not interstates or main highways because most such roads are usually not crowded.

If we must use an interstate to get to where we are going, we will rarely be found on it late on a Friday afternoon and never on a Friday afternoon before a long holiday weekend. As we mentioned earlier, we generally don't travel on weekends at all, especially in the summer. We don't need to be on the roads at these times, so why add to the crowding and why put ourselves in the situation of driving on traffic-clogged roads?

In July and August we avoid roads that are the one and only routes to popular vacation areas. If we want to visit these areas, some of which are only open or accessible in the summer, and have to use such a route, we park the trailer somewhere else and do our visiting in the truck.

Limited-access, high-speed highways such as expressways, freeways, and interstates are the best and quickest ways to travel through big cities, in spite of the heavy traffic they carry. To avoid the traffic as much as possible, we don't enter or leave a large city during the rush hours in the morning and evening, especially if we have never been there before. We've found that the noon hour is one of the least crowded times on these highways. Most of the truckers are stopped for lunch, which eliminates much of the traffic.

When we stay over in a city for a few days, we often take the truck to scout out the route we'll take when we leave.

DEALING WITH INCLEMENT WEATHER

If the weather is very bad, don't travel unless you have to, and most fulltimers don't have to. They can wait out blizzards, cloudbursts, high winds, dust storms, and fog. By the same token, we can move our rigs out of the path of hurricanes and flooding.

If you are caught in a bad storm while traveling, try to find a place where you can safely pull off the road and wait it out. The shoulder, however, is not a safe place. If you are having trouble with visibility, so is every other driver on the road. Someone may decide to pull off onto the shoulder just where you are parked. Try to find a turnout, rest area, or parking lot where you'll be well off the road.

When weather conditions deteriorate, always reduce speed. In heavy rain and blowing snow the windshield wipers may not be able to remove the rain or snow fast enough to provide good forward visibility at fast speeds.

Note instructional road signs and slow down for curves more than you normally would. Pay attention to warning signs about wind gust areas, blowing dust, and the like. Be mentally prepared for anything that can happen.

Even light rain or mist can make highways slippery. In slippery conditions reduce speed so there will be no problem with stopping should it be necessary.

HANDLING LONG, HEAVY RIGS

Both the length and weight of a rig affects its performance and handling. The length of even short rigs necessitates wider turns at corners. The weight affects slowing and stopping, requiring more braking and distance for both. Heavy head winds increase fuel consumption markedly, while tailwinds provide a boost. Strong winds that are blowing so that they hit a rig broadside require that the person at the wheel pay strict attention to his or her driving.

The pull from passing trucks affects long trailers more than shorter ones and may have an effect on motorhomes with long overhangs in the rear. Those who encounter the most problems from passing are those who are caught off-guard and who aren't prepared for the suction that may occur. When a truck is seen in the mirror in the passing lane and well behind the rig is the time for the driver to put both hands on the wheel in order to hold it as steady as possible as the truck passes. The speed at which we habitually drive, usually being less than that of the truck speed limit, helped cut down on our travel trailer's tendency to yaw. Passing trucks don't have much effect on fifth-wheels.

Get into the habit of looking in your mirrors every thirty seconds or so. That way you won't be caught off guard by passing trucks.

If your trailer starts to yaw, don't panic; the yawing can be corrected. Keep a firm grip on the wheel and try to steer as straight as possible. Don't try to correct for the yaw. The idea is to keep the trailer and the tow vehicle in the normal configuration—in a straight line. Sometimes increasing speed helps to straighten out the rig. If you feel you must brake, use only the trailer brakes (by using the manual override lever on the controller) and brake for just a second or two at a time.

Certain wind speeds and directions can increase truck suction. Be extra cautious on windy days.

Constant problems with suction caused by passing trucks call for an assessment of hitch equipment to determine if it's adequate, if it's installed correctly, or if the hitch weight is heavy enough. (The location of the water tank and the amount of water in it is a hitch-weight factor in some rigs.) If all are satisfactory, and problems still exist when trucks pass, you are probably traveling too fast.

Some who have trailers find towing them to be a chore because they don't track well. Such problems can usually be traced to the hitch area: Its size, its installation, how much tension is on the equalizer bars, or the weight of the hitch. Towing should be easy and effortless and will be if the trailer and tow vehicle are properly hitched with the right equipment.

The middle lane on your side of a six-lane highway or the lane second from the right on your side of an eight-lane highway, are the best for traveling through; however, using these lanes means you'll have to travel at the speed of the rest of the traffic. Going slower than the maximum posted speed limit is only feasible in the far right lane. Traveling in the far right lane in cities can present problems, however. Traffic may prevent you from moving to the left to make room for entering vehicles so you may have to slow down. Slowing and stopping are the causes of most chain-reaction accidents on high-speed, multilane highways. Another concern about driving in the far right lane is that nearly all lanes marked "exit only" are far right lanes. You run the risk of being shunted off the highway at a place you didn't intend to go because you may not be able to move over into another lane.

Forget about fast getaways from a standing stop with any kind of full-timing rig; it can't be done. But the rig should be accelerated as rapidly as possible when entering an interstate or other high-speed thoroughfare, whether in urban or rural areas. The safest way to merge into the traffic on such highways is by moving at the same speed as the traffic. Then the rig can be inserted into a smaller hole and the other vehicles on the road are spared having to dodge around a slow-moving entering vehicle. It's dangerous to be poky or indecisive when entering a high-speed highway.

When making lane changes or entering a highway, use turn signals and make sure they are turned off after the maneuver. In some states, failing to turn them off can result in a citation.

Making a U-turn on a highway is something rig drivers rarely plan to do, but sometimes it's the easiest or only method for correcting a navigating mistake (if the law allows). A long motorhome towing an auxiliary vehicle needs many lanes in order to execute the maneuver. We read about one motorhome/auxiliary vehicle combination that required seven lanes to make a U-turn. With our 23-footer we could negotiate U-turns on a two-lane highway as long as there were wide shoulders on both sides, so in effect we needed about four lanes for the turn. Longer trailers need more room. U-turns with a fifth-wheel trailer are a snap. The fifth-wheel driver can start from a narrow shoulder on a two-lane highway and turn into the far lane without swinging wide because fifth-wheels can be turned with the truck at a 90-degree angle to the trailer. This maneuver must be done very slowly though to avoid actually rolling the trailer tires from the rims since the trailer pivots on the tires.

Long trailers and motorhomes have a good deal of overhang on the rear, and when they are turned, the rear end makes a wide arc. Caution must be exercised so that the rear end doesn't wipe out such things as mailboxes that may be set close to the road.

Rigs with heavy weights carried on the rear bumper may yaw even when traveling on a straightaway with no other vehicles creating suction, and the rig tends to be hard to control when turns are made at too high a speed.

Too much weight too high in the RV or in roof storage pods raises the already high center of gravity that RVs have and may create handling instability. When cornering, the sensation may be one of toppling over because of the top-heaviness. High winds can affect the stability of top-heavy rigs, especially winds that hit the rig broadside. Distributing some of the weight to places lower in the rig helps alleviate the problem.

When a fifth-wheel trailer goes over a short, steep incline such as found at the entrances to some parking lots, the underside of the gooseneck may kiss the side walls or tailgate of the truck. When we're faced with this situation, instead of moving straight ahead we try to enter at an angle; this sometimes prevents kissing. The rear of any rig can drag on such an incline, but entering at an angle may prevent this too.

UP AND DOWN HILLS

When driving a motorhome or towing a trailer, you won't be able to go up and down hills as quickly as you may like. Be patient, especially on long steep grades. Because of the weight of the rig, when going uphill you may be practically crawling before reaching the top, but so what? Hills on highways suitable for fulltiming rigs are neither long enough nor steep enough to cause any significant amount of lost time because they can't be climbed at top speed.

If you are one of those who is disturbed by being passed by nearly everyone else, you had better change your attitude, stick to the flatlands, or give up driving an RV rig.

Any combination of steepness, high altitude, and hot weather can cause problems for some vehicles. We try to pick routes that don't go over the highest passes. If a steep grade is on our route, we may stop at a campground nearby and scout it out before taking the trailer over it. We check the steepness of the grade, and look for places where we could pull off the road if we needed to.

When we had our 23-footer we made one such scouting expedition at Townes Pass, leading into Death Valley from the west. The pass reaches an elevation of only about 5,000 feet, but the grade is 13 percent. On one of our maps, it was noted that it was not recommended for trailers. To reach Death Valley from our location via the only other existing route would have meant an extra 100 miles of driving on a mundane highway that did not interest us.

Other business took us to the vicinity of the pass, so we went only a few miles out of our way to check it out. Scouting in the truck, we found the uphill grade was not 13 percent all the way; in several places it leveled out to a much more moderate incline. Quite a few spots were available where we could pull off and park well off the highway. We had no worries about overheating because of hot weather since it was December.

We decided to chance it. We made it, albeit very slowly, with no problems whatsoever. No overheating occurred because almost immediately as we started the uphill climb we had to shift into second gear, then soon afterward into first gear. Every downshift lowered the temperature, which had begun to rise slowly.

On newer, computer-controlled vehicles, manual downshifting shouldn't be done. Let the computer take care of it. Otherwise the computer becomes "confused" and may take many miles to reset itself.

In the lower gears, sometimes the rig crawls up grades—we were down to eighteen miles an hour at one point on Townes Pass. If traffic behind you can't pass because the grade hasn't a slow-vehicle lane (major highways with steep grades usually have this extra lane) or a shoulder wide enough for safe travel, it's not really your problem. You can only proceed according to the capabilities

"If traffic behind you can't pass because the grade hasn't a slow-vehicle lane . . . or a shoulder wide enough for safe travel, it's not really your problem."

of your rig. Those behind will have to put up with your slowness for the few minutes it takes.

All rigs perform differently when going downhill, depending on the steepness of the grade and the weight of the rig. On certain grades, the weight of the trailer seems to hold us back; on others we need to do considerable braking.

Brakes should never be applied constantly or they will overheat. When too much heat builds up, brakes may fade or fail. It works this way: As brakes begin to heat up, more pedal pressure must be applied. Eventually, no more pedal pressure can be exerted. When this happens, no reserve braking power is left, and it may be impossible to slow down.

Trailerists can use the trailer brakes to aid in slowing, but these brakes should be activated intermittently for only a second or two at a time.

Those driving a motorhome and towing an auxiliary vehicle must be extremely cautious; the considerable extra weight of the car puts that much more load on the brakes of the motorhome.

When going downhill with a gasoline-powered vehicle, downshifting allows the engine's compression to help in slowing so the brakes don't have to be applied constantly. With a diesel engine, however, there is little effect from downshifting.

Motorhomes and tow vehicles can be equipped with an exhaust brake, or retarder, which keeps the rig from picking up speed on a downgrade.

Heed grade-warning signs, and always check the brakes before beginning a long downgrade. We make it a practice to start down steep grades at a very slow speed. If there is a place where we can pull off at the top of the grade, we often do so to allow all traffic to get around us so we can negotiate the grade at our own speed.

Useful books for traveling fulltimers are *Mountain Directory West* and *Mountain Directory East*. They describe in detail the major grades in their respective parts of the country. To order contact:

Mountain Directory, R & R Publishing, Inc., P. O. Box 941, Baldwin City, Kansas 66006-0941; (800) 594-5999.

A general checklist for safe driving appears in Exhibit 19.1.

BACKING AN RV

Backing a motorhome is much easier than backing a trailer because the motorhome is one unit and it's not necessary to contend with another unit hitched to it that often seems to have a mind of its own. If the motorhome is towing an auxiliary vehicle, either with a tow bar or tow dolly, however, it has to be unhitched before any backing is done; it's almost impossible to control the movements of a hitched auxiliary vehicle when backing.

EXHIBIT 19.1
A Driving Checklist

❑ Check tire pressures frequently. Nothing wears out tires faster than driving with them improperly inflated.
❑ Periodically check the lug nuts on all wheels for tightness.
❑ Proper front-end alignment and wheel balance is important for comfortable, safe driving and for getting the most wear from tires.
❑ The radiator should be filled to the proper level and have enough coolant.
❑ Check the transmission fluid often and the oil level regularly.
❑ Be sure the window-washer reservoir is filled.
❑ When driving, check all gauges frequently to catch developing problems before they become serious or cause damage.
❑ Adjust mirrors for the best visibility and monitor them often while traveling, paying particular attention to any wheels visible in the mirrors.
❑ Make frequent stops for driver relaxation, for the tires to cool down, and to do a quick walkaround of the rig to see that everything is in order.

Some sites are laid out so that a motorhomer backing in may wish his or her unit did bend in the middle like a trailer. In such sites, where the ability to jackknife would be an advantage, motorhomers, especially those who have a unit with considerable rear overhang, have to pay particular attention to rear of the unit. It may swing beyond the side perimeters of the site into trees, shrubbery, or posts.

Most drivers have to back up by using the side mirrors since many motorhomes don't have rear windows, or if they do, they are too far from the cockpit to provide the driver with much visibility. A rearview TV monitor is a great aid for backing. It's standard on some motorhomes, may be offered as an option on others, or can be an after-market installation.

Backing a Travel Trailer

When it comes to backing a travel trailer, here's the oft-cited way of determining wheel-turning and direction when backing: Put your hand at the bottom of the steering wheel; whichever direction you move your hand is the way the rear of the trailer will go. This is good advice as far as it goes, and the simple instruction is easy to remember, but once into the maneuvering it's no longer relevant.

Backing requires both hands on the wheel to control it during the several turns needed during the backing operation. Furthermore, the interaction between the tow vehicle and trailer is not instantaneous; some distance may be covered before the steering wheel transmits its movement to the trailer.

We would suggest placing your hands on the wheel in a normal fashion and keeping your eyes glued to the driver's side mirror so that every movement of the trailer can be seen. When the back of the trailer moves in a direction you don't want, steer in the other direction. Of course, when the trailer is lined up straight and you want to back straight, you'll need to glance at the steering wheel to see if it's in the position where the tow vehicle's wheels are straight.

Understanding the different pivot points involved in backing a travel trailer may shed some light on the seemingly mysterious subject. The tow vehicle pivots on its rear wheels. Several feet away from the rear wheels is another pivot point: the hitch. The trailer itself pivots on its wheels.

When backing, as the front wheels of the tow vehicle are turned to the right, the front of the tow vehicle moves to the left. As the tow vehicle is pivoting on its rear wheels, it forces the pivot point of the hitch (the ball and coupler) to the right. As a result, the rear of the trailer begins to turn to the left. Therefore, turn the wheels of the tow vehicle in the opposite direction from the direction the trailer is to go (step 1, Figure 19.1).

Once the trailer is in its turning mode, the situation won't remain status quo. The trailer won't continue turning in a constant circle. It will describe more of a spiral movement, which becomes progressively tighter as the turning continues, and eventually causes the trailer to jackknife. If the tow vehicle's wheels are straightened out after the initial turning effort, the trailer still will jackknife eventually. A countermovement must be started because, once into the turn, the only control the driver has is to either increase or decrease the rate of turn.

Decreasing the rate of turn is achieved by turning the wheels in the same direction as the direction of turn (step 2, Figure 19.1). The rate of turn is increased by turning the wheels in the opposite direction to the direction of the turn, just as is done in the initial turning movement (step 3, Figure 19.1). It requires considerably more distance to decrease the rate of turn than it does to increase it.

If the trailer turns too much, it can be straightened out quickly by turning the tow vehicle's wheels in the direction opposite the way the trailer is turning and pulling forward a few feet.

It may be necessary to increase and decrease the rate of turn several times before the trailer is maneuvered into position (steps 4 and 5, Figure 19.1).

> **"O**nce the trailer is in its turning mode, the situation won't remain status quo.**"**

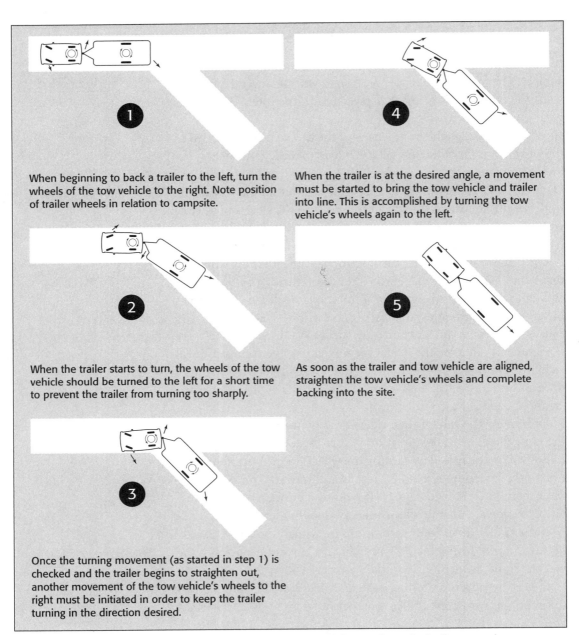

1 When beginning to back a trailer to the left, turn the wheels of the tow vehicle to the right. Note position of trailer wheels in relation to campsite.

2 When the trailer starts to turn, the wheels of the tow vehicle should be turned to the left for a short time to prevent the trailer from turning too sharply.

3 Once the turning movement (as started in step 1) is checked and the trailer begins to straighten out, another movement of the tow vehicle's wheels to the right must be initiated in order to keep the trailer turning in the direction desired.

4 When the trailer is at the desired angle, a movement must be started to bring the tow vehicle and trailer into line. This is accomplished by turning the tow vehicle's wheels again to the left.

5 As soon as the trailer and tow vehicle are aligned, straighten the tow vehicle's wheels and complete backing into the site.

Figure 19.1 Trailer backing principles are shown in the five steps above.

Backing a Fifth-wheel Trailer

Backing a fifth-wheel trailer is, in theory, the same as backing a travel trailer; the wheels of the tow vehicle are turned in the opposite direction from the way the rear of the trailer is to go. But, because the hitch pivot point on a fifth-wheel is just about over the rear wheels of the tow vehicle (its pivot point), all turning actions are much quicker and all correcting actions take longer. Given the same attitude of the tow vehicle's wheels, a fifth-wheel trailer jackknifes more rapidly than a travel trailer. Turning the tow vehicle's wheels in the opposite direction cannot unjackknife the trailer unless the trailer has many, many feet in which it can be maneuvered while backing—certainly not the situation with most campsites. The only practical way to unjackknife a fifth-wheel is by pulling forward.

The jackknifing tendency is an advantage when maneuvering into some tight sites, once you get the hang of how to control it. In fact, a fifth-wheel trailer can be more easily maneuvered into some sites than can a travel trailer.

When a fifth-wheel is backed, any adjustment of the tow vehicle's wheels is transmitted to the trailer much more rapidly than with a travel trailer. A slight turn of the tow vehicle's wheels results in a quicker, sharper turn of the trailer. Because of this tendency, it's best to make turns as shallow as possible.

When backing any trailer, don't hesitate to pull forward as often as needed if the trailer starts to turn too much, or if you have misjudged any distance or maneuver. Anyone who backs a trailer should realize that pulling forward is one of the best maneuvers for successful backing. It's the rare back-in site that doesn't require us to pull forward at least three or four times before we can maneuver easily into it.

When learning, stop the rig each time the wheels are turned and think about what is happening instead of moving constantly. Go at a very slow speed when you do move. Whenever possible, avoid extremes in turning the wheel. Overcorrecting can get you into more difficulties than undercorrecting.

"Anyone who backs a trailer should realize that pulling forward is one of the best maneuvers for successful backing."

If the campsite is edged with a curb, keep in mind that a trailer is wider than the tow vehicle. Keep the tow vehicle's wheels well away from the curb to avoid scraping the trailer tires against it. If a travel trailer's wheels are too close to a curb, neither backing nor going forward may move them away. To move out it may be necessary to ride up on the curb or go over it, neither of which does the tires any good. When parallel parking next to a curb, follow the same practice; keep the trailer wheels well away from the curb.

Some general tips for backing all RVs are listed in Exhibit 19.2.

PRACTICE MAKES PERFECT

The only way to become an expert at backing is to practice over and over. To perfect your backing technique, try practicing in a large shopping-center parking lot when there isn't much traffic in the area.

Back up with the wheel turned in either direction just to see how it affects the trailer's movement. Learn to achieve the movement desired by turning the wheel as little as possible.

EXHIBIT 19-2
Backing Tips

- If you are unsure of what is happening when backing, stop, get out, and take a look.
- When backing, do it slowly.
- Stop and analyze what movement is needed before proceeding. It isn't necessary to keep the rig moving all the time.
- Pull forward to straighten out the rig.
- A slightly angled site is easier to maneuver into than a site at a right angle to the road.
- The shorter the trailer, the more quickly it turns.
- Backing and turning to the left is easier to execute than backing and turning to the right because of better driver visibility.

Practice backing straight by looking in the left side mirror. This gives you a good feel for how to turn the wheel to make the trailer behave the way you want. You'll find that the wheel must be constantly turned—a little this way, a little that way—in order to back straight.

Try to put the trailer between the lines marking one of the parking spaces. The width of the parking space is narrower than the average campsite, so if the trailer can be put neatly into it, campsites should present no problems. Approach the space from ahead and from each side. Learn how far to pull past the parking space to allow enough room for turning into it. Notice the position of the trailer's wheels and how they track when turning into the site.

In all backing situations with either a trailer or motorhome, take your time. Stop frequently and get out to assess the situation. Develop a parking routine with your partner (if you travel with one), then rely on your partner when parking the rig. Strangers, even campground personnel, who want to be helpful can lead you astray and give you confusing directions and signals.

An economy of direction signals is better than a series of gestures. When we want the trailer to go in a certain direction, we merely extend our arm and point in that direction. In our procedure the direction-giver is often stationed on the edge of the site so the driver knows that the trailer must be positioned beyond the stationed person.

Your partner should give only three basic instructions:

1. Come back (or move ahead)
2. The direction to turn to correct a situation
3. Stop

The direction-giver should always be in view of the driver in one of the side mirrors so hand signals can be seen or walk alongside the vehicle in a position where verbal instructions can be given (which we usually do when the site is to the right of the truck and not easily seen by the driver). Those with long rigs who need someone at the

In all backing situations with either a trailer or motorhome, take your time.

rear to keep a check on what is going on back there can use hand-held, two-way radios to communicate with one another.

The best direction-givers are those who have had experience in backing the rig themselves. They better understand what the driver needs to know.

If your partner gives you the wrong directions, don't make a fuss about it; everyone makes mistakes. Discuss only what is necessary to get the job done. Spare others any denouncements of your partner's abilities. If necessary, talk over the problem later, in private, to achieve a mutual understanding so the situation won't happen again.

Perhaps this will be encouraging if you have any trepidations about backing: Every tight spot we have encountered in backing and parking the trailer has been the result of our own bad judgment in assessing the situation. Most of the problems occurred when we were novice trailerists. We have profited from our experiences—as you will profit from yours—and we rarely have any backing and parking problems any more.

DRIVING THROUGH CAMPGROUNDS

Although many campgrounds have sites for large RVs, these same campgrounds may have roads that are unsuitable for the RV to reach the site. Roads may be narrow with tight curves, have trees or other obstacles too close to the edge of the road, have ditches on either side of the road, or any combination of the above. If you have a large rig and can't see your site from the check-in office, it's prudent to walk through the campground to judge if you can make it through. If you venture onto such a road unaware of its condition, you may find yourself at an impasse, with the only way out being the way you came in, except that the getting out has to be done by backing.

Campgrounds like this are in the minority, however, and you may never encounter one.

CHAPTER 20

Customizing the Cockpit

S ince many fulltimers spend a fair amount of their time driving, the driver-passenger area, or the cockpit, should be outfitted to make it efficient and comfortable. Whether you drive a motorhome or tow vehicle, you'll want certain items near at hand. Maps and directories should be easy to consult; if fuel and service records and a trip log are kept, they should be conveniently at hand for making entries; and beverage holders and a litter bag should be within reach.

EXTRA COCKPIT STORAGE

Many motorhomes have a spacious cockpit area that can be adapted for storage of items needed while traveling. We say "adapted" because many of the motorhome builders don't take advantage of the cockpit space available, and it's often devoid of storage compartments.

On many models there is plenty of room between the driver and passenger seats for a built-in cabinet or chest, but many manufacturers don't install such storage compartments in their units, or if they do, the storage space may be scanty. We saw one motorhome in which the storage space amounted to two small map pockets and two beverage holders.

It's possible that a ready-made piece of furniture would fit into the area, such as a night table with drawers, an end table with one drawer and a enclosed cabinet in the bottom portion, or a top-opening chest.

Many motorhomes do have storage compartments above both the driver and passenger seats, but even the compartment above the passenger seat is impractical for storage of items needed during driving because the passenger must unbuckle the seat belt and stand up to retrieve such items—not a safe practice when the motorhome is moving.

Our present tow vehicle, a standard cab pickup truck, has plenty of storage space in addition to the glove box: spacious pockets that run the entire width of the doors; a well-designed, roomy console between the seats; pockets and bins behind the seats; and beverage holders. The storage was one of the reasons we purchased the truck.

Our former tow vehicles had very little storage space in the cockpit so we had to make our own. Some new trucks are also lacking in storage space. If you have one of these, perhaps you may want to adapt some of our ideas to your vehicle. Those who drive motorhomes or more spacious tow vehicles also may find some helpful ideas.

A Custom-made "Console"

The first thing we did to gain storage space in our previous trucks was to put a large container in the middle of the bench seat. This "console" was a 14-inch-square, 7-inch-high plastic crate.

The crate wouldn't stay put without something to hold it in place, so we engineered a holder into which it fit (Figure 20.1). The holder was originally made of fabric, but when it became faded and old we made another holder from more sturdy, fade-resistant vinyl upholstery material.

Figure 20.1 A homemade "console" for a pickup truck with a bench seat.

Three sides of the boxlike holder were no higher than the crate. The fourth side was an extended back, a 14-inch wide-strip of fabric that reached up and over the top of the seat back.

Four hook-and-loop material/elastic tabs were attached to the holder to keep it in place. To make the tabs, a 1-inch-long piece of hook-and-loop material was sewn onto one end of a 3-inch length of 1-inch-wide elastic. One tab was attached to each corner of the extended back and another to each of the back lower corners of the box section. The holder was secured by passing the box-section's tabs through the seat back and joining them to the extended-back's tabs with the hook-and-loop material.

The elastic's stretchiness allowed the seat back to be pushed forward without straining the holder. The hook-and-loop material made the holder easy to remove for cleaning.

Three sides of the holder had pockets running nearly the full width and depth of the sides and the back had two rows of small pockets that were sewn on another pocket that was the full width of the back and almost its height; this large pocket was sized to hold a big road atlas.

We fashioned a lid of ½-inch plywood for the crate. It rested on the top edge of the crate and was kept from shifting by cleats on the underside. The lid was hinged across the middle (with a piano hinge to make the top as smooth as possible) and covered with the vinyl. The vinyl was attached with contact cement except in the hinge area where it was left loose so it could flex when the lid was raised. The edges were finished with a cemented-on strip of the vinyl.

To keep small items from falling through the openings on the bottom of the crate, we put a thin piece of foam in the bottom, but cardboard would have done just as well.

The crate was at a convenient height for an armrest, and the covering on the lid kept clothes from being snagged on raw wood. When we were traveling, the crate served as a storage place for items we didn't want to leave in view when we were away from the truck.

Maps were kept in the side pockets. Pencils, pens, markers, magnifying glass, penlight, and scratch paper were some of the items kept in the smaller pockets.

A Beverage Container

Every time we want a drink of water we don't want to stop and go back to the trailer for it, so we keep a small, pump-type vacuum jug in the cockpit. In our present truck we have a place to set the jug so it's easily reachable. There was no such place in our previous trucks, so we set it on the floor of the passenger side. To hold it in place and upright, it was secured in a loop of one-inch wide webbing with hook-and-loop tabs (so it could be removed easily) attached to the sidewall with a screw. Such a jug can also be used for coffee or soft drinks.

Other Cockpit Storage

We had a gun rack mounted on the rear cab window of one of our trucks, but we didn't use it for guns. At times we hung items from its lower hooks, as long as they weren't so large that they interfered with visibility. Fabric hats were folded and held securely in the upper hooks.

Not having any built-in storage units behind the seats on our previous trucks, we had to make our own. For one storage unit, we cut a length of fabric to fit along the back of the cab about 18 inches wide, sewed various-size pockets on it, and put grommets along the upper edge. It was installed just under the rear window by inserting screws in the grommet holes. The bottom edge was not secured.

Underneath this storage unit, resting on the narrow shelf that ran behind the seats, were several boxes we custom made to fit the items we stored there.

Directory, Map, and Book Storage

Because we use so many different campground directories and usually refer to them every day when we travel, we need to have them contained in a storage unit, yet readily accessible. There has not been a place in any of our trucks with these attributes, so again, we had to make our own storage unit.

For the directories, we made a square-sided case from vinyl upholstery material, measuring 12 inches long, 8½ inches tall, and 4 inches wide; the opening is on the long, 4-inch side so the directories, which are stored with their spines visible, can be grasped easily. The width is large enough to accommodate all the directories we normally consult. To stiffen the case so the directories can be removed and replaced easily without the sides caving in, the case is lined with a duplicate case made of cardboard and stapled to the vinyl to hold it in place. The case sits on the floor in the middle of the cockpit in front of the seat.

At one time we stored our directories under a seat in a canvas bag and pulled the bag out by its handles when we wanted to use the directories. This was convenient, but not as much as the case.

Maps are, of course, essential items for travel, and, if you are like us, you'll refer to them frequently when under way. The technology for folding maps conveniently still hasn't been perfected, so we don't bother folding and unfolding them. Instead, we open and fold them to the general area in which we are traveling and put them on a clipboard. So the driver and the passenger (who is always chief navigator on our rig) can see and use the maps easily, the clipboard is kept on the lid of the console between us.

Since we don't cover several states in a day's travel, or even much of one state on most days, we don't have to keep changing maps often. Once one of our maps is opened to a certain area, it may stay in that position for several days or even weeks.

We like to have as many maps of a state and area as we can lay our hands on. Our basic maps are those we receive as a benefit of being a member of the American Automobile Association. We also like state-issued maps because they often have some roads that aren't included on other maps. Sometimes we purchase a state or area map, and we often have a U.S. Forest Service or Bureau of Land Management map to use for exploring backwoods roads. We also keep handy a map of the United States and a regional map of the area we are in.

We use a variety of maps because each publisher's map is different from another's. On some maps, the historic sites are well marked and include famous and not-so-famous sites. Others may have more secondary roads indicated. Some have more general informative details, such as the altitudes of cities.

When we are in big cities, we use a large-scale map of the city with all streets indicated and also another of the metropolitan area, which is often found on a state-issued map. A metropolitan-area map is handy for determining at a glance the major routes in and around the city.

We don't use a large road atlas during travel. No matter what its size, the maps aren't as big as individual road maps and it's also difficult to keep the atlas open to the needed page when traveling.

HELPFUL COCKPIT ITEMS

Instruments

Aside from the necessary instruments and gauges necessary for operating the vehicle, you may want to add some others for your own pleasure and to satisfy your curiosity.

We have a compass, an altimeter, and a clock that gives the time and date.

For a compass to be worthwhile it must be the type that can be corrected (or adjusted). Correcting is easy (instructions come with the compass). Proper correction can be done only on streets or roads that run exactly north/south and east/west, which may not be so easy to find.

The Log Book

We keep a log because we like to have a record of where we have been, the campgrounds at which we have stayed, and the people we have met.

The preprinted logs on the market don't have enough pages for extensive travel and never seem to have spaces for all the things we want to enter, so we use a spiral-bound steno notebook for a log (Figure 20.2).

The entries are written across the long measurement of the

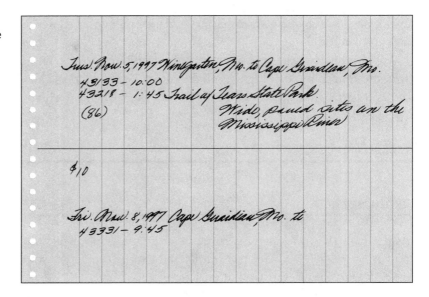

Figure 20.2 A spiral-bound steno notebook serves as the authors' log.

page. Two different entries are made on one page, using the center line to separate them.

Every time we move the trailer we make a log entry consisting of the day, date, town, or place from which we are leaving; starting mileage; and time of departure. When we arrive at our destination, we enter the mileage on the odometer as well as the actual miles driven, time of arrival, the town we are in or near, name of the campground where we are staying, and the rate. Later we add a brief description of the campground or our site, noting the number of the site if we especially like it.

Because we enjoy eating out, we enter the names of restaurants we have sampled in the area with our own rating of one to five stars. Rather than having a separate guest log, we put the names of people with whom we become acquainted in our notebook log, along with the type of rig they have. Addresses, if needed, are put in a separate address book.

Most of our log entries are merely items we may want to recall at a later date, but some entries are more valuable. By entering the

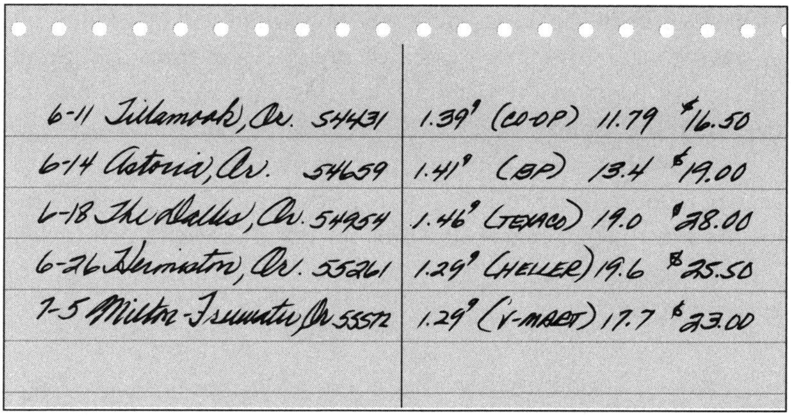

6-11	Tillamook, Or.	54431	1.39^9	(CO-OP)	11.79	$16.50
6-14	Astoria, Or.	54659	1.41^9	(BP)	13.4	$19.00
6-18	The Dalles, Or.	54954	1.46^9	(TEXACO)	19.0	$28.00
6-26	Hermiston, Or.	55261	1.29^9	(HELLER)	19.6	$25.50
7-5	Milton-Freewater, Or	55572	1.29^9	(Y-MART)	17.7	$23.00

Figure 20.3 The authors use the back pages of their log to enter fuel purchases and to keep records of maintenance performed on both their truck and trailer.

mileage every time the trailer is moved, we have a complete record of the number of miles on the trailer alone. Since we tally up the trailer miles frequently, we know when it's time to have the wheel bearings checked and lubricated.

The campground fee is an indicator of how much we may expect to pay should we return to that campground. Often we rent a site for a week or a month. Directories list only daily rates, so our records are helpful in this way too. By adding all the amounts spent for campgrounds during a year, we can determine our average daily cost.

The campground or site description serves as a reminder of desirable or undesirable features.

A number of pages in the back of the notebook are reserved for fuel and servicing logs (Figure 20.3). For these, the pages are used in the normal manner. Every time we purchase fuel, the date, mileage, cost per gallon, number of gallons purchased, and the total price are noted. The brand of fuel and sometimes the location of the service station are also entered. If we ever revisit the area, we will know where the lowest-price fuel can be found. When oil is added, the quantity—usually one quart—is entered on a line of its own in the fuel log. We know how often we are adding oil, and we have a complete record of our fuel expenditures. Some other back pages of the log are the servicing records for both the truck and the trailer.

We find that if it's convenient to enter information, the log-keeper is more likely to keep the records up to date. We store the logbook in the passenger-side door pocket and keep a pen tucked into the spiral of the notebook so we never have an excuse for not keeping up the logs.

CHAPTER 21

Recreational Transportation

In addition to a motorhome, auxiliary vehicle, or tow vehicle, many fulltimers want another form of transportation for recreation, sport, or exercise. This may be a boat, bicycle, moped, motorcycle, scooter, or all-terrain vehicle (ATV).

Unless any of these is towed on its own trailer, its weight has to be considered in the cargo-carrying capacity of the rig, as well as where it's stored, especially if it's to be kept on the rear bumper of a motorhome or trailer.

Recreational transportation items of all types should be accessible. If they aren't stored in a convenient, easy-to-get-at location, you may find you won't use them often.

BOATS

Water-oriented recreation, especially fishing, is very popular with fulltimers, many of whom transport boats with them to fish or explore the recreational possibilities of rivers, streams, lakes, and other bodies of water that abound in locations where a full-timing rig can be taken.

A boat as long as 18 feet can be carried atop the canopy of a pickup truck, but a 12- to 14-footer is a more practical size from the standpoint of weight and ease in handling (and the size of the outboard motor needed to propel it). The motor and other equipment needed for the operation of the boat may be kept inside the canopy. One fulltimer we know claims that carrying his boat on the top of his truck canopy when he is towing his travel trailer is as good as having a wind deflector. He notices a distinct difference in handling when the boat is not in position.

Those who have fifth-wheel trailers can't carry a boat this way because of the hitch being in the truck's bed, but cabtop racks are available that project out over the truck's hood (and sometimes slightly beyond) for fifth-wheelers who want to take their boats with them.

Canoes and kayaks can be carried on nearly every type of tow vehicle, including autos, and on the roof of some motorhomes.

A large boat might be stored in a favorite boating area to which you return on a regular basis, but if you prefer to take it with you, a sizable boat can be towed behind a motorhome on its own trailer. We have seen small cabin cruisers, open-console fishing boats, and cruising sailboats towed in this manner. The interiors of some of these boats can be used for storing all sorts of items—even bicycles.

In some states it's legal to tow boats on trailers behind travel and fifth-wheel trailers, but this would not be practical for fulltimers who travel extensively in many different states.

If a boat is carried on the roof of a tow vehicle or motorhome an easy way of lifting and lowering it is needed. A boat loader will do the job mechanically. The manual types that employ a crank for the raising and lowering operations require little effort and muscle power; an electrically operated boat loader will do it all.

A boat carried on its own trailer can be launched from the trailer. A boat carried atop a vehicle, once unloaded, can be transported a short distance from the vehicle to the water on a set of launching wheels.

Rigid boats aren't the only type that can be taken along. Folding and inflatable boats are exceptionally practical and take up lots less storage room than a rigid boat. Lifting and storing them is easier because when folded or deflated, the boat is a relatively small, easily maneuverable package.

The folding Porta-Bote, suitable for use as a fishing boat, is available at some large RV-supply stores and marine and sporting-goods stores. For the location of your nearest dealer contact: Porta-Bote International, 1074 Independence Avenue, Mountain View, California 94043; (800) 227-8882.

The Porta-Bote, which can be assembled in about two minutes, is suitable for rowing or use with a motor; it also becomes a sailboat with the addition of the sailing package. It's available in three sizes, which, when assembled are 8, 10, and 12 feet long, with weights of 39, 49, and 59 pounds, respectively. The weight is less than half that of a comparable aluminum boat because the Porta-Bote is constructed of polypropylene. A special mount can be obtained that allows the boat to be carried flat on the side of an RV (Figure 21.1).

Numerous brands of inflatable boats are available in many sizes and a wide range of prices. They can be propelled by a motor or

Figure 21.1 The Porta-Bote can be easily carried because it folds down into a small package, but it can be assembled in minutes.

rowed, although the rowing characteristics of some designs aren't very good. Not having any sort of keel, and sometimes having a blunt bow, none of them steers really well, but they are ideal for float trips and whitewater rafting.

Sailing can also be part of fulltiming. In small sizes, anything from a sailing dinghy to a sophisticated racing sailboat lends itself to rooftop storage.

A sailboard is extremely practical. It's easy to take along because its weight is negligible and it's not bulky.

Any boat used with a motor will embroil you in the red tape of registration, which, depending on the state, may be a problem.

BICYCLES

Bicycles seem to be as popular as boats among fulltimers. They are often carried on either the front or rear bumpers of motorhomes and trailers. If a storage compartment is in the rear of the RV, bicycles stored there may have to be removed in order to access it.

Numerous bike carriers are on the market. Depending on the type, the bike wheels fit into channels, or the bike is hung by its frame on a rack with hooks. A rear deck suitable for storing bicycles along with other items may be added to either a trailer or a motorhome.

A bicycle can be carried upright in a roof mount on some tow or auxiliary vehicles. If the bicycle is light enough so that climbing a ladder with it is not difficult, it can be laid flat on the roof of a motorhome or trailer. We saw a motorhomer who used a simple pulley arrangement attached to the roof rack as an aid for lifting up his bikes.

Bicycles and tricycles can be rigid or folding, and both are available in three-speed models. Most folding bicycles have 16- or 20-inch wheels, making them unsuitable for riding long distances and over rough or hilly terrain.

Bicycles and tricycles are ideal for use in large campgrounds where the office, recreation facilities, and even friends may be a considerable distance from your site, or for use anywhere if you are riding for the exercise.

Those who want a rigid bicycle can choose from among a wide variety of multi-speed models and a more limited selection of three-speed models.

A mountain bike is a popular bike because it's easy to ride and is as well adapted to rugged, hilly mountain trails as it is to flat, level pavement. The fat, knobby tires provide good traction on almost any surface, absorb bumps, and roll over small rocks and branches smoothly. Even though they have many gears, they are easy to operate. Most have double brakes for sure stopping power. A mountain bike weighs from 27 to 30 pounds.

Some municipalities require the licensing of bicycles and tricycles if they are used on public streets.

OTHER VEHICLES

Fulltimers can have low-cost auxiliary transportation with either a moped, a small motorcycle, or a scooter, any of which can be stored in a bumper rack. Some of those who fulltime in a motorhome find that one of these is more desirable auxiliary transportation than a small car, which must be towed.

The only practical way to take a heavier, full-size motorcycle with you is to tow it on its own trailer.

Although none of these vehicles provides the comfort and convenience of a car—it is not pleasant to be out in the open on rainy days, for instance—they are cheaper to buy and maintain, and provide a much greater range than a bicycle. They could be auxiliary transportation alternatives for those on tight budgets.

Unlike larger units, mopeds, scooters, and lightweight motorcycles don't have the speed and handling characteristics that may be needed to avoid accidents. When ridden in traffic, caution must be exercised and full safety gear—helmet, boots, gloves, jacket—should be worn.

Again, with a vehicle with an engine, the registration has to be considered, as well as insurance. All states require registration of motorcycles, and some require that certain insurance coverage be maintained. Regulations covering mopeds and scooters vary by state.

Carriers designed just for motorcycles and mopeds with a ramp for easy loading and unloading can be purchased. One type is mounted by using a standard hitch receiver.

Some fulltimers enjoy snowmobiling or driving an ATV. These vehicles need to be transported on their own trailers. Neither a snowmobile nor ATV requires registration. Fulltimers who regularly spend time in the same location where these vehicles can be used could store them there from season to season to avoid hauling them around.

HOW ABOUT RENTING?

Some of the boats and vehicles we have mentioned can be rented in many locations. Just about any type and size boat desired—sport-fishing boats, houseboats, cruising sailboats—can be chartered for a day, a week, a month, or longer.

Renting or chartering has many advantages:

- It may be less costly than owning, especially if you don't use the equipment regularly year round.
- It frees you from any registration and insurance obligations, which would be especially advantageous for fulltimers who don't reside in one place.
- There will be no worries about how your property will survive storms if stored someplace where you may not be able to take care of it.
- You have no maintenance chores and expenses.

PROTECTING YOUR EQUIPMENT

Boats, bicycles, mopeds, motorcycles, scooters, snowmobiles, and ATVs are all expensive items and attractive to thieves because of their cost and portability. If you own any such equipment, you'll need a way to protect it from being stolen when it's being transported and when you are at your destination.

Heavy chains with sturdy locks should be used to secure any vehicle carried in a rack, unless the rack itself has a locking device. Although stealing a boat from the roof of a vehicle is more trouble than most thieves would bother with, if we carried a boat on our truck roof, you can bet we would somehow chain and lock it to its rack or the truck.

If equipment is transported on its own trailer, it's not enough to secure it to the trailer. A lock should be affixed to the trailer itself so it cannot be unhitched from the tow vehicle and cannot be taken when it's unhitched. An ordinary padlock with a shank thin enough to pass through the holes in the coupler latch or one of the locks specially made for this purpose can be used.

CHAPTER 22

Safety, Security, and Protection

Fulltiming is not different from other lifestyles when it comes to the precautions you need to take to protect yourself and safeguard your belongings. Unfortunately, you can't be as trusting as you may like with your neighbors and casual acquaintances or be too open about your plans in the presence of strangers. Be especially aware of circumstances that can adversely affect your safety and security and take the necessary precautions.

LOCKS

No lock is burglarproof. Burglars can get into anything that's locked if they are allowed enough time. Because of this, your RV and other vehicles should be secured so that breaking into them can't be done easily or quickly. If your property is protected this way, thieves may give up on burgling it and move on to some other property that is not so well secured.

Entry-Door Locks

Fulltimers who don't have dead bolts on their entry doors in addition to the latches are asking for trouble. Breaking in is easy when the only thing to contend with is a latch that's locked by turning a button or pushing a lever; a screwdriver may be all that's needed to gain entry in a matter of seconds.

A dead bolt can be locked and unlocked from the outside only with a key. A crowbar will dispatch an RV door with a dead bolt, but it may take a little time, and someone attacking a door with a crowbar may arouse the suspicions of passersby.

It's a good idea to have a locksmith change the tumblers on any dead-bolt locks. Many master keys exist for these locks, and some are in the hands of people who will use them for unlawful entry.

If you are napping or sleeping with the door open or when you are alone in the RV, lock the screen door from the inside. A simple hook and eye is enough to stop someone from just walking in. For the same reason, we make it habit to lock the outside door when we are inside.

We started this practice after we became acquainted with a man in a campground who, when he wanted to see us, would rap on the side of the trailer, then just walk in. He was a friendly, well-meaning individual, but we couldn't count on any real privacy as long as he could enter our trailer at will. We realized if he could gain entry just by walking in, so could someone else who was not as friendly and well-meaning.

Any type of screen-door lock should be located high or low on the door so that no one can push back the slider and reach in to unlock it.

Compartment Locks

The locks on many outside compartments are virtually worthless as far as security goes. Not only are they flimsy, but they also have common keys. On occasion, when we have been on a dealer's lot looking at RVs unaccompanied by a salesman, we have been able to use our keys to open compartments on other RVs when we wanted to check them out for size and accessibility. Kits for changing the tumblers on outside compartment locks are available at RV-supply stores.

We had two locks on our travel trailer that would have de-layed—not stopped—anyone who wanted to steal the trailer itself. One was a padlock that was put through the holes in the coupler latch. The hitch could not be attached until the padlock was re-moved (this method works with tow dollies too). The other was a bicycle lock that fit on the wheel chock we used then, and which we continue to use (see Figure 18.4, page 461).

To protect our fifth-wheel trailer from theft, we use a metal col-lar that fits over the kingpin. The collar is held on with a padlock.

The two house batteries were on the A-frame on our travel trailer. To secure them, a small eye was put in one end of a length of stainless-steel cable (we happen to have a tool for doing this). The other end of the cable was passed around the angle iron of one of the battery supports where another eye was installed. An identical length of cable was made and installed on the angle-iron support for the other battery. The cables were just long enough to fit tightly across the top of both battery boxes, meeting in the middle. The two cables were fastened together with a padlock, the bail of which went through both eyes (Figure 22.1). Instead of purchasing a spe-cial tool for making eyes, they can be fashioned with wire-rope clamps. The clamps can be removed with a wrench, but that takes time, and if the clamps are positioned so they are difficult to get at, a thief may not bother. Lengths of chain may also be used.

Many canopies on pickup trucks can be easily broken into. Their locks also have many common keys, but thieves rarely bother with keys when the canopy is made of aluminum. Instead, they use a pry bar on the door. Fiberglass and steel canopies are sturdier than those made of aluminum but how burglarproof they are depends on the size of the windows. On some, it's easy to pop out a window and crawl through the opening. A hasp and padlock can be used on a canopy door, but it often sends the message that there is something of value inside. If anything valuable is kept in a canopy-covered bed, it should not be in view.

"Fiberglass and steel canopies are sturdier than those made of aluminum but how burglarproof they are depends on the size of the windows."

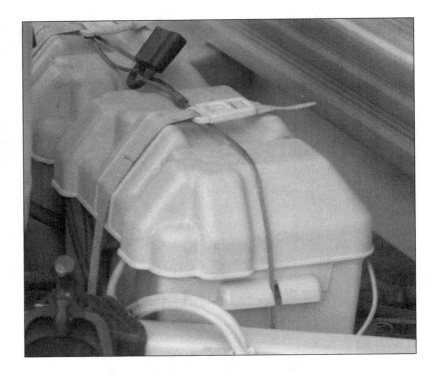

Figure 22.1 Batteries stored on the outside of an RV, as they are on many travel trailers, can be secured with a cable and a padlock.

WINDOWS

If you have an opening window adjacent to the entry door, it's a good idea to keep it closed if you leave the RV. On some RVs, it's relatively easy for someone to rip the screen, reach in, and unlock the door; no sound of breaking glass would attract anyone's attention.

Keeping the opening portion of escape windows closed when the RV is unoccupied is a good practice too. On some RVs, the spring-loaded latches that release the part of the window that swings out can be easily manipulated by reaching around through the window from the outside.

If someone was bent on gaining access to our trailer through another open window, it would take some time to bend the louver frame out of the way to make a wide enough space to crawl through. This activity, and the glass that would have to be broken, may attract someone's attention.

Sliding windows and those that open from the bottom don't provide the security of louvered windows. We once saw some trailers on a dealer's lot that had been broken into. The thieves had not bothered with any models that had louvered windows. On the other trailers, they had simply pried out windows with a screwdriver and crawled in. On some, the frames were barely damaged.

CAMPGROUND SAFETY PROCEDURES

RVers, being a friendly bunch, often display their names on the outside of their RVs. If you do this, have you considered that someone unfriendly can come to your door and call you by name? "Hey, Jim, its Fred." Most of us would assume Fred was a fellow RVer. If we can't quite remember who Fred is, perhaps seeing his face will remind us. Anyway, it would be unfriendly not to acknowledge Fred's presence by opening the door. We heard of one couple who found themselves looking into a gun barrel when they opened their door to a "Fred."

We are cautious when anyone comes to our door, day or night. At night, we turn on the outside lights, then ask any callers to identify themselves. If our suspicions were aroused, we would ask the person to show some identification through the window before we opened the door.

Security Lights

Some RVs are equipped with motion-activated, exterior security lights, so when you leave the RV, it's not necessary to leave an exterior light on just so you can see well enough to unlock the door when you return after dark. The motion-activated lights remain off until movement is sensed and then automatically turn on.

We don't usually turn on the exterior lights when we leave the trailer. An exterior light left on, with no other lights visible in the RV, is often an indication that the unit is unoccupied.

Security for Portable Valuables

If you don't want the risk of having valuables stolen, don't leave them around your campsite unless they are secured. Trusting people go away from their campsites and leave expensive coolers, barbecue grills, lawn chairs, and lanterns that can be easily stolen. Bicycles are often left where they can be simply ridden off or carried away.

If you have an expensive item that may attract thieves, such as a camera, binoculars, or a radio, don't leave it outside unless you are using it and be careful of displaying it needlessly. Even if you put it inside the RV, observant people may take note that you have such equipment and perhaps think it worthwhile to relieve you of it when you are away from your campsite.

If you have such items inside your RV, either keep them out of view or pull the draperies or blinds whenever you leave.

It's especially prudent to keep valuables out of public view in crowded public campgrounds, such as in national parks in the busy seasons, because there isn't much security provided by rangers anymore; they have their hands full just managing the crowds.

A few years back there was a gang of thieves operating in some of the state parks in southeastern coastal areas. Members of the gang would watch to see who left their RVs and alert others who would break in by various methods. This professional, well-organized group had master keys for many brands of RVs, but if they couldn't simply unlock the door and walk in, a small child was often used to gain entry by way of a roof vent.

Such thievery usually occurs in crowded public parks in the summer when RVers may be inclined to leave windows and vents open. Even though we don't normally frequent such places when they are crowded, preferring to visit them off season, any time we are in a public campground we are extra careful about protecting ourselves and our belongings.

Suspicious Characters

Sometimes people in a campground arouse our suspicions. On more than one occasion we have taken down the license plate numbers and a description of the vehicles such people were driving. One time in a city park, a carload of teenagers pulled into the site next to ours just as we were leaving to run some errands. The young men had no camping gear but they did have some beer. We figured if anything happened to the trailer while we were gone, they would be prime suspects. Fortunately, nothing did happen, but we had the information that would have allowed us to identify their car. Another time, in a state park, two young men in a car kept cruising around the camping area. They too had no visible camping equipment. We were leaving to pick up our mail in a nearby town, but first we recorded their license number and vehicle description just as a precaution.

Where you camp sometimes has a bearing on how safe you are. If your RV is the only one parked in a place, you may be considered an easy mark since there is no one around to come to your aid. At any designated campground someone comes to check it out sooner or later, so there is always a chance that thieves may be deterred by this. But if you were spending the night in a little-used rest area or at the side of a road, there may not be any protection at all, or if there is, locals up to no good may know how frequently the location is patrolled by law enforcement officers.

Although we like to be off by ourselves, we are much more cautious when we are alone anywhere. We watch anyone who comes into our area, and keep a check on them until they leave. If they don't leave, we stay alert and investigate any suspicious noises.

Firearms or Not?

Those who use firearms for sport of any kind don't have to decide whether to keep a gun aboard for protection; they already have a firearm that can be used defensively. Others often find themselves in a quandary about whether they want to have a gun solely for this reason. Many people doubt they could use a gun against another person, even in a "them-or-me" situation. Still, gun ownership may be practical because the odds are against your ever being in a situation that would turn into a shoot-out. A gun can be an effective deterrent even if it isn't loaded. Merely pointing a gun at a person may change someone's mind about what he or she intends to do. A rifle or shotgun can also be used effectively as a club. A great deterrent is the distinctive sound of a shell being loaded into the chamber of a pump-action shotgun.

If you think you might ever fire a gun, you should know how to do so. Take lessons or get instruction from someone you know who is skilled in the use of firearms. In the hands of the untrained, a loaded gun can be just as dangerous to the user as to the aggressor.

Laws governing gun ownership vary from state to state. Full-timers with firearms who do extensive traveling may find themselves in technical violation of some of these laws.

Border crossings between the United States and Canada and Mexico may present problems if certain types of guns are carried and worse problems if they are concealed and discovered by customs agents.

A firearm for protection won't be of much use unless it is readily accessible. The gun case we used in our 23-footer was designed so that when the top was lifted, the front dropped down. There was nothing to undo or move out of the way to reach the guns. Although we have no space for the gun case in our fifth-wheeler, the guns are just as accessible.

From a safety standpoint, the best practice is to keep a gun's chamber empty but with ammunition loaded in a clip or magazine and stored where it's handy. It is especially important to keep guns and ammunition separate if children are living in the RV.

AN ENCOURAGING WORD

Lest we have alarmed you by pointing out so much that could happen, be aware that RVing is a very safe activity. In all our years of fulltiming, we have never had anyone try to break into our trailer or tow vehicle, nothing has ever been stolen from our campsites, no one suspicious has ever knocked on our door, we have never been bothered by dubious-looking characters, and we have never felt our safety threatened enough to remove our guns from their storage place.

SAFETY EQUIPMENT FOR THE RV

To protect the RV and its occupants, certain safety equipment should be installed, and certain routines practiced.

Smoke Alarms and Fire Extinguishers

Smoke alarms have proven their value over and over in residences; they are just as valuable in RVs. Each RV should have at least one smoke alarm. It should be installed some distance away from the immediate galley area however, because stove-top cooking can trigger it.

Even the smallest RV suitable for fulltiming needs two fire extinguishers—one in the front and one in the rear, and they should be even more accessible than a gun. Any extinguisher should be regularly inspected to see that it's in working order; if not, have it recharged, or replace the nonrechargeable types when the test device so indicates.

Don't wait for a fire to figure out to use a fire extinguisher. Read the instructions, and reread them each time you give the extinguisher its routine inspection.

Plan how you would exit your RV if a fire broke out in any location. Chances are good that you would be able to get out of the entry door or the escape window (required on all one-door RVs). We open our two escape windows regularly to be sure they can be opened quickly.

A fire would be bad enough if you were in the RV, but it could well be disastrous if it occurred when you weren't around to take care of it. Before leaving the RV, do everything possible to make sure the RV will be safe from fire in your absence. One way to do this is to turn off everything that could cause a fire before leaving.

When we go away, no matter how hot it is, we never leave the air conditioner operating (it doesn't take too long to cool our trailer when we return). Even though the air conditioner has a circuit breaker that should trip in case of a problem, the circuit breaker itself could malfunction. In cold weather we never leave with an electric heater running or the gas furnace on. We do, however, feel safe with the catalytic heater operating, and sometimes leave it on in very cold weather when we go away for short errands. If our return were delayed, the worst that would happen is that the heater would run out of propane eventually.

We feel more comfortable if all electronic equipment—the TV, the receiver, the amplifier (if in use), and the stereo—is off when we leave the trailer because anything electrical has the potential for causing a fire. Another safety benefit: If an electrical storm occurs while we are away, there is less chance of damage to such equipment if it's turned off. Appliances, such as the coffeemaker, are unplugged. That way, there's no doubt about them being off.

We have installed a switch to select either the built-in charger or inverter. Using this switch, we turn off whichever has been in use so neither is operating while we're away.

We turn off the water pump too. If a leak developed somewhere in the line after the pump and the pump switch were left on, it would pump water out onto the floor until the tank was empty. The pump itself could become wet, short out, and perhaps cause a fire.

Again, it may seem that we are overcautious, but what if we were involved in an accident when we were out and couldn't get back to the trailer, perhaps for days? Knowing the trailer was secure would be one less worry we would have.

Gas Detectors

While RVing is a very safe activity, your very life can be threatened by something that can't be seen, heard, or smelled. That "something" is carbon monoxide (CO) gas. If there is a concentration of this poisonous gas in an RV, the occupants can become seriously ill or die.

Carbon monoxide is a byproduct of burning combustibles. In RVing, these combustibles are the propane, gasoline, and diesel fuel used in furnaces, catalytic heaters, stove burners, and automotive and generator engines.

There isn't much problem with CO when furnaces operate properly because furnaces are vented to the outside. The CO output of a catalytic heater is minimal; nevertheless, it should never be operated without adequate ventilation. Stove burners should never be used for heating, and even when cooking in a closed RV, a window should be open if the RV doesn't have outside venting through a range hood.

Built-in generators, or gensets, are the real culprits when it comes to producing the deadly gas. If the genset has a faulty exhaust system, CO can seep through minute cracks in the walls and floor of an RV. When the genset system is in order and the genset is operating properly but located near a window, the gas may come in through the window. If your neighbor is running a generator, fumes from it may reach you. We've heard of numerous instances where RVers have been affected by "second-hand" CO.

To be on the safe side, never operate a generator while any occupants of the RV are asleep; they may never wake up.

You can be aware of the presence of this invisible killer if you install a carbon-monoxide detector. All motorhomes built after September 1, 1993, are required to have carbon-monoxide detectors; however, detectors can be installed in any RV. Most RV-supply stores carry them.

Another useful accessory is a propane detector, which warns of the presence of this gas.

The CO and propane detector operate on 12-volt DC electricity, and each produces a phantom load (see Chapter 13, page 338).

Burglar Alarms

The attitude of many people these days is one of noninvolvement, so you can't count on anyone to take action upon hearing your burglar alarm go off. Nevertheless, a burglar alarm is valuable as a deterrent because thieves don't want to call attention to themselves.

Sometimes a decal on a window indicating that an RV is equipped with a alarm system may cause a thief to think twice about burgling that RV (Figure 22.2).

Portable Lights

It makes sense to have sources of light available other than the 12-volt interior and exterior lights. For one thing, in an emergency situation, a built-in light may not be available where it is needed. In any lighting conditions, we needed a flashlight to identify the fuses on the fuse panel on our 23-foot trailer. At night, if you were awakened by noise made by someone outside and you didn't want to turn on any lights, a shielded flashlight can help you make your way around inside, unnoticed, while you investigate. A flashlight is also useful to light your way at night in a poorly lit campground.

Included among the various flashlights we have are two lantern types that have exceptionally bright, long beams. One is kept in the trailer and the other in the truck. If circumstances called for it, we could use these flashlights to temporarily blind someone. The

Figure 22.2 A decal on the window of an RV indicating that it is equipped with an alarm system may deter thieves.

beam can also be used for signaling since it can be seen from quite a distance.

EMERGENCY CARDS

We carry cards in our wallets with information about who to notify in case we have an accident. Our cards are somewhat different from those of people who live in a fixed dwelling and have a telephone. For example, Bill's card reads:

> In case of emergency notify
>> Jan Moeller
>> in a (brand name), 29' fifth-wheel trailer
>> (trailer's license number and issuing state)
>> at (a local campground)
> or notify
>> (relative's name)
>> (relative's address)
>> (relative's telephone number)

There aren't too many places where campgrounds are so numerous that they couldn't all be checked out quickly.

When we register at a campground, we pick up one of the campground's business cards and keep it in the truck in an obvious place.

A RECORD OF IMPORTANT NUMBERS

A list of all our important numbers is with us at all times. The list contains serial numbers of our truck, trailer, and every piece of equipment we have that may be the target of a burglar. It also has telephone numbers for reporting lost or stolen credit cards. We each carry a copy of the list and keep another copy in the trailer in a place where, chances are, a thief may overlook it.

Whenever we purchase new equipment, it's added to the list. The copies we keep in our wallets are much-reduced photocopies made from the master list.

CHAPTER 23

Fulltiming with Children and Pets

Fulltiming with children and pets may be somewhat more restrictive than fulltiming without them, but most people willingly sacrifice some of their freedom in exchange for the joy that they bring into their lives.

Even though children and pets can enrich fulltiming, they can also bring their share of problems. Sometimes children are accepted in RV parks where pets are not. On the other hand, some parks—especially those advertised as adult parks—may accept pets but won't allow children below a certain age or have limitations on the amount of time children can spend visiting those staying in the park. Some parks, however, don't allow either children or pets, and some that do allow them impose an extra charge for each child or pet.

RV ACCOMMODATIONS FOR CHILDREN

An RV has to be proportionately larger for fulltiming with children. Each child needs to have a place to sleep, study, and relax, and space to store clothing and other possessions. Bigger children need more physical space than small ones. Two or more children when beyond the toddler stage should have equal accommodations.

Not many manufacturers have RVs suited for fulltiming with children. They regularly build units that sleep up to six people, but it's evidently assumed that the six won't be sleeping in the RV for longer than an occasional vacation, because two of the six, if they are small, are expected to use the converted dinette for a bed. This is not ideal when fulltiming. Even if the children don't mind sleeping on the dinette, an adult must make it up each night and disassemble it each morning, and the dinette is out of use for any other activities when it's made into a bed.

The only RVs truly ideal for fulltiming with children are two-bedroom units with a front bedroom and another bedroom in the rear. The rear bedroom usually contains two bunk beds, although in some models, a twin bed is incorporated into the rear bedroom as well. As far as we know, no motorhome manufacturer makes a model like this, but in recent years we have seen an upsurge in two-bedroom models in both travel and fifth-wheel trailers.

If an RV doesn't have this arrangement, it would take considerable alteration of an existing floorplan to achieve anything close to a two-bedroom layout. And, as mentioned earlier, it would be the rare manufacturer that would do this sort of customizing.

Bunk beds are ideal for children because they take up little space. The addition of a shelf or two and perhaps a curtain to close off the entire bunk compartment can turn a bunk into a personalized, private space. A bed in the cabover portion of a Class C motorhome can have the same treatment.

Ideally, a dining area should be large enough to seat all the occupants of the RV at one time. With more than four people, however, this may not be possible. As far as we know, there are no RVs with two baths, so it may be more convenient for some of those living in the RV to use campground facilities at times.

The physical space of even a large RV may be too confining when children are living in it, but extra space can be gained in several ways: A screened "room" can be attached to the outside of the RV where children can play and, perhaps, sleep; children can sleep outside in a tent; and a canopy-covered pickup-truck bed can be used for sleeping and playing. If a van is used as a tow vehicle, it might serve as a children's room.

When traveling with children, campgrounds should be selected with an eye toward activities and recreational possibilities, not only in the campground, but also in the locality. Most children aren't happy being cooped up in one place all the time; they want to get out and do things. At campgrounds where the busy season is in the winter months, the activities are usually targeted at those who are middle-aged or older. For children living in such a campground, the community should offer recreational opportunities for them.

TRAVELING WITH CHILDREN

Most children like the excitement of going somewhere—up to a point. That point is just before they whine, "Are we there yet?" If children travel too many miles in a day, they become bored, restless, and irritable. So if children are along it's especially important to keep trips short and not travel every day; lay over often for a day or two. During a day's run, make frequent stops so children can work off pent-up energy.

A standard pickup truck isn't roomy enough to use as a family tow vehicle. The extra seating capacity of a super or crew cab truck or a van may be needed. Seats with seat belts are needed for everyone traveling in a motorhome.

How Adaptable Are Children?

If children are very young, there is little to worry about as far as their adapting to fulltiming. They have little previous experience in the non-full-timing world to color their opinions about it one way or the other.

When children have spent all their years in the full-timing lifestyle, they may accept it as their way of life, but children between the ages of about eight to twelve, to whom fulltiming is a new experience, may not look upon it with nearly the same enthusiasm as their parents. Fulltiming means their world will be disrupted, they'll be thrust into an unfamiliar environment, and their friends will no longer be around. Nevertheless, most children of these ages can adapt to fulltiming and benefit from it.

Children of full-timing parents who travel considerably are usually more self-assured than others of their age. They deal with a host of different situations that stay-put children never encounter. Their experience is broader in all areas than that of children who grow up in one place. Traveling gives a child an awareness of history, nature, geography, and regional customs that no school can ever provide. Children's knowledge will be expanded if they take part in travel planning.

A problem with children's' adaptability may arise when they enter the teen years, especially if their schooling comes from home-study correspondence courses (see pages 521–522). Children who don't attend a regular high school have no opportunity to participate in the sports, activities, and social life that high school provides. They never experience belonging to school clubs, playing in the band or on the football team, going to proms, and being publicly recognized for good grades. The all-important graduation ceremony does not take place for them. Such teenagers may become resentful and intractable because of what they have been denied, creating discord that, in the relatively confined space of an RV, is not pleasant for anyone. Yet it would be the exceptional teenager who could get through this period without being somewhat dissatisfied with his or her lot.

Education

One of the major concerns of full-timing parents is how their children can be educated within the framework of a mobile lifestyle. This can be accomplished in two ways: Either plan on staying in one place during the school year so the children can enroll in school, or use home-study correspondence courses.

With home study, parents aren't tied down; they can travel as they wish. This is why many parents who fulltime opt for the home-study method.

Although it may seem desirable to be able to educate your children wherever and whenever you wish as you travel, doing so is not without its problems. The child must devote many hours a day to studying, and the parents must oversee the work and function not only as supervisors and disciplinarians but also as teachers. If the child does not follow a regular study routine, this system won't work, and such a routine is difficult to maintain when much traveling is done.

Traveling or not, home study requires much discipline on the part of the child and the parents. Children usually handle the disciplinary restrictions more easily than the parents. Many children have spent some time in a regular school before they begin fulltiming, and lessons, homework, and studying have been a regular part of their lives. Parents, though, have been away from school for many years so adapting to a study-teaching regimen may be more difficult for them.

Correspondence courses can give children as good an education, or a better one, than regular schools if the parents do their part and see that the children do theirs.

The Calvert School (105 Tuscany Road, Baltimore, Maryland 21210; (410) 243-6030) offers home-study courses for the elementary grades. Certain church-affiliated correspondence courses are also available. For over sixty years, high school curricula have been available from the University of Nebraska (Division of Continuing Studies, 33rd and Holdrege Streets, Room 269, Lincoln, Nebraska 68583-0900; (402) 472-3450). The American School (2200 East 170th Street, Lansing, Illinois 60438; (800) 228-5600 or (708) 418-2800) also has home-study courses for grades 9 through 12.

While home-study courses are expensive, it may average out to cost less than what it would to send a child to school. Children who study at home don't need a wardrobe of special school clothes and money for meals and snacks eaten outside the home. There are no transportation costs and expenses for school-related activities.

A real plus of home education is that parents have more control over their children's social environment and what they are exposed to, especially drug, alcohol, tobacco use, and the sexual mores of their peers.

In years past in some states, home education was frowned upon, even prohibited, but as public education continues to deteriorate, home schooling has gained wider acceptance.

Fulltiming with Children—or Not?

Is it really sensible or practical to fulltime with children? The answer is yes and no.

There are happy full-timing families with children of all ages (Figure 23.1), but there are also former full-timing families who could not make the lifestyle work for them.

The success or failure of fulltiming with children depends on several factors. The personalities, temperaments, and attitudes of everyone involved in the venture are important. If there isn't a harmonious family relationship in a fixed dwelling, it will probably change for the worse in an RV.

The ages of the children and their feelings are another factor. Small children are amenable to just about anything as long as the family unit remains the same. They are used to having their lives organized and controlled by their parents. They are also too young to voice their feelings about such things as a change in lifestyle.

As children advance in age, however, they have definite opinions and feelings that should be taken into account. As with a dissatisfied partner, it isn't pleasant to live day after day with a child who is not happy with the full-timing lifestyle.

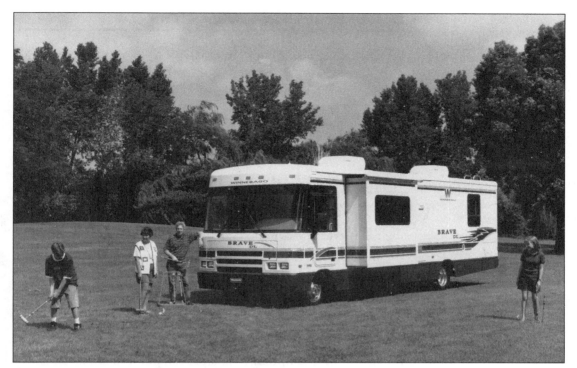

Figure 23.1 These days, it's not unusual to find full-timing families with children. (Courtesy Winnebago Industries Inc.)

Forcing children into fulltiming against their will or continuing in the lifestyle when they are terribly unhappy with it can cause long-term resentment. Never mind any benefits of the lifestyle; the child may end up feeling cheated simply because his or her life is different from that of other children.

Deciding whether or not to fulltime with children requires extensive soul searching, but there is no way of knowing for sure how it will turn out. For some families, the togetherness of living in an RV is more than their relationship can stand and it becomes a disaster. For others, this same way of living brings them closer together and is a rich and rewarding experience.

CHILDREN VISITING FULLTIMERS

It's a common practice for grandparents to invite their grandchildren to travel with them for a short period of time. If you do this, be sure to have a letter of permission from the parents and also a letter from them authorizing you to seek medical treatment for the child should it be necessary.

TRAVELING WITH PETS

Fulltimers who have a pet often must make certain adjustments in their life-style to accommodate the pet.

"No Pets Allowed"

The sign prohibiting pets is appearing more and more frequently in private RV parks, state parks, and other public campgrounds. Because of this, fulltiming with a pet can put limitations on where pet owners can stay. Very few people could bear to give up a pet they already own just for the sake of being able to stay in the places that don't allow pets. But if you are thinking of acquiring a pet, perhaps this aspect should enter into your decision making.

Some pet owners have only themselves to blame for the ever-increasing campground restrictions on pets. Too many dogs and cats have been allowed to run loose, make messes, bother other campers, and make noise at all hours of the day and night. As usual, the owners of well-behaved pets must suffer because of a minority that has soured many campground operators about accepting pets.

Most of the campgrounds where we have stayed where pets are accepted have regulations posted regarding pets, but too often they are ignored by pet owners. In our experience, the most flagrant violation is that of the leashing rule. Most campgrounds require pets to be leashed so they can't intrude on other campers' space. We have been jumped on, growled at, licked, and nuzzled by unleashed dogs whose owners were nowhere in sight. We have owned dogs, aren't frightened of them, and know how to handle them, but think how others who aren't used to dogs would feel in these situations. Very few people hate dogs; most of us like them—if they are under control.

But even if pets are leashed, they can be a nuisance. In a state park, we had a site next to the owners of two large dogs. The dogs were kept outside, tied to the trailer, day and night. The owners left early each morning and did not return until evening. Those who ventured past their trailer, or in our case, when we came out the door, were barked at and lunged at by the dogs. Their leashes were just long enough to reach our site, which meant there were many dog droppings around our picnic table. Although we didn't complain about the situation, evidently someone else did. A park ranger appeared at our neighbors' door early one morning, and they hitched up and left within the hour.

Unleashed cats have been more of an annoyance than a problem for us. They seem to like bounding about under the trailer and doorstep, creating strange noises. Many of these same cats want to take up residence with us it seems, since we have difficulty keeping them out when we open the door.

While pet owners can control where their pets do their business, they can't control the barking, whining, or meowing of animals when they go off and leave them behind. In some campgrounds, if an animal is allowed to befoul the grounds or bother others with its noise, its owner may be asked to leave. Pet owners should be considerate of their animals, but at the same time they should be considerate of other campers.

We have heard of some campgrounds that have a separate registration form for pets. On the form is all the pertinent information about the pet—breed, color, name, and such—along with a clause acknowledging that the owner understands and agrees to abide by all the campground's rules concerning pets. A deposit may be imposed as well, which would be refunded if the pet and its owner didn't violate any of the rules.

The size of the animal may affect where you can stay with a pet.

> **"W**hile pet owners can control where their pets do their business, they can't control the barking, whining, or meowing of animals when they go off and leave them behind.**"**

We have heard of some campgrounds that accept only small pets; one campground we know of stipulates that the pet can weigh no more than twenty-five pounds.

Pet Safety

Whenever pets are outside they should be leashed for their own safety. If they can't run loose, they won't be run over on a highway or wander away and get lost. It's tragic when a beloved pet becomes lost, but especially so when RVers are traveling and the pet disappears. RVers on vacation often have no choice but to leave the area and continue on, but fulltimers may be able to stay until all the possibilities in tracking down the missing pet are exhausted. If the animal wanders away and gets lost, there may be a chance of recovering it if you are able to post notices and run ads. In the case of a stolen pet, however, probably nothing can be done to recover it.

Pet thievery is not uncommon, so take every precaution against someone stealing yours. Most animals are stolen for the money they bring when sold. No animals are safe. Purebreds can be sold as pets; less desirable animals are often sold to research facilities.

Never leave your pet unattended in any public place. Mark it with some form of permanent identification, such as an ear tattoo, in addition to identification on its collar. A nose print is just as individualistic as a human fingerprint so it can be used for positive identification of an animal.

A pet should be protected by having a veterinarian give it the necessary shots. Aside from the health benefits, pets can't enter Canada and Mexico unless they have the proper inoculation certificates.

If a pet should accidentally ingest a poisonous substance or be deliberately poisoned, a twenty-four-hour hotline operated by the National Animal Poison Control Center in Urbana, Illinois, can be used for assistance. The toll-free number is (800) 548-2423. The fee is $30 and can be charged with a credit card.

Pet Accommodations

Any pet should be given time to adjust to its new RV environment. Immediately establish a place for it to sleep. In a motorhome, the sleeping place should be safe and secure for use when the motorhome is moving as well as when it's parked. Whether in a motorhome or riding in a tow vehicle, pets must be disciplined so they know the driver's area is off limits. An animal crawling around the driver's feet can be hazardous.

Some RVers have installed pet doors in their units. A ramp from the door usually leads to a fenced-in enclosure so the pet can come and go as it pleases, yet not be able to wander away when the owners are absent. So a pet can't climb over the fence and other animals can't get in, a roof of chicken wire can be put across the enclosure.

Pets should never be left in a closed-up RV or other vehicle in extremely hot weather.

Costs of Pet Ownership

Those on tight budgets should consider the cost of owning a pet before acquiring one. The initial cost can be anywhere from nothing to hundreds of dollars, but the upkeep and feeding runs into thousands. For example, a few years ago the estimated cost of owning a small dog for an average ten-year life span was $3,500. A medium-sized dog would require $6,000, and a large dog $8,350. A cat's upkeep was found to be slightly more than that of a small dog.

CHAPTER 24

The Fun and Rewards of Fulltiming

By now we should have convinced you that fulltiming is easy, and, if you thought problems were inherent in the lifestyle, we hope we have proved that they aren't problems at all, or that they can be overcome or solved one way or another by anyone who really wants to be a fulltimer. So if you want to join the ranks of fulltimers, don't delay. None of us knows how many tomorrows we have, so make the most of today and take advantage of all the benefits that fulltiming offers.

The lifestyle can expand horizons, increase knowledge, and provide opportunities to make new friends every step of the way. It can prevent you from falling into a rut and living in the same never-varying pattern day after day. Fulltimers, unlike most people, can have an ever-changing environment. Those who are adaptable and aren't afraid of change, who want to see and do new things, will be in no danger of growing old—at least mentally.

CLUBS AND CAMARADERIE

Fulltiming offers the chance to make a host of new friends. Pull into a campground in the off-season or in the South in the winter months. No doubt you'll find that many of the others in that particular campground at that time are fulltimers. It shouldn't take long to become acquainted. Maybe the other campers will even let you get settled before they introduce themselves.

All during the year you are likely to encounter vacationing RVers with whom you'll have much in common. If you don't meet again in a vacation spot, you may end up visiting them in the place where they live. Among our non-full-timing friends, many have offered us a place to park our trailer when we come to see them.

When you purchase a recreational vehicle, you may find that a club exists for owners of your particular brand of RV. Club activities often include rallies and get-togethers on the national, regional, state, and local levels; caravans; and many benefits other than the social. All Winnebago and Itasca owners, for example, are eligible for membership in Winnebago-Itasca Travelers, which has a special division for fulltimers called the 365 Club. Fulltimers may also want to join certain other clubs not affiliated with any particular RV manufacturer.

The Good Sam Club

Being members of the Good Sam Club adds to our fulltiming enjoyment. We recommend that fulltimers, as well as other RVers, join the Good Sam Club, no matter which other RV-oriented organizations they belong to. Benefits of membership are many and constantly expanding.

The current benefits are:

- A discount of 10 percent off nightly fees at more than 1,600 Good Sam Parks
- RV parts and accessories discounts of 10 percent at hundreds of locations
- Subscription to the monthly magazine *Highways*
- Sizable savings on all Trailer Life publications—magazines

and books—including the *Trailer Life Campground/RV Park & Services Directory*

- Mail-forwarding service*
- Message service*
- Long-distance calling card
- Emergency road service*
- Emergency Assistance System for medical emergencies*
- Rig insurance*
- RV and boat financing
- RV Search, a national database of RV buyers and sellers*
- Continued Service Plan, which is protection from repair bills after your manufacturer's warranty has expired*
- Lost credit card service
- Lost pet and lost key services**
- Various types of medical and health insurance including a plan for Canadians who travel in the United States*
- A Visa or Mastercard
- Volunteer campground host program
- A golf card entitling the holder to discounts and other benefits at 1,700 golf courses around the country*
- Discounts on propane, gas and diesel fuel, car rentals, and flowers
- Trip routing
- Investment opportunities*
- SamTours, a full-service travel agency
- Directory of Standby Sams, Good Samers located throughout the country who provide advice and assistance in emergencies

In addition to all these benefits, members can participate in Samborees and Caraventures that go on year-round. (Samborees are

*This benefit available at an extra charge; companies providing the services usually have special rates for Good Sam members.
**Service free but a low-cost special pet tag or key ring must be purchased.

gatherings of regional Good Sam members for socialization, good works, and fellowship, and often include seminars on various RV-related subjects. Caraventures are guided tours to world-wide locations. On some tours in the United States and Canada, members travel in their own rigs. Other tours in foreign countries include RV rentals. Sometimes the means of transportation is a cruise ship.)

The Good Sam Club also provides a voice on local, state, and national levels when legislation affecting RVers is proposed.

Within the ever-growing 2,000-plus chapters worldwide, the Good Sam Club has many special chapters. Some are service oriented; others are just for fun. Ham radio and CB groups, for instance, are numerous. People from the same profession often form their own groups. The LEOs (Law Enforcement Officers) in Minnesota are an example. Both working and retired officers can join. The Semper Fi Sams is a chapter for retired and former marines. Foster and adoptive parents can join the Caring Sams. Many chapters have been organized by single Good Samers.

Some Good Sam members belong to Kids 'n' Us chapters. These chapters are composed of families with children and were established with the focus on children. At get-togethers the children can count on having playmates of their own age, and all activities are family oriented.

For information: Good Sam Club, P.O. Box 6888, Englewood, Colorado 80155; (800) 234-3450.

Other RV clubs are open to RVers and offer varying benefits:

Escapees Club, 100 Rainbow Drive, Livingston, Texas 77351; (888) 757-2582

Family Campers and RVers, 4804 Transit Road, Building 2, Depew, New York 14043-4906; (800) 245-9755 or (716) 668-6242.

Family Motor Coach Association, FMCA, Inc., 8291 Clough Pike, Cincinnati, Ohio 45244-2796; (800) 543-3622, or (513) 474-3622; only for motorhome owners.

Family Travel Trailer Association, P.O. Box 5867, Titusville,

Florida 32783; (800) 603-1101 or (407) 264-9614; only for owners of any type of trailer.

Several clubs have been formed for RVing singles. In most of them you can neither join nor remain a member if you have a partner. They are:

Loners of America, P.O. Box 3314, Napa, California 94558; (888) 805-4562

Loners on Wheels (LOW), P.O. Box 1355, Poplar Bluff, Missouri 63902

Wandering Individuals Network (WIN), P.O. Box 2010, Sparks, Nevada 89432

Disabled RVers can join the Handicapped Travel Club, Inc., Merle Young, 12555 Lantern Road, Fishers, Indiana 46038; (317) 849-8019.

A club just for women is RVing Women Inc., P.O. Box 1940, Apache Junction, Arizona 85217; (888) 557-8464.

Active and retired military personnel may be interested in joining the Special Military Active/Retired Travel Club: S*M*A*R*T Headquarters, 600 University Office Boulevard, Suite 1A, Pensacola, Florida 32504; (800) 354-7681 or (850) 478-1986.

All the above clubs publish either magazines or newsletters, and most hold national rallies during the year, as well as some more local get-togethers.

You may already belong to a club or association because of an interest of your own that has nothing to do with RVing. Being a fulltimer may enable you to attend national and regional meetings and conventions you may otherwise have to miss because of lack of time. If the cost of expensive accommodations has limited your attendance at such functions, as a fulltimer, you'll be able to attend economically without ever leaving home.

FULLTIMERS AS CONSERVATIONISTS

A rewarding aspect of fulltiming is that those in the lifestyle automatically participate in conserving natural resources just because they live in an RV. Here are some of the ways in which RVers act as conservationists:

- Heating and cooling an RV uses little energy when compared to that required for a house or an apartment. Less electricity is used for lighting an RV, too.
- No one living in an RV uses a lot of water to flush the RV's toilet. Residential toilets use from three to five gallons of water for each flush. RVers would have to make a concentrated effort to use so much as a gallon for each flush.
- Water is conserved in another way when RVers operate from their unit's water tank. When a known quantity of water exists, even though it can be readily replenished, usage is normally conservative to make the supply last longer.
- Those with an RV don't have wood-burning stoves and so don't contribute to the polluting pall caused by such stoves that hangs over some towns in the winter months.
- Fulltimers who live exclusively in their RVs don't have lawns, therefore no watering is done, and fertilizers, many of which are environmentally objectionable, aren't used.
- Fulltimers who are interested in recycling can practice it just as easily when living in an RV-home as can those living in a fixed dwelling.

FULL-TIMING ACTIVITIES

If you think fulltiming isn't interesting or that traveling will be boring, you haven't thought the matter through. Driving long days nearly every day *is* boring, so traveling should not be done all the time. Stop often for a few days, a week, a month, or more, to explore and get to know the places in which you stay. No matter how small or isolated the place, you'll find interesting people to talk to. Let them in on your lifestyle and you may be the one doing most of the talking—answering the barrage of questions they will subject you to.

It's fun to participate in regional festivals of all kinds: ethnic, patriotic, religious, wine, food, harvest, and music—from opera to hoe-downs. New Orleans is not the only town that has a Mardi Gras, and places other than Nashville have country-music festivals.

Experiencing the diversity of our country, learning how others live—their customs, dress, habits, even differences in language—is enriching and educational.

If getting to know people doesn't interest you or isn't enough to fill all your time, pick a subject and explore it thoroughly or establish a goal and set about reaching it. As a fulltimer you are always packed and ready to go.

Ideas for Full-timers' Activities

A rather common goal among fulltimers is to visit every one of the contiguous United States. Should you want something more challenging than just ticking off states, you might combine some of the following suggestions with that activity:

- Take your own covered wagon and follow some of the trails used by the pioneers—the Oregon, the Santa Fe, the Bozeman, the Abilene, the California, the Mormon—or walk sections of the great hiking trails such as the Appalachian Trail and the Pacific Crest Trail.
- Select a war, perhaps the American Revolution or the Civil War, and visit all its battlefields and historic sites.
- Old forts may attract you. In searching them out, you'll find much diversity. The isolated, spartan Fort Fetterman in Wyoming, once on the western frontier, contrasts sharply

with the elaborate structure of Castillo de San Marcos in St. Augustine, Florida.

- All the ordered beauty of Japanese gardens in the United States and Canada serenely await your contemplation.
- Exploring all the famous gardens of the South would take years. After you've seen them, you can start on the famous gardens of the North.
- How about tracking down the largest trees of each species? They are located all over the country in nearly every state (check with local forestry offices for locations).
- Bodies of water are everywhere to explore and use for sport and recreation. Fish or swim in the biggest body of water in each state. Perhaps you would enjoy searching out the highest and largest waterfalls in the country. Some are easily accessible; reaching others presents a challenge. Do you know there are sizable waterfalls in Minnesota, Michigan, and Wisconsin?
- Discover the fascination of exploring a river from its headwaters to its mouth. Pick a major river such as the Mississippi or the Missouri; or a lesser one such as the Red, the White, the Blue; or even the Mattaponi, which provides three avenues of exploration from its headwaters: the Matta, the Po, and the Ni.
- You could make it your aim to fish in every state. Try for trout in the Battenkill in Vermont, coho in Lake Michigan, rockfish in the Chesapeake Bay, and steelhead in the Nehalem River in Oregon.
- If you're a golfer, swing through the country to play all the challenging golf courses (Figure 24.1).
- In your RV you can follow the route of the Intracoastal Waterway and watch the commercial traffic and pleasure boats making their way from the Virginia Capes, around Florida, and on to Brownsville, Texas.
- If the Intracoastal Waterway piques an interest in canals, travel inland to take a look at the remains of the James River-Kanawa Canal—started, but never finished, and intended to connect the Atlantic Coast with the Ohio River. Preserved

Figure 24.1 Playing challenging golf courses throughout the country is just one of the many activities fulltimers can pursue. (Courtesy Fleetwood Enterprises, Inc.)

sections of old canals exist in many states. The Erie Canal, now called the New York State Barge Canal, still carries boat traffic.

- If the Erie Canal doesn't interest you, maybe eerie ghost towns will. Every western state has its share.
- Board the many old railroad trains that still chuff their way along. Ride a logging train in the mountains of West Virginia, travel to a pioneer village across the Nebraska prairie, roll through the Napa Valley while dining in elegant surroundings

and sipping the fruitful beverages the valley is famous for, or clatter across breathtakingly high, narrow trestles in the mountains of Colorado.

- Are railroads too tame for your taste? If so, then take off, at least in your imagination, with the astronauts at Huntsville, Alabama; Cape Canaveral, Florida; and the Johnson Space Center in Houston, Texas. Come back to earth watching the space shuttles land at Cape Canaveral. Fly with the Wright brothers at Kitty Hawk, North Carolina, and hop with Lindy across the Atlantic in the *Spirit of St. Louis* at the National Air and Space Museum in our nation's capital.

- Birdwatchers can use every day of fulltiming to add their life list. Your RV can take you to habitats of rare, elusive, and uncommon species. Is the ivory-billed woodpecker really extinct, or do a few still exist in the swamps of South Carolina? Maybe you'll be the one to find out.

- With regional wildflower books you can identify flowers that grow in beautiful settings and in homely waste patches by the roadside. You may even develop an appreciation for the beauty of some weeds you once tried to eliminate from a lawn you used to have. You might try to find different wildflowers from each state.

- If geology is your hobby, visit the unusual geologic formations that are to be found in nearly every state. Go to the section of western Kansas that resembles Monument Valley in Arizona and the brown, volcanic-ash and lava landscape of Craters of the Moon National Monument in Idaho. On the hills surrounding Missoula, Montana, notice the ripple marks left by a huge, ancient lake formed by a glacial ice dam during the Ice Age.

- On a less grand scale, but still in the same vein, rockhounds can pursue their hobby in more places than they can cover in a lifetime. You may include in your collection a specimen that is representative of each state.

- Delve into ancient history with trips to the fossil beds that are found in several states and visit the many museums that focus on paleontology.

- Shell collectors have miles and miles of beaches to comb on the East, West, and Gulf Coasts. Don't miss Sanibel Island off the west coast of Florida.

- Your RV can be your base camp for making an ascent to each state's highest point. Some high points can be reached in a vehicle; others require mountain-climbing skills. Climbing wouldn't have to be a requirement for adding high spots to your list. You can make the rules. Perhaps it would "count" if you merely looked at some of the high spots in the mountain states. The highest points in many states are unnamed and unmarked; tracking them down can take you to interesting, off-the-beaten-path locations. Will you recognize Florida's 345-foot high spot for what it is, if you find it? You would if you were on an expedition with some of the 300 members of the High Pointers Club (P.O. Box 70, Arcadia, Missouri 63621; (573) 546-3711), a nationwide organization whose elevating purpose is to visit the highest point of each state.

- Select a famous historical person in whom you have an interest and visit the places connected with his or her life. This sort of in-depth exploration of, say, George Washington, Sacagawea, Robert E. Lee, Jim Bridger, George Armstrong Custer, or Chief Joseph can give you a new appreciation of the person and the times and take you across vast distances.

- For more history, visit the birthplaces of all our presidents; this will keep you busy for quite a while going from the East Coast to the West Coast with many stops in between.

- All sorts of museums await your visit. Pick a subject, any subject, and there will be a museum or, perhaps, many museums, devoted to it. If you're interested in RVing history you should visit the Museum of Family Camping in Allenstown, New Hampshire (603-239-4768), and the RV/MH Heritage Foundation, Inc., in Elkhart, Indiana (800-378-8694). If you are researching old RVs or just curious about the RVs of yesteryear, delve into the archives and library of Lost Highways in Philadelphia, Pennsylvania (215-925-2568).

- Check out all the state capitals. The capitol buildings are varied and interesting, and the cities in which they are located offer much in the way of both architectural and historical exploration.
- A interesting undertaking would be to visit every single national park.
- As a fulltimer, you can attend all the dog, cat, and horse shows you wish. Follow the rodeo circuit if that is more to your liking.
- Your RV can be used to carry you back in time if you attend mountain-men rendezvous held at different times of the year in many locations.
- Refresh yourself spiritually and aesthetically at great churches and cathedrals throughout North America. Many rival those in Europe. Spend some quiet moments in simpler edifices such as Bruton Parish Church in Williamsburg, Virginia, where George Washington worshipped over 200 years ago, and St. Ignatius Mission in St. Ignatius, Montana, embellished with fifty-eight paintings done by the mission cook almost 100 years ago.
- The mansions of the wealthy give you an insight into another lifestyle. See what the very rich called "cottages" on Jekyll Island on the Georgia Coast, where they went for the winter. Visit their summer homes in Newport, Rhode Island. Who has the better life—the millionaires with their vast estates or you roaming free as a fulltimer?
- Seek out the very best of the foods you enjoy. Sample hamburgers in different regions of the country to find the tastiest. Are hamburgers too ordinary? How about oysters? Chili? Barbecue? Bratwurst? Locally made chocolate ice cream?
- Visit vineyards, wineries, and attend wine festivals. Don't overlook the unique scuppernong wine in North Carolina as you

go from the more famous wine-making areas in upper New York State to the Napa Valley in California. Sample regional cheeses as you go about your countrywide wine tasting.

- Perhaps you'll want to "collect" sunrises and sunsets and preserve your memories of them on film, on canvas, or by writing your thoughts about each one in prose or poetry.
- If none of these ideas interests you, perhaps your own forebears may. Start tracking down your ancestors. The trail may lead you to places you never dreamed of. So your work won't be for naught, compile your information and send it to other family members, the Library of Congress, and genealogy libraries in the states involved.

We could go on—and on—but we're sure you get the idea.

Being a fulltimer and having the time to explore a subject thoroughly may make you an expert on it and possibly allow you to make some extra money. You might write articles or even a book about your subject, and you may find yourself giving talks and presenting slide or video shows to groups of fellow RVers, RV clubs, and other organizations. Collections made as you travel may be of value to other collectors or, perhaps, even be the beginning of a business.

You may want to take the road to learning by participating in Elderhostels for RVers, where you live in your RV while attending classes. So popular are the programs, some colleges (where many programs are held) have campus campgrounds with full hookups to accommodate RVers. Elderhostel programs are ongoing throughout the country the year round and cover just about any subjects you can think of. Elderhostel is open to anyone age fifty-five or older. For more information contact: Elderhostels, 75 Federal Street, Boston, Massachusetts 02110; (617) 426-8056.

If you want to learn more about RVs and the lifestyle, including fulltiming, you can attend Life On Wheels conferences which are held in various locations throughout the country. These classes,

> **"E**lderhostel programs are ongoing throughout the country the year round and cover just about any subjects you can think of.**"**

too, are usually held at colleges and RV parking is available on campus. For dates and locations of conferences contact: University of Idaho Enrichment Program, Moscow, Idaho 83844-3224; (208) 885-6486.

A FULLTIMER'S YEAR

We have continued our fulltiming life as we were writing this book, exploring many new places and revisiting some of our old favorites.

You may recall that we were on the Snake River in Washington when we wrote the first chapter of this book. How did we get to that location?

A year before that date we were continuing east along the Mogollon Rim in northern Arizona after spending a few days in a forest service campground atop the rim, in the company of several elk. We were on our way to visit the Very Large Array of twenty-seven radio telescopes in the middle of nowhere west of Socorro, New Mexico.

After that we took back roads across New Mexico, then angled northeast through Texas, Oklahoma, and Kansas to Nebraska, where we visited with family and friends and got to meet our new greatnephew for the first time.

Leaving Nebraska, we again headed northeast in order to explore the southeastern section of Minnesota and portions of the Great River Road that runs along the Mississippi River from Minnesota to Louisiana. We followed the River Road through Iowa and got our last view of the mammoth tows plying the river at Keokuk.

We wended our way through Indiana, Ohio, along Lake Erie in Pennsylvania and across New York, taking our time, because we wanted to arrive in New England in the fall.

Our first stop in Vermont was at the house of friends who had invited us to stay in their driveway. We hadn't visited them for many years, and the formerly clear driveway we remembered was now overgrown with branches. Not being RVers, our friends had neglected to mention this, so we spent much of the first afternoon of our visit clearing away the intruding branches so we could move our trailer off the road.

We gloried in the brilliant fall foliage as we traveled through Vermont and New Hampshire to Maine where we intended to revisit old haunts. After traveling along the coast of Maine, we were on our way south, when we pulled into a campground high on a hill overlooking a tidal river. We had intended to stay only overnight, but it was so beautiful and peaceful we ended up staying two weeks.

Our next stop was at a campground inland in Maine, where we arrived just in time to be invited to an end-of-season potluck dinner.

We followed the fall season south to Virginia, where we spent several weeks visiting friends before heading west again through the rolling green hills of the Bluegrass Country of Kentucky.

After hearing so much about Branson, Missouri, and never having been there, we decided it would be a good place to spend Christmas. We normally stop at some place about a week before Christmas and stay over until after New Year's Day. This way, we can put up our Christmas tree and enjoy it for a long time without having to stow it (or try to) for traveling.

We couldn't have picked a more Christmasy spot than Branson. The town was decorated with lights from one end to the other, and the shows were geared to the season.

Once the holidays were over, we headed south to visit another place we had never seen: the Big Bend area of Texas. We pottered about in the Sun Belt until it was warm enough to head north.

We eventually arrived on the Oregon Coast where we spent many weeks, dipped into Washington along the coast, and from there headed east again, which put us on the Snake River.

This turned out to be a pretty busy year for us because we covered so much territory, although we did so at our usual slow pace.

> **"W**e couldn't have picked a more Christmasy spot than Branson. The town was decorated with lights from one end to the other . . .**"**

In a more normal year, we wouldn't visit so many states or travel from coast to coast.

This last year, as we always do during our travels, we sought out regional foods to sample. We had pancakes with real maple syrup in Vermont; country ham, biscuits, and peanut soup in Virginia; and Lebanon bologna in Pennsylvania, along with some other Pennsylvania Dutch delicacies. Being chocolate lovers, we enjoyed our visit to Lititz, Pennsylvania, where we could get a no-calorie chocolate fix simply by inhaling: A candy factory's emissions permeates the air of this small town.

Nothing can compare with the Danish pastries found in and around the New York City area. We made a slight detour in New Jersey to a diner we knew of with a great selection of these pastries. We wanted to stock up and keep a supply in our freezer. It took quite a bit of driving through narrow streets before we found a place large enough to park our rig. We had a fair hike back to the diner, and we spent an awful lot of money, but we left with a freezerful of pastries that lasted us for several weeks.

We seek out barbecue restaurants wherever we go and enjoyed the different types and different flavors of barbecue as we traveled across the South. Years ago when we visited Canada we tasted peameal bacon (uncured back bacon with a coating of cornmeal) for the first time. When we were in New York along the St. Lawrence Seaway, we crossed over into Canada for the sole purpose of purchasing some. The supermarket had none but we were told a shipment was expected the next day. We went back the next afternoon and, since we knew we wouldn't be in Canada again for some time, purchased a supply that we could freeze. The American customs agent was in the middle of asking the usual questions prior to crossing the border, when he looked at us as if we were up to no good and said, "Didn't you come through here yesterday?" Lest he think we were running some sort of contraband over the border we explained about the pea-meal bacon. Stern and unsmiling he listened to our story, then waved us on, shaking his head and grinning, as if he didn't know whether to believe us or not.

Although we enjoy eating in restaurants, we usually have Christmas dinner at home. In Branson, we had traditional fare: turkey with all the trimmings and homemade pumpkin pie. As always, we trimmed our RV-sized tree with ornaments we have collected in our travels: Red glass chili peppers from Santa Fe, porcelain snowflakes from Livingston, Montana, Hopi beads from Sedona, Arizona, a dove carved from myrtlewood from Oregon, and a Moravian star made of folded paper from Winston-Salem, among others. The tree was draped with garlands of beads we caught as they were thrown from Mardi Gras floats in Mobile, Alabama.

We were entertained by wildlife throughout the year. A small black bear was perched in a tree surveying the landscape in Shenandoah National Park in Virginia. Gawky road runners trotted across

Figure 24.2 Nature's magnificent handiwork is evident in Providence Canyon State Park, near Lumpkin, Georgia.

the highway in Texas and often perched on our picnic table at campsites, and rattlesnakes occasionally made their presence known. Coyotes serenaded us in various places, and one came to visit our site every afternoon in a campground in Arizona. Several elk kept us company while we were camped on the Mogollon Rim, and deer were in many of the campgrounds in which we stayed.

Wherever we go in our travels, the beauty and magnificence of our country and the glories of nature never fail to awe us: In the South, mysterious swamps with the coffee-colored water overhung by tree branches shrouded in Spanish moss; the haunting marshes of Glynn in Georgia immortalized in the poems of Sidney Lanier; and on the other side of the state, Providence Canyon with its deep reaches and sculpted formations in a spectrum of tones ranging from creamy white to deep vermilion (Figure 24.2).

Then the Southwest, where an entire landscape, as far as the eye can see, is composed of red rock formations or mountains that turn to shades of pink and lavender in the setting sun. The stars are especially luminous in the high desert. We viewed the brilliant swath of the Milky Way—brighter than we had ever seen it before—high in the mountains in a forest-service campground. In the spring, the desert may be carpeted with acres of bright orange poppies.

In the Northwest, eternally snow-covered volcanic peaks dominate the skyline, from Mount Shasta in California to Mount Rainier in Washington. Closer inspection of the mountains reveals trees of towering sizes not found anywhere else on the continent. The Rocky Mountains loom large over the landscape farther east. We were in the midst of a wondrous display of lightning over the Absaroka Range when a sudden summer squall developed. After another squall in Judith Gap in Montana, the lowering sun created a double rainbow whose iridescent colors were set off against the slate-gray skies of the departing storm.

The Northeast offers a dazzling display of colors when the trees turn in the fall, and more serene vistas in the spring when the orchards of apple trees break out their pink-tinged white blossoms.

Figure 24.3 Fulltimers can enjoy the panorama of Slim Buttes, near Reva, South Dakota.

Old buildings line the streets of nearly every town. Strolling through them on brick sidewalks, it's almost like being transported back in time.

The heartland of the country, the Midwest, has it's share of beauty too. In a North Dakota campground we were treated to the wispy, undulating shimmers of the northern lights. In South Dakota, we camped in view of stark, white, chalk cliffs when the aspen trees below had turned to bright yellow (Figure 24.3). Lining our route in Kansas were field after field of sunflowers in bloom. In the western section of Nebraska, we were led across the plains by the huge rock formations used as markers by emigrants on the Oregon Trail: Courthouse and Jail Rocks, Chimney Rock, and just before entering Wyoming, the bulk of Scotts Bluff.

It's wonderful to be able to see so many sights, visit so many places, do so many things, and meet so many nice people, all without ever leaving home. These are the things that are important to us; they provide us with a continual fresh outlook, and keep us young in heart and mind. It's really what fulltiming is all about.

Although we have no idea where we will go or what we will do next year, we know that fulltiming will provide us with a host of rewarding, interesting, and fulfilling experiences.

If you want to be a fulltimer there should be no hesitation about joining all of us who are participating in this lifestyle. The only regret you may have is that you didn't become a fulltimer sooner.

Index

Page numbers in **boldface** type refer to illustrations and tables in the text.

acoustic couplers, 289–290
adapter, grounding, for 120-volt
AC electrical system, 320,
320–321, **321**, **323**,
323–324, **324**, **325**
address, personal
for driver's license, 99-101
for federal taxes, 102
for vehicle license, 97–98
adjustment to fulltiming, 13–15
children and, 519–520
air conditioner, 400–402, 512
amperage rating, 400, 401–402
maintenance, 400
voltage and, 400–401
all-terrain vehicle, 495
alternator, 341–343
altimeter, 491
American Association of Retired
Persons (AARP), 107
American Automobile
Association (AAA), 424
American Radio Relay League,
315
amperage ratings, 330–332, **331**
antenna
ham radio, 314

television, 301–302
television, coupler-splitter
for, **302**
antenna amplifier, television,
302–304, **303**
appliances, amperage ratings,
331
audiocassete storage, 272–273, **273**
automated teller machines
(ATMs), 93–95
ATM cards, 93, 96
auxiliary vehicle. *See* vehicle,
auxiliary
awnings, 403–404

backing an RV, 477–478
fifth-wheel trailer, 481–482
motorhome, 477–478
practicing, 482–484
tips on, **482**
travel trailer, 478–479, **480**
banks, 93, 96. *See also* checking
account
bathroom
cleaning, 411
fifth-wheel trailer, 188, 189,
188, **189**, **191**

usability of, 207–210
batteries, 332–343. *See also*
battery charging
amperage draw, **337**, 337–338
checking voltage, 354–356,
354, **356**
conserving power, 352–353
deep-cycle, 333, 342
discharge rate, **335**, 335–338
gel-cell, 333–334
isolators, 346–347
location of, 332
maintenance, 336, 420–421
measuring charge, 341, **342**
reserve capacity, 335
securing with locks, 505, **506**
sizes, **334**, 334–336
SLI, 333
battery charging, 340, 341, **348**
built-in, 347–348
with built-in charger,
347–348
with generator, 348–349
inverters, 360
methods, 340–341, 347–352
principles of, 339–340
with solar panels, 349–352

battery compartments, 171
battery-condition meter, 354
battery-monitoring system, 355
battery monitor panel,
        354–356, **356**
bed
    cabover, 190–191
    for children, 518
    making up, 191
    remodeling, 219, **220**
bedroom, 189–193
    for children, 518
beverage container, 488
bicycle carriers, 498
bicycles, 495, 498–499
    security of, 508
    types of, 498–499
bills, payment of, 73–77, 90–93
boats, 495–498
    carrying, 496–497
    inflatable, 496–497
    renting, 500
    towing, 496
    types of, 496–497
bookcases, 270–272, **271**, **272**,
        273, 489–490
books. *See* bookcases;
        directories, campground
boondocking, 44, 171
    batteries and, 334
    battery checking methods,
        353–356, 355
    roof-vent fans and, 403
    size of RV and, 153
    with television, 301
brake retarder, 166
breaking camp, checklist for, **446**
Bureau of Land Management,
        427
burglar alarm, 514, **515**
Bus Conversions magazine, 243

business office. *See* office, RV
*Business Traveler's Survival
        Guide, The* (Langhoff),
        298
buying an RV. *See* selecting an
        RV for fulltiming

cabinets
    for books, 271–272
    in cockpit area, 485–486
    doors, 264–265
    galley, 260–263, 266–267, **267**
    maintenance, 412
    storage under, 267–268
cable television, 304–305, 429
    connections, 304–305
Camperforce Directory, 55
campgrounds, 423–443
    campsites, 432–434
    children and, 519
    destination resorts, 46
    driving through, 484
    electrical hookups, 329,
        330–332, 400–401,
        429, 462
    electrical outlets, 320, 321,
        321, 322, 323
    fees, saving on, 38–44
    and GFCI problems, 329, 330
    highway signs, 426, **426**
    hookups, 428, 429, 432,
        462–473
    hosting at, 53–54, 55
    length of stay at, 41–43
    locating, 423–424, **425**,
        426–427, **426**
    location of, 41, 43–44
    membership associations,
        45–50, **46**
    off-season, 437–439
    private, 428–431

public, 431–433
rates, 427, 428, 429, 430–431,
        432–433, 493
reservations at, 436–439
resort, 40
restrictions on pets, 524–526
RV size and, 436
safety procedures, 507–510
selling products at, 65–66
showers, 209, 429, 436
suspicious characters in, 509
teaching at, 67
telephone hookup, 79–80,
        82–83
television hookups, 304–305,
        429
types of, 427–433
water hookup, 370, 463
work at, 53–54
camping
    in campgrounds (*See* camp-
        grounds)
    cold-weather, 441–443
    etiquette, 443
    in noncampgrounds,
        439–441
    in parking lots, 440–441
    in rest areas, 439–440
    setting up and breaking
camp, 445–463, **446**
    at truck stops, 440
campsites, 433–434. *See also*
        boondocking;
        campgrounds
    hazards, 434–436
    levelness of, 433–434
    trees, 435, 436
Caraventures, 531–532
carbon monoxide detector,
        513–514
Caretaker Gazette, The, 56

caretaking while fulltiming, 53, 56
carpenters, 66
carpet
    avoiding soiling, 409, **410**
    cleaning, 407, 408–409
    replacing, 214–217, 408
catalytic heater, 44, 391–394, **394**
caulk, silicone, 419
Cellular Connection, 291
cellular phone systems
    data transmission with, 291–292
Cellular Travel Guide, The, 88
cellular telephone systems, 84–89, **85**
    analog, 86, 87
    charges, 84
    digital, 86–87
    wattage of phones, 87–88
chairs, 210
Chandler, Arline, 55
checking account, 93. *See also* automated teller machines; banks
checklists
    breaking-camp, **446**
    driving and handling practices, **477**
    pre-travel exterior, **448**
    pre-travel interior, **447**
    using, 446–449
checks, personal, 92–93
children, 517–524, **523**
    accommodations for, 517–519
    adaptability of, 519–520
    difficulties of fulltiming with, 522–523

education of, 520–522
    visiting, 524
chocking, 460–461, **461**
circuit analyzer, **322**, 322–323
cleaning
    bathroom fixtures, 411
    carpet, 407, 408–409
    exterior, 416–419
    upholstery, 407, 409–411
cleaning supplies, 413–414
climate control, 148–149, 389–404, **394**
    See also air conditioner; fans; heater, electric; heating system; insulation
clock, 491
clothing, 126, 129–130
    cost of, 37
    storage options, 252–257, **253, 255, 256**
    washable, 259
clubs for fulltimers, 529–533
    for disabled fulltimers, 12–13, 533
cockpit area, RV
    customizing, 485–491
cold-weather situations
    camping hints, 441–443
    insulation and, 389–390
    tips for, 398–399, 441–443
    water system and, 383–384
color schemes, interior, 201–203, 214
compact disk (CD) player, 313–314
compass, 491
compatibility with partner, 16–17
computer
    data transmission, 285–294

desktop versus notebook, 281–283
    and fulltiming, 52–53
    handheld personal, 288
    modems, 285–289
    navigation systems, 317–318
    notebook, 281–282, 284, 286–289
    software for travel planning, 316-318
    storage space for, 283–285
    storing recipes on, 268
    surge protector, 328
    telephone hookup and, 287–289
    viewing photographs on, 207
computer printer, 361, 363
    multifunction, 295
    storage space for, 284, 285, 295
condensation, 395–396
"console," truck bench seat, homemade, 486–488, **487**
containers, 250–251, 278
    in galley, 263–264
contracts, membership campground, 48–49
cooling RV, 400–404
Corian, 196
Corps of Engineers, 427
correspondence courses for children, 521–522
costs. *See* expenses
counter space, 194–196
countertop materials, 196
crafts, selling, 62–65
credit cards, 90–91, 95
customizing RV, **137**, 137–139
    cockpit area, 485–491
cybercafe, 289

data transmission, 285–294
 Web-page resources, 291
dead-bolt locks, 504
debit cards, 92
dental care, 104–106
digital audio radio service
 (DARS), 314
dinghy. *See* towing; vehicle,
 auxiliary
dining area. *See* living/dining
 area
directories, campground,
 423–424, **425**, 426–427,
 429
 Good Sam, 530-531
 storage of, 485, 489–491
Direct Satellite System
 (DSS), 305–312
 aligning dish, 307–309
 automatic system, 305–306
 installing, 305–309
 nonautomatic system,
 306–307
 portable mount, 308–309, **309**
 telephone connection, 310
DirecTV, 310
disabled fulltimers, 10–13, **11**,
 34, 104
 clubs for, 13, 533
 RV adaptations for, **11**, 12–13
Dish Network, 310
dishwashing, 376–377
doctors. *See* health care
doormat, 449
doors, 210–212
 distorted frame, 211
 locks, 503–504
drafts, preventing, 399–400
draperies, cleaning, 410
driver's license. *See* license,
 driver's

driving and handling practices,
 465–484
 avoiding crowded highways,
 470
 in campgrounds, 484
 checklist, **477**
 fifth-wheel trailer, 146
 in inclement weather,
 470–471
 long and heavy RVs,
 471–474
 minimum preplanning,
 468–469
 taking it easy, 465–466
 taking it slow, 467–468
dusting, 407–408

education of children, 520–522
electrical hookups, 40, 44, 320,
 321, **321**, 322, 323, 329,
 330, 332, 400–401,
 429, 462
electrical system, 120-volt AC,
 319–332
 adapters, **320**, 320–321, **321**
 checking voltage, 325–326,
 326
 circuit analyzers, 322–323,
 322
 extension cords, 321
 generators, 358–359
 ground fault circuit inter-
 rupters, 328–330
 grounding adapters, **320**,
 320–321, **321**, 323,
 323–324, **324**, **325**
 power indicator, 327
 reversed polarity, correcting,
 323–325
 surge protectors, 327–328
 ungrounded circuits,

 correcting, 324–325, **326**
 wattage and amperage con
 siderations, 330–332, **331**
 without a hookup, 358–364
electrical system, 12-volt DC,
 319, 332–353. *See also*
 batteries
 components, 332
 inverters for, 359–364
 outlets, 356–358, **357**
 phantom loads, 338
electrical systems, RV, 319–365.
 See also electrical system,
 120–volt AC; electrical
 system, 12-volt DC
 trouble-free, tips for,
 364–365
electric heater, 394–395
electronic entertainment and
 information, 299–318
electronic equipment, turning
 off, 512
E-mail, 288, 296–297
 equipment necessary, 297
emergency cards, 515–516
emergency road service, 531
employment. *See* working
employment agencies, 52
engine maintenance, 420–421
Escapees RV Club, 78, 532
Estes, Bill, 168
etiquette, camping, 443
expenses of fulltiming, 25–50
 cellular service, 84–86, **85**
 controlling, and choice of
 RV, 25–26
 day-to-day, 36–37
 of home base, 31–36
 home-base maintenance,
 30–37
 membership camp-

Expenses, *continued*
grounds,
45–50, **46**
money-saving suggestions,
39–45
planning income to meet,
68–72
reduction of, suggestions for,
39–45
RV costs, 25–30
shelter, 37–38
taxes, 37–38
extension cords, 321
exterior
cleaning, 416–419
pre-travel checklist, **448**
refurbishing, 237–238
security lights, 507–508
storage space, 276–277
striping, replacing, 238

Family Campers and RVers,
78, 532
Family Motor Coach
Association, 78, 532
Family Travel Trailer
Association, 78, 532–533
fans, 402–403
roof-vent, 402
fax machines, 295
fifth-wheel trailer, 131, **133**, 134
backing, 481–484, **482**
baths, 188, 189, **191**
battery location, 332
bed, 191
cabtop rack, 496
catalytic heater in, 392–393,
394
doors, 211–212
floorplans, 181–183, **182, 183**
handling of, 146-147
hitching, 454–455, **454**

payload rating, 167
preventing theft of, 505
size of, 154, 155
storage space, 147–148, **148**
unhitching, 454–455
UVW, 165–166
windows, 199–201
workshop space, 61–62, **62**
financing, 174–175
fire extinguisher, 511–512
fire prevention, 511–513
fishtailing, 168
flooding, 434–435, 470
floorplans
bathroom, **188, 189, 191**
Class A motorhome, **178,**
178–179, 180
Class C motorhome,
179–181, **180, 181**
fifth-wheel trailer, 181–183,
182, 183
galley, **197**
storage space and, 186–187
travel trailer, **183**, 183–184,
184
freshwater tanks, 153
fuel. *See also* propane
consumption of, 144
weight of, 158, **159**
fuel, RV, costs, 28–30, **29**
fuel log, 493–494, **493**
full-time lifestyle
clubs for fulltimers, 529–533
delayed, 129–130
earning money for, 51–72
expenses of, 36–50
first-day experiences,
119–121
getting started in, 115–130
giving up, 34
practicing, 121–123
reading about, 115–116

talking to people about,
116–117
fulltimers. *See also* full-timing
lifestyle
as conservationists, 534
disabled (*see* disabled
fulltimers)
reasons for becoming, 5–7
retired, 13
various types of, 22–23
full-timing lifestyle, 1–23.
See also fulltimers
activities, suggestions for,
534–542
adjustment to, 13–22
advantages of, 1–9
attractions of, 7–9
authors' experiences,
542–544
concerns about, 13–15
lack of structure of, 20–21
with partner, 15–17
risks of, 6–7
seizing opportunity for, 9–10
selecting an RV for, 131–176
versus vacationing, 21–22
furnace, 390–391
cleaning, 390–391
forced-air, 390, 391
output, 390
thermostat, 44
furniture, RV, 174
fuse panel, 333
fuses
for inverter circuit, **364**
spare, 333

galley, 194–199
cabinets, 266–267, **267**
carpeting, 216
counter space, 194–196
double-duty equipment, 268

galley, *continued*
floorplans, **197**
location of, 197–199
space drawer, 265, **266**
storage containers, 263–264
storage space, 260–270
under-cabinet storage, 267–268
Ganis Corporation, 174–175
gas detector, 385, 513–514
generators, 348–349
AC, 358–359
getting started, 115–130
global positioning system (GPS), 317–318
gloves, 462
Golden Access Passport, 432
Golden Age Passport, 432
Golden Eagle Passport, 432
golfing, 536, **537**
Good Sam Club, 530–532
benefits, 530–532
chapters, 532
financing through, 174–175
Highways magazine, 116
mail-forwarding service, 78
Parks, 426
Radio Net, 315, **317**
Snowbird Service, 79
vehicle insurance through, 112, 531
grades, 474–477
gross combined weight rating (GCWR), 143
ground fault circuit interrupter (GFCI), 328–330
grounding adapter, **323**, 323–325, **324**, **325**
gun case/rack, 273–274, 489
guns, 510

ham radio, 314–315, **317**, 532

Handicapped Travel Club, Inc., 533. *See also* disabled fulltimers
health, 6, 7, 103–104, 107. *See also* disabled fulltimers
health care, 34, 103–108
locating best, 104–106, 108
locating treatment, 104–105
medical records, 106–107
health insurance, 37, 108, 531
health maintenance organizations (HMOs), 108
heater
catalytic, 391–394, **394**
electric, 394–395
heating system, 390–396
condensation, 395–396
Higby, Bill, 291
Highways magazine, 116, 530
hills, 474–477
hitch, 144, 167, 421, 454
hitching, 141, 449–456. *See also* unhitching
aids, 452
fifth-wheel trailer, 454–455
travel trailer, 450–452, 453–454
hitch weight, 168–169
hobbyists, 64–65
holding tanks, 44, 153, 172, 379–382
black-water, 381–382, 462–463
emptying, 379–382
gray water, 382
preventing freezing in, 383–384
home base, 30–36
costs of maintaining, 31, 33–36
decision to sell house, 123–124

lack of freedom and, 30–31
versus legal residence, 30
reasons for not having, 31–36
reasons given for keeping, 33–36
renting out, 32
state taxes and, 103
winterizing, 32
home maintenance, 5–6, 7–8
home-study courses, 521–522
hooks, 251–252, **252**
hookups, 462–463
electrical (*see* electrical hookups)
saving on, 40–41
telephone, 79–80, 82–83
water (*see* water hookup)
horses, work with, 59–60
hoses
for drinking water, 368–369, 371
sewer, 380–383
HoTMaiL, 297
hot weather
cooling trailer during, 400–404
site selection, 404
housecleaning tools, 407

inclines, 474–477
insulation, 44, 389–390
insurance, health, 37, 108
insurance, personal liability, 112–113
insurance, vehicle, 37, 111–113
proof of, 97
through Good Sam Club, 112, 531
interior, 177–204
bathrooms, 187–189, **188**, **189** 207–210
bedrooms, 189–193, **190**

Interior, *continued*
  color schemes, 201–203
  floorplans, basic, 178–189, **178**
  galley, 194–199, **197**
  livability of, 177, 203–204,
    205–212
  maintenance, 405–415
  pre-travel checklist, **447**
  storage space, 184, 186–187
Internal Revenue Service, 102
Internet, 296–297. *See also*
    World Wide Web
Internet service providers
    (ISPs), 285, 296–297
inverters, 359–364
  fuses, **364**
  solar panel and, 363–364
  solid-state, 359–360, 361
  transfer-switch utilization,
    360, **361**
  wiring, 362–363, **363**
isolators, battery, 346–347

jacks, for stabilization, 459–460
Juno Online Services, 297

keys, extra, 463

Langhoff, June, 298
laundry, storing, 257–259, **259**
layup periods, propane system
    and, 388
leakproofing RV, 418–419
leaks
  air conditioner, 401
  propane, 384–385
leveling, 150, 456–459
  automatic system for, 150,
    458
leveling boards, 433, 449, **457**,
    457–459
  storing, **248**, 248–249

license, driver's, 98, 99–101
  address for, 100
  personal identification for,
    100
  renewal in person, 100–101
license, vehicle, 96–99
Life on Wheels conferences,
    541–542
lights
  portable, 514–515
  security, 507–508
livability of RV, 177, 203–204,
    205–212
living/dining area, 150–151,
    193–194
  remodeling project, 230-237,
    231, 233
  windows in, 200–201
loading guidelines, 246–247
locks, 501, 503–505, **506**
  compartment, 504–505
  entry-door, 503–504
logbook, 491–494, **492, 493**
  entries, 492–494
  fuel log, 493–494
Loners of America, 533
Loners on Wheels, 533
LP-gas. See propane

mail
  certified, 76
  Express, 76–77
  forwarding services, 73–77,
    78, 98, 101
  General Delivery, 75, 76
  paying bills by, 73–77
  Priority, 76
  subscriptions, 79
maintenance of RV, 7–8,
    405–422
  doing own repairs, 405

equipment for, 422
  vehicle and engine, 420–421
manufacturer, calling for
    advice, 406
maps
  storage of, 485, 489–491
  using, 490–491
mattress, 189–190, 192
  Select-Comfort, 192–193
mechanics
  disreputable, 110–111
  RV repair and, 109–110
medical care. *See* health care
medical records, 106–107
Medicare, 108
membership, in campground
associations, 45–50
  purchasing and selling,
    47–49
membership campgrounds
  types of, 49–50
message services, 75, 89–90
microwave oven, 222, **223**
  storage in, 269
  surge protector, 327–328
*Military RV, Camping &
    Recreation Areas Around
    the World*, 426–427
modem, 285–289
  compatibility of, 290, 291
  transmission speeds,
    286–287, **287**
money-market funds, 95–96
mopeds, 495, 499–500
motorcycles, 28, 499–500
motorhome
  automatic levelers, 150, 458
  backing, 477–478
  batteries, 333
  battery compartment, 171
  carbon-monoxide detector,
    513–514

motorhome, *continued*
cargo-carrying capacity, 159–161, **161**, 495
Class A, 131, **132**, 134, 148, **178**, 178–179
Class C, 131, **132, 134, 148**, 179–181, **180, 181**, 190–191
climate control, 148-149
cockpit storage, customizing, 485–491
driving, 146
GCWR, 143
GVWR, 19, 158, 159–161
heating system, 390
leveling, 458–459
living/dining area, 150, 151, 188
propane–cylinder compartment, 172
repairs, 145–146
roof rack, 498
storage space, 147-148, **148**
towing with, 143–145
versus trailer, 141–156
UVW, 159, 160
warranty repairs, 145–146
wiring, 343
MotorHome magazine, 79, 115, 135, 136, 142
Mountain Directory East, 476–477
Mountain Directory West, 476–477
mounting tape, 206–207
moving into RV, 127–129
multimeter, 353–354, **354**
Museum of Family Camping, 539

National General Insurance Company, 112

National Oceanographic and Atmospheric Administration (NOAA), 299, 315–316
national parks, 432
work at, 53
navigation systems, computer, 317–318
NetAddress, 297
net carrying capacity (NCC), 157–158
newspapers, local, checking prices in, 41–43

odors, 414
office, RV, 194, 245–246, 281–298. *See also* computer; modem; pager; telecommunications; telephone
adding, 226–229, **227**
paper and file storage, 275–276
off-season travel, 4, 40, 437–439
oil changes, 420
operating costs, RV, 28–30
optional equipment, 172–173
oven, 197
microwave, 222, **223**, 269
overheating, 475, 476

pagers, 294–295
pant hanger, 255–256, **256**
partner
compatibility with, 16–17
compromising with, 15–16
fulltiming with, 15–17
living in close quarters with, 17
personal liability insurance, 112–113
pest control, 414–415, **415**

pets, 517, 524–527
accommodations for, 527
campground regulations, 524–527
costs of ownership, 527
safety of, 526
phantom loads, 338
pharmacies, 107
photography, freelance, 56–59
physical disabilities. *See* disabled fulltimers
picnic table as workshop, 239–243
pictures, hanging, 206–207
Porta-Bote, 497, **497**
possessions, disposing of or storing, 124–127, 129–130
post offices, receiving mail at, 75–77
prescriptions, 106, 107
mail-order, 107
pressure regulator, water system, 369–370
Primestar, 310
privacy curtains, 205–206
propane, 45
problems, 384–385
shutting off when traveling, 386–387
usage, 387
using while traveling, 386–387
propane cylinder
filling, 385–386
purging after layup, 388
refilling, 172
relief valve, 386
propane-cylinder compartment, 172
propane system, 384–388. *See also* propane; propane cylinder

Propane System, *continued*
care of, 388
propane water heater, 377–378
protection. *See* security
putty, 419

Quake Wax, 207

radio
CB, 299, 300, 315, 316
DARS, 314
ham, 314–315, **317**
weather, 299, 315–316
recipes, storing, 268
recreational transportation,
495–501
security of, 501
types of, 495–500
Recreational Vehicle Industry
Association, 157
recreational vehicle (RV). *See
also* fifth-wheel trailer;
motorhome; selecting an
RV for fulltiming; travel
trailer
advantages over home base,
34–35
cost of, controlling, 25–26
customizing, **137**, 137–139
equipping with optional
equipment, 27
handling of, 146–147
long and heavy, handling,
471–474
making products for, 65–66
operating costs, 28–30, **29**
repairs, 108–111
with slideouts, 169–170
types suitable for fulltiming,
131–134
weight-carrying capacity,
156–165

refrigerator, 456
automatic energy selecting,
342–343
propane supply, 386–387
storage in, 269
registration, vehicle, renewing
by mail, 98–99
remodeling, 213–243
exterior, 237–238
living/dining area project,
230–237, **231**
major, 225–243
office-space project, 226–229
preliminaries, 225–226, 232
storage-space project,
229–230
repairs, 108–111, 145
galley tool kit, 269–270
locating mechanic, 109
precautions, 110–111
under warranty, on
motorhomes, 145–146
reservations, campground,
436–439
residence, legal, 101–103
definition of, 102
resorts, 46
work at, 53
rest areas, 439–440
retirement
advantages of fulltiming, 13
early, 68–69
working during, 51, 54,
68–69
RJ-11 jack, 287, 288, 289, 291
roaches. *See* pest control
roads, 470, 472
*Road Work: The Ultimate RVing
Adventure* (Chandler), 55
rodents. *See* pest control
roof leaks, 419

roof vent
fans, 402, 403
maintenance, 413
RV Alliance America, 112
*RV Electrical Systems, a Basic
Guide* (Moeller), 365
RV Handbook, The (Estes), 168
RV/Heritage Foundation, Inc.,
539
RVing Women, Inc., 533

safety, 503–516. *See also* driving
and handling practices;
security
in campground, 507–510
locking doors for, 504
of pets, 526
safety equipment, 511–515
safety procedures
campgrounds, 507–510
fire prevention, 511–513
Samborees, 531–532
sanding block, 240–241, **241**
satellite communication system,
88–89
Satellite Direct magazine, 311
satellite radio reception, 314
satellites, types of, 292–294, **293**
satellite telephone service,
292–294
future, 294
options, 292–294
satellite television system,
305–312, **306**, **309**, 429
See also Direct Satellite
System (DSS)
obtaining service, 310–311
reception problems, 311–312
systems available, 310
schedules, lack of
adjustment to, 18–19
advantage of, 8, 19, 468–469

Schedules, *continued*
  and campground reservations, 47
scooters, 495, 499–500
sealant, 418, 419
seasons, and full-time RVing, 4–5
seats
  recliners, 220–221
  refurbishing, 220
securing accessories, 207
security
  exterior lights for, 507–508
  locks, 503–505
  of recreational vehicles, 501
  windows, 506–507
Select-Comfort mattress, 192–193
selecting an RV for fulltiming, 131–176. *See also* shopping for RV
  checking before buying, 203
  cost control, 25–26
  interiors, 177–204
  optional equipment, 172–173
  partner and, 16–17
  renting before, 118–119
  size and weight considerations, 152–161
  used RVs, 173–174
serial numbers, list of, 516
servicing log, 493, **493**
setting up/breaking camp, 445–463
  checklists, **446**, 446–449, **447, 448**
sewer hookup, 379–383, 462
shelves, 249, **249**
shopping for RV, 135–140. *See also* selecting an RV for fulltiming

tips, 175–176
where to purchase, 139–140
showers, 209, 376, 429–430, 436
shower supplies, 208–209
Simple Green, 411
single fulltimers, clubs for, 533
sink
  bathroom, storage under, 258–259
  galley, storage under, 260–263, **262, 263**
sinks, 195–196
site selection, hot-weather considerations, 404
size of RV, 152–156
  fifth-wheel trailer, 154, 155
  motorhome, 152, 153, 156
  travel trailer, 153–156
skirting, 398–399
skylight, 204, 397–398
slideout rooms, 169–170, 184, **185**, 193, 199
  considerations, 169–170
smog inspection, 98
smoke alarms, 511
snowmobiles, 500, 501
Soft Scrub, 411, 418
solar system, 349–352, **351, 352**
  and inverter, 363–364, **363**
  regulator, 351–352, **352**
  selecting and installing, 350–352
Special Military Active/Retired Travel Club, 533
spice drawer, 265, **266**
spouse. *See* partner
stability, and hitch weight, 168
stabilizing RV, 459–460
state parks, 431–433
  work at, 53–54
stereo equipment, 313–314

storage space, 124, 125, 126, 130, 184, 186–187, 245–279
  adding, 229–230
  under bed, 219, **220**
  for boats, 496
  for books, 270–272, **271, 272**
  for business papers, 275–276
  checking RV for, 186–187
  for clothing, 252–257, **253, 255, 256**
  cockpit area, 485–491
  compartments, **248**, 248–249
  for computer, 283–285
  containers, **250, 251**, 278
  on doors, 264–265, **265**
  exterior, 276–277
  in galley, 260–270
  gun case, 273–274
  hooks in, 251–252, **252**
  increasing, 247–252
  motorhome, 147, **148,**
  organizing, 278–279
  partitioning, 247–249, **253, 254–255, 255**
  RV loading and weight distribution guidelines, 246–247
  for soiled laundry, 257–259, **259**
  truck bed, 148, **149,** 156, 277
storm windows, 396–398
stoves, 197
structured lifestyle
  freedom from, 3–5, 20–21, 30–31, 468–469
  need for, 18–19, 20, 21
surge protector, 327–328
  with GFCI, 328
surgery, 108
suspension system, 421

suspicious characters, 509, 511

tables, 210
   remodeling, 221–222
taxes
   federal, 102
   home base and, 103
   sales, 37–38
   state, 38, 101–102, 103
   vehicle registration, 37
Telecom Made Easy (Langhoff),
   298
telecommunications, 285–294
   analog and digital transmis-
      sions, **286**
   modem, 285–291
   telephone hookups, 287–294
telephone, 79–90, 285
   alternate operator services,
      80–81
   calling cards, 80–81
   campground hookup, 79–80,
      82–83
   cellular, 84–89
   cellular, data transmission
      with, 291–292
   listening device for, 81–82
   message services, 75, 89–90
   pay phone, 80–82
   satellite service, 292–294
television
   antenna amplifier, 302–304,
      303
   antennas, 301–302
   cable, 304–305
   campground hookups,
      304–305, 429
   location of, 194
   satellite systems, 305–312
   size of, 301
   storage of, 301, 302
   surge protector, 328

weather reports, 299–300
thermostat, furnace, 391
thievery. *See* security
tire maintenance, 421–422
tools
   for housecleaning, 407
   for maintenance and repair,
      422
tourist areas, off-season, 4, 40,
   437–439
tow bar, 143–144
tow dolly, 143–144, 449
towed vehicle. *See* vehicle,
   auxiliary
towel holders, 208
towing
   costs of, 28–29, **29**
   with motorhome *versus*
trailer, 143–145
towing equipment, 142–143
tow package, 168
tow vehicle, 141, 143–145
   brake retarder, 166
   equipping, 26–27
   fuel consumption, 29, **29**
   GCVR, 158
   GCWR, 166–167
   hitching with, 453–454
   manufacturer's literature on,
      167
   passenger cars, 168
   proper, selecting, 165–168
   purchasing, 25, 26
   tow package, 168
   truck as, 165–168
      See also truck
trailer, fifth–wheel. *See* fifth–
   wheel trailer
trailer, travel. *See* travel trailer
trailer electrical connector
   cable, 343, 345, 347, 355

Trailer Life Books, 168
Trailer Life Directory, for
   Campgrounds, RV Parks
   & Services
   423, 424, **425**, 426, 531
Trailer Life magazine, 79, 115,
   135, 136, 168, 452
Trailer Life's Towing Guide, 142
travel trailer, 131, **133**, 134
   backing, 478–479, **480**
   back-jack placement,
      459–460
   batteries, 335
   battery compartment, 171
   cargo-carrying capacity,
      161–163
   climate control, 148–149
   customizing, **137**, 137–139
   floorplans, **183**, 183–184, **184**
   GVWR, 161–163
   handling of, 146-147
   hitching, 450–452, 453–454
   hitch weight, 168–169
   living area, 150–151
   locks, **461**, 505
   versus motorhome, 141–156
   size of, 153–156
   towing with, 144
   unhitching, 452–454
   units to avoid, 139–140
truck
   bench-seat "console,"
      486–488, **487**
   canopy, 505
   light-duty, 165, 166, 167
truck, *continued*
   locks, 505
   medium duty, **165,** 166, 168
   storage space in,
      147–148, **149,**156, 277
   as tow vehicle, 165–168
truck stops, 440

unhitching
    fifth-wheel trailer, 454–455
    travel trailer, 452–454
United Parcel Service (UPS),
    77–78
unloaded vehicle weight
    (UVW), 157–158
upholstery, 202
    cleaning, 407, 409–411
    replacing, 217–218
used RVs, 25–26, 27, 173–174
    problems in gas or water
        systems, 367, 372–374
    remodeling, 213–243
    roaches in, 415
    sanitizing water system,
        372–374
USSB (U.S. Satellite
Broadcasting), 310

U-turns, 473

vacations, versus fulltiming,
    21–22
vacuum cleaner, 407
valuables, portable, security of,
    508–509
vehicle
    licensing, 96–99
    maintenance, 420–421
    registering, 96–99
    repairs. See repairs
vehicle, auxiliary, 140, 141–145
    backing, 477
    hitching, 449
    leasing, 145
    restrictions, 142
    towing considerations, 28,
        143–145
    U-turn with, 473
vehicle insurance. See insurance,

vehicle
ventilation, 204, 396, 401–403
    for microwave, 222, **223**
    water heater, 378
    windows for, 200
vents
    blocking in cold weather,
        399–400
    roof, 397–398, 413
veterans, 108
videocassette player (VCP),
    312–313
videocassette recorder (VCR),
    312–313
    built-in, 312–313
voltmeter, 354–356, **356**
voltmeter, AC, 325–326, **326**

wall coverings, maintenance of,
    412
Wally Byam Caravan Club RV
    Service Net, 315, **317**
Wandering Individuals
    Network, 533
wardrobe, 252–257
warranty, 145–146, 156
washer-dryer, 173, 209
washing RV, 416, 417
wastebaskets, **263**, 274
water
    conservation of, 376–377
    holding tanks, 379–382
    quality, 371–375
    weight of, 158, **159**
water faucets, 222–225, **224**
water filter, 374–375, 422
water heater, 44, 377–379, **379**
water hookup, 370, 463
water pressure, 369–370
water pump, 512
water purifier, 375

water system, 367–384
    accessories, 368–371
    cold weather and, 383–384
    pressure regulator, 369–370
    sanitizing, 372–374
water tanks, 44
water thief, 370
weather, 470–471
    cold, and plumbing, 383–384
    radio reports, 315–316
    and satellite TV reception,
        311–312
weather reports, 299–300,
    315–316
weight
    of accessories, 160, **160**
    distribution and storage
space, 246–247
    and handling, 471–474
    keeping to minimum,
        163–165
    of RV, 156–161, 471–474
    of slideout rooms, 169
    of towed recreational
        vehicle, 495
    of wet consumables, 158, **159**
weight labels, 157–159
wheel chock, 461, **461**
window cleaner, for exterior
    cleaning, 416–418
window coverings, 201
    awnings, 403–404
    privacy curtains, 205–206, 403
    replacing, 218–219
    shades, 403
windows, 170–171, 199–201
    burglar alarm decal on,
        514,, **515**
    leakproofing, 419
    picture, 200-201
    security provisions, 506–507

Windows, *continued*
  stone shields on, 237–238
  storm, 396–398
  tinted, 403
winds, 471, 472, 474
wiring, electrical, 343–346
  "ampacity" of, **346**
  battery-charging, 343, 345
  gauges, and voltage drop,
    343, **344**
  inverter, 362–364, **363**
  for transfer-switch utiliza-
    tion, 360–361, **361**
  upgrading, 345–346
wiring harness, 168
women, club for, 533
*Woodall's Campground
    Directory*, 423–424
woodwork

tools, 240–243, **241**
  using picnic table, 239–243
woodwork maintenance, 412
Workamper News (newsletter),
  55
Workers on Wheels (newsletter),
  55
working while fulltiming,
  51–72
  campgrounds as market,
    65–66, 67–68
  caretaking, 53, 56
  crafts, selling, 62–65
  early retirement and, 51
  employment resources,
    55–56
  fifth-wheel trailers and,
    61–62

finding employment, 54–56
  as manufacturers' reps, 59
  plan for early fulltiming,
    68–69, **70**, 71–72
  potential income, 69, **70**,
    71–72
  seasonal opportunities,
    52–54
  teaching, 67
  various options, 52–54,
    56–68
workshops in trailers, 61–62, **62**
World Wide Web
  browsers, 296–297
  sites, 23
writing, freelance, 56–59

yawing, 472, 474